Professing Criticism

Professing Criticism

ESSAYS ON THE ORGANIZATION
OF LITERARY STUDY

John Guillory

THE UNIVERSITY OF CHICAGO PRESS

CHICAGO AND LONDON

The University of Chicago Press, Chicago 60637
The University of Chicago Press, Ltd., London
© 2022 by The University of Chicago
All rights reserved. No part of this book may be used or reproduced
in any manner whatsoever without written permission, except
in the case of brief quotations in critical articles and reviews.
For more information, contact the University of Chicago Press,
1427 East 60th Street, Chicago, IL 60637.
Published 2022
Printed in the United States of America

31 30 29 28 27 26 25 24 23 22   1 2 3 4 5

ISBN-13: 978-0-226-82129-0 (cloth)
ISBN-13: 978-0-226-82130-6 (paper)
ISBN-13: 978-0-226-82131-3 (e-book)
DOI: https://doi.org/10.7208/chicago/9780226821313.001.0001

The University of Chicago Press gratefully acknowledges
the generous support of New York University and
the Abraham and Rebecca Stein Faculty Publication
Fund toward the publication of this book.

Library of Congress Cataloging-in-Publication Data

Names: Guillory, John, author.
Title: Professing criticism : essays on the organization of
literary study / John Guillory.
Description: Chicago : University of Chicago Press, 2022. |
Includes bibliographical references and index.
Identifiers: LCCN 2022012453 | ISBN 9780226821290 (cloth) |
ISBN 9780226821306 (paperback) | ISBN 9780226821313 (e-book)
Subjects: LCSH: Criticism—Study and teaching. | Humanities—
Study and teaching. | Literature—History and criticism.
Classification: LCC PN94.2.G85 2022 | DDC 801/.95071—dc23/
eng/20220510
LC record available at https://lccn.loc.gov/2022012453

Contents

Preface

The title of this volume argues that if literature is *studied* in the university, it is criticism that is *professed*. My title alludes to that of Gerald Graff's landmark work, *Professing Literature*, which I have respectfully amended to bring out an unresolved problem in how literary study understands its purpose. The distinction between "studying" and "professing" is not trivial. University disciplines identify objects of study by differentiating these objects from others, by specialization, but professions establish the requisites and perquisites common to all the disciplines. As different as physics and literary study are, their disciplinary distinctions are submerged in the form of the profession, the notional parity of literature professors and physics professors. Where Graff offers an institutional history of our discipline, I attempt to analyze this history within the framework of a sociology of professions. The professionalization of disciplines organizes the work of teaching and research, a process that for literary study has been fraught with unintended consequences. The essays in this book consider how literary study has been organized, both historically and in the modern era, both before and after its professionalization. The sometimes adventitious and opportunistic solutions to problems in this volatile history have solidified into permanent features of our institutional landscape. For the most part, the discipline succeeds in its efforts to preserve, transmit, and study literature, yet it continues to be troubled by the relation between its disciplinary protocols and its identity as a profession. I argue in this book that the discipline's enthusiastic embrace of professionalism betrays an ambivalent relation to its amateur past, its earlier identity as *criticism*. Literary study attempts to resolve this ambivalence by *professing criticism*.

In the twentieth century, criticism was transformed into a discipline and a profession—but not in that order. As I demonstrate in part 1 of this book, our discipline inverted the usual sequence between these two processes: *Literary study became a profession before it became a discipline.* Driving this anomalous sequence was the belated attempt to determine the object of study in the English and modern foreign language departments, which only during the interwar period were identified with literature. The study of literature is very old, one of the oldest in Western history, but the object of the discipline, as we know, wavered in the later nineteenth century between literature and language. It was not obvious that literature was a legitimate object of disciplinary study, whereas the vernacular languages could boast a highly developed body of scholarship, an undoubted entitlement to the status of a discipline. So uncertain was the process of defining an object that for several decades in the earlier twentieth century, the discipline had no settled name at all. Teaching and research into literature were poised to achieve disciplinary status with the choice of a surprising array of names: philology, belles lettres, rhetoric, literary history. When the discipline was finally baptized, in the period after World War II, it took a new name: *literary criticism.*

This story is well known; it is in essence what Graff's institutional history reveals. And yet when we look at this account from the comparative perspective of other disciplines, its oddity is the chief impression. One might suppose that "literature" is the inevitable correspondent to the objects that define the most nearly allied disciplines of art history and music history. Even today, however, the position of literature as disciplinary object is not wholly secure, as Graff acknowledges in a new preface to his book: "The very phrase *teaching literature* is misleading, since what teachers and students produce in literature courses is not literature, but *criticism*—that is, discourse about literature."[1] Graff goes on to affirm Chris Baldick's earlier observation in *The Social Mission of English Criticism* that criticism is "the real content of the school and college subject" that goes by the name of literature.[2]

The currency of the term "literary criticism" is a legacy of I. A. Richards's transformative intervention into literary pedagogy. Richards saw literary criticism as a practice that could be put on a scientific basis, which would certainly have established its disciplinary credentials, but Richards did not see himself as establishing a corps of professional critics. Literary criticism was on the contrary regarded as a practice in which every reader of literature was engaged; criticism was another name for reading, whether done well or badly. His successors saw the possibility of the moment differently. In the famous statement of John Crowe Ransom, "Rather than occa-

1. Gerald Graff, *Professing Literature: An Institutional History* (Chicago: University of Chicago Press, 1987, 2007), xviii.

2. Chris Baldick, *The Social Mission of English Criticism, 1848–1932* (New York: Oxford University Press, 1983), 4–5.

sional criticism by amateurs, I should think the whole enterprise might be seriously taken in hand by professionals."[3] The chapters of this volume ask, What does it mean to "profess criticism"? This question has never, in my view, been systematically addressed in the context of a sociology of professions. It is my hope that this framework of analysis will help to explain the perennial churn in literary study, the constant revolutionizing of its methods and objects, the agon of its professional identification. I should say at the outset, however, that my intention is not to come down in favor or disfavor of "professionalism." I take the profession of criticism as given, an accomplished fact, but no less subject to analysis for that reason.

The chapters in this collection were composed initially in the hope of producing a sociologically informed history of literary study, a history that would proceed as a linear narrative. That plan ultimately proved impractical, largely because of my limitations as a scholar of English literature. The asymmetric relation between English and the modern foreign languages in the Anglo-American university makes the history of literary study very difficult to integrate into one narrative. For related reasons, the converging and diverging histories of British and American literary study are equally difficult to integrate. I write, therefore, as an American scholar of English literature, acknowledging where possible prior or parallel developments in the history of literary study in the United Kingdom and in modern foreign languages. Some moments in the story, such as the work of I. A. Richards already mentioned, were assimilated in the United States differently than in the country of their origin, where the university system permitted a more casual relation to the procedures of credentialization. For better or worse, British universities have more than caught up in recent decades with their American peers in the effort to professionalize university teaching; it is my hope that my analysis will prove relevant to that convergence in the end.

There are other reasons for rejecting a linear, "monographic" presentation of the argument. Chief among these is the fact that literary study in the past did not take the form of a professional activity at all; for most of its history, literary study was a set of practices with many different sites, both within and outside the university. Only in the later nineteenth century did it intersect with the emerging form of new professions, and then only fully after the First World War. These two histories interacted in ways that were highly contingent and fraught with problems. I offer an account of this process in chapter 2 of part 1, with the caveat that some moments in this story call for separate and more detailed examination. Part 1 should thus be read

3. John Crowe Ransom, *The World's Body* (New York: Charles Scribner's Sons, 1938), 329.

as the core argument from which radiate the semi-independent studies offered in the following two sections of the book. If I have had to forgo the linearity of the monographic form, I have exchanged that tidiness for the possibility of studying close-up a number of developments in the discipline only schematically noted in part 1. Some of these developments—such as the decline of rhetoric or the globalization of English—have unique contexts and timelines, which could only with multiple digressions have been integrated into a single longitudinal narrative.

It will be helpful to set out briefly in this preface some of the main points of part 1, "The Formation and Deformation of Literary Study," in order to give the reader some coordinates for what might seem otherwise a sprawling collection of essays on many different topics in literary study. The first chapter of part 1, "Institution of Professions," establishes a foundation for analysis of the discipline in the theory and history of professions. Literary scholars are strongly committed to the ideal of professionalism, but they often speak with more enthusiasm than knowledge about the organizational form of the profession. In order to recover a more grounded understanding of what it means to profess criticism, I begin with the very basic concept of *specialization*, from which the social forms of "occupation," "discipline," and "profession" all developed. The premise of my argument is that the most highly specialized, highly skilled forms of cognitive labor entail a correlative disability, or what has sometimes been called a "professional deformation." To put what is implicit in this phrase in the form of a proposition, all professional *formation* is also *deformation*. The social benefits of professionalization are immense, but the costs are real. Professions invoke the benefits directly in the expression of their aim or purpose. The scholarly professions are unusual in that they are highly prestigious at the same time that their aims are more difficult to specify than other occupations. I take a hint here from Nietzsche's discussion of scholars in his work, his recognition that precisely because their aims have been difficult to specify, scholars have often been led to overestimate the benefits of their work.

The overestimation of aim gives me the working hypothesis for an analysis of literary scholarship with the emergence in the nineteenth century of "professional society." During this period, occupations aspiring to professional status sought to institutionalize professional training in the university. The theory and practice of professionalization was a hallmark of the Progressive Era, when the university gathered an extraordinary number of disciplines and professions within its pale, organizing them in the bureaucratic form of the "department." Among these new departments were English and the modern foreign languages. Concurrent with this development was the decline of another occupational type, the "critic," whose locus of operation was the periodical public sphere. The critics of the nineteenth century achieved great visibility and influence without depending upon academic credentials. They were in that sense truly amateurs, representatives of the common reader. They possessed a kind of expertise that was *self-authorized*. Critics succeeded in the public sphere, as they still do today, by creating their public. In the nineteenth century, the scope of their criticism extended far beyond literature, to the whole of society. When literary study later sought to identify itself as "literary criticism," it fused the nineteenth-century identity of the critic with the professional identity of the twentieth-century scholar. In 1942, the social theorist Joseph Schumpeter responded scornfully to the emergence of these professional critics, dismissing their criticism of society as "the profession of the unprofessional."[4] Schumpeter's provocation betrays an attitude prevalent among the social scientists at the time and suggests why it was so important for literary critics to insist on their professional credentials. As the heirs of the self-authorized critics of the nineteenth century, they needed to find a way to *profess* criticism.

This narrative is already severely abbreviated, and at this point, I must offer an even more foreshortened account of the sequence of events that culminated in the establishment of a discipline called "literary criticism." During the interwar period of the twentieth century, a cadre of teachers of literature in the Anglo-American university—among them, a number who maintained parallel careers as critics or poets in the periodical domain—advanced what sociologist Andrew Abbott calls a "jurisdictional" claim over literature.[5] Many of these teachers did not possess the doctoral degree, but the lack of the credential was common in the university teaching corps of the earlier twentieth century and not finally an impediment to the claim of jurisdiction. This moment was the first of two pivots in the history of the discipline in the twentieth century. A cohort of teachers strongly identified with the practice of criticism successfully competed with other claimants in the "language and literature" departments (the philologists and literary historians) to jurisdiction over literature. The subsequent development by the critics of a new *method* (or more precisely, an array of related methods) for the study of literature backed up the claim to professional status, or "professing criticism." These new methods entailed redefining criticism—formerly understood as the practice of *judgment*—as a *method of interpretation*. In this way, the profession of criticism became a discipline. The new

4. Joseph Schumpeter, *Capitalism, Socialism, and Democracy* (New York: Harper and Brothers, 1942), 148.

5. Andrew Abbott, *The System of Professions: An Essay on the Division of Expert Labor* (Chicago: University of Chicago Press, 1988), 59–85.

methods raised criticism above mere opinion by specifying *the verbal work of art* as criticism's proper disciplinary object. The result of this strategy was finally to disambiguate the relation between language and literature that characterized the formation of the modern language departments. I further track the consequences of this strategy in what I call the "postwar settlement," the reorganization of literary study as a fusion of period-centered scholarly research with the interpretive essay.

This phase of relative stability was in turn upended by the convergence of an externality, the new social movements of the later 1960s, and an internality, the assimilation of continental theory into literature departments, beginning with comparative literature. This second pivot—*away* from the postwar settlement—determined much of what followed in the next half century. The chief result of this convergence was a reassertion of the critical motive in its strongest, predisciplinary form. The reassertion of criticism, however, entailed a reversal of its original orientation to literature, a *volte-face*. So far from being the proper object of criticism, literature came to be regarded as constraining the scope of critical assertion, its mission as the criticism of society. The disappearance of older public venues of criticism paradoxically acted as a spur to the overestimation of aim to which the scholarly disciplines were always inclined.

The new social movements provided literary study with specifically *political* aims but not the means of their expression in the public sphere. This deficit did not matter in the end, however, because the object of criticism was deflected back upon literary study itself: *the discipline became the object of criticism*. The discipline and its institutional structures, especially the curriculum, were reimagined as surrogates for the social totality. The canon debate of the 1980s and '90s was the major consequence of this surrogational politics. Although this debate seemed to subside by the turn of the century, it remained dormant only long enough to permit its resurgence of late as a nearly verbatim repetition of the earlier debate. The literary curriculum is once again the scene of conflict in our ever ongoing culture wars.

Equally prominent among the strategies of surrogacy was the emergence of what I call "topicality," the foregrounding of political thematics in teaching and scholarship, along with claims for the socially transformative effects of these thematics. The aims of topicality are laudable, but the realization of these aims is limited by their mediation through the university itself, an institution that channels only a small percentage of its students through literature courses, and which has cultural and political effects that transcend those of any one discipline. Students who pass through the postsecondary system emerge having acquired what I describe in chapter 1 as a *professional profile*, the cognitive skills, manners, values, attitudes, and cultural references that are less specific to individual fields of study than to the "college-educated" generally. If topicality in literary study participates in the construction of this profile, it hardly controls its content. Topicality has had more conspicuous effects upon the discipline itself, enlarging it in some directions while contracting it in others. It has reoriented much teaching and scholarship to concepts and problems defined by their contemporary relevance.

There is no question that topicality, in concert with the methodological innovations of high theory, energized the discipline in the wake of the postwar settlement's exhaustion. But it has done so, I argue, by ignoring the altered historical condition of literature. At the same time that criticism has amplified its claim to socially transformative effects, the proliferation of new media has displaced literature itself from its historical position as the premier medium of entertainment and edification. This media condition is in my view a matter of existential concern, but as long as the professoriate evades the question of whether its object is, or will continue to be, *literature*, it has no incentive for thinking through the place of literature in the media system. It does not matter how politically ambitious the aims of literary study might be if literature itself continues to contract in social importance.

In these circumstances, a crisis of legitimation was inevitable. This crisis is not the one that usually goes by this name—the collapse of the job market for PhDs, funding reductions, or a decline in the number of majors—but rather the one that is internal to the development of the discipline, the question of its *justification*. I suggest that in the absence of a means to assess literary study's real effects in the world, the discipline has been forced into the position of *justification by faith*. It does not appear that this faith is either warranted or likely to sustain the discipline in the future. In chapter 3, I approach the recent tendency of "postcritique" as an expression of this crisis of faith, instanced as a surprising turn away from the "professional" discipline of reading to an idealization of the "amateur" reader. The postcritical moment belatedly acknowledges our responsibility to the clientele of literary study, the readers of literature. How well has our profession served them? The return of the amateur reader, the "lover" of literature, is a curious unintended consequence of the profession's overestimation of its aims. The rejection of disciplinary methods of reading in the postcritical moment is unlikely to return literary scholars to the position of social prominence occupied by the nineteenth-century critics. The postcritical tendency might in the end look more like another version of Schumpeter's "profession of the unprofessional"—or, more precisely, a sign that our "justification by faith" has failed us.

In part 2, I examine a number of concepts and categories that enter into the historical process of "organizing" literary study, beginning in chapter 4 with the concept of the "humanities," a term that derives from antiquity but that organizes a set of related disciplines in the twentieth-century university, including the literary disciplines. I do not proceed in these chapters in precise chronological order but in a fashion that circles around the central category of literature itself. In chapters 5 and 6, I examine the categories of study that preceded the disciplinary and professional forms of literary study: rhetoric, philology, and belles lettres. These studies have various survivals in literary study, but my argument is that literary study had to supersede these discourses in order to establish literature as a disciplinary object. In chapter 7, I examine the process that accomplished this supersession, which I call the "delimitation of literature." This was the process by which literature shed older significations and gained new ones, and by which it was ultimately transformed into a disciplinary object.

Part 2 concludes with an chapter that examines the pressure on the curriculum exerted by the explosive growth of literary writing in English as a result of the language's globalization. Curricular revision is undertaken today on an even larger scale than in the 1990s, because the scene has shifted from national to transnational literatures. The implications of this shift are hugely significant. Without question, it will be necessary to reconstruct the curriculum in order to accommodate literary writing on a global scale. This effort risks, however, repeating the error of the first wave of canon revision, which too easily conflated authors with contemporary social identities and was focused too exclusively on the question of which authors to add and which to drop from the curriculum. In this chapter, I propose that we think of the curriculum alternatively as a global cultural commons. Our aim should be to democratize access to literary works, whatever their time or place.

In part 3, I consider several problems or sources of discontent in the professionalization of literary study, beginning with the collapse of the job market for new PhDs and the effect of that economic calamity on the culture of graduate education. Other essays in part 3 take up the professionalization of composition and its relation to literary study, the evaluation of scholarship and teaching in the context of promotion, and finally the question of lay reading in relation to professional reading. The latter essay is an attempt to provide a theoretical backing for the argument in chapter 3, concerning the "postcritical" tendency. Inasmuch as this tendency raises profound questions about the nature of reading, a reconsideration of the fundamental distinction between "professional" and "lay" practices is very much on the agenda for literary study.

The occasional nature of these essays allowed me to approach certain problems by zooming in, as it were, on moments in the long history of literary study. I have attempted to sustain the connection between these more local analyses and the core argument presented in part 1, at the cost of sometimes addressing the same issues or events in more than one essay. The form of the essay permits, I hope, some allowance for this looser organization. I have found in writing these essays that passing back and forth over the same terrain has sharpened the resolution of the argument presented schematically in part 1. In any case, the nonlinear organization of the book will support a nonlinear procedure of reading. I expect that some essays will be more relevant to some constituencies than others.

One other caveat is worth adding here: the reader should not look in this book for an exhaustive survey or assessment of literary study as it exists at the present moment, with all of its diverse fields and subfields. It was rather my purpose to give an account of the profession's formation and deformation according to a guiding principle of what the Greeks called *parrhesia*, or speaking the truth freely. It is my hope that this account will be of service to literary study in negotiating its perennial crises, above all the crisis looming before us, the probable contraction of the literary disciplines in the face of overwhelming social and economic forces.

The first three sections of the book comprise chapters that focus on what is problematic in the discipline, what has both inflated and undermined its aims. This is the bad news. But there is also good news, which I offer in the conclusion, "Ratio Studiorum," an outline of rationales for literary study deeply rooted in the whole history of education in the West. These rationales underlie our teaching and research even today. My point of departure here is the historical fact that literary study has not always taken the form of a discipline or a profession. In retrospect, this fact suggests the possibility that literary study in the future might no longer take the form it takes today, a university discipline. I do not offer this scenario as a prediction but as the motive for developing the most historically expansive account possible of our engagement with literature. The conclusion sets out a kind of primer for literary study understood as a practice that originated millennia ago, achieved a maximal state of organization in the twentieth-century university, and now faces an uncertain future. The point of the existential outer frame is not to exacerbate the anxiety of the professoriate but, on the contrary, to insist on the immemorial functions performed by literary study.

The conclusion describes five rationales for literary study: (1) linguistic/ cognitive, (2) moral/judicial, (3) national/cultural, (4) aesthetic/critical, and (5) epistemic/disciplinary. The last of these rationales fully emerges only with the era of professionalized literary study and the correlated overestimation of the discipline's aims. Together, the rationales constitute what I hope will enable a *reestablishment* of the discipline, a credible estimation of its aims. I do not mean to suggest in my conclusion a new subject for literary study but to remind the professoriate of what we already do, and often do well. The rationales operate at the level of a deep infrastructure, much less visible than the constant turnover of topics and methods. The rationales remind us that literary study, in one form or another, is foundational for *all* education and that there is no need to overestimate the social effects of the discipline in order to affirm what it has to offer. At present, literary study oversees a domain that is large, but shrinking. At the boundaries of this domain is a world of new media in which literature discovers its identity as an "old" medium—writing—and in which literary study affirms its role in transmitting the arts of reading. My hope is that this book will serve as a preliminary clearing of the ground for an effort that cannot be undertaken within its covers, a resituating of literary study and of literature itself in a transformed cultural field.

[PART ONE]

*The Formation
and Deformation of
Literary Study*

CHAPTER 1

The Institution of Professions

No man forgets his original trade: the rights of nations and of kings sink into questions of grammar, if grammarians discuss them.
SAMUEL JOHNSON, *Lives of the Poets*

Every craft makes crooked.
FRIEDRICH NIETZSCHE, *The Gay Science*

THE SCHOLAR'S HUNCHED BACK

The premise of this chapter is that all professional formation is also, necessarily, deformation. As a legacy of French usage, *déformation professionnelle* is more current in French than in English, perhaps because it has a wider scope of application and is less thoroughly pejorative in its implication. If one can judge from the example given by Larousse online, it can even be understood playfully: "Ne fais pas attention, c'est de la déformation professionnelle!"—which the translators render freely as "Don't worry, it's just my job!" It would be difficult to imagine so casual a usage in English, in part because of the term's relative rarity for us but also because the French *formation* can designate any occupational training (*formation professionnelle*), a sense the word does not usually invite in English.[1] Conversely, *déformation* can bear the general meaning of *changement de forme*, which contrasts with the tendency of the English word to converge simply on deformity. Throughout the argument of this chapter we ought to hear the French expression underlying the English in order to recover the full spectrum of these meanings, from the neutral "professional training," which like all learning changes the learner, to the harsher sense of "deformation," invoking the ways in which professional training produces

---

1. For a comment on this aspect of the French concept of *déformation professionnelle*, see Bruce Robbins, "Deformed Professions, Empty Politics," *Diacritics* 16 (1986): 67. Robbins is skeptical of the concept's utility as an analytic tool, a caveat I have borne in mind in emphasizing formation and deformation as complementary concepts.

a certain bias of perspective, a way of seeing the world from within an occupational enclosure.

The concept of "professional deformation" is a placeholder for a fuller
elaboration of the sociology of professions, a much larger task than the
analysis of literary study. I have integrated as much of this sociology as
seemed necessary into my analysis, although little of this research employs
the French term directly. "Professional deformation" has always straddled
the domains of disciplinary discourse and ordinary usage, sometimes sinking in the latter realm merely to a complaint the laity like to make about
professionals and bureaucrats. This complaint has been studied infrequently by sociologists.[2] A rare early consideration of *déformation professionnelle* can be found in an essay of 1934 by the Belgian sociologist Daniel
Warnotte, "Bureaucratie et Fonctionnarisme," which is concerned with the
sometimes disagreeable behavior of bureaucratic functionaries, their se-
cretiveness, rudeness, and self-importance.[3] These traits might be discovered among functionaries of many professions, but Warnotte's analysis is
directed chiefly toward government bureaucracy. Although Warnotte describes a familiar "insolence of office," he does not tell us whether this distortion emerges entirely from the bureaucratic organization of professional
knowledge workers or from some other source more deeply embedded in
intellectual labor itself. As soon as we have opened this question, we see
that bureaucracy and profession are distinguishable historical forms, if almost always joined together in the twentieth century. Most professions are
bureaucratically organized today, with the expected deformations named
by Warnotte.[4] These behaviors have the peculiar quality of appearing to be
both modern and very old. The epigraph from Samuel Johnson testifies to
an awareness of something like professional deformation long in advance of
the term's appearance, and in advance of the bureaucratic organization of
professions. (The great exception is the clergy, which was bureaucratized

2. For a curious early use of the term *professional deformation* in English, see Hubert
Langerock, "Professionalism: A Study in Professional Deformation," *American Jour-
nal of Sociology* 21 (1915): 30–44. This essay attests to the currency of the term, which
Langerock uses to launch a diatribe against professionalism.

3. Daniel Warnotte, "Bureaucratie et Fonctionnarisme," *Revue de l'Institut de Sociolo-
gie* 17 (1937): 219–60. Warnotte describes *déformation professionnelle* as an "*adaptation
du fonctionnaire à sa profession*" (245). The sense of "adaptation" here can easily bear
the evolutionary connotation that the concept is given, as we shall see below, in Dewey
and Burke.

4. For the most strenuous critique of the professions in these terms, see Magali Sarfatti Larson, *The Rise of Professionalism: A Sociological Analysis* (Berkeley: University of
California Press, 1977).

very early.)[5] The concept of professional deformation draws our attention to behaviors that arise as the by-product of occupational training generally, or more broadly, *specialization*. If we are to understand the formation of literary study in the context of a sociology of professions, we must inquire at the same time into this immemorial foundation of the division of labor. Beneath the sociology of professions, there is an anthropology of specialization, in particular the specialization of cognitive labor. For the purpose of this argument, it will be necessary to construct the anthropology of specialization and the sociology of professions in tandem, the former as the condition of the latter.

In the premodern world of craft labor, the specialization of occupational behaviors could be manifest as a visible difference, even as a sartorial difference in the case of livery. For the medieval "clerks," their garb set them apart from the laity as both priests and scholars (the latter meaning persons who could read and write Latin). All scholars descend from this occupational group and carry over into modernity a visible symbology of specialization, however muted. The distinction of livery was of course common to most occupations, sometimes as signals such as clerical garb and tonsure, sometimes even as bodily deformations resulting from particular kinds of physical labor, or what we might call *stigmata*. These stigmata lie behind the metaphor of professional deformation. We might recall here the "dyer's hand" by which Shakespeare famously troped his theatrical career in Sonnet 111 as socially down-classing, unfitting him for the company of the young aristocrat to whom he is writing: "My nature is subdued / To what it works in, like the dyer's hand." The sonnet offers an early example of the figurative extension of occupational stigmata employed by Nietzsche in the passage from which my second epigraph is drawn, which I quote here more fully:

> Almost always the books of scholars are somehow oppressive, oppressed; the "specialist" emerges somewhere—his zeal, his seriousness, his fury, his overestimation of the nook in which he sits and spins, his hunched back; every specialist has his hunched back. Every scholarly book also mirrors a soul that has become crooked; every craft makes crooked [*jedes Handwerk zieht krumm*]. Every craft, even if it should

---

5. The tendency of authority to evolve into "office" is of course an old theme in sociology and the "insolence of office" an even older theme. The greatest theoretician of bureaucracy, Max Weber, returns often to the bureaucratization of the clergy in order to construct his sociology of institutions. See Weber, *Economy and Society: An Outline of Interpretive Sociology*, 2 vols., ed. Guenther Roth and Claus Wittich (Berkeley: University of California Press, 1978), 1:241–54.

have a golden floor, has a leaden ceiling over it that presses and presses down upon the soul until that becomes queer and crooked. Nothing can be done about that. Let nobody suppose that one could possibly avoid such crippling by some artifice of education.[6]

Nietzsche says the worst that can be said of the scholar as "specialist," but he goes on to argue conversely that something valuable is to be gained in exchange for deformity: "On this earth one pays dearly for every kind of *mastery*. I bless you [scholars] even for your hunched backs . . . because your sole aim is to become masters of your craft" (366–67). Whatever we might think about the language of mastery, which has its own complexities, Nietzsche's assertion of the indissoluble union of mastery and deformation is sound sociology; only with the recognition of this difficult union will it be possible to understand professional *formation*.

Nietzsche's remarks on the scholar in *The Gay Science* pose one further difficulty that must be confronted at the outset of our inquiry. The scholar whom Nietzsche depicts is a familiar figure, born in antiquity, but his deformation has a puzzling relation to that of the bureaucrat described by Warnotte. Unlike the bureaucrat, Nietzsche's scholar—the conventional "Western" scholar—is a solitary, a creature of the "nook," where he seldom lifts his eyes from his heavy volumes and so acquires his telltale stigma.[7] This constitutional solitariness would seem on the face of it to defy professionalization, much less bureaucratization, inasmuch as these are fundamentally forms of *association*. Nevertheless, the solitariness of the scholar is itself only another kind of association, one that accommodates periods and places of withdrawal but has its own forms and sites of sociability. The image of the scholar in the carrel encourages us to forget these other places—the schools, academies, institutes, learned societies, colleges, universities, professional associations—but only for a moment. It suits Nietzsche's purpose to consider the scholar's deformation as an effect of seclusion, because he sees this space as the locus of specialization, or the cultivation of the scholar's *craft*.

6. Friedrich Nietzsche, *The Gay Science*, trans. Walter Kaufmann (New York: Vintage Books, 1974), 366.

7. This scholar is Western, in contrast to the Chinese literati, who were by definition political functionaries, quite unlike the monks of the medieval scriptorium. For an interesting and witty study of the characterological deformation of the Western scholar, focusing on the examples of Isaac Casaubon, Mark Pattison, and the fictional "Dr. Casaubon" of George Eliot's *Middlemarch*, see A. D. Nuttall, *Dead from the Waist Down: Scholars and Scholarship in Literature and the Popular Imagination* (New Haven, CT: Yale University Press, 2003).

Although it is possible to figure the deformation of the scholar as the result of solitary labor, the figure of the hunchback hides the relation between specialization and bureaucratization and so gives us two contrasting versions of professional deformation, one linked to solitariness, the other to a highly organized, even byzantine form of collectivity. In order to advance our account of deformation, it will be necessary to relocate Nietzsche's solitary scholar squarely in a milieu of professional organizations, the structures of which are correlated to the increasing *formalization* of the scholar's intellectual labor, its increasingly elaborate and precisely focused craft.[8] The more intensively expertise is cultivated, the more likely that experts will be credentialed and their work assessed in an institutional setting. Specialization in fields of expertise tends to intensify over time, driving the development of more complicated structures of association and culminating inevitably in the form of bureaucracy. The coordination of these tendencies is attested in the history of the university by the fact that the division of knowledge during the nineteenth century into ever more specialized disciplines necessitated the reorganization of university faculty into departments, the most conspicuous feature of our institutional geography. Departmental structures in turn enabled the cultivation of still more refined specializations, such as our "period" concentrations in literary study. These in turn have spun off still other professional associations. The relation between specialization and bureaucratization, then, is mutually intensifying.

The tendency of abstract or intellectual labor to become more specialized and, consequently, more organized, conforms to the tendency of the division of labor as a whole, which exhibits in most domains of work a similar double movement. In this context, the problematic distinction between intellectual and manual labor is less determining, if also scarcely irrelevant.[9] Nietzsche's word for the scholar's craft, *Handwerk*, reminds us that we think with our bodies, that scholarly work is work with the eyes, ears,

---

8. The concept of "formalization" will concern me later, but for the present we can understand by it the various standardized techniques of research, styles of argument, and modes of publication that mark given activities and writing as "scholarly" in nature.

9. The intensification of specialization in the division of labor does not always move in the direction of transforming manual into intellectual (or abstract) labor and might well move in the opposite direction, as it has with many former crafts. This circumstance suggests that the tendency of specialization is a direct expression of the supervening division of labor in modernity, which breaks down craft production into the smallest, sometimes mindless tasks at the same time that it encourages ever more focused specializations in abstract fields.

and hands.[10] Later we shall look more closely at the relation of craft to other conceptions of work, including the concept of *occupation*. In the meantime, we can hypothesize that the disagreeable traits observed by Warnotte are produced by the interaction of specialization with the tendency of intellectual labor to become increasingly organized. The pathology of character is specific to the type of work and its mode of social organization. If bureaucratic organization produces a certain "insolence of office" across the spectrum of occupations, the specialization of the scholar has other characterological features. Nietzsche speaks of the scholar's *zeal, seriousness,* and *fury,* traits that are quite unlike the indifference of Warnotte's state functionaries and sound more like those of the Protestant reformer. The features Nietzsche cites conform to a familiar topos of scholarship: even as late as the 1880s, scholars still occupied a place in the social imaginary close to that of clerics.[11] If these two professions were diverging, the formation of the scholar could follow the trajectory, as it did for Nietzsche, of a deviation from theology. As the schools moved decisively away from the church during this period, new forms of association began to produce new types of institutional identity. Without losing sight of the ancient relation of scholarly to clerical identity, I propose now to take up another hint in Nietzsche's remarks, concerning the scholar's estimation of the *aim* of scholarship.

Uncertainty about the social aim of scholarship is the condition for the deformation that is expressed as the compensatory assertion of the very grandest aims. Nietzsche's comment on the scholar's "overestimation [*Überschätzung*] of the nook in which he sits and spins" specifies the inflection of narcissism specific to scholarship, as opposed to medicine or other professional fields. Such overestimation manifests itself in the scholar as a *species* of narcissism, like but also unlike the hubris of the medical doctor. In either case, this species of self-regard is the expression of a corporate identity. It might be amusing to observe the vanity of particular scholars, but this stigma is anything but an idiosyncratic aberration. Such behaviors

10. For this reason, the "stigma" of the scholar should not be understood as only a metaphor. See Carolyn Steedman's discussion of the notorious *mal d'archive,* "'Something She Called a Fever': Michelet, Derrida, and Dust," in *Archives, Documentation, and Institutions of Social Memory: Essays from the Sawyer Seminar,* ed. Francis X. Blouin Jr., and William G. Rosenberg, (Ann Arbor: University of Michigan Press, 2007), 4–19. Steedman is interested in the illnesses induced by archival dust as well as the extensive medical literature on diseases associated with occupations.

11. Warnotte's functionaries inherit forms of bureaucratization that descend from the Catholic Church, while Nietzsche's scholars descend, I suggest, from the model of the Protestant clergy.

can only come to characterize the scholarly type as a result of the *forma-tion* of the scholarly identity (*formation professionnelle*), as determined by the *forms* of scholarly association, the institutional structures within which scholars are produced.

Although the vanity of professionals and bureaucrats (and experts gen-erally) has always provoked irritation among the laity, sociologists have tended to dismiss this as a minor concern. But the question of professional character might instead serve as a point of entry for sociological analysis, along the lines suggested by the retooling of the concept of *habitus* in socio-logical theory.[12] If the inward turning of the profession—the deflection of aim—betrays a corporate *habitus*, its condition is the relation of professional groups to the superordinate social forms that threaten the autonomy of such groups. Professional deformation is an unavoidable by-product of the asser-tion of that autonomy enabling the cultivation of professional expertise to begin with and that insulates such expertise to some extent from the tyranny of the market and from the draconian interventions of the political system.[13]

In the case of the scholar's narcissism, what Nietzsche calls "overesti-mation" is a type of professional self-regard determined by the unique so-cial relations of the scholarly profession. The overweening self-regard of the scholar is the behavioral correlative of an overestimation of the aim of scholarship, which is in turn an attempt to cope with radical uncertainty about this aim. If only it were enough to say, with Aristotle, that the desire to know is all the reason of the scholar's labors! Because it has never been enough to say this, scholars have formed associations to remedy the impo-tence of knowledge in the face of power, along with the relative poverty of those who produce "useless" knowledge.[14] Literary study is not alone

12. The refunctioning of *habitus* is associated with the work of Pierre Bourdieu (passim), but it descends ultimately from the Aristotelian concept of *hexis* by way of Aquinas's Latin analogue, *habitus*.

13. I have allowed in my schema, I hope, for the sunnier view of professional groups one finds in Durkheim, and also in Veblen, both of whom placed much faith in the future of scientific professionals as a bulwark against the predations of the entrepreneurs. I do not think that this faith has been justified, but neither do I think that Durkheim's notion of "professional ethics" is a delusion. On this question, I have been most influenced by the position of Alvin Gouldner, *The Future of Intellectuals and the Rise of the New Class* (New York: Continuum, 1979), who gives us a more favorable account of the contri-butions made by the professional, technical, and managerial groups, as opposed to the entrepreneurs.

14. The distinction between useful and useless knowledge is a bit of ideology that works endless mischief in the market for intellectual goods. It is a scandal that the dis-tinction has been associated with the division between the sciences and the humani-ties. A good deal of science is in market terms "useless"; conversely, literary knowledge,

among the humanistic disciplines in its struggle to define a social mission that would justify its corporate identity as a profession or to resort to over-estimation as a compensatory response to uncertainty of aim.

In Nietzsche's time, it was still possible to regard one discipline—philosophy—as representative of the scholarly field itself, although this moment was rapidly closing. Given the historically privileged position of philosophy among the humanistic disciplines, it will be helpful to adduce an example from the history of philosophy to clarify further what Nietzsche means by overestimation. Perhaps the most fraught invocation of professional deformation in writing of the past century can be found in Hannah Arendt's 1971 essay "Martin Heidegger at Eighty," in which Arendt tries to come to terms with the scandal of the philosopher's excursus into politics, which she sees as arising from an overestimation of philosophy itself. Arendt situates Heidegger's mistake in a long line of such errors, beginning with Plato's ill-fated excursions to Syracuse and his conceit of the philosopher-king. She hints that Plato already had a sense of the "philosopher" as a social type and so an intimation of the corporate identity that would one day take the form of a profession. Arendt identifies the tendency toward overestimation in philosophy's totalizing drive: "Philosophers have exhibited an annoying inclination toward system building." In most philosophers, this "system building" might provoke no *more* than annoyance—Arendt's term resonates here with Warnotte's description of the professional—but in Heidegger's case it was much more than this, the gambit of a would-be philosopher-king:

> We who wish to honor the thinkers, even if our own residence lies in the midst of the world, can hardly help finding it striking and perhaps exasperating that Plato and Heidegger, when they entered into human affairs, turned to tyrants and Führers. This should be imputed not just to the circumstances of the times and even less to preformed character, but rather to what the French call a *déformation professionnelle*. For the attraction to the tyrannical can be demonstrated theoretically in many of the great thinkers (Kant is the great exception).[15]

No doubt this statement is exculpatory (as many have complained). The reduction of Heidegger's crimes to a professional deformation assimilates

---

understood as imparting certain cognitive skills, is much more useful than is often acknowledged.

15. Hannah Arendt, "Martin Heidegger at Eighty," trans. Albert Hofstadter, *New York Review of Books* (October 31, 1971), 50–54.

those crimes to a tendency exhibited by nearly all the great philosophers, provoking "exasperation," echoing Arendt's earlier "annoyance." For the most part this deformation has been harmless, but under certain historical conditions the *déformation professionnelle* can explode into something much more ominous.[16]

The scholarly disciplines, including philosophy, have a very different relation today to their social and political contexts than Heidegger's philosophy in the 1930s. And yet the expression of deformation is not dissimilar in its trajectory, as it arises from the same condition of uncertainty as to aim, and a compensatory inflation of aim. This scenario can still play out in many of the humanistic disciplines as the strategy of "politicization," which is a painfully accurate descriptor in the context of Heidegger's trajectory. Arendt's sensitivity to this tendency led her to refuse the name of philosopher—she claimed only to be a political theorist, someone who thinks (not without the aid of the philosophers) about the *vita activa*. But where precisely does that leave philosophy as a discipline, or as a profession? Arendt's struggle with her own professional formation under Heidegger's tutelage compelled her after a fashion to quarantine philosophy in her work—it would seem, just in order to avoid deformation. But this is not a generalizable solution to the problem of professional deformation, which finally has to be redressed by a better *estimation* of the aim of philosophy, as of any scholarly discipline.

I have attempted here and in the other chapters in this volume to submit the problem of overestimation to analysis. I hope to offer an alternative estimation of the aims of our discipline that calls the discipline to a rethinking of its primary institutional instruments, its *curriculum*, its *pedagogy*, and its *program of research*. A fuller account of this reestimation of the discipline is offered in the concluding essay. No doubt this effort will seem preliminary and crude; so it seems to me. But it should at least be useful for the purpose of further debate to have such a sketch in hand. In the meantime, I turn to the trajectory of formation and deformation in literary study, during the period in which specialization passes through the phases of discipline, profession, and bureaucracy.

16. In Arendt's most controversial work, *Eichmann in Jerusalem: A Report on the Banality of Evil* (New York: Penguin Books, 1963), she introduces the concept of "administrative massacre" (218), a term that invokes without naming it a notion of professional deformation as the underlying dynamic of what she otherwise calls the "banality of evil." It might be said that this formulation betrays the absence of a theoretical reconciliation between a philosophical account of ethics and the sociology of organizations. We can thus understand professional deformation as a subset of the general theory of behavior in groups, but a behavior (or set of behaviors) peculiarly resistant to analysis.

THE SOCIOLOGY OF PROFESSIONS
IN THE PROGRESSIVE ERA

I remarked that the notion of *déformation professionnelle* has not found an important place in sociological theory, because the phrase seems to refer mainly to behavioral traits of professionals and bureaucrats that seem marginal to social function. Historian of education John Higham, for example, describes a "matrix of specialization" consisting (in the American educational context) of the PhD degree, the departmental organization of universities, and various funding arrangements supporting research activity.[17] Such accounts tend to emphasize the end of research rather than the character of professionals. The process by which the school superinduces a common professional *habitus* onto diverse individual personalities is inherently mysterious, occurring more as a by-product than as the aim of professional training. This question touches bottom on the ground of learned behavior as such, the complex process by which any skill or art is transmitted. The dynamic of specialization is much older than the school, as old as human culture itself. Any account of its long history would require a negotiation among three possible disciplinary frames of explanation: *psychology*, *anthropology*, and *sociology*—the former two necessarily preliminary to the latter in the sense of grasping universal human conditions of learned behavior. The sociology of professions takes up this question in societies with complex divisions of labor and educational systems designed to produce highly specialized forms of action. The actions in question—forms of cognitive specialization—were present in antiquity but achieved a permanent institutional home in the medieval university.

For my purposes, however, it will be necessary to focus on the concept of professions emergent in the Progressive Era, when new professions both displaced and transformed the system of the three "ancient" (that is, medieval) professions: law, medicine, and divinity. Other essays in this volume will return to the earlier history of the study of literature, necessarily out of historical sequence, because the event of professionalization has so thoroughly transformed our relation to literature. It is difficult to see *through* the professionalization of literary study to its long prehistory. This condition, in which a kind of screen drops down between us and the era before "professional society," demands that we acknowledge an epochal

17. John Higham, "The Matrix of Specialization," in Alexandra Oleson and John Voss, eds., *The Organization of Knowledge in Modern America, 1860–1920* (Baltimore: Johns Hopkins University Press, 1979), 3–18.

break. Claims to professional identity by a proliferation of new technical and managerial workers effectively entailed a reconceptualization of cognitive labor itself, expressed in a great burst of theorizing that lasted from the later nineteenth century until the Second World War.

I begin with one small but representative example of this theory in the work of Robert K. Merton, his essay on "Bureaucratic Structure and Personality," composed in 1940.[18] Merton's work, along with that of Parsons and Park, belongs to the great age of sociological synthesis, after which the discipline moved in other, less theoretical directions.[19] Merton adopts the notion of professional deformation from Warnotte, attracted no doubt by its resonance with Merton's interest in the idea of social "role"; the latter term is only lightly invoked, however, in the essay on bureaucracy. Like Warnotte, Merton is concerned with the bureaucratic personality type as a symptom of the "dysfunctions of bureaucracy," a focus that permits him to bring related notions in the work of John Dewey and Thorstein Veblen into association with Warnotte's earlier use of *déformation professionnelle*:

> The transition to a study of the negative aspects of bureaucracy is afforded by the application of Veblen's concept of "trained incapacity," Dewey's notion of "occupational psychosis" or Warnotte's view of "professional deformation." Trained incapacity refers to that state of affairs in which one's abilities function as inadequacies or blind spots. Actions based upon training and skills which have been successfully applied in the past may result in inappropriate responses *under changed conditions....*
>
> Dewey's concept of occupational psychosis rests upon much the same observations. As a result of their day to day routines, people develop special preferences, antipathies, discriminations and emphases. . . . These psychoses develop through demands put upon the individual by the particular organization of his occupational role. (562)

Merton tells us that he owes the correlation of Veblen and Dewey to Kenneth Burke's *Permanence and Change*, which he follows closely in his exposition, and to which he adds the reference to Warnotte.[20] I will turn to Burke presently, along with Dewey and Veblen, but would like first to bring out Merton's general purpose in associating the three notions of "profes-

18. Robert K. Merton, "Bureaucratic Structure and Personality," *Social Forces* 18 (1940): 560–68.

19. See Alvin Gouldner, *Coming Crisis of Western Sociology* (New York: Basic Books, 1970), 142–43.

20. Kenneth Burke, *Permanence and Change: An Anatomy of Purpose*, 3rd ed. (Berkeley: University of California Press, 1954), hereafter cited as *PC*.

sional deformation," "trained incapacity," and "occupational psychosis." Merton's constellation of terms gives us a clue about the peculiar marginality of the concept of professional deformation. Correlating the three phrases strengthens them theoretically and allows Merton to scale up the theory of "bureaucratic personality" into a theory of human action as such, seemingly taking us far away from the particular forms of profession and bureaucracy: "The concepts of Veblen and Dewey refer to a fundamental ambivalence. Any action can be considered in terms of what it attains or what it fails to attain."[21] This thought is further developed with a quotation from Kenneth Burke's *Permanence and Change:* "'A way of seeing is also a way of not seeing—a focus upon object A involves the neglect of object B'" (562). Merton endorses Burke's view that all trained human action is characterized by partiality of perspective. This core notion of social theory yields what we might call a *general* theory of specialization, an idea that is illuminating if also vertiginous. The notion of a "fundamental ambivalence" in human practice points to a universal perspectival bias to which all human beings are condemned by virtue of their species being.[22]

In the particular case of bureaucracy, "partiality" refers to the familiar deformation of the bureaucratic official, considered as analogous to the limitations of species being. As with much social theory of the period, this conception of organization leans tacitly on evolutionary notions of adaptation and maladaptation in organisms, upon which a functionalist ideology is typically overlaid. Merton offers as the exemplary instance of "dysfunction" the bureaucrat's dogged adherence to institutional rules, which becomes an end in itself, resulting in the "familiar process of displacement of goals."[23] This deflection of investment from the end onto the means is described as a "formalism" that renders the functionary "unable to assist many of his clients," threatening the mission of the organization itself (563). The conservatism of functionaries arises from their very training, from the very fact of what they *know:* "They have a pride of craft which leads them to resist change in established routines" (565). None of these observations is surprising, but Merton is laying a foundation here for a more interesting and ambitious generalization. The theory of bureaucratic organization serves as a model of social organization per se, an equivalence that momentarily raises Merton's expectations for sociology itself: "Studies of religious, educational, military, economic, and political bureaucracies dealing

21. Merton, "Bureaucratic Structure and Personality," 562.
22. The logic of this argument would seem to imply that only God can escape this species being, pointing us to the significance of "god-terms" in Burke's thought.
23. Merton, "Bureaucratic Structure and Personality," 563.

with the interdependence of social organization and personality formation should constitute an avenue for fruitful research. On that avenue, the functional analysis of concrete structures may yet build a Solomon's House [sic] for sociologists" (568).

The hopeful Baconian allusion leads one to wonder why this "Solomon's House" was never built, why it was not possible to construct a general sociology of organizations setting out from the revelatory instance of bureaucratic *dysfunction*. In retrospect, one might hypothesize that the Weberian stress on rationality inherited by American sociology made it difficult to account systematically for the vagaries of "personality formation." But more is implicated in this difficulty than the weighty inheritance from Weber, who balanced his concept of bureaucratic rationality with a pessimistic account of rationality's social effects, famously expressed in his image of the "iron cage." American sociology of the mid century was by contrast disposed to affirm the efficiency and functionality of organizations and to see these forms of association as mainly benign. Because the social sciences themselves were professionally and bureaucratically organized, their practitioners exhibited the same "pride of craft" as those they studied. It would seem, then, that professional deformation names a blind spot in the self-observation of organizations and for that very reason tends to fall outside the compass of theory.[24]

But not entirely. A concern with professional deformation as a consequence of specialization is close to the center of Burke's argument in *Permanence and Change*, from which Merton borrowed the association of Dewey's "occupational psychosis" with Veblen's "trained incapacity." Burke seems not to have been aware of the analogous French expression, *déformation professionnelle*, but he did not need it to make his argument. Rather than attempt to reprise his argument at greater length, I will say

---

24. In the much later volume in which the early essay on "Bureaucratic Structure and Personality" was collected, *Social Theory and Social Structure* (New York: Free Press, 1968), Merton gives an account of the earlier essay that moves its argument toward a "systems" perspective: "In this chapter, bureaucratic dysfunctions are regarded as stemming not only from an overly-close and static adjustment to a set of conditions which no longer obtain, but also from the breakdown of ordinarily self-regulating social mechanisms (e.g. the orientation of bureaucratic officials toward a well-ordered career may in due course make for excessive caution and not merely for the technically most efficient measure of conformity to regulations). In my view of the recently growing interest in mechanisms of self-regulation in social systems—social homeostasis, social equilibrium, feedback mechanisms are among the varied terms registering this interest—, there is all the more need for studying empirically conditions under which such mechanisms, once identified, cease to be self-regulating and become dysfunctional for the social system" (178).

only that Burke begins here to outline a theory of motives, the master term organizing so much of his work. That theory is grounded in a principle asserting the "partiality of perspective" inherent in all human perception and action. Or, as he describes his subject in the subtitle to the first section of the book, citing both Dewey and Veblen: "How a society's ways of life affect its modes of thinking, by giving rise to partial perspectives or 'occupational psychoses' that are, by the same token, 'trained incapacities'" (*PC, 3*). Here, as in so much Progressive Era theory, the professional organization serves as a model for society itself. This assumption might be questionable, but it can be understood as an attempt to grapple with the predominance of the new professions in modernity.

"Partial perspectives," then, are said to characterize entire societies; even more ambitiously, the rule of partial perspective is extended to all living things and grounded in a certain paradox of learned behavior. Burke begins his argument by invoking an imaginary Pavlovian experiment in which chickens learn to assemble for feeding at the ringing of a bell with a certain pitch. If later one rings the bell "not to feed the chickens, but to assemble them for chopping off their heads," their imprudent response to the bell has to be understood as a consequence of what these chickens have *learned:* "Chickens not so well educated would have acted more wisely" (*PC, 6*). This "representative anecdote" is a serious joke about the paradox of learning. All education can be understood as a process of habituation, the embodiment of knowledge. What one learns changes one's behavior, but it can also induce a maladaptive hardening of behavior over time. It might seem unnecessary to insist on this scenario with hapless chickens when so many examples from human life offer themselves, but the point of the anecdote would be to enlarge the scope of the scenario, so that it might obtain for every creature capable of learning and for every form of association in which learning is requisite. The very generality of the scenario reinforces its application to the special case, the case of *specialized knowledge*, because the more specialized the knowledge, and the more effort someone puts into acquiring a particular knowledge or skill, the greater the risk of behavior that responds inflexibly or inappropriately to a change of circumstance.

Now, there is probably in this scenario a less than fully worked out dependence on an evolutionary narrative; evolution requires, after all, vastly greater stretches of time than occur in the process of learning, which occurs during a single lifetime. Learned behaviors are furthermore precisely those that depart from heritable behaviors. We are really dealing with an analogy, then, which must prove its worth when recontextualized as a hypothesis in social science. In that context, Veblen's problem of "trained incapacity" can be reformulated in Burke's terms as the question of how much bureaucrats are, so to speak, like chickens—or to put this question more abstractly: How can we measure the debilitating effects of "trained incapacity" as human organizations become more complex over time and demand ever longer and more difficult periods of learning?

Burke relies for his initial formulation of this problem on an early essay by John Dewey, entitled "Interpretation of Savage Mind," published in 1902.[25] The influence of this essay after Burke is likely a result of Burke's circulation of the phrase "occupational psychosis," which he attributes to Dewey but which actually appears nowhere in Dewey's essay.[26] Dewey does speak of occupations, and also of psychoses, defining both in terms peculiar to tribal societies. In this setting, occupations are "ways of getting a living," but in a far less specialized sense than in modern societies. Dewey is concerned with the orientation of a tribal society to one particular mode of sustaining life, such as hunting. We are a long way from the ordinary sense of *occupation*, but as we shall see, also very close. Because the behavioral patterns associated with hunting differ from those associated with agriculture (the alternative tribal means of "getting a living"), Dewey hypothesizes that these differences come to impress themselves upon the psychic orientation of tribal members, so that "we may well be able to speak, and without metaphor, of the hunting psychosis, or mental type." Burke contracts this line of reasoning to the phrase "occupational psychosis." Dewey does not mean by "psychosis" a mental pathology, a sense that becomes current later, but rather "a pronounced character of the mind," a meaning consonant with the etymology: *psyche* + *-osis* (state of). Nonetheless, for Burke the later pathological sense inflects the compound term. In this respect, the word *psychosis* does some of the same lexical work as *deformation*.

Dewey argues that the prevalent psychosis of his hypothetical "hunting society" enabled the transference of "hunting language" to other social domains, such as courtship—a crude moment of sociologizing, perhaps but echoed in extrapolations of commerce to an analogous "marriage market." Setting aside the now outdated ethnology in Dewey's essay, we can see that what drew Burke's interest was the implication of Dewey's idea for "complex" societies, a subject that Dewey himself brings out only at the end of

25. John Dewey, "Interpretation of Savage Mind," *John Dewey: The Middle Works, 1899–1924*, vol. 2, *1902–1903*, ed. Jo Ann Boydston (Carbondale: Southern Illinois University Press, 1976), 39–52.

26. Burke does not cite the essay by name, and every text I have found that invokes "occupational psychosis," beginning with Merton, cites Burke rather than Dewey, leading me to conclude that few of Burke's readers have read the source text.

his essay. There he remarks how the later development of occupations obscures the relation between occupation and psychosis, the anthropological basis of which social science might recover: "This is the problem of mental patterns appropriate to agricultural, military, professional and technological trade pursuits, and the reconstruction and overlaying of the original hunting schema" (52). Recovering such a "hunting schema" beneath these later occupational forms may or may not be persuasive, but the observation of behaviors correlated with occupations is common in the realm of what we might call lay sociology, or more simply, the discourse of everyday life. Ordinary conversation is full of statements invoking diverse occupational stereotypes, not always accurately, of course, and sometimes descending to the level of mere prejudice. This kind of lay sociology long predates the organized social sciences and is particularly fixated on the problem of character as at once individualized and stereotypical.[27]

Burke is most interested in expressions of a modern psychosis, "which might be variously called capitalist, monetary, individualist, laissez-faire, private enterprise, and the like"—a list that betrays the critical intention of his argument. This motive leads him to activate the pathologized sense of psychosis in order to explain certain social puzzles: "Its psychotic force [that of the modern psychosis] is probably best revealed in the professionalization of sports, and in the flourishing of success literature during the late-lamented New Era" (PC, 41). The eager identification of so many occupations with the form of the "profession" confirms the social preeminence of that form over other kinds of labor. Perhaps with similar cases in mind, Burke moves away from his initial nomination of the occupational psychosis of modernity as "capitalist," settling instead on a term that will prove to be closely associated with the concept of the profession: "In and about all these, above them, beneath them, mainly responsible for their perplexities, is the technological psychosis. It is the one psychosis which is, perhaps, in its basic patterns, contributing a new principle to the world" (PC, 44). The promotion of the "technological" to the forefront of the argument seems to be a result of Burke's striving for the widest possible scope; he posits in the pages to follow a kind of Viconian history of human rationality in three phases: the magical, the religious, and the scientific or technological. Technology names modern society's mode of subsistence (on the anal-

27. The "character books" of the Renaissance, for example, give us portraits of these occupational types, who bear not only the stigma their labor impresses on their bodies—the dyer's hand—but that other stigma as well, their occupational *character*. For a sampling from the character books of Sir Thomas Overbury, Samuel Butler, John Earle, and others, see Isobel Bowman, ed., *A Theatre of Natures: Some 17th Century Character Writings* (London: Geoffrey Bles, 1966).

ogy of Dewey's hunting), but it is also powerfully associated in the social imaginary with the emergence of new *cognitive specializations*, those kinds of intellectual labor that come to be called "professions," including most conspicuously the new scientific, technical, and managerial professions.

It is not a simple matter to determine the relation between these new professions and—to cite a term from another lexicon—the *mode of production* that divides the world between capital and labor. But posing this question does give us an entry to the problem that so engaged the Progressive Era, that is, the social value of *expertise*, those specialized forms of work that are at once integrated into the market and strive to stand apart from it, are sometimes even hostile to it.[28] In the later nineteenth century, a sector of occupations split off from the market in wage labor and attempted to control the assessment of its labor by cultural strategies such as the distinction between "intellectual" and "manual" labor. This ideology of professional expertise is in some ways as constitutive of modernity as the rise of the natural sciences. The sciences lent their prestige to all forms of expertise, but the domain of expertise was never restricted to the sciences. The new division of labor is more accurately represented in social theory as the appearance of a new class, the "professional-managerial class." This is the occupational sector that arrogates "intellectual" labor to itself.

In Burke's view, the technological psychosis leads directly to the condition of "occupational diversity. . . . We have the doctor's point of view, as distinct from the lawyer's, the chemist's, the sandhog's, and the reporter's" (*PC*, 47). Despite the manifest diversity of these occupational types, Burke argues that the technological psychosis is impressed upon the character of the society *as a whole*; this "psychosis" overwrites the manifest diversity of occupations. For the Progressive Era, expertise defines the most valuable mode of labor as well as the distinctive character of labor in modernity: the society of new professions.

The new professions can be said to have emerged out of crafts, leveraging their claim to cognitive expertise for higher social position and market compensation.[29] Occupations, on the other hand, arise out of an immemorial division of labor. All occupations realize partial perspectives, but not all occupations successfully assert cognitive expertise or successfully claim identity as professions. Some occupations—most notably those associated

---

28. My analysis here defers to the great study of this period, Burton Bledstein's *Culture of Professionalism: The Middle Class and the Development of Higher Education in America* (New York: W. W. Norton, 1978), which establishes in rich detail the existence of the "culture" of its title.

29. On the claim to "abstract" labor, see Abbott, *The System of Professions*, 98–108.

with factory production—require a limited course of training that assumes the infinite fungibility of individual workers. On the other hand, the struggle to professionalize is fraught with difficulties and not always successful. This circumstance is responsible for a certain incoherence in the claims to professional identity, as with the "professional sports" mentioned by Burke, or "professional dry-cleaning." Those seeking to professionalize any particular occupation must persuade potential clients that their occupational expertise is more than craft, sometimes by derogating the very craft practice upon which professions are often based.[30]

It is not Burke's aim to critique the professions as such but to posit an alternative analysis, along Nietzschean lines, to the specialism or partiality of perspective he sees in the technological psychosis of modernity. This alternative does not entail the eradication of specialization and therefore is not the expression of antiprofessionalism: "Any performance is discussable either from the standpoint of what it *attains* or what it *misses*. Comprehensiveness can be discussed as superficiality, intensiveness as stricture, tolerance as uncertainty—and the poor *pedestrian* abilities of a fish are clearly explainable in terms of his excellence as a *swimmer*" (*PC,* 49). Burke's argument calls into question the "antiprofessionalism" or "antispecialization" asserted sometimes in the higher regions of social criticism. In the spirit of this anthropology, I hope to avoid either of the argumentative straw men represented by the positions called "professionalism" and "antiprofessionalism"—this is a spurious opposition.[31] And in any case, "professionalism" circulates as a normative concept that holds professional labor to desirable technical and ethical standards.

Nonetheless, as Burke saw, all new learning is also the inception of new ignorance, the widening of a blind spot that, if it does not engulf the visual field, can dangerously contract it. This is what led Burke to borrow Veblen's notion of "trained incapacity," extending the notion in one direction to the whole of mankind and in the other to those whose "intensive knowledge"

30. For this argument, see John Ehrenreich and Barbara Ehrenreich, "The Professional-Managerial Class," in *Between Labor and Capital,* ed. Pat Walker (Boston: South End, 1979), 5–48.

31. Arguments for or against "professionalism" in literary study are unfortunately not always informed by a knowledge of the sociology of professions. An exception to this rule is Stanley Fish, in numerous works, among which I cite as particularly relevant the two essays "Profession Despise Thyself: Fear and Self-Loathing in Literary Studies" and "Anti-Professionalism," both included in *Doing What Comes Naturally: Change, Rhetoric, and the Practice of Theory in Literary and Legal Studies* (Durham, NC: Duke University Press, 1989). Fish invokes work on the sociology of professions, mainly that of Magali Sarfatti Larson, and mounts a very effective case against antiprofessionalism.

is "restricted to small groups." More than any other sociologist of his time, Burke relentlessly exposed the dynamic of professional formation and deformation in partiality of perspective.[32] It will be worth entertaining his notion of a countervailing strategy, his "perspective by incongruity," in order to complete this theoretical sketch and to extend its reach to literary criticism as an academic specialization.

Burke's inquiry into "partiality of perspective" as a universal feature of human societies is without doubt evidence of his struggle to understand the ideology of professional society emergent in the Progressive Era. When he turns his gaze upon academic disciplines, however, he can seem thoroughly "antiprofessional," seemingly contradicting the premise of his theory of specialization. Upon closer inspection, however, his target is the blinkered perspective of *particular* disciplines such as economics, which he sees as especially corrupted by industrial capitalism. In *Attitudes Toward History*, for example, he denounces those "orthodox economists hired by business to provide the scholastic rationalization of its procedures."[33] This kind of statement employs a familiar topos in order to produce "incongruity"—economic theory is debunked as a kind of scholasticism. Burke is warming up for an even more aggressive exercise in perspectivism; he goes on to characterize economists as latter-day "cameralists"; they are like the bureaucrats of "semi-feudal Germany" who were "concerned solely with the 'internal adjustments' of the bureaucratic order" (*Attitudes Toward History*, 308). The aim of Burke's incongruous description is to expose the professional deformation of economics, its inability to see that its theoretical constructions amount to a narcissistic projection onto the real world of its self-certainty. Such a critique may be unfair as a generalization

32. Burke will later come to analyze the specialist's partialism with reference to his theory of identification. In *A Rhetoric of Motives* (Berkeley: University of California Press, 1969), he argues that the specialist's identification with his function disables a wider moral perspective that would check the tendency of his "occupational autonomy": "If the technical expert, as such, is assigned the task of perfecting new powers of chemical, bacteriological, or atomic destruction, his morality *as technical expert* requires only that he apply himself to his task as effectively as possible. The question of what the new force might mean, as released into a social texture emotionally and intellectually unfit to control it, or as surrendered to men whose *specialty* is *professional killing*—well, that is simply 'none of his business,' as specialist, however great may be his misgivings as father of a family, or as citizen of his nation and of the world" (30). The example is lurid and resonates with Arendt's account of "administrative massacre." Yet Burke does not need an example so extreme to make the larger theoretical point that all forms of expertise are subject to deformation.

33. Kenneth Burke, *Attitudes Toward History*, 3rd ed. (Berkeley: University of California Press, 1984), 308.

about the contributions of the economic discipline tout court, but it would be hard to deny that recent history has dispelled substantial segments of economic theory as disciplinary fantasy. For the economy *in theory*—as envisioned, for example, by the "efficient market hypothesis"—the market resembles nothing so much as a society in which all actors are economists. Every craft makes crooked.

Burke goes on to consider more positively two other academic disciplines, praising "the perspective by incongruity to which the historian or sociologist is automatically pledged" (*PC,* 107). It seems doubtful, however, that these two disciplines are exempt from professional deformation. In order to be thoroughly consistent, Burke would need to concede the inevitable deformation even of the most self-critical disciplines. Elsewhere Burke speaks suggestively of how "perspective by incongruity" is produced when "a given classification cuts across other classifications on the bias" (*PC,* 102). This would be the point of offering a sociological analysis of economics: to bring the lexicon of one discipline to bear against another.[34]

In the end, Burke does not identify his "perspective by incongruity" with any one academic discipline but rather with a practice that is difficult to locate on any map of modern disciplines: *poetry.* The gesture toward what seems a transcendent positioning of poetry seems a surprising idealization, when the reach of Burke's theory exceeds its grasp, but we may want to see it rather as a necessary error. Burke argues that the practice of poetry is the least "psychotic," that is, the least deforming: "After all, the devices of poetry are close to the spontaneous genius of man" (*PC,* 66). But what can this mean? Poetry is not being represented here as a privileged "occupation"; it is rather a figure for perspectivism itself. Poetry yields a *terminology* for perspectivism, which Burke unfolds from the concept of metaphor: "The poetic metaphor offers an invaluable perspective from which to judge the world of contingencies" (*PC,* 266). The semantic polyvalence of the trope constitutes a means "to designate the architectonic nature of either a poem, a social construct, or a method of practical action." All of these human things are best described with a "vocabulary of tropes"—a prescient thought (*PC,* 264)![35] At the same time, Burke wants to shield his perspectivism from reduction to just another occupational specialization:

---

34. There is something to be gained in theoretical precision by invoking "cross-disciplinary" rather than "interdisciplinary" in this context, as I have in mind, with Burke, a deliberate crossing of disciplines, in order to produce perspective by moving at a tangent to a disciplinary bias.

35. It is a measure either of Burke's subtlety, or his lack of clarity, that it remains difficult to tell whether his metaphor is the realization of perspectival incongruity, or only a metaphor—to the second degree—of this perspectivism.

"The corrective of the scientific rationalization would seem necessarily to be a rationale of art—not however, a performer's art, not a specialist's art for some to produce and many to observe, but an art in its widest aspects, an *art of living*" (*PC*, 66). The invocation of this art recalls Nietzsche and his ancient precursors, but we moderns must also make a living.

For a *poiesis* that takes nothing less than the "art of living" as its aim, there can be no question of professional deformation. But what of those who *study* poems, those who profess *reading for a living*? For these professionals, something like Burke's claim to perspectival incongruity is asserted in their signature disciplinary practice, which is not poetry, or literature, but *criticism*.

THE NEW UNIVERSITY AND THE NEW CLASS

Their faith in education was so full of pathos that one dared not ask them what they thought they could do with education when they got it. Adams did put the question to one of them, and was surprised at the answer: "The degree of Harvard College is worth money to me in Chicago."

HENRY ADAMS, *The Education of Henry Adams*

Professionalism is one of the public *ideologies* of the New Class, and is the genteel subversion of the old class by the new.

ALVIN GOULDNER, *The Future of Intellectuals and the Rise of the New Class*

The specialization of human action or *poiesis* lies at the foundation of all organized forms of human effort, including all forms of intellectual labor. The career of the university academic today is further defined and organized socially by the concept of the *profession*, which, as we know, descends from the credentialing procedures of the medieval university and other schools of the period. In the modern world, professions have proliferated vastly, and most of them harbor their programs of training in the university system. Despite the copious scholarship on the history of higher education, as well as on the sociology of professions, the explosion of professions in the Progressive Era is still difficult to explain. Beyond dispute is the fact that all forms of expertise in modernity aspire to the condition of the profession. If some of these forms do not require college or university degrees, the state will usually step in to validate training programs and dispense licenses, but these professions are the exception that proves the rule. For most professions, the university has become the venue of credentialing.

Without question, this system has immensely improved the quality and reliability of expert practice. Nonetheless, a certain ambiguity afflicts the category of profession, which is in part an effect of the medieval inheritance, as well as a consequence of the university's engrossment of the credentialing function. The fact that the category of "profession" now stretches from "professional baseball" and "professional dry-cleaning" to law, physics, engineering, finance, music, the study of literature, and very many other forms of expertise confronts the sociology of professions with a challenging incoherence.

Although many professions train their apprentices in university programs, the professionalization of teachers themselves—the professors—is a special case of professional formation, as well as of social prestige. The profession of scholar is correlated with the form of the *discipline*, that is, a mode of organizing intellectual inquiry according to object and method. Until the later nineteenth century, this organized effort of inquiry might or might not reside in the university or might straddle the school and other kinds of association. But the intellectual disciplines came finally to reside permanently in the university, where they have solidified into the bureaucratic form of departments. Disciplines are thus nested within the form of the profession, facing outward, and the department, facing the college or university. If it has been possible nonetheless to think of disciplines as though they were nothing but autonomous discourses or practices—the history of physics, the history of philosophy, the history of sociology—we should not forget that these histories have always been as much institutional as intellectual, as much the story of the *organization* of inquiry as of the ideas and theories of individual scientists and scholars.

The institutional conditions of intellectual inquiry have long been acknowledged by historians and no less for literary study than any other discipline. But in the case of literary study, there exists a complication that confounds attempts to explain its history. Burke indirectly acknowledges this problem in setting the idea of *poiesis* in opposition to the idea of specialization. Burke's *poiesis* does not name any discipline in the university system, though it seems to be connected for Burke with the practice of "criticism." But that suggests that we know what criticism is, because it names a university discipline and, moreover, a profession. These are just the occupational concepts that need to be examined. "Literary criticism" is not the only form in which literature has been studied historically. The organization of such study into the form of a university discipline occurs very late in its history, not until the middle of the twentieth century. The reason for this fact is correlated to what I have called the "delimitation of literature," discussed in chapter 7, "The Location of Literature." Only when literature itself is restricted to the "imaginative" or "fictional" genres does it become possible to organize "literary criticism" as a university discipline.

In the received history of literary study, this sequence has been perennially misrepresented. The "critics" of the nineteenth century were supposed to have become the literary professors of the twentieth; the study of literature became one profession among many. But critics did not evolve like dinosaurs into academic birds by renouncing their former journalistic role as the arbiters of taste and purveyors of opinion in the public sphere. The difference between their former "profession" as writers for the reviews and quarterlies of the nineteenth century and that of university professor is just the problem that has drawn so much commentary in recent decades. It is crucial to recall here that in the nineteenth century, both "criticism" and "literature" were "extracurricular" kinds of writing. As Gerald Graff, Chris Baldick, Francis Mulhern, and others have shown so persuasively, the discourse called criticism was not an easy fit for the university, and its relocation from the public sphere of journalism was a complex affair. In achieving a perspective on this transition, it will be necessary to ascend to a considerable height, where the structures of interest to the sociology of professions are most clearly visible. From that altitude, what matters most to this history is the category of the *discipline* as a transitional form, the organization of diverse intellectual enterprises according to the differentiation of their objects and methods. This form mediated the reconstruction of the university in the later nineteenth century, when the "new university" with its constellation of new disciplines replaced the classical and theological courses of study in the older institution.

In retrospect, the establishment of new disciplines in the university system, and their ultimate bureaucratic organization into departments, was premised on a normative conception of knowledge identified with what the age called *science*.[36] The conception of science was very expansive and included both the "natural sciences" and other forms of empirical investigation, such as history and philology.[37] This construction of science is no

36. This is a view of science that matured with William Whewell, famously responsible for the neologism "scientist." For Whewell's view of science, see *The Philosophy of the Inductive Sciences*, 2 vols. (London: J. W. Parker, 1837); and on university subjects, see *On the Principles of English University Education: Including Additional Thoughts on the Study of Mathematics* (London: J. W. Parker, 1838).

37. See Michael Warner, "Professionalization and the Rewards of Literature, 1875–1900," *Criticism* 27 (1985): 1–28: "We no longer think of ourselves as scientists, but our notion of what interpretation is and why we do it was the creation of a philological community that *did* think of itself as scientific" (14).

longer available to us, and for that reason early empirical disciplines such as philology ceased in the twentieth century to claim the identity of science. The recategorization of all knowledge discourses as "sciences" in the early phase of transformation was a necessary condition for the development of university disciplines and ultimately the means by which the sciences themselves were successfully professionalized. It is easy for us to forget that scientific inquiry before the nineteenth century was, like criticism, pursued largely outside the university, by experts who were ipso facto amateurs.[38] By the beginning of the twentieth century in the United States, university disciplines took over the looser formal functions of the scientific associations of the previous century. Throughout this period of transition, many nonscientific professions came increasingly to imitate the scientific form of knowledge production through *disciplinarization*, that is, by the strategy of locating the production and reproduction of their expertise in the university.[39] This is how the university became the monopolistic agency for the *institution of professions* and so of the proliferation of professionalized occupations.

The mediating function of the disciplinary form, correlated with an understanding of knowledge as "scientific," enabled what the sociologist Harold Perkin called "the rise of professional society."[40] If the temporary identification of "discipline" with "science" mediated the reformation of the university, these categories later separated and the disciplines were sorted out on the basis of other principles of categorization. The form of the discipline, however, endured in the university as the bureaucratic unit for all

38. On the absence of science education in the British university, see Brian Simon, "Systematization and Segmentation in Education: the Case of England," in *The Rise of the Modern Educational System*, ed. Detlef K. Muller et al. (Cambridge: Cambridge University Press, 1987), 94–99.

39. See Magali Sarfatti Larson, *The Rise of Professionalism*: "A Profession's cognitive base can evolve in complete independence from the profession itself and from its production of professional producers, *until the production of knowledge and the production of producers are unified into the same structure*. Or, in other words: the link between research and training institutionalized by the modern model of university gives to university-based professions the means to control their cognitive bases" (17). Peter Dobkin Hall, in "The Social Foundations of Professional Credibility: Linking the Medical Profession to Higher Education in Connecticut and Massachusetts, 1700–1830," in *The Authority of Experts: Studies in History and Theory*, ed. Thomas L. Haskell (Bloomington: Indiana University Press, 1984), 107–41, observes that medical schools were compelled to incorporate within universities in order to maintain their credibility.

40. See Harold Perkin, *The Rise of Professional Society* (London: Routledge, 1989), and *The Third Revolution: Professional Elites in the Modern World* (London: Routledge, 1996).

forms of inquiry, defined by the union of teaching and research functions. This form of organization was achieved early in the American university; the universities of Great Britain and the continent evolved more slowly in this direction. Henceforth nearly all would-be professions, however distant their connection with science, were compelled to locate their credentialing operations in the university or risk extinction. The university thus brought the professions into permanent fusion with the system of the disciplines, which in turn transformed the university itself. The form of the discipline— instantiated as a program of college or university study—thus articulated the form of scientific knowledge with the form of the profession.[41]

Scientific inquiry and professionalism are nonetheless distinct social forms, despite their convergence in the institutional form of the discipline, with its bureaucratic instantiation, the department. Science may not have been the only discourse of knowledge, but it acquired immense social prestige on the basis of its vaunted method, however difficult it was on the ground to define this method. A profession is by contrast a mode of *association*, a social arrangement by which those who possess specialized forms of knowledge associate with one another and organize their actions. Although not all professions produce scientific knowledge, all professions share in sociological terms an identity as *expert cultures*. Experts possess a certain rarified knowledge, distinct from the knowledge of the "laity," but it is only certain kinds of experts at certain historical moments who become professionals.[42] Just as we might understand the category of the expert as larger, more abstract, than that of the profession, so the profession is larger than that of science. The fact that there are many nonscientific cultures of professional expertise gave rise to one of the great epistemic problems of modernity, the tension between the heterogeneity of expertise and the enormous social authority wielded in the name of science.

This problem has never yielded to a philosophical solution, a successful negotiation of the value relation between different kinds of knowledge. In the place of that epistemological resolution we have practices of coexistence within "professional society," practices that permit the professionalization of heterogeneous kinds of expertise, expressed, for example, as the nominal equivalence of lawyers and scientists as professionals. The university thus became the agency for reducing the tension between the

41. Bledstein, *The Culture of Professionalism*, points out that during this period knowledge of the law begins to be represented as a "rational science" (186).

42. The fusion of expertise with professionalism in the nineteenth century is signaled by the new pejorative sense of "amateur," as the opposite of professional. See Bledstein, *The Culture of Professionalism*, 31.

normative status of science as the premier discourse of knowledge and the social authority of the many other expert cultures granting credentials in the university. There, all forms of knowledge possess a notional institutional parity.

Historians of higher education in America like to observe that the emergence of the new university is in retrospect surprising, given the fact that the nineteenth-century American college was largely irrelevant to the cultural and socioeconomic life of the nation. Lawrence Veysey, in his authoritative history of the American university, notes that the goals of the early American college, in addition to its task of training clergymen, were to instill Christian piety and a sense of self-discipline in students and in a general way to maintain the cultural status of a small social elite.[43] In *The Culture of Professionalism* Burton Bledstein also describes the early American college as "a form of moral apprenticeship for the children of the gentry."[44] One might suppose that the purpose of this institution was to reproduce that elite, but in fact, attendance at college mattered little to its survival. What Bledstein calls the "gentry" was not, after all, an aristocracy or *rentier* class, whose social authority might be reinforced by its claim to the old high culture of the classics. On the contrary, in the nineteenth century the upper strata of society in the United States consisted of successful commercial and industrial entrepreneurs; the "old-time college" offered very little of use to this class beyond the veneer of European civility. Within this stratum, the colleges were regarded with some ambivalence; they were not necessarily seen as effective avenues of up-classing in the same way that the English bourgeoisie came to regard Oxford or Cambridge; much less were they ports of entry for positions in government, as in imperial Britain.[45]

43. Lawrence Veysey, *The Emergence of the American University* (Chicago: University of Chicago Press, 1965); see also Veysey, "Stability and Experiment in the American Undergraduate Curriculum," in *Content and Context; Essays on College Education*, ed. Carl Kaysen (New York: McGraw Hill, 1973), 1–64. For abundant bibliography and learned commentary on myriad issues relating to the university and professional labor, see Alan Liu, "Palinurus," http://palinurus.english.ucsb.edu/index2.html.

44. Bledstein, *The Culture of Professionalism*, 209.

45. The university in the United States never took on the social task of preparing a civil service, in the manner of the French and German universities. Because the latter systems were linked to qualification for state functions, they retained a predominantly humanistic or language-oriented curriculum longer than in the United States. At the same time, this curriculum was compatible, in the case of the German system, with the development of "research." But the German "mandarins" produced by this system, as Fritz Ringer has shown in *Decline of the German Mandarins: The German Academic Community, 1890–1933* (Middletown, CT: Wesleyan University Press, 1990), were less

In the very irrelevance and decrepitude of these institutions one can see the enabling condition of their transformation. Like Czarist Russia, their backwardness ripened them for revolution. Throughout the nineteenth century, the curriculum of Greek, Latin, and theology provoked increasing resistance and calls for reform. When reform came, it was radical. In the era of the great university presidents—Charles William Eliot of Harvard, Daniel Coit Gilman of Johns Hopkins, Andrew Dickson White of Cornell—the Latin and Greek curriculum was replaced by the system of electives, which permitted specialization directed toward a career. Specialization was instituted at the level of curriculum as a means of supporting the aims of new disciplines. With electives, and later majors, came the modern divisional structure of sciences, social sciences, and humanities. The professoriate too was transformed; it was no longer devoted for the most part to the task of teaching but also now to research. Professors no longer taught courses in any or every subject but only in their field of specialization. The department emerged as the bureaucratic unit organizing teaching and research around the form of the discipline. Graduate and professional schools were established, and the degree system was revised. The PhD became a professional or research degree rather than just a credential for teaching. After 1900, the higher educational system began slowly to expand, as a larger percentage of the population sought out education rather than entrepreneurship as the path to upward mobility. The old college disappeared, and what replaced it, though deferring to the aims of piety and self-discipline, was a very new social institution, one that became a powerful agent of social change in its own right.

The strongest impetus for reformation came from a sector of the professoriate itself, not the scientists only but those who identified with science more broadly, especially philologists and historians. This cadre might be described, as I indicated above, as identified with science in the nineteenth-century sense, meaning that they saw themselves as engaged in *empirical research*. These professors acquired sophisticated new conceptions of research in part as a consequence of study abroad, primarily in the German universities. This version of reform was so successful that by the turn of the century, as Edward Shils has remarked, "science and the universities

---

inclined than their American counterparts to specialize in the natural sciences. Finally, it should be pointed out that in the European system research of all kinds is conducted in research institutes alongside universities. On science education in the British university, see Brian Simon, "Systematization and Segmentation in Education: the case of England," in *The Rise of the Modern Educational System*, ed. Detlef K. Muller et al. (Cambridge: Cambridge University Press, 1987), 94–99.

became almost identical for the broader public."[46] This identification ultimately undermined the association of the philologists themselves with science. Frederick Rudolph cites in this context the Darwinian biology professor in Colorado who "was fond of telling his students that in Colorado
'the beet root took precedence over the Greek root.'"[47] And yet during the
same period, philology represented itself as just another science.[48]

The outlines of this narrative, which I have briefly reprised here, suggest
that the success of the sciences in the university can be attributed to its
cultural position. What Bledstein notably calls the "culture of professionalism" was premised on the social value of science as a practice: "Science as a
source for professional authority transcended the favoritism of politics, the
corruption of personality, and the exclusiveness of partisanship."[49] Science
in short provided an *ethic* for professionalism, one based on principles of
honesty, mental discipline, and self-control.[50] The university was dedicated
to the transmission of this ethic and so established the system of profes-

46. Edward Shils, "The Order of Learning in the United States: The Ascendancy of
the University," in Oleson and Voss, *The Organization of Knowledge in Modern America*, 32.

47. Frederick Rudolph, *Curriculum: A History of the American Undergraduate Course
of Study since 1636* (San Francisco: Jossey-Bass, 1977), 180.

48. Bledstein, *The Culture of Professionalism*, notes the congruence of the disciplines
as sciences: "The physical scientist who engaged in intellectual research often felt professionally closer to the classicist pioneering in philological studies or the Shakespeare
specialist than he did to the businessman scientist" (302). This fact explains why, in Bledstein's view, the Huxley-Arnold debate attracted little attention in nineteenth-century
America. See also Stephen Brint, *In an Age of Experts: The Changing Role of Professionals
in Politics and Public Life* (Princeton, NJ: Princeton University Press, 1994): "During the
course of the nineteenth century, the appeal to science became a keynote and not just an
accompaniment of professionalizing activity. A 'scientific' base served as a prima facie
argument for incorporation. Even law and management, both so clearly based on human
institutions and human judgment, claimed a scientific base" (35).

49. Bledstein, *The Culture of Professionalism*, 90; Bledstein further notes, "It became
the function of the schools in America to legitimize the authority of the middle class by
appealing to the universality and objectivity of 'science.' The fact that most Americans
learned to associate the scientific way with democratic openness and fairness made the
relationship convincing" (123–24).

50. The possibility of generalizing professional ethics was already explored by Emile
Durkheim in his lectures of the 1890s, *Professional Ethics and Civic Morals*, trans. Cor-
nelius Brookfield (London: Routledge, 2019). In the United States, Thorstein Veblen
argued for the ethics of the professions in opposition to the mores of the capitalist entrepreneurs in *The Engineers and the Price System* (New York: B. W. Huebsch, 1921).
John Dewey made a similar argument in *Democracy and Education: An Introduction to
the Philosophy of Education* (New York: Macmillan, 1916), as did Parsons throughout
his work. Gouldner remarks in *The Future of Intellectuals*, "Indeed, Talcott Parsons' vast

sions on the foundation of the system of disciplines. In Thomas Haskell's formulation, "The university provided the keystone for the great expansion and elaboration of expert authority that inaugurated the contemporary division of labor."[51]

This judgment affirms the analysis of Alain Touraine, in *The Academic System in American Society*, that "by the end of the nineteenth century," the university was "more an instrument for shaping a new type of society than the means of reproducing an established order."[52] Touraine makes a very particular claim for the difference of the American university from its European peers—that it was *a new kind of school*, no longer defined exclusively by the function of social reproduction dissected with such anatomical precision in the work of Pierre Bourdieu and Jean-Claude Passeron.[53] We broach here another category of analysis, that of culture, which is crucial for understanding the subsequent history of the academic profession. The university became a *culture-making* institution. But this culture was not what we mean by its European correlate: the "high arts" of poetry, painting, music, architecture. This difference was to have large consequences

---

oeuvre can best be understood as a complex ideology of the New Class, expressed by and through his flattering conception of *professionalism*" (37).

51. Thomas L. Haskell, *The Authority of Experts: Studies in History and Theory* (Bloomington: Indiana University Press, 1984), xxvi. See also Stephen Brint, *In an Age of Experts: The Changing Role of Professionals in Politics and Public Life* (Princeton, NJ: Princeton University Press, 1994): "For all intents and purposes, it is the universities that define the professions. During this period, economic power describes the world of entrepreneurial industry and commerce, while cultural legitimation with or without economic power describes the world of 'the professions" (35). Bledstein notes that "any occupation and any subculture of American life achieves recognition and status when it became deserving of study" (*The Culture of Professionalism*, 125) so that it is possible now to receive degrees in a vast number of occupational fields, many of them quite remote from scientific knowledge. Perhaps bemusedly, Bledstein cites the example of the "degree in radio announcing" (126). See also Rudolph, *Curriculum*, 9, for a discussion of the variety of degrees now awarded in the American university. It is important to emphasize in this context that "professional society" is inclusive of much more than the traditionally most prestigious professions, such as doctor, lawyer, scientist, etc.

52. Alain Touraine, *The Academic System in American Society* (New Brunswick, NJ: Transaction, 1974), 19. Because the new curriculum shared a similar ethical agenda across the disciplines, it was not necessary for students to specialize exclusively at the undergraduate level. This arrangement had the effect of making an undergraduate degree a desirable means of upward mobility (the point of the anecdote from Henry Adams).

53. The social effects of the university were out of proportion to the size of its constituency. Larson, *The Rise of Professionalism*: "At the beginning of the twentieth century, only a minority of the professional and managerial middle class had passed through the university; but it was a particularly active, cohesive, and significant minority" (154).

for all of the disciplines of the university but especially for "humanities" disciplines such as literary study.

If it was the case, as Bledstein proposes in his study, that "the American university came into existence to serve and promote professional authority" (x), it is in this context that we must understand the implications of the early alliance of the humanities and social sciences with the natural sciences. Edward Shils argues that "scholarship in the humanities and the social sciences gained from this association."[54] Lawrence Veysey notes that in the twenty-four leading graduate schools of 1896, the single largest contingent of graduate students, "amounting to a third of the total," was engaged in the study of language from a philological perspective.[55] It was a golden age for language study, and language study dominated over literary study, as even a cursory examination of the early record of Modern Language Association proceedings would confirm. By comparison with the popularity of language study, only a quarter of graduate students were working toward degrees in the natural sciences. The late nineteenth-century enthusiasm for science fashioned the system of the disciplines in accordance with the norm of research, muting the difference between what we might think of now as "humanistic" fields and the natural sciences. But this was only a temporary rapprochement.

If science was indeed the embodiment of a cultural norm for a new professional society, professionalism itself was nonetheless much more than a mimesis of scientific practice. As I have already suggested, some professions would prove capable of enlarging their social authority without necessarily claiming to be scientific. Rather, that authority came to be based on the very institutional and cultural forms science had helped to establish: the professional association, the academic discipline, the department, professional and graduate schools, the higher degree.[56] These forms became permanent features of the university system and of the professions. They survived beyond the immediate conditions of their emergence because

54. Edward Shils, "The Order of Learning in the United States," 32.

55. Veysey, *The Emergence of the American University*, 173.

56. Lawrence Veysey, "The Plural Organized World of the Humanities," in Oleson and Voss, *The Organization of Knowledge in Modern America*, points to the reorganization of the professions into more homogeneous forms of association through the university: "The rise of academia encouraged a new style of professionalization. . . . The social effect was to transfer cultural authority, most crucially over the printed word and what was taught to the sons and daughters of the elite, away from the cultivated professions as an entirety and toward a far smaller, specially trained segment within them, those who now earned Ph.D. degrees" (63).

the underlying social force that ensured their success was less science itself than the culture of professionalism.

This circumstance had enormous consequence for all academics, including literary scholars. It meant that the initial association of literary study with science (as in the discipline of philology) could be discarded when other social and institutional forces no longer supported this identification. The *professional* form of literary study persisted long beyond the alliance of science and professionalism in the early Modern Language Association, dominated as it was by the scientific study of language. In the end, professionalism triumphed even over science; it determines disciplinary protocols now more than ever.[57]

The category of the "professional-managerial class" has been vigorously contested from every possible position, left and right, but it has survived, at least as an ongoing topic of research.[58] However it is to be defined or explained, the professional-managerial class is without doubt the majority clientele of the twentieth- and twenty-first-century university. Although the expansion of the higher educational system over the course of the twentieth century, especially the growth of two-year colleges, opened higher education to a larger population, the university remains unmistakably oriented toward professional occupations by virtue of holding out the promise of upward mobility to those entering the system from lower-income households. Whether we like to acknowledge this fact or not, students who study literature are moving toward a wide array of professional-managerial careers; only a very small fraction of this clientele will seek to become pro-

---

57. Arguably now as powerful as the norm of scientificity. The professions of business and law, for example, draw vast monetary resources to their professional schools without ever having to make claims to scientific truth.

58. My discussion will make reference directly or indirectly to the following studies: Alvin Gouldner, *The Future of Intellectuals*; John Frow, *Cultural Studies and Cultural Value* (Oxford: Clarendon Press, 1995); Abbot, *The System of Professions*; Brint, *In an Age of Experts*; Milovan Djilas, *The New Class: An Analysis of the Communist System* (New York: Frederick A. Praeger, 1957); Eliot Freidson, *Professionalism Reborn: Theory, Prophecy and Policy* (Chicago: University of Chicago Press, 1994); B. Bruce-Briggs and Robert L. Bartley, eds., *The New Class* (New Brunswick, NJ: Transaction, 1979); Arthur J. Vidich, ed., *The New Middle Classes: Life-Styles, Status Claims, and Political Orientations* (New York: New York University Press, 1995); Perkin, *The Rise of Professional Society*; Perkin, *The Third Revolution*; Hansfried Kellner and Frank W. Heuberger, eds., *Hidden Technocrats: The New Class and New Capitalism* (New Brunswick, NJ: Transaction, 1992); Ash Amin, ed., *Post-Fordism: A Reader* (Oxford: Blackwell, 1994); and Jorge Reina Schement and Terry Curtis, *Tendencies and Tensions of the Information Age: Production and Use of Information in the United States* (New York: Routledge, 2017).

fessors of literature. Even these students pursue graduate study in part because they know that professors have a relatively high social standing as professionals.

The occupational categories of the professional-managerial class—doctors, lawyers, scientists, engineers, teachers, administrators, managers, and others—have long constituted an interesting, though seemingly intractable problem for sociological analysis. It has always been difficult to determine the common features of this aggregate, even whether it constitutes a "class" in any historical sense of that word. Alvin Gouldner, in his important work *The Future of Intellectuals and the Rise of the New Class*, argues that the twentieth century saw the emergence of a genuinely new class formation, in conflict with the old bourgeoisie and destined to replace its rule of money capital with the regime of knowledge or cultural capital.[59] Gouldner's presentation of this transformative scenario is very ambivalent. The New Class is in his view a "flawed universal class," a different version of what the old bourgeoisie *believed* itself to be, but it is also emphatically not a revolutionary class, as the proletariat was *supposed* to be.

Gouldner's work is indebted to the seminal article by John and Barbara Ehrenreich, "The Professional-Managerial Class," which takes a somewhat less hopeful view of its subject. The Ehrenreichs see the New Class as less in conflict with the old bourgeoisie than with the working class itself. For the Ehrenreichs, the New Class is defined by the "expropriation of the skills and culture once indigenous to the working class," with which it thus has objectively antagonistic relations (17). The Ehrenreichs cite, for example, the displacement of craft production by the science of the engineers, which proletarianized former craft workers or displaced them altogether. Other New Class occupations, such as journalism (credentialed by the university), and significantly the humanities fields themselves, are associated by the Ehrenreichs with the dissemination of ideology. For them, the New Class as a whole is committed to "the reproduction of capitalist culture and capitalist class relations" (12). This thesis obviously contradicts Gouldner's assertion of a "genteel subversion" of the older class structure.

Some commentators, such as Peter Drucker and Robert Reich, identify the rise of "intellectual labor" with a new class system, even with, in Drucker's view, the inception of a "post-capitalist society."[60] While this

---

59. For documentation on the growth of professionals and managers as a sector of the workforce, see Ehrenreich and Ehrenreich, "The Professional-Managerial Class," 18–21.

60. Robert Reich, *The Work of Nations: Preparing Ourselves for 21st-Century Capitalism* (New York: Alfred A. Knopf, 1991); Peter Drucker, *Post-Capitalist Society* (New York: Harper Business, 1993).

notion does not seem to me credible, it testifies to significant changes in the organization of the economy.[61] Professionals and managers command large portions of the total wealth of industrialized societies, not simply because intellectual labor has greater social status, but because certain kinds of intellectual labor enter into the economy as new means of creating wealth, or as a more efficient means of managing the process of production, or as new means of marketing commodities. Certain kinds of knowledge, information, or skill (though not all kinds) circulate as highly valued in the market for labor. At the same time, scientists, administrators, and policy experts have come to exercise considerable influence on the total system of wealth distribution through the bureaucratic agencies of the welfare state, and through the disposition of capital projects without, however, transforming "knowledge workers" into a new *ruling* class.[62] In fact, there still exists no necessary correspondence between intellectual labor and the ownership of capital, or between intellectual labor and political power.[63]

Further clarification of this tangle of social conditions lies beyond any conceivable theoretical horizon within my ken.[64] Nonetheless, I should like to advance just a little further toward this horizon by revisiting briefly the arguments of the Ehrenreichs and of Gouldner, for whom the question of status is definitely connected to that of culture. The Ehrenreichs posit class as defined by two characteristics, *economic* and *cultural*, the former a "com-

61. The new division of labor is sometimes conceived as a relation between the production and service sectors of the economy. This distinction seems to me quite useful for understanding certain aspects of the division of labor, but I do not think that the professional-managerial class can be adequately grasped simply by means of the category of service.

62. See here Amin, *Post-Fordism*; Frank Webster, *Theories of the Information Society* (London: Routledge, 1995); Michel Aglietta, *A Theory of Capitalist Regulation: The US Experience* (London: New Left Books, 1979); Daniel Bell, *The Coming of Post-Industrial Society: A Venture in Social Forecasting* (Harmondsworth: Penguin, 1973); Fritz Machlup, *The Economics of Information and Human Capital* (Princeton, NJ: Princeton University Press, 1984).

63. For a critique of the more extreme claims about the new rule of technocrats and managers, see Gil Eyal, Ivan Szelenyi, and Eleanor Townsley, "The Theory of Post-Communist Managerialism," *New Left Review* 222 (1997): 60–92. See also Schement and Curtis, *Tendencies and Tensions of the Information Age*, 213.

64. My analysis here differs from that of John Frow, in *Cultural Studies and Cultural Value*, who views class as "the effects of struggles structured by objective conditions that are simultaneously economic, political, and ideological" (104). This formulation produces an illuminating taxonomy of social struggles, inclusive of potentially every sort, including those of gender, race, and ethnicity. Class here is a meta-category of classification, with no inherent or exclusive relation to the economic. In my own analysis, I prefer to maintain economic and cultural categories as distinct fields of classification.

mon relation to the economic foundations of society," the latter "a coherent social and cultural existence" (11).[65] But what is the relation between these two features of the professional-managerial class? Does one determine the other, or is it just that they appear together?

Gouldner, by contrast, argues in *The Future of Intellectuals and the Rise of the New Class* for the *cultural constitution* of the New Class by positing knowledge as a form of cultural capital that enters directly into the economic process: "The special culture of the New Class *is* a stock of capital that generates a stream of income (some of) which it appropriates privately"[66] The difference between the Ehrenreichs and Gouldner is that for the former, culture is to be found at the site of consumption, while for the latter it defines an organic involvement in production itself. This distinction is of great consequence. The identification of a new class of professionals raises the possibility that it is a class for which the cultural constituent is uniquely related to what it produces, which is something of *value*. Every profession, even if it uses its expertise to produce a service, still *produces something*, goods or services that can be assigned a value in exchange. This demand for product troubles some professions in peculiar ways, perhaps none more so than scholarship, for reasons already implicit in the argument of this chapter. Scholars who are both teachers and researchers produce goods (publications) and services (teaching), both of which are difficult to assess, even in comparison to each other. University scholars, among them literary scholars, are called upon to justify their place among the disciplines in terms of product (the value of the knowledge they produce) as well as productivity (how many books published, how many students taught). A question arises from this reflection about the comparability of various forms of knowledge as product. We know that this is not an easy question to answer and that different objects of knowledge have different perceived values. What buoys up diverse forms of knowledge, what maintains their minimal value, is in the end the form of professional identity itself, the fact that all forms of professional expertise are rarified, and acquired with difficulty, by the path of the "discipline." This makes the product of humanities schol-

---

65. In a response to their critics, the Ehrenreichs in *Between Labor and Capital* defend their joining of cultural and economic concepts in the category of class. There, it is evident that what is at stake for them in the cultural determination of class is the political: "a person's political consciousness and loyalties" (135).

66. Alvin W. Gouldner, *The Future of Intellectuals and the Rise of the New Class* (New York: Continuum, 1979), 19. The difference between Gouldner's sense of the relation between the economic and the cultural and the Ehrenreichs lies in his identification of cultural capital as "specialized knowledge."

arship comparable to the knowledge commodities in other professional-managerial fields, even if this product is only very distantly connected to the economy. At the same time, this account of the intertwined history of the university and the professional-managerial class reveals the weakness of the humanities in the reckoning of social value and the reason for the vulnerability of humanities disciplines to devaluation and "deprofessionalization" within the system of the disciplines.

FROM THE CULTURE OF PROFESSIONALISM TO THE PROFESSIONAL PROFILE

If the New Class can be defined in part by its possession of knowledge as a commodity, it attempts to ensure the value of that commodity mainly by *cultural* strategies. The most successful of these strategies by far has been professionalism itself, which Magali Sarfatti Larson defines in her exemplary study of professionalization as "the process by which producers of special services sought to constitute *and control* a market for their expertise" (xvi), or "an attempt to translate one order of scarce resources—special knowledge or skills—into another—social and economic rewards" (xvii). As the analysis above demonstrates, this strategy doesn't always succeed. The nominal equivalence of professionals *as professionals* masks a difference in the perceived social value of different kinds of knowledge. These discrepant valuations establish the terms of employment for the contract professoriate, what is perceived as their "deprofessionalization." I will return to this question in chapter 9 below.

The cultural strategies entering into the constitution and valuation of professional identity are capable of being distinguished from the kind of lifestyle choices exercised in the domain of consumption and establish the "social cohesiveness" of the professional-managerial class. I will turn to the latter aspect of the culture of professionalism presently, but I offer here a summation of the strategies constituting this culture inasmuch as it is addressed to the domain of production and to the market for the assessment of its knowledge product:

- The labor of the professions is constructed as *cognitive* or *abstract*. It necessarily involves, as one theorist of professionalism, Andrew Abbott, has noted, "applying somewhat abstract knowledge to particular cases."[67] We should understand this as a necessary but not sufficient condition

67. Abbott, *The System of Professions*, 8.

for defining professional work. Cognitive labor also underwrites the demand for a certain measure of work autonomy and encourages resistance to the routinization of labor.

- The strategy of *specialization* reinforces claims to control over certain tasks by demarcating exclusive fields of knowledge and competence, what Abbott calls the "jurisdictional" claim. The division of intellectual labor is related to the desideratum of constant improvement or "progress" in knowledge, which lies behind the pressure continually to raise the market value of professional goods and services.

- Modes of *professional organization* are developed in order to certify the validity of professional knowledge and to control the standards for credentialing practitioners. This organizational mode entails a very different principle of exclusivity than the one that characterized guild or craft associations. Whereas the guild controlled its knowledge by keeping it *secret*, passing it on from master to apprentice, the professions seek to ensure the social credibility of their knowledge by *publication*, by opening knowledge (in principle) to public scrutiny. Consequently, publication becomes the singular most effective marker of professional success for many professional fields, including those, like literary study, that do not enter directly into the exchange of traditional commodities. The exclusivity of professions is on the other hand sustained as a consequence of the manifest difficulty of acquiring this knowledge, by the requirements imposed upon candidates for entrance into a given profession and by the delegation of credentialing to the university system, with its complex hierarchy and array of social filters. Credentialization through the university system has thus become the requisite for entrance into nearly all professions. This is what I mean by the "institution of professions."

- The professional organization is *bureaucratized* in order to ensure uniform procedures, practices, and standards for large groups of professionals (with supplemental reinforcement by state laws regulating accreditation and licensing), to structure the working life into the form of the "career," and to establish minimum rates of exchange for professional labor. While the professional organization is quite unlike the labor union in many respects, from another point of view it serves an analogous function of negotiating the value of expert labor in the market. Professional organizations do not need to undertake this negotiation directly with employers, because the compensation for most professional labor is individually negotiated on the basis of certain socially established scales of compensation.

- Finally, professions develop *ideologies* of social presentation or legitimation, for example, the ideal of "public service."[68] The ideology of professionalism is also often expressed as an "ethic" of intellectual rigor,
honesty, and service. If these ethical principles can be regarded as constituting an ideology of legitimation, this ideology can hardly function
in that capacity if it does not also describe a real aspect of professional
culture, the necessity of that culture to be accountable ultimately to the
consumers of its services, and second to reflect critically upon its own
practices in the same way that it reflects critically upon the field of objects or practices over which it claims jurisdiction. In *The Future of Intellectuals*, Gouldner calls this the "culture of critical discourse" (28). One
might argue (gesturing here to Durkheim or Veblen) that the professions
have crafted an ethic that arises out of the innermost secularizing and
rationalizing tendencies of modernity. This ethic descends from, without
being reducible to, the principles of scientific reason that came to be recognized for these same features in the nineteenth century.

If these strategies are dedicated ultimately to ensuring the market value of
professional knowledge and the labor required to produce it, this value is
not only or inevitably determined by these cultural strategies. Money capital has, so to speak, the last word on the market value of the knowledge-
worker's labor. We are attempting to grasp here the complex relation between knowledge and the market for knowledge, a relation in which no
definite result is guaranteed and in which cultural strategies for the valori-
zation of knowledge can succeed or fail.

Most of these strategies can be said to characterize professional-
managerial fields in general, rather than specifically the humanities or literary study. Here I set out some of the implications of the institution of professions for the latter fields. The social condition of greatest consequence is
the distance of the professionalized humanities from commodity production and from the market for goods and services provided by the scientific,
technical, and managerial fields. In these professions, there is a relatively
stable range of values that can be assigned for goods and services, testify-
ing to their relatively secure claim to professional identity. For some fields
in science and engineering, the traffic between academic research and the

68. The notion of "public service" is both ideology and reality. Stephen Brint, *In the
Age of Experts*, argues that the history of the professions has been characterized by a
movement away from the ideal of public service and toward a market concept of the
professional service as a private transaction between provider and consumer.

market is very busy. Everyone concedes the high value range for new phar-maceuticals, new information technology, which in turn supports the valu-ation of the university disciplines that support these knowledge industries. There are, on the other hand, some products of "basic research" even in the sciences that are more like the results of humanities scholarship—in astronomy or zoology, for example, which are not accidentally among the more poorly funded of the sciences. The claim to professional identity can only go so far as insurance against devaluation if the profession in question is itself uncertain about the value of its products and services, a circum-stance, as I have noted, that can result in a compensatory overestimation of those values. The converse circumstance is also worth remarking: the fact that humanities disciplines are vulnerable to a severe *underestimation* of their value, which amounts nearly to a refusal to acknowledge their place among the professions. We are all familiar with the perennial version of this "crisis" that, since the collapse of the alliance between humanistic and nat-ural scientific disciplines, has occasioned a perennial rhetoric of defense. (I return to this question in chapter 4, "Monuments and Documents.")

As a general principle, we can say that professional goods and services can command a professional level of compensation to the extent that this labor conforms to the recognizable norms of professionalism. As we have seen, this is the condition that makes it possible to sustain the comparabil-ity of professional labor in the university stretching across the spectrum from a new and potentially lucrative discovery in chemistry to a new read-ing of Joyce's *Ulysses*. It is no wonder, then, that so much depends on the maintenance of professional identity, especially when that identity is in part the result of cultural strategies.

What is the value of the knowledge produced by literary scholars? This knowledge does not enter directly into the field of the production of goods, nor does the fact that scholars also teach—a necessary social function—explain its assessed value in the university. We know that teaching alone does not account for compensation; research claims the greater margin of compensation above a nominal "base pay," because it is the locus of what is perceived to be the more professionalized practice. The value of literary scholarship is assessed according to the norms of professionalism and by virtue of the employment of literary scholars in the university. To be a free-lance scholar, no matter the quality of one's scholarship, is precisely to be excluded from the system of rewards. Professionalization, as we have seen, insulates some kinds of knowledge work to a certain extent from the vola-tility of the market. In these cases, the value of scholarship is assessed in-directly, in the context of *the university's internal consumption of knowledge goods*, which results in the further intangible good of institutional prestige.

Of course, we are not speaking here of the hypothetical value of knowledge as a *social good* but only of the value of knowledge in exchange, that is, in a given market. Many kinds of "useless" knowledge—useless from the standpoint of the market—might be defended as social goods. It is a social good to have an educated citizenry but a different kind of social good than that of a diabetes drug or, for that matter, the aggregate increase in the GDP that might result from an increase in the number of persons with higher degrees. The social good of knowing how to read and enjoy works of literature is very difficult to enter into this calculus and in fact does not usually enter into the assessment of the value of literary study at all. That value is almost always assessed in the university's internal market, where it can be reduced to quantitative measures such as the number of students taught or books published and, ultimately, to a measurable index of institutional reputation. The existence of this market permits both literary scholars and the consumers of university education to avoid thinking through the relation between the *social* value of literary study (that is, nonmonetized social benefit) and its *market* value (personal compensation and institutional prestige). The norm of professionalization, which without question makes possible the partial insulation of literary study from the market for material goods, also confounds attempts to translate the production of literary knowledge into a social good, capable of circulating outside the market of internal consumption constituted by the disciplines, the university, and the professional associations that bind each of these to the others.

Despite the insulating effect of professionalism, those fields that do not have an organic relation to the economic system suffer from an inherent vulnerability, with which we are only too familiar. Professors of literature who are classified as teachers rather than researchers are subject to "deprofessionalization" and much lower compensation. It is thus possible for the university to impose economies of scale by adjusting downward the ratio of its research professoriate to a teaching professoriate. This strategy saves a remnant of professionals, whose labor is assessed on the market of institutional prestige at the expense of a larger number of contract teachers who will likely not have the time to undertake the research that circulates in the university's internal market and who are thus excluded from full recognition as a professional cadre.

Three further consequences follow from this systemic arrangement: First, strategies of professionalization tend over time to become highly standardized, universalized, ritualized, and above all compulsory. The "culture of professionalism" consists of a set of social arrangements virtually identical in form for all professions: university apprenticeship, academic degrees, legal procedures for licensing and accreditation, national associations, conventions and conferences, and the use of publication or other forms of public recognition such as prizes to distribute rewards. The advantages of professionalization are such that professional fields must conform to these practices, even sometimes when they are not entirely appropriate or not wholly convincing. Recall that the disciplines of the later nineteenth century were compelled to advertise their knowledge as "scientific," because the scientific norm was culturally dominant and professionalization depended on this norm. But the requisite claim to scientific status disappeared as a way of defining professional identity for all but those disciplines conforming to a much narrower definition of science emergent in the twentieth century. The norm of professionalism overtook science itself and absorbed it into the new universe of disciplines, identical to the university itself.

Second, if success for a given field of knowledge work follows from the degree of professionalization, then professionalization becomes an interminable, competitive, constantly innovative process, at the same time that it can suffer distortion of its knowledge-producing aims, loss of public accountability, and the proliferation of sometimes meaningless professional rituals. Professionalism manifests a kind of wheeling social dynamism—an index of its social value, and as such, of the appeal the professions have for those coming up through the educational system. Students in the colleges and universities very much want to enter into professional fields because they have internalized conceptions of success and failure that make any other kind of working life undesirable. The competition for entry into these fields is thus always increasing. In these circumstances, the institutions of apprenticeship impose ever greater burdens on applicants for entry. This too is a condition with which we have become familiar in literary study, though it is not unique to our discipline. As time goes on, the requirements for entry into the professions become more rigorous at every level of the system, including the phase at which PhD holders apply for jobs.

Third and finally, the system of professions shapes the aims of the higher educational system by imposing a universal *cultural* requisite for entry into professional-managerial occupations. This requisite is not formalized in the same way that tests or letters of recommendation formalize qualification or achievement. And yet it is a requisite nonetheless. Students who move through the colleges and universities acquire something more than a body of disciplinary knowledge—they are also *socialized* into professional society in a process that is diffuse and indirect, the responsibility of no one and everyone they encounter in their postsecondary education. Students learn to internalize something I will call a *professional profile*, a set of cognitive skills, manners, values, attitudes, and cultural references that are not so much specific to individual fields of study as to the "college-educated" generally. Of course, the components of this profile vary to some extent across different fields of study and across the diverse institutions in higher education. But the profile consists of core features similar enough to establish the college-educated as a real demographic. Among the component skills of the profile, the most important is surely the ability to analyze or make complex arguments, in spoken or written form. This intangible good, which is not guaranteed by a college education but is a common aim, is the core of Gouldner's "culture of critical discourse." The differences between this "culture" and older conceptions of the culture bestowed by higher learning mark the difference between class formations, the "genteel subversion" of the old bourgeoisie that Gouldner sees in the transition to the professional-managerial class. Gouldner's "culture" converges on what we mean today by the term "critical thinking," but that term only grasps a part of what belongs to the professional profile, perhaps the most aspirational of its features.

Gouldner's association of the word "critical" with a core aspect of the professional profile shines a kind of ultraviolet light on the historical concept of "criticism" secreted in his "culture of critical discourse." The literary professoriate desires to effect social change directly through the critique expressed in literary criticism, but the reality is more complex, *a mediation of criticism through the professional profile.* This mediation is further complicated by the residual effects of the origin of criticism in the realm of the fine arts, as the cultivation of taste or *aesthetic judgment,* a component of the professional profile more closely identified with the humanities than with the natural sciences and social sciences, and closer to what the Ehrenreichs mean by the "social and cultural cohesion" of the professional-managerial class.[69] Although it is doubtful that the culture of which they are thinking has much to do anymore with the cultivation to which the old European *haute bourgeoisie* aspired, some residual features of that culture nonetheless survive in a domain apart from the working life, a domain of what is trivially called "lifestyle." This culture is closer to what Burke means by an "art of living," an art that is even more difficult to assess as a social good than the "critical thinking" skills university disciplines inculcate among the other features of the professional profile. All of these meanings descend from the root concept of "criticism," and they circulate turbulently, clashing with one another in the discipline that names itself "literary criticism."

69. Ehrenreich and Ehrenreich, "The Professional-Managerial Class," 11.

CHAPTER 2

Professing Criticism

From the criticism of a text to the criticism of a society, the way is shorter than it seems.

JOSEPH SCHUMPETER, *Capitalism, Socialism, and Democracy*

What we do, under pressure, and especially what we do as professionals, is what we have been trained to do, what we have got used to doing, what at deep levels we can take for granted so that we can get on with an immediate job. And there is no profession which can fail to learn from someone making explicit just the training, the usage, the taking for granted, that underlie all practice. This is how all rigorous professions work.

RAYMOND WILLIAMS, "Isn't the News Terrible?"

THE ARCHIMEDEAN STANDPOINT OF CRITICISM

The profession of literary criticism is committed to its scholarship and teaching as instruments for realizing larger social and political aims, far beyond the interpretation of literary texts. Criticism, as many understand it, is an Archimedean lever for moving the world. What the realization of those aims actually means outside the academy will concern me later, but in the meantime, the possibility of the "overestimation" discussed in chapter 1 is obviously signaled by the very concept of criticism. This word at once reaches back to capture the antecedent senses of criticism dominant in the nineteenth-century public sphere and forward to the interpretive practice of an academic discipline *specialized to the literary object.* The overlapping of these two senses of "criticism" focuses a contradiction in the standpoint of the discipline, which in no way disables its everyday practice but, rather, as we shall see, troubles its effort at *justification.* This trouble defines the unique position of literary study among the disciplines; no other discipline incorporates the concept of criticism into its name.

The situation of "criticism" in the nineteenth century, as we know, was very different. Criticism named a mode of writing in the public, journalistic sphere rather than the university. As writers for periodicals, the journalist-critics of the era did not require university training, though they were sometimes graduates of universities, nor did they hold degrees in journalism, as these did not yet exist. They were "professionals" in the sense of working for money, a sense that survives in locutions such as "professional sports." The *self-authorization* of the critic-journalists licensed the diverse subjects of their criticism, which were not restricted to the literary. The critics of the great nineteenth-century periodicals, the so-called "Victorian sages," saw all of society as their legitimate concern. Such was the prestige of their discourse, we might say that all of literature aspired to the condition of criticism (in Arnold's famous phrase, the "criticism of life"). Conversely, criticism itself was a genre of literature and continued to be regarded as such well into the twentieth century.[1] But the decline of the great periodicals deprived this supergeneric discourse of its institutional base, and criticism came to be distinguished from literature with the emergence in the 1920s of academic literary criticism.[2]

Setting aside the received narrative of criticism's supposed decline into mere academic discourse, it is worth recalling that criticism as a university discipline continued intermittently to assert the *motive* of its ambitious precursor, the criticism of society as a whole. This positioning of criticism has been described by Stefan Collini as "an assertion of the superiority of the literary sensibility as a basis for cultural criticism."[3] Collini goes on to observe the peculiar interplay between the restricted domain of literature and the unlimited universal scope of academic criticism: "One of the most interesting questions in mid-twentieth-century intellectual history is how the prolonged exposure to the kind of verbal artifact that is a 'world by itself' [that

---

1. The specification of criticism to the literary artifact is a corollary effect of the redefinition or delimitation of the literature concept itself, a trajectory charted below in chapter 7, "The Location of Literature."

2. This point can be confirmed by looking at the subjects of essays published in *PMLA* and other journals of the 1920s. The journal articles at that time address indifferently works of criticism and of literature, with the clear implication that criticism is being regarded as a genre of literature. For a consideration of this issue, see Brian McCrea, *Addison and Steele Are Dead: The English Department, Its Canon, and the Professionalization of Literary Criticism* (Newark: University of Delaware Press, 1990). McCrea sets out to explain the decline of interest in Addison and Steele as writers of discursive prose. I would say that Addison and Steele are still in some sense canonical, though much less read, and that *many* earlier works of criticism have suffered the same decline of interest as Addison and Steele. The earlier history of criticism is regarded as largely irrelevant to what literary scholars do today, and most graduate students leave graduate programs having read little in this genre.

3. Stefan Collini, "On Highest Authority: The Literary Critic and Other Aviators in Early Twentieth-Century Britain," in *Modernist Impulses in the Human Sciences 1870–1930*, ed. Dorothy Ross (Baltimore: Johns Hopkins University Press, 1994), 159.

is, the literary work] came to seem to be a privileged position from which to conduct the critical scrutiny of the failings of one's own society" (159). This is a question, to underscore Collini's point, not of the legitimacy of social critique but of the relation between literature as the object of a *discipline*, and critique, as a name that gestures toward the *aim* of that discipline.

If criticism is a kind of Archimedean lever by which literary critics hope to move the world, it must be a wonderful device indeed, wherever one stands in order to push down on this lever. But where the critic stands in social space is just the point of greatest consequence in estimating the effectiveness of criticism. The differentiation of cognitive labor into "professions," with their diverse claims of expertise, crowd this space, fill it to its borders. In this universe of disciplines, the old discourse of cultural criticism must inevitably appear weaker than it did when it dominated the periodical public sphere—or rather, only as strong as the particular field of professional expertise where it plants its flag. This weakness is not so much intrinsic to criticism as a discourse as it is the structural effect of the differentiation of knowledge disciplines and the professionalization of these disciplines in the university. We can evoke the condition of structural weakness summarily by pointing to the division in the university between the humanities and the social sciences, which carved up the human world unequally along the border surrounding the empire of natural science.[4] The position of criticism—that is, *literary* criticism—in the disciplinary system by no means confers upon literary scholars the authority to speak on social and political matters in public venues.

The circumscribed position of literary criticism following the division of the disciplines was evident by the interwar period. The public reputation and influence of scholars such as F. R. Leavis evince the extent to which the limits of criticism could be defied or exceeded. More predictive of criticism's future were the comments of the prominent social theorist Joseph Schumpeter in his celebrated *Capitalism, Socialism, and Democracy* of 1942, a work that argues for the authority of the social sciences over the humanities. Schumpeter comments in particular on the discourse of criticism, which he regards with suspicion. A partisan apologist for the economic system Kenneth Burke deplored, Schumpeter nonetheless took literary scholarship more seriously as a competitor than social scientists have since. Turning a jaundiced eye on the critics, he traces their overreach back to the humanist philologists of the Renaissance: "The humanists were primarily philologists but . . . they quickly expanded into the fields of man-

---

4. Even that division has been encroached intermittently over the last century by developments in the natural sciences, especially in psychology and cognitive science.

ners, religion and philosophy. This was not alone due to the contents of the classic works which they interpreted along with their grammar—from the criticism of a text to the criticism of a society, the way is shorter than it seems."[5] Philology names an undoubted expertise; it is arguably the first of the modern disciplines. But is the criticism of a text a sufficient basis for the criticism of society? In the Renaissance, such criticism was unlikely to look anything like a work by Arnold, Burke, or Leavis, much less their successors in twentieth-century departments of literature, nor did it look like the works of the philologists of the same period. The criticism of society was perhaps best exemplified in the premodern world by Thomas More's *Utopia*, the work of a powerful state functionary and humanist scholar. His ironic travel narrative was closest to the classical genre of satire.

Criticism—as the name of a *genre of writing*—did not appear as such until late in the seventeenth century, when authors began to call judgments about plays and poems by that name. The purpose of critical writing was to judge the success or failure of a literary work, to identify its good or bad parts, its "beauties" or "defects." In the eighteenth century, the growing popularity of criticism as a genre of writing ultimately liberated the idea of criticism from its early restriction to literary forms such as the drama; other kinds of literature, other aspects of society, and finally society itself came to be "criticized." Something that we call "critique" emerged, though still known in English as "criticism." Along a parallel trajectory of intellectual history, the idea of criticism was elevated by continental philosophers such as Kant into a radical procedure of philosophical inquiry, nothing less than a determination of the conditions of knowledge. Schumpeter is not interested in the details of this history, and he runs together the history of criticism and philology, two discourses that were distinct, if sometimes intertwined. In his irritable caricature of the critics, he is thinking less of Renaissance philologists or of Kantian critique than of his contemporaries in humanities disciplines. His polemic belongs to a moment in an ongoing struggle between social scientists and humanist intellectuals over the authority to make claims about society as a whole.[6] This struggle, however, was not waged in a vacuum, as a matter only of the "history of ideas"; its immediate context was the professionalization of all intellectual labor as the university system sorted specializations into disciplines and departments.

---

5. Schumpeter, *Capitalism, Socialism, and Democracy*, 148. For a related argument about criticism, see Reinhard Kosellek's *Critique and Crisis: Enlightenment and Pathogenesis in Modern Society* (Cambridge: MIT Press, 1988).

6. For an important account of this struggle, see Wolf Lepenies, *Between Literature and Science: The Rise of Sociology* (Cambridge: Cambridge University Press, 1992).

Schumpeter exhibits the new attitude of the Progressive Era intellectual at the same time that he inherits the capacious learning of a European scholar. But as a social scientist, he feels moved to scoff at criticism, which he describes as the "profession of the unprofessional." His quarrel with criticism reveals how difficult it was for the critics of the earlier twentieth century to find their place in a universe of knowledge disciplines. The authority of criticism in this institutional universe was a *new* problem, emerging out of a "conflict of the faculties" unimagined by Kant, a contention between the social sciences and the humanities. It is the latter *cultural* authorities whose credentials Schumpeter questions, *their* extension of the criticism of the text to the criticism of a society.

If Schumpeter speaks for social science, the burden of his complaint is that criticism plays both sides of the street, pretending to be a specialization among other specialized disciplines but tacitly *specializing in everything.* This is what he means by the "profession of the unprofessional." The tendency of literary criticism to grasp the whole world in grasping its particular object of study seems to confound the very principle of specialization upon which the disciplines are based. It would be difficult to deny that criticism fell into this contradiction as soon as it competed for territory among the academic disciplines. This difficulty cannot be finessed by the sort of claim made by Leavis on behalf of an "English School": "Its special—but not specialist—discipline is to be the literary-critical, a discipline of sensibility, judgment, and thought which, of its essential nature, is concerned with training a non-specialist intelligence."[7] Academic literary criticism has by and large rejected the Leavisian notion of a "special—but not specialist" discipline in favor of a discipline asserting parity with other specialized disciplines of the university. As we will see, the problem of the relation between this special status and specialization played out as a different kind of border conflict than that between the humanities and the social sciences: the difference between the profession and the discipline.

PROFESSION AGAINST DISCIPLINE

The Formalization of an Amateur Discourse

What, then, is the relation between the discipline called "literary criticism" and the "criticism of a society"?[8] What authority is arrogated by a

---

7. F. R. Leavis, *Education and the University* (London: Chatto and Windus, 1943), 43.

8. Henceforth I will drop the article before "society" in this phrase, in recognition of the elevation of the word *society* to an abstraction that hovers behind critical practice in the later twentieth century.

discipline that names its particular expertise as literary criticism? Although Schumpeter would probably consider literary criticism of recent decades an even more extreme instance of the "profession of the unprofessional," it must be said that there is nothing unprofessional about the behavior of contemporary professors of literature. They have long since embraced with the greatest enthusiasm the occupational identity of professionals, with both the responsibilities and privileges belonging to that status. Yet the very insistence of the discipline on its professional status raises the question of whether the academic study of literature can in fact be comprehended under the name of criticism and whether this name really legitimizes a special claim on the criticism of society. It will be evident from the essays in this volume that I do not believe the criticism of society is the province of any particular discipline, much less that it can be institutionalized in departments of literature. I suggest on the contrary that the legitimacy of criticism depends on its indeterminate position, equivalent to the perspectival dislocation Burke calls "incongruity." In this sense, criticism is the privilege of no one discipline and the obligation of all.[9]

But many believe otherwise, as Collini remarks, and have staked much on the distinctive social mission of the discipline called literary criticism. The resolution of this question will depend in part on our understanding of how criticism came to be professionalized in the first place, that is, its professional *formation*. The history of the university reveals no discipline called "literary criticism" until as late as the Second World War. René Wellek and Austin Warren remark in their *Theory of Literature* (published in the same year as Schumpeter's volume, 1942) that there is still no single term for the "systematic and integrated study of literature" and that "the most common terms for it are 'literary scholarship' and 'philology.'" The first term is "objectionable" for Wellek and Warren because it excludes "criticism," while the second term seems to exclude literature itself in foregrounding a chiefly "linguistic" disciplinary object.[10] As Gerald Graff reminds us, the "word *criticism* was not added to the Modern Language Association's constitutional statement of purpose until 1950."[11] In the previous hundred years, the most common names that circulated in connection with the study of literature were *philology, rhetoric, belles lettres,* and *literary history,* any of which

9. For another take on the relation between text and society, see Paul Ricoeur, "The Model of the Text: Meaningful Action Considered as a Text," in *Hermeneutics and the Human Sciences,* ed. John B. Thompson (Cambridge: Cambridge University Press, 1981), 197–221.

10. René Wellek and Austin Warren, *Theory of Literature* (New York: Harcourt, Brace, 1942), 29.

11. Graff, *Professing Literature,* 283.

might involve teaching or research in literature.[12] Moreover, the relation between criticism and academic forms of literary study was, so far from being one of identity, openly conflictual, the struggle between "scholars and critics" recounted by Graff.[13] This conflict emerged in its first iteration during the eighteenth century, though not as a conflict between university disciplines. Critics and literary historians were not opposing intellectual types but rather *gens des lettres* composing in different genres of writing. Critics and literary historians might be found within the university or without. But in the twentieth century, the divergence of the two discourses defined a conflict *internal* to the literary professoriate.

Here it will be necessary briefly to rehearse this sequence, even though it is relatively well known. As the historians of our discipline have noted, the scholars moved away from philology after World War I (in part because of its Germanic associations) and tended to identify their discipline thereafter as "literary history," or in Wellek's term, "literary scholarship." Being a literary scholar meant practicing a version of research in which literary texts were read more or less like other kinds of historical documents. Being a critic, on the other hand, when criticism was no longer a dominant discourse of the periodical public sphere, meant something quite different. The critics who taught in the university at the time practiced a mode of criticism descending from the "belletristic," a style disparaged by T. S. Eliot and his followers as merely impressionistic. Criticism as a discourse was otherwise not well defined in the university until the revolutionary work of I. A. Richards in the 1920s, in which he repudiated belletrism, along with the philology and literary history taught in piecemeal fashion at Cambridge and elsewhere. In this oft-told story, Richards's followers in England, along with the New Critics in America, inaugurated a polemical struggle with the scholars, a deliberate attempt to dislodge them from their authoritative positions in English and modern foreign language departments. Yet in the two decades after the war, conflict between the scholars and the critics came to a peaceful conclusion, and a new discipline coalesced that called itself by none of the earlier names enumerated above, but a new name: *literary criticism*. How did this happen?

Our understanding of the social and institutional dynamic impelling both the conflict and its resolution is still imperfect. Looking back on the struggle between the scholars and the critics, I argue that *professionalization* was the solution to the problem of integrating criticism into the existing organization of literary study—or rather, *disorganization*. For what

12. Wellek and Warren, *Theory of Literature*, 29.
13. Graff, *Professing Literature*, 121–44, 183–94.

criticism accomplished by means of its successful struggle with scholarship was to organize the disorganized discourses of philology, literary history, and belletristic appreciation into the *one* discipline of literary criticism. But this happy conclusion entailed asserting first a claim to professional identity, in support of which the critics then devised a method of teaching addressed to the specificity of the literary object. This methodology, however, could not be a formalization of *judgment*, which was too easy to dismiss as mere opinion.

The unstated aim of thus organizing literary study was to reconcile criticism, as a discourse of *opinion*, with scholarship, as a discourse of *knowledge*. The status of opinion was always the impediment to raising the status of criticism, as Samuel Johnson acknowledged centuries before in stating that "the task of criticism" was "to establish principles; to improve opinion into knowledge."[14] Johnson's comment points forward to the possibility of criticism as a *discipline*. Literary scholarship had already achieved at least protodisciplinary status when Johnson was writing, in the forms of philology and literary history.[15] When the scholars of vernacular literature later began to find places in the universities, they came to regard the critics as amateurs—even those critics who were journalists by "profession," as were the writers for the great reviews of the nineteenth century.[16]

Johnson's hope for raising criticism to knowledge was frustrated by the rapid development of the disciplines themselves. Yet criticism did finally become established as a discipline in the "modern language" departments of the twentieth century, a surprising outcome, given the existing disciplinary forms for the study of language and literature. We can identify the conditions for the critics' happy reversal of fortune by recalling, first, that a certain inherited exigency weakened the regime of scholarship at the moment of the critics' challenge. This exigency was simply the fact that with the retirement of classical Greek and Latin as the required course of study, and the replacement of the classics by a vernacular curriculum (discussed at

14. Samuel Johnson, *The Rambler*, no. 92, in *The Yale Edition of the Works of Samuel Johnson* (New Haven, CT: Yale University Press, 1969), 4:122.

15. The qualifier "vernacular" distinguishes literary scholarship from the predecessor form of classical philology. The reason for this distinction is argued in my "Literary Study and the Modern System of the Disciplines," in *Disciplinarity at the Fin de Siècle*, ed. Amanda Anderson and Joseph Valenti (Princeton, NJ: Princeton University Press, 2002), 19–43.

16. For an informative account of the struggle for cultural authority between the critics and the scholars on the American side of the Atlantic, see Kenneth Cmiel, *Democratic Eloquence: The Fight over Popular Speech in Nineteenth-Century America* (Berkeley: University of California Press, 1991).

greater length in chapter 5, "The Postrhetorical Condition"), the classically trained teaching corps of the university system had to be recommissioned for the new vernacular curriculum. Their numbers were insufficient for this task, and other teachers, some of them critics and poets who wrote for belletristic journals, joined university faculties after the First World War. This teaching professoriate did not always possess the doctoral degree, which was held by a smaller percentage of the faculty, more or less identical with the "scholars." Their training was in vernacular—at the time, usually English—philology and literary history. This was the situation prevailing in the years preceding the two great transformative movements in the interwar period, "practical criticism" in England and the "new criticism" in America. At this point, however, we must suppress the details in this story in order to see a very big picture: the institutional purchase afforded by the *teaching function* allowed the critics, whatever their credentials, to adopt and conform to the institutional norms of professionalism, that is, the protocols governing the career of the college professor. *Criticism thus became an academic profession before it became a discipline.*

Despite the success of the critics in professionalizing as academics, the absence of an elaborated methodology of criticism—something analogous to the methods of philology or of historical research—remained problematic and might have resulted in the permanent division of the literary professoriate into higher and lower cadres, the scholars above, the critics below. For a period of time the critics did indeed occupy this secondary position in university faculties. But in the 1930s, the critics opened a second front in their conflict with the scholars by developing criticism itself as a *formal discourse of knowledge*, different from both its belletristic predecessor and from the literary history of the scholars. I. A. Richards's reinvention of "practical criticism," and the New Critics' development of this technique into a method of interpretation, imparted rigor and iterability to a course of study that seemed at the time nothing more than an (often inept) effort to cultivate the judgment of students. When R. P. Blackmur defined criticism in his well-known 1935 essay "A Critic's Job of Work," as "the formal discourse of an amateur," he signaled the transitional strategy of *formalization*.[17] John Crowe Ransom made the stakes in this procedure explicit: "Rather than occasional criticism by amateurs,

---

17. R. P. Blackmur, "A Critic's Job of Work," in *Selected Essays of R. P. Blackmur*, ed. Denis Donoghue (New York: Ecco, 1986), 19. See also Foucault on the threshold of formalization, in *The Archaeology of Knowledge*, trans. A. M. Sheridan Smith (New York: Pantheon, 1972), 186–89.

I should think the whole enterprise might be seriously taken in hand by professionals."[18]

The critics undertook to formalize their discourse in two venues: first, in the classroom, where they developed those iterable techniques of interpretation that later came to be aggregated (not always accurately) under the name of "close reading," and second, in new periodical publications like the *Sewanee Review* and *Scrutiny*, where they conducted a polemic against the scholars on behalf of criticism as a rigorous discourse that fused judgment with interpretation.[19] Importantly, the "formal discourse" of criticism was premised in both venues on the construction of the literary text as a *verbal work of art*, a conceptualization that subordinated the documentary aspect of literary texts to an aesthetic ontology, thus distinguishing the *object* of literary criticism from that of literary history.[20]

Although the critics achieved considerable success in developing criticism into such a formal discourse, the scholars continued to express a low opinion of criticism by comparison to literary history, with its established empirical methods of archival research. The scholars might very well have

18. Ransom, *The World's Body*, 329.

19. See René Wellek, in *The Attack on Literature and Other Essays* (Chapel Hill: University of North Carolina Press, 1982): "The method of close reading became the pedagogical weapon of the New Criticism" (97).

20. See Wellek and Warren, "The Analysis of the Literary Work of Art," in *Theory of Literature*: "This raises an extremely difficult epistemological question, that of the 'mode of existence' or the 'ontological situs' of a literary work of art" (141). The specificity of the "literary work of art" is Wellek's perennial theme. His qualifier "literary" begs certain questions that I have tried to keep open by opting usually for the "verbal" work of art. The definition of literature was still somewhat fluid during the interwar period, in part because it was one of the stakes in the ontological move. The notion of a "verbal work of art" does not settle the definition of literature but frames the question better for the purpose of understanding both the history of literary study and its developing theoretical premises. In retrospect, the polemics of the critics in the interwar period tell us that the delimitation of literature was finally a question of a *media* form, though the significance of this fact is only just becoming apparent. But here is Blackmur, writing not atypically of literature in "A Burden for Critics," *The Hudson Review* (Summer 1948): "In our own time—if I may be permitted the exaggerations of ignorance and of poetry— almost everything is required of the arts and particularly of literature. Almost the whole job of culture, as it has formerly been understood, has been dumped into the hands of the writer. Possibly a new form of culture, appropriate to a massive urban society, is emerging: at any rate there are writers who write with a new ignorance and a new collective illiteracy: I mean the Luce papers and Hollywood" (173). It is only against emergent mass media that literature becomes burdened with the full weight of Arnold's "culture"; the critic is correlatively burdened with supporting high culture against its degradation in mass media. This "burden" is in the end an overestimation of the "critic's job of work."

prevented criticism from achieving disciplinary status, yet by the 1950s, the critics succeeded in imposing the name of *criticism* on the discipline itself. It is this reversal of fortune that compels us to recognize the importance of the anomalous sequence by which criticism became a profession before it became a discipline. A shared commitment to professional identity gave the critics a staging ground for contesting scholarship's claim to jurisdiction over the literary object and for asserting a counterknowledge of formalized aesthetic judgment specific to this object.[21] This was a question at base of what the sociologist Andrew Abbott calls "professional jurisdiction."[22] The scholars, the critics argued, could not produce an expert discourse about the literary object because they failed to grasp fully the aesthetic nature of this object. Insisting upon the verbal work of art as the proper object of the discipline, the critics were able to assert a claim to expertise or "jurisdiction" in relation to this object.

This claim was powerful in its day not only because it was plausible in its own terms but also because it resolved an ambiguity left over from the foundational moment of the "modern language" disciplines in the 1880s. The construction of the disciplinary object as the literary work of art finally disambiguated the relation between language and literature that had long perplexed a coherent conceptualization of the modern language disciplines' object of study. Was this object language or literature? The older relation between these terms survives now in the name of the Modern Language Association itself, which foregrounds the object of study dominant in the 1880s, when the association was formed. Even the foreign-language disciplines, which are committed to the teaching of language as such, have reconciled this study to the dominance of literature by dividing the professoriate into the two cadres of literary scholars and language instructors. By the end of the Second World War, both English and the modern language disciplines were decisively reoriented to literature as the name of their principal object.[23]

21. The documentary record of this struggle is copious, but for the purposes of this account, the most interesting polemic was the one conducted jointly in *The Southern Review* and the *Kenyon Review*, entitled "Literature and the Professors." Also instructive in retrospect is F. R. Leavis's exchange with F. W. Bateson in *Scrutiny*.

22. Abbott, *The System of Professions*, 59–85.

23. The resolution of this ambiguity was temporary, and the question of the relation between language and literature was reopened with the emergence of high theory. Language, however, was understood by theory in a way very different from the old philology. In New Critical practice, language was subsumed to a set of familiar figurative devices, such as irony, ambiguity, and paradox, all drawn from rhetoric. If interwar scholarship recuperated only a small fragment of rhetorical practice, this recupera-

From a longer perspective, the reorientation from language to literature brought to completion a tendency dating from the turn of the century. Literary study was already moving away from philology toward literary history in the earlier twentieth century. The reasons for this tendency in the discipline are too complex to take up here, but the critics were positioned to take advantage of it; by the 1930s, they no longer needed to struggle with the philologists, as had the belletristic professoriate (unsuccessfully) before them. Their conflict was for the most part with the literary historians. By means of a formalized technique of reading, the critics were now able to assert a jurisdictional claim over literature and to overcome, once and for all, their residual identity as amateurs. It was as a professional cadre, then, that the critics were spurred to develop a disciplinary method of reading in the mid-twentieth century, reversing the sequence followed by other disciplines before them. They hammered out the principles of a formalized discipline of criticism in the course of their conflict with the scholars, ramping up their theoretical output like factories during wartime. Only in this way were they able to catch up with the scholars, who had long since asserted professional status on the basis of an older, positivistic conception of disciplinary knowledge. That conception, as Burton Bledstein has shown, was common both to scientists and humanist scholars in the later nineteenth century, but it was increasingly subject to question among the cultural disciplines by the interwar period.[24] The critics joined the movement against positivism gaining strength in other historical and social science disciplines, but they lacked a full articulation of criticism as a positive knowledge, with a program of research. Their theory was largely a theory of practice, achieving its initial success in the classroom.[25] In consequence, certain underlying epistemological questions were deferred, and criticism

---

tion still sufficed to generate very powerful new work, beginning with Empson's *Seven Types of Ambiguity*. For a concise account of the victory of literature over the philologists' sense of language in the midcentury departments, see Catherine Gallagher, "The History of Literary Criticism," in *American Academic Culture in Transformation: Fifty Years, Four Disciplines*, ed. Thomas Bender and Carl Schorske (Princeton, NJ: Princeton University Press, 1997): "The New Critics changed our subject matter from language to literature, and they changed our skill from scholarship to criticism" (153). The first half of this statement is correct, but the second half needs to be qualified, as we shall see.

24. See Bledstein, *The Culture of Professionalism*, 302.

25. The basis of New Critical theory in a technique of reading continued to be controversial for some, long after the reconciliation of literary history and literary criticism. Hugh Kenner, for example, remarks in "The Pedagogue as Critic," in *The New Criticism and After*, ed. Thomas Daniel Young (Charlottesville: University Press of Virginia, 1976): "The curious thing is how a classroom strategy could come to mistake itself for a critical discipline" (45).

remained in some respects suspended between opinion and knowledge. The lingering effects of this irresolution argued for a rapprochement with the literary historians, the scholars.

The Postwar Settlement

The conflict between the scholars and the critics is now ancient history, and on the surface, it would seem that scholarship has long cohabited peacefully with criticism. Scholarship and criticism merged in the postwar period into a single discipline uniting the two most conspicuous features of professional formation in both practices: *period specialization*, carried over from literary history, and *a technique of reading closely*, the legacy of criticism. This composite discipline had much to recommend it because the turn to interpretation freed literary history from its residual positivism at the same time that literary history provided the readings of the critics with a sounder basis in historical scholarship. The process of reading became a *model* for new scholarly writing, the projection of reading into "readings," that is, interpretations. Of course, this is an "ideal type" description of the discipline; individual scholarly works could be tilted heavily to one practice or the other. In any case, the study of literature in the university rechristened itself by the 1950s as "literary criticism."[26]

Along with this new disciplinary formation, a new figure appeared in the later 1950s, the "scholar-critic," who embodied in one person the reconcili-

---

26. We tend to forget today that the postwar settlement also entailed a rewriting of the history of literary criticism itself. Although the term "literary criticism" began to appear with some frequency in the later nineteenth century, it meant just what "criticism" had always meant—judgment. The critics of the time possessed the freedom to range over multiple domains of social and cultural life, while retaining a kind of anchor in the literary field. These critics have more or less dropped out of the history of criticism after World War II. Examples of this critical mode include Randolph Bourne, Wan Wyck Brooks, Paul Elmore More, H. L. Mencken, Edmund Wilson, Malcolm Cowley, Philip Rahv, Delmore Schwartz, Alfred Kazin, and others. Some of these critics were academics, others poets or creative writers, but they do not fall into the line that extends back to T. S. Eliot, who is, nonetheless, the most famous example of their kind. With the postwar settlement, this sort of "public intellectual" became increasingly rare; exceptions worth noting include Lionel Trilling, Norman Podhoretz, and the "New York Intellectuals," as well as Susan Sontag. Perhaps this is the place also to register a difference in this story for British literary critics, who never moved quite so far away from their identity as social critics as their American peers. For an indispensable account of the persistence of this strain of critique in British literary critics of the twentieth century, see Stefan Collini, *The Nostalgic Imagination: History in English Criticism* (Oxford: Oxford University Press, 2019). Professionalization, at least in the American style, came later to the British professoriate, often imposed from "above," by the government.

ation of scholarship and criticism. Jacques Barzun celebrates this figure in an essay of 1958 in which he looks back on the earlier conflict: "People outside the academic profession as they know it today are always surprised to hear the distinction made between the scholar and the critic. . . . Yet it was not much more than thirty years ago that inside the university the name of critic was a bar to advancement."[27] The editor of the volume in which Barzun's essay appeared, Lewis Leary, remarks summarily that "there is no longer reason for invidious distinction between the scholar and the critic" (9).[28] Statements of this sort, which were common in the later fifties and early sixties, seemed to reassure the professoriate that it had satisfactorily resolved the conflict of the preceding decades. The program of graduate education was restructured in accordance with the terms of this resolution, retaining only a residual commitment to philology in the form of the "Old English" course. The curriculum was expanded to include modernist works, and all students were inducted into the art of the interpretive essay.

The postwar settlement, however, was not as stable as the concept of the scholar-critic indicates. I suggest that at some perhaps less than fully

27. Jacques Barzun, "The Scholar-Critic," in *Contemporary Literary Scholarship: A Critical Review,* ed. Lewis Leary (New York: Appleton-Century-Crofts, 1958), 3. An English Institute of 1966 explored the newly established amicable relations between historical scholarship and criticism, with the proceedings published the following year as *Literary Criticism and Historical Understanding,* ed. Phillip Damon (New York: Columbia University Press, 1967). In another testament to this amity, F. W. Bateson, who was a principal in the conflict between the historians and the critics, extolled the hybrid figure of the "scholar-critic" in his volume of this name in 1972, *The Scholar-Critic: An Introduction to Literary Research* (London: Routledge and Kegan Paul, 1972). It is worth a side-glance at the parallel but also very different trajectory of French literary scholarship, which also turned away from philological and positivistic literary historical modes with the emergence of "la nouvelle critique." The turn is punctuated by the famous dispute between Raymond Picard and Roland Barthes on the interpretation of Racine's oeuvre. Barthes executed a deft pivot away from standard French literary pedagogy in his essay "Reflections on a Manual," in which he repudiates the methodology derived largely from Gustave Lanson (though Lanson is not named) and transmitted faithfully in the manuals used in the French school system. This essay was first published in 1969 and is translated by Richard Howard in *The Rustle of Language* (Berkeley: University of California Press, 1989), 22–28.

28. For further discussion of the relationship between scholarship and criticism from the period, see George Whalley, "Scholarship and Criticism," first published in 1959 and reprinted in *Academic Discourse,* ed. John J. Enck (New York: Appleton-Century-Crofts, 1964), 150–62. Whalley tries to develop a theoretical framework for the reconciliation of scholarship and criticism. Looking back on the statements that proliferated on this subject in the later 1950s and early 1960s, it is undeniable that the two modes are increasingly fused in scholars who were the products of postwar graduate programs in literature.

conscious level of the professional imaginary, criticism remained inimical to the very form of the academic discipline. If there was no longer a conflict between the scholars and critics, a struggle began at a more inward site where we might say that the discipline of literary criticism was in conflict *with itself*. In the later sixties, this struggle broke out into the open with the emergence of the "new social movements." A favorable response to these movements was prevalent among younger faculty hired at the time to address a shortfall in faculty, a consequence of the rapid expansion of the university system. The result of these convergent tendencies was not only the reassertion of criticism but a growing uneasiness in the professoriate about the postwar settlement, what I will describe as an *internal alienation of disciplinarity*.

The events of the later sixties clarified the size and nature of the gap between disciplinary practice and the arena of social and political action—but not just for literary study. As I have already observed, all scholarly professions are distanced from the sphere of political action by the very institutional structures sustaining the relative autonomy of these professions in society. This distance, however, has different effects for different professions. In our society, there is no "political profession" per se, for example, but there are professions that typically channel credentialed specialists into agencies of government, or into the media public sphere. Other professions are by contrast distanced from these functions by virtue of the particular nature of their autonomy; among the latter are most humanities disciplines, including the study of literature. This kind of autonomy can be experienced at once as a privilege and as a source of disempowerment. The latter effect is especially strong for literary criticism, for the obvious reason that its predisciplinary history was distinguished by the dominant place of criticism in the journalistic public sphere, where the critics were free to address any and all social and political problems.

Looking back on this history, it is possible to understand why the postwar settlement was so fragile: the merger of criticism and scholarship drove the criticism of society underground, as the cost of compromise. Precisely because criticism had to establish its disciplinary credentials, it suppressed *judgment* in favor of its "formal discourse," a technique of interpretation.[29] Judgment was the predicate for the criticism of society, but

29. On the displacement of judgment by interpretation, see the excellent account of Wallace Martin, "Criticism and the Academy," in *The Cambridge History of Literary Criticism*, vol. 7, *Modernism and the New Criticism*, ed. A. Walton Litz et al. (Cambridge: Cambridge University Press, 2000), 269–321. The earlier understanding of criticism as judgment is still prevalent in the anthologies of criticism published in the 1940s and 1950s, for example, *Criticism: The Foundations of Modern Literary Judgment*, ed. Mark

its disappearance from academic literary study was a loss for other reasons as well. We are perhaps only just beginning to understand the cost to the discipline of abandoning the effort to formalize *aesthetic* judgment. But I must leave this question to the conclusion of this volume. In the meantime, we can observe in passing that the preeminence of interpretation in the postwar settlement vitiated the historical allegory of the New Critics that tacitly expressed the criticism of society. This allegory was a transitional construction, a preliminary relegation of judgment to covert messaging. Moreover, this allegory never quite escaped from the crudity of its formulation in Eliot's theory of the "dissociation of sensibility." The "readings" of literary works that proliferated in the postwar period had no need for this allegory, its implicit condemnation of modern society.

Further complicating this transition was the fact of literature's division into modernist and avant-garde writing on the one side and popular genres on the other. The case for modernist literature was always unlikely to succeed when coupled to the indictment of *popular* literature—or, for that matter, denunciation of new media such as film, radio, and television. The notorious difficulty of modernist literature further undermined the ground of authority for critics in the public sphere. The criticism of society followed modernist literature itself into less public venues, remote from the common reader. Where this criticism survived in the work of "public intellectuals" such as Edmund Wilson, Lionel Trilling, or Susan Sontag, it failed to model interpretive practice for the literary professoriate.

Although criticism in the form of reviewing endured in journals and newspapers, radio and television were rapidly creating a new public sphere, where the position of the nineteenth-century style critic was reoccupied by the electronic "pundit." Credentialed experts in various fields are often given a platform by the pundits, but literary scholars are very rarely among those so invited.[30] For the literary professoriate, print venues continue to offer the primary and nearly exclusive venues for literary critics in the public sphere, but even these are limited. For every Edward Said, Stanley Fish, David Bromwich, Michael Bérubé, Judith Butler, or

---

Schorer et al. (New York: Harcourt, Brace, and World, 1948). For a recognition of the new meaning of criticism, see E. D. Hirsch Jr., *Validity in Interpretation* (New Haven, CT: Yale University Press, 1967): "The fact that the term 'criticism' has now come to designate all commentary on textual meaning reflects a general acceptance of the doctrine that description and evaluation are inseparable in literary study" (209). This chapter of Hirsch's book was first published in *PMLA*, September 1960.

30. Allan Bloom and Harold Bloom are exceptions, not accidentally because they were reliable critics of the adversarial academic culture that was perceived to have repudiated the great works and normative values of "western civilization."

Louis Menand, there are thousands of scholars who have little access to venues beyond their classrooms and specialized scholarly journals. Yet this same circumstance permits literary critics a great measure of intellectual autonomy, the obverse of their relative marginalization.[31] This paradox is a structural feature of the organization of disciplines in the university that is very difficult to overcome. Consequently, there are few Marxist economists in economics departments, just as there are few neoliberal apologists in literature departments. The relation between marginalization and autonomy is a powerful effect of the university's success in engrossing all of the arts and sciences into one immensely complex institution. The university permits the expression of a broad range of opinion—otherwise known as "academic freedom"—at the same time that its very structure exercises tacit control over the interfaces between disciplines and the public sphere.

The Reassertion of Criticism

By the later 1960s, the literary professoriate had begun to tire of producing "readings" of literary works, the manifest redundancy of which was becoming an embarrassment for the postwar settlement and a problem for the very category of literature that emerged out of the modernist ferment.[32] In retrospect, the interpretive essays of the previous decades seemed to circulate as endlessly repeated celebrations of great literature, usually exalting the "unity" of the work or the coherence of thematic and formal elements. But with the infusion of new structuralist and poststructuralist "theory" by way of comparative literature departments, the posited unity of the work was, in the mannered language of the time, "called into question." The interpretive strategy of demonstrating unity was rejected in favor of detecting moments of contradiction or incoherence that in turn raised interesting new interpretive questions. The readings that emerged from this redirection of interpretive practice were often more interesting than their predecessors. In any case, they pointed the way beyond the postwar settlement.

Theory arrived on the Anglo-American scene at the same time that the new social movements of the 1960s were transforming the university and the society this institution served. Without rehearsing once more this well-

---

31. For an account of the question of autonomy, see my "Literary Critics as Intellectuals: Class Analysis and the Crisis of the Humanities," in *Rethinking Class: Literary Studies and Social Formations*, ed. Wai Chi Dimock (New York: Columbia University Press, 1994), 107–49.

32. See Jonathan Culler, "Beyond Interpretation: The Prospects of Contemporary Criticism," *Comparative Literature* 28 (1976): "If there is one thing we do not need it is more interpretations of literary works" (246).

rehearsed episode at length, I want mainly to emphasize the convergence of "high theory" with the social movements of the time, a convergence that was sometimes a clash, but more often a merging of aims. One result of this unique set of circumstances was *the reassertion of criticism*, the recovery of what had lapsed since the interwar period and the postwar settlement. It is worth recalling once more that during the interwar period, the literary work's posited organic cohesion functioned as critique, permitting the literary work to stand as an *implicit* indictment of an inorganic "mass civilization" (Leavis's term) dominated by the supposedly inferior works of mass media. But the convergence of theory with the social movements of the 1960s inverted this paradigm of interpretation. Incoherence in the literary "text" resonated with social conflicts and revealed these conflicts in ways that no longer justified the celebration of the literary work's organic unity.

Theory injected new energy into the discipline and seemed to inaugurate a new role for literature as well. Unfortunately, literature itself was no longer quite what it was during the interwar period. It was now much less central to the sphere of cultural production and consumption by comparison to new media. Further, the "language paradigm" that emerged with theory, and that seemed to reduce all of culture to a kind of literature, collapsed under the weight of its overstatement and intensified uneasiness with the object of the discipline.[33] If the iconic status of the literary work of art—*the verbal icon*—disappeared with the rise of iconoclastic theory, a surprising *volte-face* was imminent: whereas criticism first achieved professional status by claiming jurisdiction over literature, the professoriate now began to express discontent with the *restriction* of the discipline to that object. The earlier celebration of the literary work of art, crucial to literary study's claim to professional status and disciplinary credibility, turned over into a subtle alienation.

High theory was itself an inaugural move in this direction, setting out from the hypothesis that the language artifact or "text" did not need to be a work of literature at all in order to exhibit "literariness." This immensely generative conception, deriving from antecedents to theory extending back to Russian formalism and Prague structuralism, had unwitting consequences in the era of high theory. A door was opened leading beyond literature to all of culture, reduced to various species of textuality or literariness. But having passed through this magic portal, it was difficult to return to literature, to be content with that object.

Long-standing frustration with the constraint imposed on literary study

---

33. For a persuasive critique of the paradigm, see Geoffrey Galt Harpham, *Language Alone: The Critical Fetish of Modernity* (New York: Routledge, 2002).

by its specialized focus on literature argues for many, half a century later, that the coherence of literary study ought to be located in its *method* rather than its object. The name of this method is of course "interpretation," a practice that theory complicated without displacing. The long road of theory and its successors ended in a dry place of uncertainty about the object of the discipline and about the condition of disciplinarity itself. I take this to be what Gerald Graff means when he describes the state of the discipline as "coherence without disciplinarity," proposing that henceforth the discipline might "be made to cohere around the terms *reading* and *writing*."[34] Graff's suggestion returns the discipline restoratively to its classroom practice—not on the face of it an unreasonable strategy. But the shift of orientation to the terms "reading" and "writing" effectively severs these terms from literature in order to set the discipline free of a perceived impediment to its greater mission. In his suggestion for reimagining the discipline, Graff responds to a desire for immediacy of impact but at the cost of relegating literature to a kind of disciplinary ballast.

The subsequent extension of criticism to cultural works in general with the emergence of "cultural studies" was a consequence of unresolved tensions in the formation of the discipline, evidence of its simultaneous deformation. Cultural studies was the name of a solution, one of many solutions since the decades of the sixties through the eighties, all of which offer literary critics an escape from the shrinking island of literature. The preeminence of method over object is a general feature of literary study today, despite the fact that literature continues to occupy the position of nominal object in the institutional structures of the discipline—the curriculum, period specialization, categories of hiring, professional associations, and journals. Despite its survival in these institutional forms, literature bears the burden of ambivalence in the discipline, even as literary scholars continue to assert their professional identity with ever greater intensity.

The volatile relation between interpretation as *method* and literature as *object* is evident in the trajectory of high theory, which was notable for conjuring alternative disciplinary objects such as *signifier, textuality, subject,* and *discourse.* The preeminence of each of these alternative objects eventually waned, or fell victim to changes in intellectual fashion, the consequence of an initial overestimation. For this reason, despite the extraordinary ferment of "high theory" in the decades of the seventies and eighties, theory

---

34. Gerald Graff, "Coherence without Disciplinarity," in *English as a Discipline, or, Is There a Plot in this Play?*, ed. James C. Raymond (Tuscaloosa: University of Alabama Press, 1996), 24.

has come finally to have a less prominent role in the discipline, often diminished to the relatively stunted pedagogic form of various "approaches" to literary or other kinds of cultural works. These applications might be reanimated by staging them as a *conflict of theories*, to which the response might be, in Graff's recommendation, to "teach the conflicts." But is there really any longer much of an investment in the stakes of these conflicts? At present, theory is disseminated largely by means of anthologies that offer theoretical approaches to interpretation, like choices on a menu (I invoke this banal simile to underscore my point). The reduction of theory to "approaches" suppresses what was actually at stake in the difference between structuralist and post-structuralist readings, Marxist and feminist readings, Derridean and Foucaultian readings, deconstructive and new historicist readings. These differences no longer rise to the level of conflicts about which anyone really cares and serve instead as a set of performative routines graduate students internalize in the course of their professionalization. Looking back at this history, I would argue that the most interesting disciplinary work has always arisen out of intense investment in the *object* of study and a belief in the value of producing knowledge about this object. In the absence of this investment, it is not surprising that methodological conflicts proved insufficient to constitute the content of the discipline and that conflicting methods were reduced in the end merely to routines.

Arriving at a moment of repetition and fatigue, literary critics today seem no longer much interested in debating either a method or an object. We have even arrived at the possibility of settling for "no method," the real stake in what has been called inaccurately the "method wars." Disenchantment with the form of the discipline has thrown literary study back even more strongly upon the name of criticism, which offers a *motive* for the discipline but does not prescribe its object or method. At the same time, exhaustion with the proliferation of methods has driven the discipline by default back to the research methodology that once supported the disciplinary form of literary history. In much recent scholarship, the research agenda predominates, but the *motive* of scholarship remains the criticism of society. Often the critical motive seems less than convincing, despite being vigorously asserted. It is as though criticism and scholarship face one another once again in an unwitting replay of their historical conflict. This curious state of affairs might be fine for some, but it puts the discipline on weak ground vis-à-vis the knowledge claims of other disciplines. Louis Menand points to this disadvantage in an essay entitled "The Demise of Disciplinary Authority," which telegraphs its argument in its title, affirming that literary study's institutional and social authority reside necessarily in its claim to *be* a discipline and presumably not only a profession.[35] Is it possible to imagine an academic profession for which there is no corresponding discipline? In an admirably honest statement, discussed at greater length in chapter 10 below, Barry Sarchett affirms just this, that "we have a profession without a discipline" and that "professionalism is all that remains for us to use as a set of criteria to judge the relative merits of graduate and subsequent careers in literature when our discipline itself, which has never been as coherent as the sciences, becomes so fragmented as to virtually disappear."[36] Even conceding the difficulty of establishing "criteria" for the purpose of evaluation, is there no sense in which we can be said to transmit disciplinary knowledge?

If the repudiation of disciplinary constraints seems very contemporary, it is really the complacency of this position that is new. The profession's ambivalence about its disciplinary identity was a perennial theme in postwar reflection on literary study, though usually expressed as an anxiety. The very same condition that Sarchett regards favorably, for example, was deplored by Richard Ohmann in his watershed book of 1976, *English in America,* in which he laments the displacement of disciplinary coherence by what he sees as an apolitical professionalism: "There is no common core of knowledge, no 'discipline,' no theoretical framework, no central pragmatic problem to be solved. As in most academic fields, the profession of the MLA members is simply whatever activities have grown up round certain academic subjects and have somehow become respectable. . . . So 'professional standards' means simply the standards of those who have achieved prominence in the profession."[37] Although Ohmann condemns what Sarchett celebrates, they agree about the fact that the profession has triumphed over the discipline. Criticism is what we really profess. Although some version of this story no doubt characterizes other disciplines in the humanities, ambivalence about the disciplinary object is more intense in literary study, for reasons that are peculiar to the history of criticism. The same degree of disciplinary self-doubt does not seem to trouble art history or music history. We are thrown back on the concept of criticism, then, in order to explain this exceptionalism in the self-understanding of literary study.

35. Louis Menand, "The Demise of Disciplinary Authority," in *What's Happened to the Humanities,* ed. Alvin Kernan (Princeton, NJ: Princeton University Press, 1997), 201–19.

36. Barry Sarchett, "Preprofessionalism and Disciplinarity," *ADE Bulletin* 133 (2003): 44.

37. Richard Ohmann, *English In America: A Radical View of the Profession* (New York: Oxford University Press, 1976), 39.

Setting aside for a moment the question of disciplinary object, I want to look more closely now at the relation of academic literary critics toward professionalism itself. The embrace of professionalism has occasioned unease among the professors, as with Ohmann, but that attitude is exceptional. If literary study is weakly or ambivalently identified with the form of a discipline, it has long been, I suggest, overidentified with the form of the profession. The interaction of these opposing identifications magnifies professional deformation by setting in motion an oscillation between a (largely phantom) antagonist—antiprofessionalism—and a contrary tendency toward an ever more intense affirmation of professionalism. Ohmann saw professionalism as excessive, a betrayal of the higher mission of criticism, but this moment of antiprofessionalism was short lived and relatively exceptional thereafter. We have mostly forgotten now that antiprofessionalism was associated with the inaugural phase of left-wing assertion in the discipline, especially in the epochal year of 1968, when the annual MLA conference was temporarily occupied by an insurgent group of professors. In an important volume of essays that emerged from this event, *The Politics of Literature*, the editors, Paul Lauter and Louis Kampf, made very clear their view that professionalism diverted literary study from its true mission: "Mass education has helped to finance and accelerate professionalism and its attendant vices of inordinate publication and empire building; has helped produce the growing disparity between the concerns of professionals and those of students."[38] In their consistently anti-institutional and antiprofessionalist polemic, Kampf and Lauter expressed a conspicuous tendency of the new left, an unwillingness to accept the authority of established institutions. Suddenly it became possible to reimagine disciplines such as literary study altogether, beginning with Lauter and Kampf's recommendation that the curriculum must be revised to include working-class and minority writers. In the light of the canon debate to follow, the volume offers an explicit statement of the antiprofessionalism motivating canon revision at its inception, which the discipline has largely forgotten.[39] Professionalism eventually became once again the *ally* of criticism, as it was during the interwar period. Another *volte-face*.

The reassertion of professionalism and its reunion with the motives of criticism had an obvious historical basis in the failure of the social move-

38. Louis Kampf and Paul Lauter, introduction to *The Politics of Literature: Dissenting Essays in the Teaching of English*, ed. Louis Kampf and Paul Lauter (New York: Vintage, 1970).

39. The injunction to include "working-class writers" in the canon was forgotten as well, reminding us of the split between the new left and the old left, a prominent feature of the new social movements.

ments of the sixties to achieve their most ambitious transformative ends or even to protect their substantial incremental successes from the backlash politics of the Reagan era and after. Still, it is remarkable in retrospect how quickly professionalism ceased to be cast in the role of adversary, a diversion from the proper aims of criticism, and was reconceived as itself a platform for goals of social transformation. When antiprofessionalism was expressed in the eighties and after, it tended to emanate not from the professoriate but from a nonacademic coalition of journalists and legislators; their right-wing antiprofessionalism was only weakly seconded by some in the academy itself. Together, these antiprofessionalists saw themselves as defending an older notion of literary study closer to that of the belletrists, whom they believed to be unconcerned with the criticism of society. About this they were wrong, but on the other hand the belletristic professors at the turn of the nineteenth century did sometimes praise the figure of the "amateur" in defiance of what they saw as the self-involvement and social irrelevance of the specialized professoriate.[40]

For the professoriate today, professionalism in no way subverts or distracts from the political aims of criticism; by default, however, these aims have come to be realized intramurally as an operation *upon the discipline itself*—its object (the literary curriculum), or method (a technique of reading), or thematics (topics of research and teaching). The critique of the discipline from within came to *constitute* its criticism of society, its political intervention. If this tactic seems to imply a kind of emptying out of the discipline, this hardly implies inactivity. On the contrary, the literary professoriate is busier than ever. Ambivalence about the discipline is accompanied by scrupulous adherence to the protocols of professionalism: courses must be taught, books and essays published, journals edited, professional associations run, conferences organized, departments administered, faculty hired or evaluated for promotion. These activities make up the *professional-institutional field*, which takes the same form for literary study as it does for every other academic discipline.

In this uniformity of activity, the organizational form of the profession can be contrasted sharply with that of the discipline. Disciplines are defined by their *differences* from one another, the specificity of their objects and methods, but professions, though founded on specializations, evolve toward an *identity* of institutional practice. In their important essay on this subject, sociologists Paul J. DiMaggio and Walter W. Powell name this effect "institutional isomorphism," which they define thus: "Once disparate

40. See Bliss Perry, *The Amateur Spirit* (Boston: Houghton Mifflin, 1904).

organizations in the same line of business are structured into an actual field (as we argue, by competition, the state, or the professions) powerful forces emerge that lead them to become more similar to one another."[41] These forces are "environmental"—in the case of academic disciplines the organizational forms of department and university that impose a uniformity of professional practice on all academic disciplines.

DiMaggio and Powell also argue that the processes that "make organizations more similar" do not necessarily result in "making them more efficient" (64). On the contrary, the uniform practices that are imposed on the disciplines are always relatively deforming, relatively disruptive of disciplinary aims; these impositions cannot be ignored, though they might be resisted. For this reason, the relation between a discipline and the form of the profession is determined by a certain ratio of strength to weakness. To adduce another hypothesis from the analysis of DiMaggio and Powell, *"The more uncertain the relationship between means and ends, the greater the extent to which an organization will model itself after organizations it perceives as successful"* (77; italics theirs). The strategy of imitation is more likely when the "goals" of an organization are said to be "ambiguous" (77). These hypotheses provide a much-needed framework for analyzing the relation between the phenomenon of overestimation and literary study's happy conformity to professional practices. In the absence of a more realistic estimation of disciplinary aims, the literary professoriate wants to see the expression of critical motives as somehow confirmed by the tokens of professional success. A stronger discipline, one that is more certain of its means and ends, even if these ends are more modest, might not need to make as great a show of professionalism in order to confirm its disciplinary goals or to assess the quality of its scholars.

The role of specialization in literary study underlies the paradox of its critical motives, given that our discipline has no generalists as such; we are all specialists *in literature*, as opposed to other arts. Specialization founds the discipline as such, and the anthropological dynamic of specialization still operates underneath the sociology of professions. Nevertheless, we

41. Paul J. DiMaggio and Walter W. Powell, "The Iron Cage Revisited: Institutional Isomorphism and Collective Rationality in Organizational Fields," in *The New Institutionalism in Organizational Analysis,* ed. Walter W. Powell and Paul J. DiMaggio (Chicago: University of Chicago Press, 1991), 65. DiMaggio and Powell seek to move beyond a way of looking at professional fields that emphasizes their differences from one another, as defined by the different objects or practices over which they claim expertise. What they seek to explain is the "startling homogeneity of organizational forms and practices," which overlays the constitutive differences between professions.

might argue that the development of period specializations constructs literature itself as a category of a more "general" practice.[42] Period specialization relegates literature to a domain of generality that nobody claims. I will take up this question at greater length in several of the chapters below, but here I want only to point out the fact that period specialization is not just a given of literary study; it is also an expression of that institutional isomorphism to which all academic professions tend in greater or lesser measure. The profession exerts an isomorphic pressure on the discipline to generate intradisciplinary specializations that constitute new ways for literary scholars to identify as professionals. These specializations bring literary study into conformity with other disciplines that exhibit intradisciplinary specializations. Accentuating *differences* in specialization paradoxically expresses and reinforces the *uniformity* of professionalism across the system of disciplines in the academy. Such homogenizing tendencies are blindly structural and have unintended consequences. If intradisciplinary specializations in literary study isolate period cohorts, for example, in such a way as to make it difficult for scholars to communicate across their specializations, this is an instance of professional deformation.[43] For literary scholars, the triumph of period specializations has driven period specialists, as we like to say, into ever smaller "silos." Correlatively, the interest of period specialists in literature broadly or in scholarship outside their period field is ever declining. In this, as in other instances we might cite, the profession dominates structurally over the discipline.

Although literary study is far from unique in yielding to the isomorphic pressure described by DiMaggio and Powell, the effect of these pressures is compounded for our discipline by the interaction between intradisciplinary specialization and the motives of criticism. Period specialization widens the gap between the professional field of scholarly publication and the public sphere in which the professors imagine they might realize the motives of criticism. Works of scholarship are addressed first and last to others in the same period field. The closed circles of these internal audiences make it

---

42. Wellek and Warren, *Theory of Literature*, express the opinion of the New Critics that period concepts "constitute an indefensible jumble of political, literary, and artistic labels" (276–77). In their chapter offering recommendations for revamping graduate education (285–98), Wellek and Warren argue vigorously against period specialization as a basis for the graduate curriculum. They lost this battle, of course, with the establishment of the postwar settlement.

43. We might say that for a time theory bridged the gap between period specializations and so constituted an "inter"-disciplinary form of intradisciplinarity. But theory too became a specialized field, and for some time the concept of "theorist" became a category of employment.

nearly impossible for period scholarship to realize the motives of criticism in the larger arena of a presumptively literate public. Ironically, the reading public continues to express a high regard for literature. Without being able to rely on this regard, however, period scholars must settle for the *declaration* rather than the realization of their critical motives; these declarations of motive circulate among the professoriate, but rarely further.

By default, the critical motive tends to be expressed as a kind of imaginary fiat, imputing to even the most recondite scholarship the capacity to function as a criticism of society, an Archimedean lever. In the event, however, the reassertion of criticism, as a discourse intended to leap the gap between specialized scholarship and a larger public sphere, is undermined by the rumor that the professoriate is for some reason attacking its object of study, literature itself. This rumor is not literally true, but it captures a certain truth nonetheless, in the upside-down perception that what scholars call the critique of society is really an "attack upon literature." This misprision detects the ambivalence of the professoriate about the literary object as a constraint upon criticism. Ambivalence is not an *affective* animus, a supposed dislike of literature, but a structural consequence of the conflicting relation between the grand motives of criticism and the specialized practice of scholarship.[44] The tendency to overestimate the aims and effects of literary study is in this way subject to an extraordinary displacement or inward turn. The criticism of society is expressed as a criticism of the disciplinary object, the deep meaning of canon critique; the curriculum becomes the site of a proxy war. Thomas Bender rightly connects this intradisciplinary turn of critique to the failure of the most radical agendas of the 1960s: "Many of these academic intellectuals redefined politics in cultural terms; the campus became the world. This move made academic culture and the syllabus, more than the class system and the conditions of community life, the locus of political energy."[45] So the discipline became a surrogate for society in the "criticism of society." What is needed now is a critique of the *discipline as surrogate*.

Surrogational politics was preeminently instanced, as Bender remarks, at the site of the curriculum. This is to say that the interest of the professoriate in literature (as opposed to the professors' interested in their special-

44. This rumor was communicated to a wider public first by those within the discipline who disapproved, not always on well-considered grounds, of most theoretical and political modes of criticism emergent in the 1970s and after. See, for example, René Wellek, "The Attack on Literature," in *The Attack on Literature and Other Essays* (Chapel Hill: University of North Carolina Press, 1982), 3–18.

45. Thomas Bender, "Politics, Intellect, and the American University," in *American Academic Culture in Transformation*, ed. Bender and Schorske, 39.

ized research projects) is excited mainly by literature's role as surrogate. The relation between literature and society is obviously not one of identity but of asymmetric distinction: literature belongs to the totality of society as one of its domains. We do not need to enumerate here the social trans-actions of literature—that would be a vast labor—in order to argue that one cannot simply impute to the literary canon a surrogate role without consid-erable distortion of the complex relations between literature and society. And yet our discipline has become attached to this rhetoric, with manifest ill effects. Not the least of these is the tendency to relegate older "historical" literature to a zone of the nonpolitical, or sometimes even of the politically retrograde. Much better, in the view of many, to let some of this older lit-erature go in favor of contemporary writing, which transports one more directly to the front of critique by virtue of exhibiting the diversity that older writing inevitably fails to manifest.

In addition to the critique of the canon, the forms of surrogacy in the last four decades include the displacement of the literary object by artifacts of mass or popular culture (cultural studies) and the movement out from text to "context" with new historicism.[46] The result of these displacements was supported by something we might call "low theory," a rearticulation of theory but with less conceptual elaboration. In the works of low theory, representation disappears into the discourse of "identity," text disappears into "context," the subject disappears into "power." Or rather, the concepts of high theory reappear in these new guises. The later theoretical terms came to constitute a new-old paradigm, subordinated to the motives of criticism, at the same time that this paradigm seemed to vacate theory as an ongoing intellectual effort within the discipline.

To address for a moment only one example of ambiguous consequence, we might observe how new historicism opened a path for literary study back to the archival research of an earlier generation of scholars. With this difference, however: that the archival materials found would be only indi-rectly related to the history of literature as such. This archive had little to do with formal or generic questions or with the transmission of literary texts. The archive that opened up for literary study was rather that which related directly to social and political matters; it was a path beyond literature, even when it illuminated literary texts. The result was that archival texts them-

---

46. See Kampf and Lauter, *The Politics of Literature*, 41. Courses such as these are taught all the time in literary study today, though usually attached to period specializa-tions or specializations that emerged directly out of the identity categories named in Kampf and Lauter's statement.

selves ceased to be merely documentary and took on the energy and inter-est of the literary, that is, "literariness."

My analysis here is not intended to be dismissive; it implies nothing about the value of the scholarship based on this configuration of concepts. My observation is rather about the configuration itself, nowhere more conspicuous than with the emergence of "context" as the chief concep-tual operator in literary scholarship of the 1980s and after, displacing the concept of "text" regnant during the era of high theory. This displacement comes into better focus when we look at scholarship from a certain orbital distance, where we can observe the larger structural features of the disci-pline and the slow paradigm shifts that look very sudden only when they acquire a name. Individual works of scholarship can always rise above the paradigm, or struggle with it in interesting ways, as might be confirmed, for example, by rereading the earlier work of Steven Greenblatt with an aware-ness of the extent to which New Critical techniques of close reading contin-ued to animate his engagement with literature. The use of these techniques allowed Greenblatt to offer interpretations of found poetry in the archive, like the phrase "invisible bullets." The most successful examples of this scholarship reanimated the composite figure of the scholar-critic, estab-lishing the relation between these component identities on a new ground.

As the principal conceptual operator of the new historicism, "context" is also an expression of surrogacy in that it permits archival text to function as the stand-in for "society" in the "criticism of society"—closer than literature itself ("text") to the reality of the social. Again, I invoke these stratagems of surrogacy without impeaching the legitimacy of the research agendas to which they gave rise or questioning the value of scholarship that emerged under these headings. Many very important works of scholarship, probably the most important of recent decades, have been produced setting out from premises that do double duty, at once shedding new light on literature and *implying* the political efficacy of this scholarship. Those who were best able to accomplish these dual aims were best able to *profess criticism*.

Justification by Faith

The word "profession" has a long and interesting history, including the concept of the "profession of faith." Sometimes this is strengthened to a "confession of faith"—in the age of the religious wars in Europe, this might be a confession of the *wrong* faith. In any case, I want to activate here the religious sense of "profession" to suggest that the professional career of the scholarly critic today functions simultaneously as a covert *prophetic* career, the secret redemption of the critic's amateur past, when the critic stood over against society in the reoccupied position of prophet. Versions of this scenario can be found in all scholarly fields, as Nietzsche saw. But the fact that literary study was baptized with the name of *criticism*, a metonymy that designates not the discipline's object but its motive, tells us why this discipline stands out from other humanities fields, and is so often the target of denunciation in the public sphere. The backstory for this shift has been ably recounted by historian Carl Schorske, in an essay from which I draw the following observation on the consequences for literary study of the new social movements:

> Economics, in its prewar, descriptive aspect often a center of social criticism, had left that function behind in the analytic consolidation of the 1950s. In a strange reversal of roles, however, younger members of literature departments, abandoning their aesthetic detachment, took up social-critical functions when the New Critical umbrella was shredded by the storm.
>
> The shift in the disciplinary locus of engaged criticism from economics to literature, however limited, was appropriate enough. In the 1930s the discontents were strongly social and economic; in the 1960s, they were social and cultural.[47]

I would revise this backstory only by pointing out that the turn to "engaged criticism" was in fact the reassertion of its earlier role, from a time long before criticism was the name of an academic profession. The turn to a "cultural" politics in the 1960s made it possible to take literature as a major instance of this politics, ironically just when literature was ceding its cultural preeminence to the works of the new media. Cultural politics was a strategy for arresting this tendency, but with disappointing results. The underlying problem, *the relation of literature to new media*, failed to be addressed, with consequences we have scarcely begun to acknowledge.

The situation of criticism during the phase of its reassertion is complex enough for it to be misunderstood on all sides, especially in the public sphere. Other disciplines engage in the criticism of society, but only one names itself "criticism." The critics take up their megaphones, however, in a micropublic sphere of like-minded professors. The problem is not that these voices cannot be heard outside the professional enclosure, like a shout from a distant stadium, but that their effect and meaning are

47. Carl E. Schorske, "The New Rigorism in the Human Sciences," in *American Academic Culture in Transformation*, ed. Bender and Schorske, 325.

distorted. The messages that pass through the filters of publicity emerge strangely mangled on the other side, reductively phrased and even parodic.

The tendency of humanistic scholarship generally to aspire to the form of prophecy was well described in the earlier twentieth century by Max Weber in his moving lecture "Wissenschaft als Beruf," usually translated "Science as Vocation," but which for our purposes we can translate as "Scholarship as Profession." The "calling" that figuratively underlies the scholarly "profession" (both words translate *Beruf*) is a call to knowledge. But more ambiguously, it has also been a call to a spurious form of prophecy, the religious trope by which Weber grasps the politicization of the lecture hall and of scholarship. Weber was opposed to the confusion of scholarly and political motives in his own day for very good reasons, which proved to be predictive if not prophetic. To the would-be "professorial prophet" he famously responded: "If he then asks why he cannot deal with both sets of problems [scholarly and political] in the lecture room, we should answer that the prophet and the demagogue have no place at the lectern. We must say to both the prophet and the demagogue: 'go out into the street and speak to the public.'"[48] This message is not likely to be welcome to the humanities professoriate today, but Weber is making a valid point about the *autonomy* of scholarship. History was on Weber's side in deploring the pretention of what he called the "petty prophets" of German academia, who believed, no doubt, that they were engaged in nothing other than the criticism of society, and never more so than when, only a few years later, they welcomed the *Gleichschaltung*, the total sacrifice of their intellectual autonomy. Their criticism was heard far beyond the academy, but only because it was joined to the voice of the state.

In literary study today, the prophetic career and the professional career are fused and at the same time compartmentalized in the scholarly imaginary. The work of scholarship is *judged* in its institutional setting according to the most rigorous standards, but scholarship is *justified* to those without and within by invoking the critical motive. *Judgment* and *justification* have different occasions, but together they reveal how literary study understands itself. I want to correlate these two terms now with the two other terms at the center of my argument: scholarship and criticism. If scholarship and criticism were reconciled in the postwar period, that process was obviously never complete. Scholarship belongs to the world of disciplines and the university, but criticism in its oppositional form has no *necessary* disciplinary home. Literary scholarship aims to say something new about

48. Max Weber, "Science as Vocation," trans. Rodney Livingstone, in *The Vocation Lectures* (Indianapolis: Hackett, 2004), 20.

the literary work, which makes it seem worthwhile to publish even the smallest insight, the most unpretentious conjecture about a moment in a work of literature. But criticism claims to wield an Archimedean lever; it wants to move the world.

Because literary scholarship is a rarified form of writing, with a vanishingly small sphere of dissemination, we cannot easily know its effects beyond that sphere. What we accomplish in the classroom may seem more capable of demonstration, but even those effects are difficult to determine with any precision, given what we know about how memory works and about the psychic resistances that accompany learning. In what way students are changed by what they learn, and what part humanities disciplines such as literary study play in the aggregate effects of their passage through the educational system—these are still little understood. It seems reasonable to suppose, however, that teaching in humanities disciplines has had a significant impact on political *attitudes* in the demographic of the "college-educated." But the domain of "attitude" needs to be specified more precisely. Literary study, along with all other university disciplines, contributes to the formation of what I have called the "professional profile" of the college-educated, the skills, manners, values, attitudes, and cultural references common to the professional-managerial class. These effects are not minimal. They have propelled a great shift in attitudes toward minority groups in our society; they have encouraged universally among the college-educated a desire to move beyond the injustices visited upon minority populations. Unfortunately, the success of this attitudinal shift, especially in the field of speech, does not mean that the college-educated fully understand the structural bases of social injustice or see clearly what must be done politically to transform these structures. The professional profile coexists with the reproduction of systemic modes of oppression, because this profile is not by itself a solution to them. We live with this contradiction, but we are at a loss to address the structural relations that seem to limit social criticism to a demographic and the effects of that criticism often to the realm of speech acts.

In the professional imaginary, however, there is little time for puzzling over complexities of mediation in the dissemination of the professional profile, including those forms of critique in which we have invested so much hope. For the professoriate, the trajectory of criticism has been imaginarily foreshortened, if not actually shortened (Schumpeter: "the way is short"), by recourse to a *political thematic* in the choice of topics for scholarly research or for college courses. I propose now to consider the emergence of such thematics, what I will call *topicality*, as an innovation of great consequence for the discipline, the most widely disseminated and enduring tactic of surrogacy by which criticism has been reasserted in scholarship and teaching.

The emergence in the post-sixties university of political topicality attests to a desire very much of its moment. The basic idea of the topically organized course was already set out by Kampf and Lauter: "To break out of our closed-in specialties, we might consider teaching courses like 'Revolutionary Literature,' 'Imperialism,' or 'The Antislavery Struggle'—in addition to courses in black, Chicano, or female studies—as much to educate ourselves as our students" (41). All of this came to pass, but the antiprofessional agenda implied by "closed-in specialties" was discarded along the way. Although protest against these familiar thematics from some quarters has long since disappeared, I believe it would be fair to say that faith in their efficacy too has declined and that the impression of disappointing results is not mine alone. The profession's fatigue with its critical discourse betrays an unintended consequence of the reassertion of criticism, along with renewed uncertainty about the justification of the discipline.

The reassertion of the critical motive in literary study was registered initially by a sweeping repudiation of the postwar settlement, which was characterized as mere "formalism" and so indicted as culpably apolitical. The established protocols of scholarship were untouched by this reformation, however, for reasons that follow from the professional organization of scholarship. The reassertion of criticism did not, as Kampf and Lauter hoped, result in the professoriate's breaking out of its "closed-in specialties." On the contrary, specialization continued to organize the relation between literary study as criticism and as profession. What was desired, then, was a new way to professionalize the critical motive, a new alliance of criticism and professionalism. Of course, we know the end of this story: the political topics urged by Kampf and Lauter became new specializations. These new specializations in turn entered into competition with older specializations. As political topicality came more widely to organize teaching and research, its reach extended to otherwise resistant materials in what became a ubiquitous motif of recategorization, signaled in the favored template for a multitude of books and essays and courses: "The Politics of X." This formula works so well because the relation between the two terms, "politics" and "X" is *nonobvious*. What criticism reveals is the fact that "X" is, after all, just as political as everything so called in ordinary language. The tactic itself was inaugurated in the title of Kampf and Lauter's volume, *The Politics of Literature*, and it has continued to dominate the discipline down to the present. But again, there is evidence that its force is weakening, and that has left the discipline strangely becalmed.

In retrospect, there is no question that the emergence of political topicality reenergized the discipline, allowing it (along with the innovations of high theory and usually in concert with those innovations) to move beyond a moment of stagnation in the postwar settlement. Let me hasten to add as well that political thematization is never illegitimate in itself as a way of constructing projects for research or as the subject matter of courses; scholarship must remain open to all domains of interest, including the political, without foreclosure. Moreover, the political implication of literary works is an inescapable fact of their social relations. The problem is not with the politics of literature but with the politics of the profession—that is, the *collective understanding* of political thematics by the professoriate, or what I am calling "justification."

With regard to justification, political topicality follows from the reassertion of the critical motive in the expectation of producing a desired effect in the world. Because we cannot know the larger effect of the strategy of topicality, we might say that such teaching and scholarship are *justified by faith*. With this formula, I mean to capture how topicality operates in the discipline as the expression of surrogate politics; that operation is highly problematic for the discipline over the long term. For, supposing that topicality were a necessary and effective instrument for the critique of society, on what grounds might we justify scholarship or teaching that *does not* foreground a political thematic? Scholars should be able to assume that domains of culture possess sufficient relative autonomy to sustain inquiries not based on topics that refer directly to the political categories of contemporary society. Works of earlier periods of literary history fit very imperfectly into contemporary political categories—at least, not without complex mediations. Constructing these mediations has become a major project for those who work in early fields; otherwise, the work of these scholars will be, so to speak, left out of the game. If topicality seemed to open the discipline to new arenas of inquiry, it has also exerted a contrary pressure on the scope of the discipline, constraining its thematic categories to those that can be instrumentalized for the criticism of *contemporary* society.

The long-term effect of this pressure is twofold: the contraction of the disciplinary field *historically* to modern or contemporary literature and *generically* to the form of representation—prose narrative—most amenable to interpretation within a political thematic. These historical and generic contractions bring teaching and research into conformity with an orientation toward the categories of social identity enumerated by Lauter and Kampf. Nor is this tendency a response to student demand only, as is sometimes argued. We ourselves are the creators of demand, both in our students and among ourselves.

Although the discipline has contracted in the earlier periods of literature, it has at the same time expanded at the other end, in contemporary literature and world literature, along with the work of social minorities formerly excluded from access to writing or venues of publication. This converse of the discipline's contraction is welcome, though it discloses the fact that we have a finite amount of time for the study of an ever-greater accumulation of writing (see chapter 8 below, "The Contradictions of Global English"). Granted the inevitability of this dilemma, the question before the discipline is whether topicality is or should be the principal strategy for organizing the study of this literature. Students who enter into literary study today are the products of a system in which the representational function of literature and the criticism of society are axiomatic; the same motives of criticism have been replicated, to some extent, in the primary and secondary schools. This system now reproduces itself at every level without having to rely on the reformist energies of the generation of Lauter and Kampf. Those who advise doctoral students, for example, feel that they must press their advisees to choose dissertation topics with an eye toward the job market, thus reproducing the topical orientation of the professoriate. Advisors may feel that they are acting in the best interests of students, but it ought to be acknowledged that these good intentions are the result of professional deformation. Every craft makes crooked. We might hope that the near total collapse of the job market for new PhDs would liberate students to write about whatever truly interests them and free advisors to encourage them in this path. But the more likely outcome of vanishing tenure-track employment will be even greater pressure to tailor scholarship to the tyranny of the job market.

The interaction of criticism with the structures of professionalism has deformed the discipline in other ways. It will be news to no one that just as the system of rewards favors scholarship over teaching, it favors teaching graduate students over undergraduates. However necessary for the purpose of reproducing the professoriate, graduate teaching constitutes a reward that exceeds its reproductive purpose. Graduate teaching allows professors to address their scholarly discourse primarily to other scholars and to graduate students, and thus to distance themselves from the scene of undergraduate teaching that constitutes their first and chief opportunity for reaching a public of nonprofessional readers.[49] The rewards for success

49. To be honest about this matter, we ought to admit that teaching at the secondary level is more consequential for the political formation of the young adult population than teaching at the postsecondary level. In my experience, students arrive in the colleges and universities more or less formed politically by their familial and social experience as adolescents. The further influence their university teachers have upon them, though it is not negligible, is also not timed optimally as a formative intervention. And

in scholarship go beyond even this involution of aim. As we all know, the greatest reward for reputational success in scholarship is relief from teaching altogether. And yet the system of rewards encourages us to imagine that we are being rewarded *for* the criticism of society. I think we might expect such rewards in heaven. Surely the political well-being of our society is better served by producing one informed, insightful, and habitual reader than by the publication of any number of scholarly essays and books, however devastating these might be as criticisms of society. The absurdity of the situation should be evident to all of us: as literary study wanes in public importance, as literature departments shrink in size, as majors in literature decline in numbers, the claims for the criticism of society are ever more overstated. In these circumstances, we ought not to pretend that the university is actually rewarding the *political* work of scholarship.[50] This complacency is no longer acceptable, and literary study stands to gain a far better purchase on its effects in the world if it can be overcome.

---

most students are in any case embarked at this point on specialized courses of study that take them only occasionally, and for some students not at all, into courses in literature.

50. David Bromwich, in *Politics by Other Means: Higher Education and Group Thinking* (New Haven, CT: Yale University Press, 1994), grasped the essence of this deformation in a kind of Swiftian "working maxim" still operative for the professoriate: "The maxim says that *one need do nothing but be oneself, nothing outside one's personal and professional routine, in order to conduct politics of the most effectual and admirable kind*" (223).

CHAPTER 3

Critique of Critical Criticism

The common reader, as Dr. Johnson implies, is different from the critic
and the scholar. He is worse educated, and nature has not gifted him so
generously. He reads for his own pleasure rather than to impart knowledge or to correct the opinions of others. Above all, he is guided by an
instinct to create for himself, out of whatever odds and ends he can come
by, some kind of whole—a portrait of a man, a sketch of an age, a theory
of the art of writing.

        VIRGINIA WOOLF, "The Common Reader"

The literary professoriate struggles with the burden of a certain irony in
the very enjoyment of its professional privilege: the same autonomy that
makes possible the intellectual freedom of critique, yielding sometimes
brilliant and persuasive analyses of our troubled society, also relegates
these efforts largely to the professional venues of the discipline. There, our
works of criticism are greeted with mutual acclaim, but little expectation
for an audience beyond the discipline. This predicament might seem to be
the effect of nothing other than the crude fact of numbers: the size of the
discipline, how many students we teach, the extent to which scholarship
is read beyond the academy. Yet it is also the consequence of our failure to
understand the place from which we speak, as though the school were the
world. Those who see only the school do not see the school. The institution
and its organizational forms of discipline and profession filter and sometimes even transmogrify the messages that emanate from it.

    The overstatement of aim is the principal form of professional deforma-
tion resulting from uncertainty about the social effects of literary study.
There are other instances of deformation worth noting, however, such as
the difficulty of critical language, the prevalence of a rebarbative dialect
that sometimes has a more performative than communicative function.
Literary criticism is certainly entitled to employ a technical lexicon, develop highly complex arguments, or address texts that lie well outside the
domain of the general reader. But perhaps it is time for the professoriate to
question whether its normative language overcompensates for its marginalization, whether this language is not in some measure the defense mecha-

nism of an inward-turning profession, a response to the disappointment of its great expectations.

Relatedly, some scholars have begun to express second thoughts about the ambivalence that clings to literature itself, the legacy of a discipline that secretly fears the irrelevance of its object of study. In this moment of doubt about justification, there might be a possibility, at least, to face the reality of the discipline's media situation. Let us begin with the recognition that literary critics can enter the realm of publicity only as experts *on literature*. Perhaps the future of literary criticism will depend more on what we make of literature than what we make of criticism. If literature is the basis of our entitlement to enter the public sphere, what does this imply for our public-facing representation of what we do?

I do not mean to suggest that the literary professoriate should confine its scholarship and teaching to literary texts, narrowly defined by the concepts of imaginative or fictional writing. Many literary scholars have competence in multiple forms of cultural expression, a fact that has characterized the discipline since long before the era of high theory and cultural studies. What I do mean to say is that literature needs to be *recentered* by the literary professoriate in order to reestablish its public claim to expertise. The recentering of literature will depend ultimately on how we define literature, a question addressed further in chapter 7, "The Location of Literature," and in the conclusion. For the present, I would stipulate that the recentering of literature does not entail the assertion of its superiority as a cultural or aesthetic form to any other cultural or aesthetic form. The filiations of literature with other kinds of artifacts, like social relations themselves, stop nowhere. But our responsibility to literature is not abrogated by the virtual infinity of these relations. Literature is the ground of our professional authority to make arguments about any artifact or subject whatsoever.[1]

In any case, "justification by faith" is no longer sufficient to assure ourselves of the social value of literary criticism. Works were necessary, after all, demonstrable effects in the world. The discipline's Archimedean lever has broken, or perhaps it never really worked. And yet there is little evidence to date that the everyday practice of our discipline has changed in any substantial way. On the contrary, teaching and research continue to be dominated by topicality, by political thematics that look familiar and

1. I take a certain risk of misinterpretation in putting forward the notion of "recentering," knowing that the gesture of *decentering* is the default move in much criticism of the last half century. Recentering is offered here as a reorientation of literary study's discourse about itself, the premise of a better public-facing rhetoric than currently circulates. In any case, I believe it would be difficult to deny that the gesture of decentering has become too easy, that its marginal return as a mode of critique is rapidly declining.

often tired. Granted that literary study is not alone in having arrived at this place, that the humanities generally are also struggling, it is significant that a number of literary scholars have attempted in recent years to reestablish the discipline on different grounds. The interest of this development at the moment is largely symptomatic, but it is an important symptom, and for that reason I conclude my analysis of the formation and deformation of literary study with a consideration in this chapter of several key efforts to move the discipline beyond what is perceived to be its dominant, if often tacit, premises. I do not intend here a general survey of new movements or fields, such as digital analysis, ecocriticism, disability studies, animal studies, affect studies, or studies based on cognitive science or evolutionary biology, among many other new subfields. I am concerned rather with a tendency that most nearly concerns the fundamental question of justification, insofar as the overestimation of aim deforms the discipline.

If some literary scholars have begun to doubt that we should continue to profess criticism, what do these scholars imagine lies beyond this practice? That is hard to discern, but interestingly, our conception of literature itself seems to be on the table. What would it mean actually to *profess literature*? Would the literature so professed really constrain the intellectual freedom of the professoriate? Whatever the implications for literature, there is considerable unhappiness with business as usual, amounting to an old-fashioned "legitimation crisis," serious enough to elicit calls for an altogether new mode of criticism, as attested in the issue of *Representations* on "surface reading," published in 2009, or Rita Felski's *The Limits of Critique*, published in 2015. These manifestos and their successors summarily reject the reigning paradigms of literary study extending all the way back to New Criticism, including the practice of "close reading." The question before us is whether these efforts have cleared the ground for a major reconstruction of the discipline.

In the event, it has proven difficult to move beyond the manifestos to a new program of teaching and research, for two reasons: first, because we have not rethought our conception of literature as the object of our discipline—that would require, in my view, a new theoretical account of literature's place in the system of media. And second, because criticism will likely continue to share an agenda with the goal of "critical thinking," still a very desirable component of the professional profile. The problem the discipline faces has never been the analytic skill assumed by the concept of criticism, but its expression in the form of political surrogacy. If the problem has always been the overestimation of aim, its remedy can only be a proper *estimation* of how literary study is articulated with larger social structures. I have attempted in the conclusion of this volume to outline what I believe to be plausible rationales for literary study, most of which are already implicit in our practice and mainly need to be acknowledged. These rationales do not so much contradict the motives of criticism as they demonstrate how large the scope of literary study actually is, how much it already accomplishes and has accomplished in the longer history of disciplinary and predisciplinary modes of study.

Given the persistence of surrogacy, efforts to move beyond the current becalmed state of the discipline deserve serious consideration. The fact that nothing fully programmatic has yet emerged is evidence of how difficult it is to understand the forces that mediate literary study as a university discipline in relation to the massive abstraction of "society." And yet we are not where we were when Lauter and Kampf launched their attack on professionalism in the 1960s. The professoriate is no longer inclined to attack professionalism, but a cadre has been bold enough to raise questions about "criticism," if by that is meant the critique of society by way of a critique of the literary text. This polemic is correlated even more surprisingly with a turn away from the methodology of interpretation. It is not a question now of a contest between theories of interpretation but of the difference between reading *within the academy and without.* The shadow that has fallen upon criticism has put reading itself into a new light. It has raised a question about professionalism by virtue of identifying disciplinary reading with the prevalent mode of its practice, with "critique." The effect of this identification has been to bring into sudden view the world of reading outside the academy. This is not a case of "profession against discipline" but of the conjoined fate of professional identity and the disciplinary mode of reading.

To put this point in the most explicitly sociological terms, the literary professoriate has begun to recognize its professional deformation in just the way such deformations are typically recognized by the laity: as a turn away from the profession's proper clientele. For our discipline, the identity of this clientele is neither the professoriate nor society as a whole but *the readers of literature,* and the question before us now is how well we have served them. Stating the question in these terms does not imply the rejection of any subjects for teaching or research—on the contrary! To name our clientele as the readers of literature argues rather for the reestimation of aim, a better understanding of how literary works are read, both in the schools and without, and what literary study might do to improve the reading of literature, even reading as such.

The question of reading has been posed in what I will call a *new tendency* in criticism. I try to describe this tendency by working through in some detail several major statements in this line of inquiry. The origin of the tendency can be traced to the argument advanced in Eve Sedgwick's influential essay of 1997 titled "Paranoid and Reparative Reading," terms that are now reverberant in the discipline.[2] I will look at this essay presently, which circulated for some years before its explosive significance became apparent. That significance is acknowledged in the full-throated annunciation of a new era in literary study by Rachel Sagner Buurma and Laura Heffernan, writing in a 2012 issue of *New Literary History*: "In the new millennium a new figure beckons to the literary critic: the figure of the common reader."[3] These scholars do not shrink from the implied question: "Such a widespread celebration of deprofessionalized reading practices should lead us to ask: how have we become so down on our professional practices?" (113). And yet it is not so clear whether the target of this polemic is professionalism as such or the practice of reading as critique, now identified so inextricably with "professional practices" that to imagine reading as something other than critique is to imagine it as something other than professional. That equation is mistaken, I believe, but it may be a necessary error, the evidence of a transitional struggle.

In titling this chapter "Critique of Critical Criticism," I have borrowed from Marx a typically facetious expression to suggest the difficulty of exiting the cul-de-sac in which literary study finds itself today. Marx's phrase (the subtitle of his polemic against Bruno Bauer, *The Holy Family*) grapples with the task of surpassing the "critique" of the young Hegelians, which did not go far enough, Marx thought, as a critique of the political and economic structures of bourgeois society. The "critique of critique," however, is always in danger of spiraling into fruitless recursion—hence Marx's witty expression. There is, further, a lexical difficulty for us in the translation of "*Kritik der kritische Kritik*": Is "criticism" the same beast as "critique"? Marx's German has only the one word, *Kritik*, but English allows for a distinction. That has been convenient for recent critics of the discipline, as it suggests the possibility of identifying "critique" as the problem with criticism. But what would a criticism that rid itself of critique look like? If the new millennium brought the "common reader" onto the stage for

2. Eve Sedgwick, "Paranoid Reading and Reparative Reading, Or, You're So Paranoid You Probably Think This Essay Is about You," in *Touching Feeling: Affect, Pedagogy, Performativity* (Durham, NC: Duke University Press, 2003). An earlier version of this essay was published in *Novel Gazing: Queer Readings in Fiction*, ed. Eve Kosofsky Sedgwick (Durham: NC: Duke University Press, 1997), but I cite here the version in *Touching Feeling*.

3. Rachel Sagna Buurma and Laura Heffernan, "The Common Reader and the Archival Classroom: Disciplinary History for the Twenty-First Century," *New Literary History* 43 (2012): 113–35.

applause, literary scholars are by no means ready to give up their position as professionals or their jobs as professors. What is it, then, that they are to do? Are the professors looking for a new way of keeping the discipline going, perhaps a new version of Schumpeter's "profession of the unprofessional"?

Attempts to overcome this impasse include new defenses of the aesthetic, versions of "new formalism," "surface reading," the notion of "weak theory," and most ambitiously, the "post critique" advocated by Rita Felski and others. These theoretical efforts were effectively supercharged with the publication in 2003 of Bruno Latour's essay "Why Has Critique Run Out of Steam?" Yet Latour's intervention is curiously orthogonal to Sedgwick's argument and to literary study as a whole—as we shall see, a problematic fact. That some literary critics have embraced Latour's position suggests that a hypothetical postcritical practice is in need of a theory that leaves something for critics to do after superseding critique. Latour's critique of critique has little on the face of it to say about what this might be for literary study, but it seems likely that the enthusiastic response to his essay discloses unmistakably what literary critics *think* criticism meant, that is, some version of the criticism of society.

Gestures toward the postcritical are hard to characterize collectively as anything other than a loose alliance of interests. Some of these efforts, such as attempts to rehabilitate the concept of the aesthetic, predate the breakthrough essay by Sedgwick, betraying long-standing discontent with the reduction of criticism to a form of "ideology critique" aimed at revealing the aesthetic as illusion, a subterfuge for political interest.[4] Defenses of the aesthetic as well as the "new formalism" also responded to the severely epistemological orientation of high theory, especially in the mode of deconstruction, and these defenses have gained momentum in recent years with the waning of theory. Sedgwick's essay appeared contemporaneously with these polemics, but not explicitly in support of them. In fact, Sedgwick's turn in her 1997 essay emerged from a vanguard field of ideology-critique: queer theory. Her essay attempts to nudge queer studies away from its interpretive strategy of exposing entrenched and often masked homophobic currents in literature and culture and toward a more affirmative engagement with cultural works. Importantly, this affirmative

---

4. See, for example, James Soderholm, ed., *Beauty and the Critic: Aesthetics in the Age of Cultural Studies* (Tuscaloosa: University of Alabama Press, 1997); Michael P. Clark, ed., *The Revenge of the Aesthetic: The Place of Literature in Theory Today* (Berkeley: University of California Press, 2000); and Francis Halsall, Julia Jansen, and Tony O'Connor, eds., *Rediscovering Aesthetics: Transdisciplinary Voices from Art History, Philosophy, and Art Practice* (Stanford, CA: Stanford University Press, 2009).

mode of response was already to be found in queer culture, in the form of "camp" and presumably other affectively positive styles of engagement such as "fandom." Although Sedgwick is not concerned immediately with camp, which she does not mention until near the conclusion of her essay, these modes of engagement *outside the academy* hover over her argument as its deferred other scene. In the meantime, she hews to the style of critique, and to the scene of theory, basing her argument on a figure with a distinguished (if unorthodox) theoretical pedigree, Melanie Klein. This heretical disciple of Freud advanced a version of Freudian theory that yields the terms Sedgwick appropriates: the paranoid and reparative positions in psychogenesis. These terms are transposed to the field of reading, as announced in the title of the essay: "Paranoid Reading and Reparative Reading." The polemical force of the essay is directed toward this displacement, which risks some awkwardness in its deracination of analytic terms: "The flexible to-and-fro movement implicit in Kleinian *positions* will be useful for my discussion of paranoid and reparative critical *practices*" (128).

Without wandering too far from the scene of high theory, Sedgwick looks at literary study from a certain disinvested perspective, aiming to uncover some of its unquestioned assumptions and attitudes. Taking D. A. Miller's *The Novel and the Police* as exemplary (but Sedgwick allows that her own work belongs to the same genre), she interrogates its "hermeneutics of suspicion"—now a ubiquitous borrowing from Paul Ricoeur—for its assumption of political efficacy, the discipline's "faith in exposure . . . as though to make something visible as a problem were, if not a mere hop, skip, and jump away from getting it solved, at least self-evidently a step in that direction" (139). The momentary shift to the register of the demotic is itself evidence of the collapsing paradigm, a loss of faith in the style of criticism that was so often coupled with grandiosity of aim. The turn in the essay to affect studies, based on the work of Sylvan Tomkins, adumbrates a possible way forward for the discipline, a recovery of positive affects at the opposite end of the spectrum from its habitual posture of suspicion or detachment.

The turn to affect, which had other occasions than Sedgwick's essay, has been very generative of scholarly work. Its filiations are complex, involving both feminism and book history, which were united in a pioneering early work, Janice Radway's *Reading the Romance*. It was perhaps inevitable that this conjuncture would begin to interest scholars in the question of the lay reader. Sedgwick did not intend to celebrate this reader, as she saw the development of "reparative" criticism more narrowly in disciplinary terms, as the possibility for scholarly projects "less oriented around suspicion." She notes that this kind of scholarship is "actually being practiced" by some of the same scholars otherwise associated with the paranoid pole; it is just a matter of bringing out this subordinate tendency in the best scholarship. Only after having traversed the defile of paranoid theory does Sedgwick propose a revisionist account of nonacademic modes of reading such as camp, arguing at the conclusion of her essay that we should take at face value the "love" for certain cultural works that paranoid criticism debunks as masking camp's "self-hating complicity with an oppressive status quo" (149). Camp might be seen, contrarily, as "the communal, historically dense exploration of a variety of reparative practices" (150).

Sedgwick's essay recirculated Ricoeur's notion of a "hermeneutics of suspicion" in an environment of increasing unease with the claims of high theory and its new historicist successor. The notion of "reparative reading" has since been taken up as a new lever of change, this time an instrument for toppling the reigning mode of criticism. I want to look now at the next major episode in this development, Sharon Marcus and Stephen Best's manifesto, "Surface Reading: An Introduction."[5] Their essay, and the accompanying essays in the volume of *Representations*, follow Sedgwick in attempting to move beyond "suspicion" and the theoretical and historicist modes of interpretation seen to support that orientation. As ambitious as this move seemed when it first appeared, and despite an astonishing number of responses to the essay, it has been, I will suggest, a *false start*. The failure of surface reading to catch on is instructive for our purposes, as this failure further exposed an underlying problem in the waning of theory itself, a deep uncertainty about the effect of reading techniques at once recondite and ambitious for impact in the public sphere.

The proximate target of Marcus and Best's polemic is Fredric Jameson's "symptomatic reading," a term indebted to Freud and ultimately to Marx by way of Althusser. Jameson's catchphrase resonates with Ricoeur's "hermeneutics of suspicion," but the assumption that Jameson's version of theory has widely governed critical practice seems to me mistaken. Jameson's allegorical mode of interpretation, privileging Marxism as master code, was never established as the norm for the discipline. Nor is it evident that the concept of "symptomatic reading" entails a notion of "depth" that forecloses attention to the "surface" of the text. Jameson's technique, like most versions of high theory, was premised on a textualist injunction: "Don't look through the text, look at it." In Marcus and Best's argument, one trope has been substituted for another doing much the same work. Meaning now is to be found not *beneath* the words of the text but *behind* the screen of symptomatic reading: "Surface reading broadens the scope of critique to include the kinds of interpretive activity that seek to understand the complexity of literary surfaces—surfaces that have been rendered invisible by symptomatic reading" (1). Decoupling the tropes of surface and depth has the peculiar effect of literalizing them, as though meaning were being shuffled around in a shell game. Perhaps this objection is not to the point, however, as Marcus and Best really want to loosen the hold of *any* master code or metalanguage on the practice of interpretation, all those "approaches" constituting what the discipline calls theory. Surface reading is not just an alternative possibility for the discipline but a root and branch petition, a radical reformation.

Marcus and Best's argument is driven at base by a disappointment in criticism that reveals just how extremely the effects of criticism have been overestimated in literary study:

> We find ourselves the heirs of Michel Foucault, skeptical about the possibility of radical freedom and dubious that literature or its criticism can explain our oppression or provide the keys to our liberation. Where it had become common for literary scholars to equate their work with political activism, the disasters and triumphs of the last decade have shown that literary criticism alone is not sufficient to effect change. This turn raises the question of why literary criticism matters if it is not political activism by another name, a question to which we return in the last section of this essay. (2)

The last section to which this passage alludes is entitled "Freedom in Attentiveness," a formula that hints at an affinity with affect studies without explicitly raising that flag. Marcus and Best focus on the notion of "freedom," which has obvious political resonance at the same time that its referent is less than precise. After cautiously positioning their project in relation to the "new formalism" and to Adorno's argument for the autonomy of the work of art, they go on to specify more precisely its divergence from the ideology critique of Jameson. The point here again is to reject a master code or metalanguage in order "to stay close to our objects of study" (15). The tactic means finally resisting the temptation to *interpret at all* in favor of what reading Marcus and Best simply call "description," a term that has since become a key signifier in the new tendency of criticism. The turn to description is at the same time the restoration of critique by other means, because it holds out the hope that "producing accurate accounts of surfaces is not antithetical to critique." Without elaborating further how or when critics might follow the path back to critique, Marcus and Best

conclude their essay with an invocation of Bruno Latour, whose anticriti-
cal polemic has been in the background. The argument for surface reading
suspends any definite assertion of political effectiveness, without entirely
giving up the desire for such effect. Marcus and Best call this "political realism," which it surely is, at the same time that the extent of this qualification
is uncertain.

The difficulty of deriving a clear procedure from the notion of "surface reading" is the probable reason for the outcome I have called a false
start. Marcus's related concept of "just reading," advanced in other work,
might seem to imply that surface reading is nothing more than *uninstructed*
reading and hence needs no method at all; but what Marcus has in mind
is something more deliberate, an ascetic refusal to interpret. Attending to
the "surface" of the text, if that means "the words on the page," is not the
wrong place to begin but, as we have noted, that is where much theory began too. More problematically, surface reading is shadowed by an antecedent that looks alarmingly similar, namely "close reading." Unlike surface
reading, however, close reading was compatible with the trope of depth,
which was taken simply to indicate the meaning of the words on the page.
Heather Love enters the fray here with the aim of getting rid of "depth"
while retaining "close." Her essay "Close but Not Deep: Literary Ethics and
the Descriptive Turn," offers a corrective to Marcus and Best by disambiguating their version of reading from its historical precursor, thus bringing
the terms "close" and "surface" into alignment with a mode of reading that
simultaneously rejects the notion of "depth."[6] Dispensing with the ancient
trope of "depth" entails a sacrifice of sorts, the loss of a certain "richness" of
meaning indicated by that trope, but Love sets out to show what is gained
in recompense for this loss.

The necessity of her revisionist move arises from what Love sees as the
fact that New Critical close reading trails unwelcome ideological baggage,
which she names "humanism": "Disengaging from the operations of close
reading promises a more fundamental rethinking of the grounds of the
discipline than earlier challenges to the human subject, the canon, or the
referential capacities of language. Because they address the key techniques
of the discipline rather than its explicit ideology, these new methods are
more effective than structuralist and poststructuralist theories in challenging
the residual but nonetheless powerful humanism of literary studies" (374).
Setting aside the fact that the New Critics themselves were vehemently
antihumanist—their religious convictions forced them to be explicit on this

---

6. Heather Love, "Close but Not Deep: Literary Ethics and the Descriptive Turn,"
New Literary History 41 (2010): 371–91.

point—one might still concede that postwar literary study was character-ized by a vague humanism that served to prop up the claims for literature in competition with the derogated works of mass media. In Love's account, the survival of close reading, with its attendant ideology, undermined the radical aims of theory. If close reading perpetuated a retrograde humanism as the content of the text's "depth," then perhaps a different kind of close reading—and here Love corrects Marcus and Best's "surface reading"—might succeed. For Love, it is not enough simply to attend to the surface of the text, which might well lure the scholar into an interpretation, and thence into the interdicted region of "depth." What is needed is a mode of reading that breaks with the tradition of *literary* reading, and so effectively resists the temptation to interpret. Hence Love turns for a model of reading to the social sciences, specifically to "ethology, kinesics, ethnomethodol-ogy, and microsociology" (375). The method imputed to these social sci-ences is said to be descriptive rather than interpretive, only "descriptions of surfaces, operations, and interactions." This self-limitation of method would guarantee a kind of reading that would be "close but not deep" (375).

Is this a positive program of reading? Imitation of the descriptive method derived from social science would need to confront the difference between the objects of description in the several disciplines—on the side of social science *human behavior*, on the side of criticism the *literary text*. But this problem does not detain Love. It will in any case be resolved among schol-ars of the new tendency such as Rita Felski by recourse to Latour's "flat ontology." Love invokes Latour along with the work of Erving Goffman. To get a sense in the meantime of what Love means by descriptive reading, we can look briefly at her presentation of Toni Morrison's novel *Beloved*, which is offered as an exemplary text for a descriptive reading: "I argue that a descriptive rather than an interpretive account of *Beloved* draws attention to qualities of the text that critics have tended to ignore, particularly its exteriorizing and objective account of social life. Reading the novel at the surface brings into focus its critique of historical reclamation. A flat reading of *Beloved* suggests the possibility of an alternative ethics, one grounded in documentation and description rather than empathy and witness" (375). The example of Morrison's novel is overdetermined in an obvious way by the author's minority identity, which gestures toward the "reclamation" conversely declined by the novel's flat narration. The work of critique goes on cannily enough just in the choice of text. But this choice is equally over-determined as an instance of novelistic discourse, which always passes as closer to an account of human action than other forms of literary writing. *Beloved* is said to offer an "objective account of social life," by which Love means that the mode of narration at certain moments is devoid of interpretive markers, the hints and signals that literary critics might be tempted to work up into an interpretation. Instead, the novel exhibits in the exemplary passages singled out by Love a "flat" mode of narration, or "neutral, detailed description," that mimics an ethnographic style: "Such moments in the novel draw us up short, turning our attention to the flatness, objectivity, and literalism in this famously 'deep' novel. I would suggest that reading *Beloved* at the surface allows us to see Morrison's project as registering the losses of history rather than repairing them" (386). It is not easy to gauge the distance here between "registering" and "repairing," if the implication of the former is that a certain political work is better accomplished by that merely descriptive mode. What does seem evident is the circularity of the argument, which conflates a *mode of narration* with a *mode of reading*. This observation can be offered in objection to Love's argument, but I would rather say that what Love offers here is an "allegory of reading," something we often find at the foundational moment of a new critical school.[7] The circularity of the argument, then, is not so much a logical problem but just what the "turn to description" requires, the promise that what we want most from criticism—some kind of political efficacy—might be delivered by this new mode of doing it. As with Marcus and Best, Love's new mode of reading responds to a sense of political disappointment with high theory and its successors, betraying the extent to which an overestimation of aim continues to distort the efforts of the new tendency.[8]

Interestingly, Love hedges against her bet at the end of her essay, in much the same gesture of qualification offered by Marcus and Best. She is perhaps not quite ready to make the transition to mere description or to give up the "riches" to be found in a "depth hermeneutics," figured now as a ghost (echoing Morrison's novel) haunting critical practice: "A turn from interpretation to description might be one way to give up that ghost. But who among us is willing to exchange the fat and the living for the thin and the dead?" (388). If the transition to "surface reading" or the "turn to

7. Two other examples of this inaugural strategy are Cleanth Brooks's reading of Donne's "The Canonization" in *The Well Wrought Urn* and Paul de Man's readings of Rousseau and Proust in *Allegories of Reading*.

8. This is true, for example, of Caroline Levine, *Forms: Whole, Rhythm, Hierarchy, Network* (Princeton, NJ: Princeton University Press, 2015). Her reassertion of a formalist aesthetic is accompanied by a strong assertion of political aim: "But in fact the primary goal of this formalism is radical social change" (18). Such change is accomplished, Levine argues, by bringing forms into "collision" with one another, and there is no question that one form is preeminent in that task: "The form that best captures the experience of colliding forms is narrative" (19). The trajectory of this argument reinstates justification by faith, that just by reading novels, we engage in transformative political work.

description" seems to stumble at this foundational moment, a false start, that mischance is itself testimony to the ambition of the new tendency, its desire to overthrow all that has gone before it.

Looking back at this point to the terms put into play by Sedgwick, Marcus, Best, and Love, it is possible for us to represent the radical oscillation exhibited by the new tendency schematically:

From:	*To:*
Paranoid reading	Reparative reading
Negative affect/detachment	Positive affect/attachment
Depth	Surface
Interpretation	Description
Professional reading	Amateur reading

Although these antinomies can be found variously in the new tendency, the second and fifth seem to me to engineer the most radical shift in hinting at the correlation between affect and the social location of reading. The professoriate is said to approach literary works with detachment, suspicion, a disposition toward negative affect. Amateur readers—or "lay readers"—are supposed to be characterized conversely by *love* for what they read. Now this difference is in some measure empirically disputable. Literary scholars are in my experience just as given to positive attachments to literary works as nonprofessional readers. And conversely, amateurs are sometimes given to vehemently negative judgments, often disdaining works of literature they do not find immediately entertaining or moral. Nonetheless, the association between affect and the social location of the reader will tell us much of what we need to know about what impels the new tendency.[9]

For assistance in moving the argument forward on this point, I turn briefly to an important and timely essay by Michael Warner entitled "Uncritical Reading," published in 2004.[10] Warner is writing early on in

9. Amanda Anderson, "Therapeutic Criticism," in *Novel: A Forum on Fiction* 50:3 (2017), suggests that "surely it is also undeniable that the case against suspicion is overstated" (321). In addition to works of criticism in the last several decades that do not express this affect, she points to the concurrent emergence of "therapeutic culture" during the same period. This is an important and plausible contextualization of what I have called the new tendency in criticism and deserves further inquiry than I can pursue here.

10. Michael Warner, "Uncritical Reading," in *Polemic: Critical or Uncritical*, ed. Jane Gallup (New York: Routledge, 2004), 13–38.

the emergence of the new tendency. His aim is to confront head-on the "worlds of reading" that exist outside the academy. As it happens, we have ready access to this mode of reading through our students, who "read in all the ways they aren't supposed to. They identify with characters. They fall in love with authors. They mime what they take to be authorized sentiment" (13). And the list goes on. It includes, among many other items, the fact that students often "condemn as boring what they don't already recognize," a mode of resistance with which all teachers must struggle. Worst of all, Warner suspects that the category of "literature" itself lies behind the resistance to our favored modes of critical reading, nothing other than "a widespread disenchantment with the idea of literature, which students in a technologically changing climate increasingly encounter as archaic" (14). Warner is not directly concerned in his essay with this more distant horizon, however, but with the heterogeneous attitudes of our students, who fairly represent reading outside the academy. Their exhibition of "uncritical reading" leads him to a reconsideration of Sedgwick's essay and the question of whether her conception of "reparative reading" might offer a programmatic alternative to "critical reading." To this question, he unhappily concludes in the negative; Sedgwick's reparative reading, Warner writes, is "not so much a method as (principled?) avoidance of method" (18).

If Sedgwick's celebrated recommendation seems a dead end for literary pedagogy, it does open up for Warner an inquiry into alternative, nonacademic modes of reading that ought not simply to be dismissed as "uncritical." I forgo reprising his valuable survey of these modes—chief among them is the religious, which has a much longer history than literary criticism—in favor of pressing the question that seems most urgently to emerge from his survey. If "critical reading" is just one mode of reading among many possible, its location in the academy has blinded the literary professoriate to its narrow jurisdiction: "The self-interest of professionalized critics is insufficient to explain how a profession oriented to the teaching of critical reading could justify itself as a necessity to non-professionals" (23). The implication of this fact for the discipline's *self-justification* is meant to shock, and the bad news is delivered in the unmistakable style of "paranoid reading": "Uncritical reading is the unconscious of the profession; whatever worlds are organized around frameworks of reading other than critical protocols remain, for the most part, terra incognita" (33).

I do not take Warner to be arguing for "uncritical reading" as a new *model* for reading in the academy, but if he means that the discipline has not begun to study these other "worlds of reading," we might ask why that should be the business of literary criticism at all. In any case, reading outside the academy has been studied extensively by book historians such as Leah

Price and Andrew Piper as well as by historians such as Roger Chartier and Anthony Grafton (to name only a few representatives among many). Additionally, quantitative analyses are disclosing interesting new insights about historical trends in reading outside the academy. When Warner says that uncritical reading is the "unconscious" of the profession, he must mean that it is the professoriate's typical disregard for these worlds that constitutes a repression, a threat to critical reading itself. The problem for literary scholars is not that we are unaware of reading outside the academy, but rather that these modes of reading reveal the *limit* of the discipline's reach, the failure of its great expectations, our delusory self-justification.

This problem brings us finally to Rita Felski's manifesto, *The Limits of Critique*, which mounts a thoroughgoing critique of "critical reading" on several grounds, most vehemently on the ground of its disposition toward negative affect.[11] This construction of critique opens up for Felski the possibility of an antithetical mode of "postcritical reading" premised on the attachment of readers to texts, and related positive affects. Such reading seems to be favored outside the academy, once again bringing the figure of the "amateur" into contestation with the professional. I mean to question in my account of Felski's manifesto the correlation of affect and the site of reading, which I believe has been a *wrong turn* for the new tendency, diverting it from the recognition of what might actually connect literary scholarship with social domains outside the university. But it will be necessary first to give an account of her argument, in which we see again the radical oscillation of criticism toward the pole opposite to its long-standing practice.

The concept of "critique" in Felski's manifesto includes much of what constitutes literary criticism in the past fifty years, including both high theory and its successor, new historicism. Felski does not propose a return to the New Criticism but something even more radical, a reading practice that from a certain angle looks closest to belletrism. Yet postcritical reading is not exactly a reprise of belletrism, because it is obviously conceived *after theory*. Writing in this posthumous moment, Felski invokes belletrism as a practice that shadows the history of academic criticism: "Even at the high point of suspicious reading, there has always been a counter-trend of critics working within a more belletristic tradition, combining detailed, sometimes dazzling, literary commentary and appreciation with a declared animus toward sociological, theoretical, or philosophical argument" (11). As Felski does not name any figures here, we can only speculate about whether she is referring to particular academic critics or to "amateurs," that is, writ-

11. Rita Felski, *The Limits of Critique* (Chicago: University of Chicago Press, 2015).

ers for reviews or other nonacademic venues (these might, of course, be professional journalists). In any case, Felski wants to make a friendly distinction between her position and that of the belletrists, as she too, like Marcus, Best, and Love, makes the turn from interpretation to description. I suggest that belletrism functions in the new tendency as a figure for an imaginary fusion of the professional and amateur reader, both sharing the same practice of reading and the same distaste for the sour notes of critique. In this world of "common readers," literary criticism might even recover its lost social authority.[12]

I do not think this scenario describes a likely future for postcritical reading, because a postcritical program of teaching and scholarship cannot practically be modeled on reading as it actually happens outside the academy. Differences will subsist. I have attempted in chapter 12, "The Question of Lay Reading," to give a schematic account of these differences, conceding that such an account cannot capture all the sites in which academic and amateur reading might intersect. Granted the limits of such a descriptive schema, the world of amateur readers conjured by the new tendency remains for the literary professoriate a *projection* of our desire. This is why postcritical reading is forced to default to a "critique of critique," or the rhetorical form of the manifesto, which imagines a new program for academic literary study that *looks like* the best case for amateur reading. Deidre Lynch, whose important monograph *Loving Literature* examines the history of affective attachment to literary works, helpfully reminds us in this context that "over the last century and a half . . . each new call for the

---

12. Eric Hayot notes the implicit turn to belletrism in his contribution, "Then and Now," to *Critique and Postcritique*, ed. Elizabeth S. Anker and Rita Felski (Durham, NC: Duke University Press, 2017): "The road back to relevance would thus involve a turn away from scholarly publishing, a movement toward belle-lettrism, novel-writing, and other forms of public scholarship and digital engagement, all this amounting to a general undoing of the Theory mistake and a renewed relationship to activism, outreach, and engaged criticism" (291). Presumably the rise of "public humanities" responds to the desire for social impact, though this movement does not seem to me aligned with the new tendency's plan for a transformation of academic scholarship. Related to the belletristic urge of the new tendency is Joseph North, *Literary Criticism: A Concise Political History* (Cambridge, MA: Harvard University Press, 2017). North makes a counterintuitive argument that the expressly political, historicist turn in criticism actually represented a turn away from the politically more effective education of sensibility he traces to I. A. Richards. This is an interesting argument, though unconvincing (to me) on the representation of Richards, who was notably reserved about the politics of his criticism. Richards's political investment was expressed in his advocacy for the "Basic English" project, by means of which he hoped to make a common language available on a global scale. In this project, he was disappointed. North's argument seems closer to that of F. R. Leavis, despite the ambiguity of Leavis's political position taking.

professionalization that might better secure the English professor's claim to expertise has been followed, in another swing of the pendulum, by a new round of amateur envy."[13] With the new tendency in criticism, literary study finds itself again at the latter vertex of the pendulum's swing.[14]

Although Felski states that she does not want to offer a "critique of critique," the proportion between the work of dismantling and that of constructing in her manifesto is overwhelmingly in favor of the former. This fact does not in itself diminish the value of an account of critique that observes its limits; these should indeed be acknowledged. I quote the opening formulation of the argument in *The Limits of Critique*: "As we shall see, the idea of critique contains varying hues and shades of meaning, but its key elements include the following: a spirit of skeptical questioning or outright condemnation, an emphasis on its precarious position vis-à-vis overbearing and oppressive social forces, the claim to be engaged in some kind of radical intellectual and/or political work, and the assumption that whatever is *not* critical must therefore be *uncritical*."[15] Felski here touches the third rail, so to speak, of our discipline, its cherished political aims, and that must have taken some courage. These aims were always improbable of accomplishment; they always fell short of demonstrating the precise articulation of literary study with the social and political domain. The sites of articulation host an array of mediations that are absent from much literary criticism but also missing from Felski's restorative plan. That plan is focused on the affective orientation of critique, or what she calls "critical mood," which is supposed to be founded on detachment, an unwillingness to feel or express attachment to a literary text (*The Limits of Critique*, 20). Discreetly perhaps, Felski avoids discussing actual examples of critique in favor of metaphorical characterizations, indicated by the organizing tropes of chapters, such as "detection of crime," or "digging deep." The mood or attitude of critique is figuratively embodied in an "intellectual persona," a *personification*, that comes across as thoroughly unappealing: "suspicious, knowing, self-conscious, hardheaded, tirelessly vigilant" (6). The per-

13. Deidre Lynch, *Loving Literature: A Cultural History* (Chicago: University of Chicago Press, 2015), 2.

14. For a prescient study of literary study's longtime secret affair with amateur reading, see Marjorie Garber, "The Amateur Professional and the Professional Amateur," in *Academic Instincts* (Princeton, NJ: Princeton University Press, 2001), 3–52. As Garber's title hints, the relation between amateur and professional has been a kind of submerged dialectic in the history of literary study.

15. Anker and Felski, introduction to *Critique and Postcritique*, remark on the style of reading "where characters in novels are reduced to the indexical function of signaling some larger social injustice (sexism, imperialism, heteronormativity)" (7).

sonification of the critical mood raises an uncomfortable question about the rhetoric of Felski's manifesto, which deploys a generalized subtextual *ad hominem*. The implicit or sometimes explicit feminism allied to affect studies resurfaces in the argument as preemptively defensive, difficult to analyze because it is difficult to recover real-world practitioners of critique beneath the mounting accumulation of denunciatory language: "What afflicts literary studies is not interpretation as such but the kudzu-like proliferation of a hypercritical style of analysis that has crowded out alternative forms of intellectual life. Interpretation does not have to be a matter of riding roughshod over a text, doing symbolic violence to a text, chastising and castigating a text, stamping a single 'metaphysical' truth upon a text. In short, it is a less muscular and macho affair than it is often made out to be" (10). The hermeneutics of suspicion devolves here into a caricature of the *suspicious person*: "This entrenching of suspicion in turn intensifies the impulse to decipher and decode. The suspicious person is sharp-eyed and hyperalert; mistrustful of appearances, fearful of being duped, she is always on the lookout for concealed threats and discreditable motives" (33). Despite the arbitrary distribution of gender pronouns, the figure described is too obviously a certain recognizable type, stigmatized earlier as "macho." Personification carries too much of the argument here, deflecting it from what could have been a different and more useful critique of critique. That critique might well begin with a question of ethos or "character," which is where I began with Nietzsche, provided we recognize that we are speaking of a professional deformation; otherwise "mood" has no discernible substance other than a mannerism of theory.[16] What I have called the overestimation of aim is in truth composed in equal measure of good intentions and the constitutional narcissism of the professional, the expert. It would be helpful to distinguish these characterological fixations in the case of the literary scholar from interpretation as such, which surely *requires* a certain detachment in order to proceed, without necessarily implying disdain for the literary work.

I would like to believe that the value of criticism inheres in its discovery of a truth in literary or other cultural works, whatever feelings of affection or disaffection the critical reader might have about a given work. That truth might well concern overt political position taking, or it might point to an

---

16. For another view of this question, see Amanda Anderson, *The Way We Argue Now: A Study of the Cultures of Theory* (Princeton, NJ: Princeton University Press, 2006), and Amanda Anderson, "Thinking with Character," in Amanda Anderson, Rita Felski, and Toril Moi, *Character: Three Inquiries in Literary Studies* (Chicago: University of Chicago Press, 2019). The essays in this book provide an interesting basis for consideration of how the notion of character has reentered literary study.

implicit politics in the text's situation. These possibilities can be arrayed along a spectrum, say, from William Blake's blast against priests and kings to Jane Austen's more oblique politics. This is the sense in which, as I have said, the criticism of the text can also be the criticism of society, with the proviso that arguments about the political implication of literary works are distinguishable from the *politics of scholarship itself*, from the estimation of its aims or effects. In any case, criticism that deals with political implication need not entail the expression of negative feeling toward the literary work, any more than it necessarily entails extravagant claims for the political work of scholarship.

Still, if some criticism exhibits the negative affect Felski describes— again, this is an empirical matter, but the observation can be conceded— the question arises as to whether such affect is intrinsic to "critical reading." Is it in fact crucial to the substance of the argument? If the latter, critique so marred is not likely to be credible. On the other hand, we will have to ask the same question on the side of postcritical reading: Is the argument of such reading carried by its *positive* affect, as registered by words such as "incandescent, extraordinary, sublime, utterly special" (11)? This is language, of course, some version of which we might very well employ in our classes or in our conversations about cultural works, and which I myself have no hesitation employing in these contexts. The question is whether affective expressions of this kind can carry an argument. For whatever we mean by reading *in the discipline*, it must make an argument. It cannot simply rest with approbation.

"But how, we might ask, is such talk of affect to be incorporated into literary studies as a scholarly subject and a form of academic credentialing?" (178). In answer to her question, Felski turns to Bruno Latour and "actor-network theory." The greater part of Latour's apparatus is in my view irrelevant to the practice of literary criticism, but my reasons for this reservation will have to remain largely implicit.[17] Felski proposes three components for postcritical criticism, roughly as follows: (1) a repudiation of historical context as the premier operator of interpretation and as the driver of period specialization. This disciplinary practice, in Felski's presentation, fails to develop "models of textual mobility and transhistorical attachment," or in other words, accounts of how literary works continue to engage readers

---

17. I refrain here from a longer consideration of Bruno Latour and actor-network theory, noting only that my reservation about the utility of this theory concerns its ontology, which asks scholars to substitute a lexicon of "actors" (or "actants") for all other current or former lexicons of social analysis. This demand seems to me unreasonably totalizing.

across centuries. (2) Literary texts should be seen as *"nonhuman actors,"* according to Latour's flat ontology, which will restore to texts their agency and their numerous affiliations with the social world. And (3) postcritical reading must "do better justice to the transtemporal liveliness of texts and the coconstitution of texts and readers—without opposing thought to emotion or divorcing intellectual rigor from affective attachment" (154).

It is easy enough to endorse these recommendations in whole or in part, although also easy to recognize in them areas of research or teaching currently or formerly part of the discipline. The first component calls in effect for greater attention to the *longue durée* of literary transmission in contradistinction to the more circumscribed contextual projects so common today. In another lexicon, we would recognize this subject as *literary history*. It is, in fact, a more or less neglected field in recent decades, despite the availability of sophisticated theoretical formulations such as those developed by the Russian formalists. Literary history today is being revived by digital analysis, which requires long timelines for the accumulation of its massive textual corpora, but it is not certain that this field of scholarship will move to the center of the discipline. In the meantime, Felski is surely right in arguing that "context" has been too confining a framework for the discipline, but what would help most is not to mock it but to give an account of its history, of how it came to occupy the position it holds in literary study. I suspect that such an account would discover a rather more interesting and complex story than is indicated by the notion that "context stinks."[18]

The second component, imputing agency to literary texts, is the closest in its language to the system of Latour. Reframing our engagement with literary texts in Latour's terms would require seeing texts as "actors" in a network of associations defined by the various "attachments" of the literary work, or the "reader-text" relation.[19] Extending this argument to works of

18. In the work of the New Critics, the term "context" almost always refers to the immediate textual environment of a given passage. How did "context" come to mean exclusively the *social* environment of a text? We have as yet no account of this semantic mutation.

19. One puzzling aspect of Felski's appropriation of Latour is the representation of "texts" and "readers" as the principal actors in the networks that interest her. The figure of the "author" drops almost completely out of her account, despite the fact that readers themselves often establish attachments to authors that overdetermine their relation to individual works. These author loyalties enable authors to circulate in literary culture with considerable autonomy. Authors are "makers of difference" (to use the Latourian term) who organize large realms of consumption. This problem would not be so troubling if texts were acknowledged as the *acts* of authors rather than exclusively as actors, as demanded by Latour's flat ontology.

art in general, Felski asserts that "art works can only survive and thrive by making friends, creating allies, attracting disciples, inciting attachments, latching on to receptive hosts" (166). However persuasive (or not) the language of textual agency may be, this component of the program again points us to work with a long tradition in literary study. We might once have called this field "reception history," as instanced in the work of Hans Robert Jauss, or the work already mentioned by Janice Radway and Deidre Lynch.[20] And the "reader-text" dyad points as well to an enormous volume of research into reading, both scholarly and "common." Here we might cite the work of Wolfgang Iser, Michael Riffaterre, or Stanley Fish. But perhaps most relevant to Felski's agenda is the oeuvre of Louise Rosenblatt, whose interest was precisely in affective responses to literary works. This work had a great impact on primary and secondary schools, and it has been unfortunately neglected by the postsecondary professoriate.[21] My point here is that the new tendency in criticism does not look upon closer view as necessarily entailing quite so radical a reorientation of practice as is contemplated in Felski's manifesto. Nor does it require our subscribing to the system of yet another *maître-à-penser*, like Bruno Latour.[22] It rather demands a sober assessment of the cyclical fashions of the discipline, which make it possible for rediscovery to function as innovation.[23] Felski is right to point to the fallow ground in literary criticism today, but much of this ground was once cultivated. The history of scholarship already knows much that our current practice has forgotten.

The third component of Felski's program, postcritical reading, is less an account of the actual procedures of reading than "a placeholder for emerging ideas and barely glimpsed possibilities" (173). For particular strategies of reading, we are referred to recent French critics, such as Mariel Macé and Yves Citton, who posit "the text's entanglement with its readers. The text is no longer a monument to dead thought (*histoire*) nor a self-referential web of linguistic signs (*écriture*). Rather it springs to life via a mundane yet mysterious process, in which words are animated by readers

20. For the major statement, see Hans Robert Jauss, *Toward an Aesthetic of Reception*, trans. Timothy Bahti (Minneapolis: University of Minnesota Press, 1982).

21. If Felski rediscovers a version of "reader-response" theory, we might also affirm the relevance of uncited recent work in the cognitive science and neurophysiology of reading by Stanislas Dehaene, Maryanne Wolf, and Daniel T. Willingham.

22. For a study that is sympathetic to Felski's position but different in its theoretical coordinates and style of reading, see Toril Moi, *Revolution of the Ordinary: Literary Studies after Wittgenstein, Austin, and Cavell* (Chicago: University of Chicago Press, 2017).

23. For a comment on "intellectual fashion" in relation to the "rise and fall of Theory," see Eric Hayot, "Then and Now," in *Critique and Postcritique*, ed. Anker and Felski, 292.

and reanimate readers in turn" (175). If only this process of interanimation, which Coleridge described two centuries ago and I. A. Richards made the basis of his theory of reading, could be given new content and sophistication! Reading is indeed a process both mundane and mysterious, but the mystery has nothing to fear from a research program, either historical or linguistic.

Here is Felski's summation of the third agenda of postcritical reading: "Reading, in this light, is a matter of attaching, collating, negotiating, assembling—of forging links between things that were previously unconnected. It is not a question of plumbing depths or tracing surfaces—these spatial metaphors lose much of their allure—but of creating something new in which the reader's role is as decisive as that of the text. Interpretation becomes a coproduction between actors that brings new things to light rather than an endless rumination on a text's hidden meanings or representational failure" (173–74).[24] The hopeful enumeration of procedures in this statement reverts almost immediately to the derogation of the critical alternative: "It is not a question of . . . but of. . . ." Inasmuch as postcritical reading "brings new things to light" or forges "links between things that were previously unconnected," it is difficult to say how it is different from what the best criticism has always been. In the absence of further elaboration, postcritical reading relies tacitly on an idealized "reader's role," but as academics are readers too, the idealization seems founded on the "amateur envy" remarked by Lynch. The most urgent question before us is not how to reform disciplinary reading to be more like amateur practice but how the discipline of literary study can serve the reading of literature. Just here is where Felski's version of the new tendency takes a wrong turn. The literary professoriate might as well surrender whatever political claims it wants to make for the reading of any particular literary work if a readership for

---

24. In a later essay, "Introduction" to *New Literary History* 47 (2016), Felski offers a different program for her practice of reading, now to consist of "curating, conveying, criticizing, composing" (216). Some of these activities are familiar, as the first two converge with modes of textual transmission and the third with judgment. The activity of composing is drawn directly from Latour as "an alternative to critique" (221). It gestures toward "the possibility of composing a common world." It is difficult to discern what is implied here specifically for the practice of reading. Felski defines composing by reiterating the notion of "a forging of links between things that were unconnected" (222), as in the passage quoted above from *The Limits of Critique*. More helpful, perhaps, is the enumeration offered in *The Uses of Literature* (Malden, MA: Blackwell, 2008): recognition, enchantment, knowledge, shock. These terms identify hypothetical relations of readers with literary works and useful signposts for criticism.

that work no longer exists. We need first to understand literature as a living medium, with pleasures and challenges equal to those of the new media, before asserting the social and political benefits of our scholarship. Ultimately, this is a question of *reading in general*, the advancement of reading across all the sites of its practice. But for further consideration of this matter, I refer to chapter 12, "The Question of Lay Reading."

Despite the false starts and wrong turns of the new tendency, and the fact that it has failed to move beyond the phase of manifesto, it has succeeded in bringing the problem of reading into view. If the "critique of critique" has in some ways been misdirected, the new tendency is right to press the question of reading in contradistinction to that of interpretation, and even of criticism. Although I do not believe that interpretation can be discarded in favor of description, or that the criticism of society has no place at all in literary criticism, I support what I take to be the lesson of the new tendency: the way in which academics read literature needs to be understood in relation to the larger world of reading practices. Much as we wanted to see the guarantor of our impact and relevance in strategies such as topicality, that self-understanding has deceived us. We scholars have been mesmerized by the mirror of culture, in which we have seen society both represented and remade. In consequence, we have failed to recognize the real site of articulation between the discipline and its social environment—that site is the *practice* of reading. It is only by tracing the filiations of this practice as they extend from literature to the system of education, and beyond that, to the venues of the new media, that we might find a better way to estimate and realize our aims.[25] Long ago, literary education was the chief requisite for a voice in the public sphere; that day is over. The institution of professions

25. Recent decades have seen new efforts to bring literature into systematic relation to media, including work by N. Katherine Hayles, Jessica Pressman, Johanna Drucker, Matthew Kirschenbaum, Franco Moretti, Stephen Ramsay, Ted Underwood, and others too numerous to name. But it is my sense that these efforts have not yet been assimilated into literary study as a new paradigm for teaching and scholarship and that scholarship on the literature-media relation remains for the present a subfield of the discipline. For a presentiment of what such a new paradigm might look like, however, see Alan Liu, *Friending the Past: The Sense of History in the Digital Age* (Chicago: University of Chicago Press, 2018). Liu attempts in this work to build a "network archaeology" that would be inclusive of all media forms, and wherein literary studies would find a new place. The difficulty of this theoretical enterprise is indexed by the difficulty of the technical knowledge it involves. My fear is that the demands of this technical knowledge will debar most literary scholars from participating in what needs to be a very broadly based effort, suggesting that the theory (for now) requires something theologians used to call a language of "accommodation."

and the proliferation of new media have irreversibly transformed the social conditions of literary study and relegated literature to a smaller place in the educational system and in society. These conditions must be acknowledged if the professoriate is ever to overcome its tendency to construct literary study as something more than it can be and less than it should be.

[PART TWO]

Organizing Literature

FOUNDATIONS, ANTECEDENTS,
CONSEQUENCES

CHAPTER 4

Monuments and Documents

On the Object of Study in the Humanities

And for short time an endlesse moniment.
EDMUND SPENSER, "Epithalamion"

HUMANISMS

If there is one feature that most recent discussions of the humanities have in common, it is surely the rhetorical form of the defense. The prevalence of defense suggests—not without evidence—that the humanities are under attack, and have been perhaps since their inception. Perennially declared to be in a state of crisis, the humanities seem to have emerged as university disciplines by a different route than the natural and social sciences, both earlier than these disciplines and *left over* after the sciences achieved preeminence at the turn of the twentieth century. This is the view of the historian Lawrence Veysey, who writes that what we call the humanities were in fact "what was left" after the social sciences separated from the American Council of Learned Societies and formed their own organization, the Social Science Research Council, in 1923.[1] The natural sciences had established their professional autonomy much earlier. Veysey goes on to question whether these remaining disciplines can be credited with any coherence at all: "We are left with the possibility that the grouping of the fields of history, English, classical and modern languages, philosophy, art,

---

1. Lawrence Veysey, "The Plural, Organized World of the Humanities," in Oleson and Voss, *The Organization of Knowledge in Modern America 1860–1920*, 57. The argument of this essay is addressed to the situation of the humanities in the American university system and secondarily to the British system, which is suffering from a similar effort to devalue the humanities on the basis of monetized outcomes. It is my hope that at least a part of this argument will prove relevant to the European university as well. This extension of the argument depends in part on how comparable the Anglo-American concept of humanities is to notions such as *les sciences humaines* or *Kulturwissenschaften*, terms that orient disciplines in somewhat different ways than the tripartite division of the Anglo-American system into natural sciences, social sciences, and humanities.

and music may at bottom be nothing more than a growing convenience—perhaps especially for deans and university presidents in neatly structuring their organizations" (57). This institutional nominalism is bracing, but it leaves the humanities with a very difficult task of defense.

This task has become both more difficult and more urgent as a consequence of the residual effects of the 2008/2009 financial crisis, which gave policy makers an excuse to question the value of university degrees in the humanities. In recent decades, a meme emerged in public discourse, asserting that English and other humanities majors fail to get jobs and that students would be wiser to major in STEM fields and other practical subjects such as business or communications. Several governors even proposed tuition penalties for students in their state universities who major in humanities. Not surprisingly, these attacks provoked a torrent of books, articles, reports, and blogs in defense of the humanities, all reaffirming the value of critical thinking and other skills produced by humanities study.[2] Many of the attacks on the humanities were no doubt opportunistic, motivated as much by partisan anti-intellectualism as by concern for the employment of graduates. And as researchers pointed out, claims about the failure of humanities graduates to find jobs are simply not true.[3] Yet these defenses had little effect in changing public opinion. Universities across the country saw enrollments in humanities fields drop by significant percentages, confirming the success of the attacks. If the strategy of defense has indeed reached an impasse, I suggest that it is time to consider a different way of representing the humanities in the public sphere. The weakness of current

2. Contributions to the debate are far too numerous to list. Typical among them, and most substantial, is the 2013 report of the American Academy of Arts and Sciences entitled "The Heart of the Matter," representing a broad consensus of scholars, artists, and policy makers on the value of both humanities and social sciences. Yet despite its vigorous defense and helpful marshaling of statistics, the report breaks no new rhetorical ground. We are told that the humanities "teach us to question, analyze, debate, interpret, synthesize, compare evidence, and communicate"—all of which is true. While it is always worth reiterating these points, it is also worth noting that similar claims can be made for the natural sciences. In order to distinguish their value, the humanities have often been forced to go beyond the "skills" defense to the more high-minded aims of character formation and citizenship. For a judicious historical survey of value arguments from the nineteenth century to the present, see Helen Small, *The Value of the Humanities* (Oxford: Oxford University Press, 2014). See also Paul Reiter and Chad Wellmon, *Permanent Crisis: The Humanities in a Disenchanted Age* (Chicago: University of Chicago Press, 2021).

3. For employment statistics, see Robert Matz, "The Myth of the English Major Barista," *Inside Higher Education*, July 6, 2016, https://www.insidehighered.com/views/2016/07/06/cultural-implications-myth-english-majors-end-working-permanently-starbucks-essay.

defenses of the humanities arises above all from their failure to describe the objects of study in humanities disciplines, to make the demand of these objects upon our attention vivid and undeniable. Humanities scholars have devoted too much effort to declaring the purpose or value of humanities study—the *why*—and too little to giving an account of *what* they study. It is my contention that a better description of what we study will yield a better understanding in the public sphere of why we study these objects.

In this chapter, I propose to reorient discourse about the humanities to the objects of our disciplines by putting back into circulation two terms first employed by Erwin Panofsky in an essay published in 1940, entitled "The History of Art as a Humanistic Discipline."[4] These two terms are "document" and "monument." By the former term, Panofsky means all of those artifacts or traces of human making, action, or thought surviving into the present, the whole world of human artifacts, events, and ideas. By "monument," Panofsky refers to those artifacts, events, or ideas that have the most urgent meaning for us at any present moment, that most demand our recognition or study. Panofsky's terms do a different kind of work than defense. The absence of these terms from our public discourse reminds us that little effort has been devoted to conceptualizing the object of humanities study across the breadth of the disciplines enumerated by Veysey. As a consequence, discourse about the humanities typically defaults to high-minded but vague claims about social value, claims that are less effective than they should be in the public sphere because they are so disconnected from objects of study in the humanities, from the very things that motivate scholars in the first place.

Before considering at length Panofsky's use of the terms *monument* and *document*, however, it will be necessary to clear the ground of the discussion by looking more closely at the presuppositions of current defenses, the underlying reasons for their failure in the public sphere. Almost always scholars rise to the task of defense by making two closely related claims for the value of the humanities. The first is that the humanities are uniquely valuable for their use in making better persons, or more specifically, better citizens. This claim has a long history, which traces the humanities to the program of the Renaissance humanists, who did indeed make such claims for their new ways of teaching. The humanists called their program *studia humanitatis*, or sometimes *litterae humaniores*. The invocation of the

---

4. Erwin Panofsky, "The History of Art as a Humanistic Discipline," in *The Meaning of the Humanities*, ed. Theodore Meyer Greene (Princeton, NJ: Princeton University Press, 1940; reprinted in Erwin Panofsky, *Meaning in the Visual Arts* (Woodstock, NY: Overlook, 1974). I cite page numbers from the later volume.

"human" signaled their embrace of the classical notion of *humanitas*, real-ized above all in rhetoric, the art of "speaking well." The crucial connec-tion of *studia humanitatis* with rhetoric reasserted the classical conception of the human being as distinguished from the animal by speech. Thus was born the first version of "humanism," the conception of a unique human being defined over against the animal.

For the Renaissance humanists, the invocation of *humanitas* reiter-ated the classical conception of the human, but the humanists had an-other equally important purpose: to pry open a space for their teaching in an educational system dominated at its summit by theology—hence the comparative degree of *litterae humaniores*: "more human learning." The humanists saw themselves as more concerned with human learning than with divinity; at the same time, they did not want to place their *studia* in competition with the truths of revealed religion. Thus emerged a second version of humanism, in which the realm of "human learning" was set over against the domain of revealed religion. Importantly, human learning was inclusive of everything that we would call the humanities today, but also of natural philosophy. This too was human learning, and equally with moral philosophy established a version of humanism exalting the achievements of human beings in the realm of learning.

Although the humanism that emerged in the twentieth century and be-queathed its name to the humanities derived its moral and philosophical claims from its Renaissance precursor, it departed significantly from that comprehensive notion of human learning. The "New Humanism" espoused by Irving Babbitt, Paul Elmore More, Norman Foerster and others during the Progressive Era was the rallying cry for those who were fiercely op-posed to the utilitarian culture of industrial capitalism and to the correlated dominance of the natural sciences in the new university.[5] This version of humanism presupposed the division of disciplines that gave rise in the nineteenth century to the great debate between Huxley and Arnold, the first of the "two cultures" debates. Ultimately the humanists identified their disciplines with the very concept of culture, defined in opposition to the domain of nature, the object of natural science. At the same time, they were careful to distinguish their version of humanism as modern, and hence they rejected any retreat into religious belief. A "secular" version of humanism emerged in the uncertain gap between fading religious certainties and the confident assertions of science, and it was this third iteration of humanism

5. For the locus classicus of the "New Humanism," see Irving Babbitt, *Literature and the American College: Essays in Defense of the Humanities* (Cambridge, MA: Houghton-Mifflin, 1908).

that bequeathed its name to the "humanities" in the midcentury university. In this context, Veysey is right when he insists on the belatedness of the name for the "humanistic" disciplines: "In fact, not until the 1940s does one discover a sudden outpouring of books and manifestoes with 'the humanities' in their titles, using the word with an entirely new frequency and insistence" ("Plural Organized World of the Humanities," 57). What Veysey notes as "insistence" betrays the motive of defense, which owes perhaps too much to the third phase of humanism, orienting the disciplines around the opposition of nature and culture. The natural sciences gained the upper hand in this struggle by the end of the nineteenth century, and they retain this position today, long after the reconfiguration of the cultural disciplines as the "humanities."

In retrospect, the invocation of the uniquely civilizing or morally improving mission of the humanities relies on a weak humanism, insufficiently informed by the complex history of the three versions of humanism and distorted today by a defensive relation to science. In consequence, claims for the social value of the humanities, however true these claims might be, have unwisely been pitted against the social benefits of the sciences. This was always, so to speak, an unfair fight. So long as there are scientists at work on a cure for cancer, the humanities will have a nearly insurmountable task in making a case in the public sphere for their great, if less obvious, social benefits. The difficulty of putting across the reality of these benefits is inseparable, as we shall see, from conveying the value that inheres in the object of humanities study.

The problem that troubles the rhetoric of defense is even more evident in the second major line of defense, the argument that the humanities deal uniquely with human things, or the human world. This second defensive theme only emerged after the dubious partition of "human learning" into the two domains of the nature and culture. The notion that the humanities have a privileged relation to the human world has never been less true. The social sciences have long since confounded the binary that underlies the weak humanism of this defense. And the "natural" sciences of psychology and biology have long since taken aspects of human being as their object of study. The humanities cannot ignore the findings of science about human beings any more than humanists can deny that human beings are animals and belong to the natural world. The humanities are concerned with human things, to be sure, but what sort of things, and what sort of claims are justified on the basis of studying these things? This definitional or *ontological* problem remains unresolved today, long after the disciplines of the humanities were set adrift in their divisional boat, like Prospero and his books.

If it is true, as Veysey argues, that the humanities have no organic coherence, that they exist as a mere organizational convenience, their status among the disciplines will likely remain as troubled as it is today. The
humanities will continue to be an unequal divisional partner in the distribution of resources in the university, repeatedly submitted to existential
challenge in the public sphere. But there is no necessity to choose between
Veysey's institutional nominalism and a weak humanism. As we shall see,
Panofsky's meditation on the disciplinary object discloses a coherence that
organizes the disciplines enumerated by Veysey according to a logic far
more credible than that of convenience. If we cannot give an account of
this coherence, there can be no credible basis for a defense of the humanities generally, as opposed to the individual disciplines collected under this
category. We have more to gain, I believe, by offering a careful description of our object of study than by repeating the usual assertions of social
value or by making proprietary claims to speak about the human world. I
take it as a given that the humanities are concerned with the human world.
But they enter this world from a particular locus of interest; they do not
overlook the whole of it as though it were a kingdom. It is time now to
discard the weak humanism that motivates defenses of the humanities and
clear some conceptual space for another kind of rhetorical strategy. Let us
consider the possibility, with Panofsky's help, that the humanities might
possess a coherence that can be described more richly than an aggregation
of nonscientific disciplines.

PANOFSKY'S OBJECT

Although Panofsky's essay is well known to art historians, it will probably not be obvious to readers why a turn to this moment in his oeuvre is
demanded by the perennial crisis of the humanities. But clearly, defenses
of the humanities have reached a dead end, and a new framework for discussion is needed. It is fortunate for our purpose that Panofsky's contribution to the discourse of the humanities was written at a time just before
the consolidation of the humanities as disciplines, when they were not
yet burdened by the resentments and frustrations of the present institutional situation. His description of humanistic disciplines is cheerfully
nondefensive.

Panofsky's essay is typically learned, as luminous an example as one
might find of the scholarship produced by his generation, writing when the
lights were going out all over Europe. The historical interest of the essay is
great, but I am concerned mainly with recovering Panofsky's development
of the terms "monument" and "document" in relation to humanistic dis-

ciplines generally.[6] My inquiry therefore is avowedly unoriginal. It would not serve my purpose if scholars did not recognize what they do in Panofsky's or my description of our disciplines. I propose, then, to explore the theoretical scope and power these terms might possess beyond Panofsky's immediate concern with the visual work of art.

Perhaps because Panofsky did not undertake this elaboration himself, or only hinted at it, his terms have had an intermittent afterlife in scholarship.[7] If the concept of monument was not adopted widely, recent scholarship has evinced an extraordinary and productive interest in the category of the document, along with that of the archive. Studies of the document and the archive constitute a lively subfield across a number of humanities disciplines today, as attested by Carolyn Steedman's *Dust*, Ben Kafka's *The Demon of Writing*, Marizio Ferraris's *Documentality*, and Lisa Gitelman's *Paper Knowledge*.[8] The current interest in the document suggests that the moment is right for a reconsideration of Panofsky's reflection on the relation between document and monument.

6. I note by way of caveat that I attempt in this chapter to dislodge Panofsky's argument about monuments and documents from the general context of his iconology and, further, from his philosophical investments as a neo-Kantian close to the position of Ernst Cassirer. It is my sense that this particular argument, while compatible with these other investments, can stand alone, but that, of course, is a judgment my readers must confirm for themselves.

7. The pairing of "monument and document" was employed by Foucault, who gave the terms a rather different sense than Panofsky, in *The Archaeology of Knowledge*, trans. A. M. Sheridan Smith (New York: Pantheon Books, 1972), 7. Gary Gutting notes in his *Michel Foucault's Archaeology of Scientific Reason* (Cambridge: Cambridge University Press, 1989), that in "Sur l'archéologie des sciences: Réponse au cercle d'épistémologie," *Cahier pour l'analyse* 9 (1968): 231, Foucault attributes the monument/document pairing to Georges Canguilhem. The terms have since been taken up by Jacques Le Goff, directly following Foucault, in his account of "*nouvelle histoire.*" Jacques Le Goff, "Documento/monumento," in *Enciclopedia Einaudi*, ed. Ruggiero Romano (Turin: Einaudi, 1978), 5:38–48; and Le Goff, "L'histoire nouvelle," in *La nouvelle histoire.* ed. Jacques Le Goff (Paris: Editions Complexe, 1978), 63; see also Paul Ricoeur, in *Memory, History, Forgetting* (Chicago: University of Chicago Press, 2004), 534.

8. Carolyn Steedman, *Dust: The Archive and Cultural History* (New Brunswick, NJ: Rutgers University Press, 2002); Ben Kafka, *The Demon of Writing: The Powers and Failures of Paperwork* (New York: Zone Books, 2012); Maurizio Ferraris, *Documentality: Why It Is Necessary to Leave Traces*, trans. Richard Davies (New York: Fordham University Press, 2013); Lisa Gitelman, *Paper Knowledge: Toward a Media History of Documents* (Durham, NC: Duke University Press, 2014). See also Francis X. Blouin Jr. and William G. Rosenberg, *Archives, Documentation, and Institutions of Social Memory: Essays from the Sawyer Seminar* (Ann Arbor: University of Michigan Press, 2006), and Cornelia Vismann, *Files: Law, Media, and Technology* (Stanford, CA: Stanford University Press, 2008).

Panofsky assumes, like most of his contemporaries, a distinction between nature and culture descending from the nineteenth-century division of the disciplines, and therefore also a version of humanism I have
described as its third iteration: "From the humanistic point of view, however, it became reasonable, and even inevitable, to distinguish, within the
realm of creation, between the sphere of *nature* and the sphere of *culture*"
(5). But this version of humanism, though it defers to the term current in its
day, is crucially qualified by subsequent remarks; the "sphere of culture" is
identified not with the totality of human experience but with what Panofsky specifies as "the *records left by man*" (5). Now this domain is larger than
the accumulation of works of art but *restricted* to a particular kind of human
activity: "Man is indeed the only animal to leave records behind him, for
he is the only animal whose products 'recall to mind' an idea distinct from
their material existence" (5). The question of what a "record" is—what kind
of *thing* it is—remains open.

Panofsky goes on to emphasize the function of records in relation to the
"stream of time" or the pastness of the past: "These records have therefore
the quality of emerging from the stream of time, and it is precisely in this
respect that they are studied by the humanist. He is, fundamentally, an historian" (5). By equating the humanist scholar with the "historian," Panofsky locates the humanistic disciplines in the field of a long temporality, not
that of memory but of *memorialization*. Only this time beyond the lifespan
of the individual can establish the domain of "culture": "The cosmos of culture, like the cosmos of nature, is a spatiotemporal structure" (7).[9] The
work of art does not yet appear within this structure, only records. But
again, what are they?

First of all, they are objects in the world, and it is these objects that establish the relevant difference between the sciences and the humanities.
Panofsky then delimits this object more precisely in relation to the object
of natural science, without resorting to invidious comparison: "When the
scientist observes a phenomenon he uses *instruments* which are themselves
subject to the laws of nature which he wants to explore. When the human-

9. Panofsky is close here to a statement of Ernst Cassirer in *The Logic of the Cultural
Sciences: Five Studies*, trans. S. G. Lofts (New Haven, CT: Yale University Press, 2000):
"The object [*Objekt*] of nature appears to lie immediately before our eyes. To be sure,
keener epistemological analysis soon teaches us how many more and more complicated
concepts are required in order to determine this object, the 'object' [*Gegenstand*] of
physics, chemistry, and biology in its particular nature. But this determination proceeds
in a certain steady direction: we approach the object, as it were, in order to get to know
it ever more exactly. But the cultural object requires a different observation; for it lies,
so to speak, behind us" (85).

ist examines a record he uses *documents* which are themselves produced in the course of the process which he wants to investigate" (8). Documents are not analogous to objects found in the "sphere of nature"—these objects exist whether or not humans are there to perceive them—but to *instruments*. Documents are also instrumental. Both documents and scientific instruments are constructed, then, but instruments disclose what is *not constructed*—the cosmos of nature—just by virtue of submitting to the same laws that govern those natural objects. Documents, on the other hand, emerge from the stream of time as the evidence of something that is *not ontologically different* from the documents themselves, that is, other works of human beings. Both instruments and documents are artifacts, then, but the ones called *documents* are produced, as Panofsky says, "in the course of the process" the humanist wants to investigate. Their instrumentality lies precisely in the fact of their self-referential construction (if documents existed in the natural world, it would be as though light could report on its own speed), and this means that documents must be investigated themselves before they can yield any reliable knowledge. They do not bear with them the assumption of truth telling, as do scientific instruments, which are designed to say only what they *must* say. Documents, on the other hand, can be wrong or even mendacious.

In our current intellectual milieu, we are accustomed to modes of criticism that make it their business to call into question the truth-telling of instrumentalities generally, and documents in particular. What I want to pursue in Panofsky is not this critical theme, however, but the pairing of the concept of document with the concept of monument. Neither of these two objects appears within the field of natural science's objects. Panofsky is led to propose the second concept of the "monument" because the document, though it grasps a sense of the "record," is not in itself an adequate name for the art historian's object. Here Panofsky offers an example: a German altarpiece of the fifteenth century, found in a small town in the Rhineland, in the Church of St. James. The art historian does not approach such an object as though it had no relation to any other object in the world. On the contrary, the scholar tries first to confirm the identification of the work by means of something else—a document—in this case a written contract, dated 1471, for what appears to be the very same altarpiece. But this document, Panofsky says, "may be an original, a copy, or a forgery" and can only be validated by a complex inquiry that is itself fraught with uncertainties (8). At this point, Panofsky lacks a term to distinguish between the altarpiece and the contract or to describe the relation between the two. There are two objects to name, then, but as yet only one concept, the document.

To solve this puzzle, Panofsky settles upon the term *monuments*, provisionally distinguished here from documents. "Records," then, can be described as documents *or* monuments. Curiously, we have already heard an oblique invocation of the latter word three pages earlier, in the sentence that begins this line of analysis: mankind "is the only animal whose products 'recall to mind' an idea distinct from their material existence" (5). The phrase "recall to mind," set off in quotation marks, describes the function of the "record," but the word *monument* is hidden in this phrase as well, because monument is etymologically a calling (*monere*) to mind. Both the document and the monument "recall to mind." So what is the difference between them? It remains for Panofsky to develop this intriguing distinction with and without a difference: "However we may look at it, the beginning of our investigation always seems to presuppose the end, and the documents which should explain the monuments are just as enigmatical as the monuments themselves" (9). The objects we find in the "sphere of culture" can be described by two words, both of which mean "recalling to mind." Or rather, documents and monuments give us two necessary ways of looking at the same kind of object, the "record."[10]

But is it the case that this object, the monument/document, can be described as the same kind of object in all of the humanities disciplines? Panofsky implicitly endorses such an extrapolation in the final two short paragraphs on the monument/document concept, before devoting the remainder of his essay to the object of study in his own discipline, the visual work of art. It is in a way easy to see the path to this extrapolation: "I have referred to the altarpiece of 1471 as a 'monument' and to the contract as a 'document'; that is to say, I have considered the altarpiece as the object of investigation or 'primary material,' and the contract as the instrument of investigation, or 'secondary material.' In doing this I have spoken as an art historian. For a paleographer or an historian of law, the contract would be the 'monument,' or 'primary material,' and both may use pictures for docu-

---

10. It is possible that Panofsky is remembering, at least distantly, Nietzsche's *On the Advantage and Disadvantage of History for Life*, in which Nietzsche develops a typology of historical motivations, the *monumental*, the *antiquarian*, and the *critical*. The first two would map roughly onto Panofsky's monument and document, but with significant differences. For Nietzsche, monumental history is a linking together of great heroic moments in history for the purpose of imitation in the present, especially in the circumstance when contemporary heroic models are not available. Antiquarian history expresses a communal, ethnic, or national motive, the desire to preserve a sense of relation to, and continuity with, with the peoples of a homeland. Nietzsche's little treatise is too complex to consider further, and as its title implies, it is concerned ultimately with what humans both gain and lose by living historically. Inasmuch as in Nietzsche's view, humans do lose something from their consciousness of history, he offers at least in part an "antihumanist" argument.

mentation" (10). This observation brings Panofsky to the furthest point of extrapolation: "Everyone's 'monuments' are everyone else's 'documents' and vice versa. . . . Many a work of art has been interpreted by a philologist or by an historian of medicine; and many a text has been interpreted, and could only have been interpreted, by an historian of art" (10). The object of study in the humanities can be subsumed to the category of "record," but to study it means seeing it in a world of objects (Panofsky's "cosmos of culture"), actualized as either monument or document depending upon the relation of objects to one another. This is not merely a matter of perspectival ambiguity but of something much deeper, nothing less than a recognition of the demand that objects of this complex sort make upon us.

The object described by Panofsky at once establishes the humanities disciplines on the ground of this ontology and declares open borders between them. Such a geopolitics of the disciplines is possible because the condition of reversibility between document and monument obtains for *all of the objects of study in the humanities.* Although methodological differences, institutional competition, and intellectual inertia obscure in practice the underlying ontological identity of objects in the humanities disciplines, this unhappy situation does not undo the constitutive and universal duality of the monument/document.

If Panofksy's line of reasoning is persuasive, the humanities should not be regarded as an arbitrary aggregation of disciplines, united only by the fact of not being sciences but on the contrary as an organic expression and necessary ramification of the monument/document into different disciplinary enterprises. These disciplines coalesced historically around an *objective* unity; at the same time the process itself was obfuscated by a residual humanism that failed to grasp the limitation of the disciplinary object, its equivalence not to the human world entirely, but to those objects that make a particular demand upon us, whatever in human experience, past or present, that says "Remember me!"[11] The weak humanism that supplies the rhetorical terms of our defense might now be discarded without taking anything away from the humanities, certainly not their relation to the human world. The seemingly chaotic assemblage of objects that define humanities disciplines—works of art, music, literature, philosophical theories, the vast accumulation of historical events and processes—can all

11. We have no word in English that would cover all of the instances of the monument/document, but ancient Greek had the concept of *poiesis*, meaning both *acting* and *making*, intriguingly close to Panofsky's complementary concepts. Our transliterated term, "poetics," though suggestive, falls back into the realm of making only, with reference mainly to verbal artifacts, which was for the Greeks a discrete subset of action.

be understood as manifestations of the monument/document, an object of study that has its own irreducible specificity.[12]

This clarification offers terms of peace with the sciences too, which are different not because of putatively superior knowledge claims but because the sciences proceed first from a method, not an object, and this method *discloses* the object. Physics today, for example, yields a notion of matter that is very different from the notion prevalent in the early modern period, for which matter was small, hard, and inert. Later versions of the same experimental method that gave us Galileo's mechanical materiality give us today a "matter" that eludes natural languages altogether and bears little relation at all to the perception of matter on the macro scale of the human sensorium. The discovery of the Higgs boson particle is a good example of the priority of method to object, as the existence of this object was posited by nothing more than theoretical need. Method, so to speak, *called for* the object, and after some considerable coaxing, it finally appeared. This priority of method is reversed in the humanities, because in these disciplines the object is *given*; or better, it is *given in time*; it is what "recalls to mind" from a past that falls away from us only moments ago and recedes to the very earliest records of human existence.[13] Moreover, we need not understand this past as only behind us; it may be ahead of us, in the notional future that constructs our present moment as the past of some future. This

12. Panofsky's use of the words *monument* and *document*, it must be noted, is actually modern, standardized only a century before. As Charles W. Hedrick Jr. helpfully recalls in his *Ancient History: Monuments and Documents* (Malden: Blackwell, 2006), 19, the two words were nearly reverse in meaning in antiquity. The Romans used *monumentum* to refer to any "material objects, including written texts, which recall the past," whereas *documentum* referred to anything that could be considered an exemplary lesson about something (activating the root *docere*, to instruct). So it would seem that the two words themselves more or less exchanged places, in a process that Hedrick suggests was not complete until the later nineteenth century: "Thus as late as the 1820s, the great collection of historical texts from various archives in Germany was inaugurated with the title *Monumenta Germaniae Historica*" (19).

13. It may seem that I have sidestepped in my argument the question of method, but I assume throughout that individual disciplines are defined by a relation *between* object and method. My argument is that we take the object for granted and focus too exclusively on the method of "interpretation" as defining humanities disciplines. Methods in the humanities are perennially the subject of controversy, because they are difficult, if not impossible to specify for all humanities disciplines. No such specification is necessary, in my view, only a commitment to the *adequation* of method to object. On the other hand, I want to insist that the object in the humanities can be specified to the extent that the object manifests the dual ontology of the monument/document. In practice, this means that objects in the humanities can be enormously diverse, as will be evident from my discussion below.

demarcation of a past, present, and future is what I will call "long time," the time that exists beyond the human life span, but not beyond the time in which human beings have left traces of their existence, in the form of the monument/document. Long time means that scholars in the humanities can study objects in the present too, by asserting the calling of the object to a future present, when the object in question will fully manifest its dual nature as monument and document. It does not matter, finally, that all of these callings can be exposed for their fictional agency, that we must impute to the object its capacity to call to us over a gap in time.[14] What matters is that we *experience* this calling in the present; what we human beings have made and done and thought returns to us with a demand. We feel it right to answer, and that if we fail to respond, the calling will only become more urgent, a warning. This is the other meaning of *monere*: to warn.

Now I must admit that in offering this description of an underlying unity of humanities disciplines, and of a noncompetitive relation with the sciences, I have painted in many respects a counterfactual picture. Disciplinary politics both within the humanities and between the humanities and the sciences are not peaceful. If it is perhaps too much to ask of Panofsky's terms that they establish the conditions of peace, it would still be desirable to begin negotiations with greater clarity about what we humanities scholars do. Panofsky's virtuoso bit of theorizing offers such a clarification, which I will elaborate further in the remainder of this chapter. Such an elaboration is necessary because Panofsky's paired concepts did not pass into the general repertoire of theory in the humanities; only the concept of the "document" came to circulate widely in the critical reflection of scholars on their practice, a reflection that owes something but not everything to Panofsky. Yet in the absence of the complementary concept of the monument, the document can give only a partial account of what defines humanities

---

14. In a characteristically generous response to this essay, Geoffrey Galt Harpham, "Response to John Guillory," *History of Humanities* 1 (2016): 41–45, remarks rightly that my (and Panofsky's) reorientation to the "object" of study in the humanities is correlated with a subjectivism arising necessarily from the constructedness of this object. This construction can sometimes go disastrously wrong, as Harpham reminds us happened with the philologists' construction of "race" as an object in the nineteenth century. (The scientists were equally wrong in their positing of this object, which they constructed by a different route.) There is no way to remove this fallibility from humanities discourse, except by the rigorous application of a principle of personal accountability. The object of study in the humanities is never in any simple sense "objective." Harpham's reservation reminds us that humanities scholarship is not just play without rules and that its irreducibility to mere fact does not deliver it from responsibility to truthfulness (*parrhesia*) in all of the tasks of research and interpretation that constitute the work of these disciplines.

scholarship. It makes little sense to say that scholars in the humanities study documents, in and for themselves, when we know that documents are always instrumentalized in the process of scholarship, that they are studied because they tell us about *something else*. This something else is what Panofsky means by a monument. Art historians would not take notice of the contract for Panofsky's hypothetical German altarpiece if this work of art could not be distinguished from the contract by a descriptor that indicated its *relation* to the contract. Without actualizing this distinction, both objects—altarpiece and contract—might fall back into the stream of time; both objects might fail to "recall to mind" their complementary relation.

If the disciplines do not cut nature (or culture) precisely at the joints, they might still constitute a practical grammar of knowledge, not just a rhetoric of spurious distinctions, historical accidents that throw us into the situation of defending what we do not truly believe in, the legitimacy of the humanities as disciplines of knowledge. Against the tendency of this nominalism, I adhere to Panofsky's insight into the duality of the object of humanistic study and propose to elaborate this duality further by elevating the terms *monument* and *document* into the qualitative abstractions of *monumentality* and *documentality*. This tactic will permit us to distinguish clearly between the conventional objects in the world designated by the words *monument* and *document* and the bundle of qualities that define Panofsky's disciplinary object. We can easily see that by *monument* Panofsky does not mean only a certain kind of metal or stone structure, a memorialization of a great event. Conversely, Panofsky does not mean by *document* a piece of paper only, or even writing. For a religious historian, the altarpiece itself may be a document, a means of inquiring into some other object of study, for example, devotional practices. For that scholar, such practices possess monumentality, and the altarpiece documentality. The reversible nature of the "records left by man" is a condition of possibility for their study, whatever name we choose to give to this study.

LONG TIME

At this point, I take leave of Panofsky's essay, though still standing, as it were, on his shoulders, and attempt to elaborate the theoretical implications of the monument/document concept, or the unity and duality of the object of study in the humanities. I argue, to begin, that every object of study in the humanities has the two properties of monumentality and documentality, whether or not these objects are material artifacts, like paintings, or immaterial objects, like those historians study: events, processes, tendencies, formations. This specification of the object in its abstract character will permit us to see how even objects of study that are inferred from documents, such as "the fall of the Roman Empire," *must* possess the qualities of both monumentality and documentality. Whatever material or immaterial form the object of study might take, this object can always be located on an axis of relation between monumentality at one pole and documentality at the other. Objects of study are not fixed at any point on this axis, however, which is why a work such as Gibbon's *Decline and Fall of the Roman Empire* can be understood instantly as both monument and document. The axis of relation might just as accurately be figured as a circle, in which polarity is transformed into direction: in one direction, monumentality, in the other, documentality. This helps us to see how ontological duality characterizes objects such as historical "events," objects that exist only as inferences from surviving documents. All of the historian's objects are monuments in spite of the ephemerality of events, the very condition that drives human beings in the first place to memorialize events in monuments of stone or metal.

It is worth insisting too that if all of the objects that humanities scholars want to study come to their attention because they have been "recalled to mind"—that is, they have the quality first of monumentality—these objects can only be recalled insofar as they have been materially embodied in some fashion, a quality that we can identify with documentality. Nothing survives over long time that does not leave some material trace. Such material embodiments are of course inclusive of much more than paper documents—documentality encloses the entire world of traces, all the markings and reshapings of the physical world that can tell us about any given object of study. The duality of monumentality and documentality thus characterizes all objects of study in the humanities: Buddhism, Descartes's *cogito*, the Boxer Rebellion, the "bonfire of the vanities," the novels of Austen, the Hegelian dialectic, the Civil Rights movement, or an Andean folk song.[15] The diversity of these objects conceals an ontological unity as

15. On occasions of delivering this essay as a lecture, I have been asked whether we can any longer include philosophy among the humanities, given the position of many analytic philosophers today that philosophy is an extension of natural science and has broken tout court with its history. I would argue, however, that the break with history is an illusion, if perhaps a necessary one for some philosophers. It may even be that the strategy of temporal deracination is a "monumental" feature of analytic philosophy and will become the object of study for some historians of philosophy of the future. For a comment on the general problem, see Bernard Williams, "Philosophy as a Humanistic Discipline," in Bernard Williams, *Philosophy as a Humanistic Discipline* (Princeton, NJ: Princeton University Press, 2006), 180–99. Williams offers a strenuous critique of "scientism" along with an argument for the necessity of philosophy to engage with its history.

possible objects of study. The monument can be an abstraction, an event or an idea, but it cannot reach across long time without a material trace. The document conversely is defined not by its particular substance, paper or stone, but by its materiality as such; it is the medium by which what is monumental reaches us.

As we have broached the question of materiality, we can now take fuller account of just what is implied by the usual substances metaphorically associated with Panofsky's complementary concepts: in the case of the monument, *metal* or *stone*, and of the document, *paper*. In ordinary usage, the monument might be a thing of stone, but with the concept of monumentality, stone functions as a metaphor: the stoniness of the monument is a figure for defense against decay and the passage of time. Further, the opacity of the monumental surface solicits interpretation but resists its finality, as though every monument were a puzzle like Stonehenge, even those monuments made of words that seem to say only, "I mean what I say." No monument is simply unequivocal, because every monument is historical, immersed in the stream of time. This figure is a commonplace, but not trivial. Panofsky recurs to it when he speaks of the humanities as "enlivening what otherwise would remain dead. . . . Gazing as they do at these frozen, stationary records of which I said they 'emerge from the stream of time,' the humanities endeavor to capture the process in the course of which those records were produced and became what they are" (24).

The metaphorical stoniness of the monument can also convey the opposite effect, what we might call the condition of *stonification*, the loss of the monument's ability to attract interpretation, inviting rather indifference or contempt. Such monuments mutate into silent surfaces later generations will pass by without a second glance. Robert Musil famously and amusingly commented on this condition in a brief essay on monuments, by which he meant the proliferation of statuary and plaques that populate our built environment: "There is nothing in this world as invisible as a monument."[16] If such monuments so often seem to be hopeless attempts to coerce recollection, their failure gestures toward the much larger stakes of monumentality. The metaphoric potentiality of the monument stretches across all of the possibilities of remembering and forgetting and justifies our taking the

16. Robert Musil, *Posthumous Papers of a Living Author* (New York: Archipelago, 2006), 64. I thank Scott Newstok for drawing my attention to Musil's piece. The situation Musil describes with regard to material monuments is not exclusively an expression of old Europe's monarchical culture, despite John Quincy Adams's famous quip, that "democracy has no monuments." A visit to Washington, DC (or any American town square, for that matter), would disabuse anyone of Adams's whimsical notion.

risk of calling the great works we revere and great events we do not want to forget *monuments*, knowing the potential banality of that compliment.

Documents, by contrast, find their metaphoric association in substances such as parchment or paper, at once fragile and yet surprisingly enduring. Documents also have the purpose of recalling to mind, but they do not necessarily make any demands. They are defined by their instrumentality, their capacity to store up messages, some of which may never be read, or if read, never understood. Documents make monumentality possible, but they speak with many and contradictory voices. They are voluble, chatty, full of information but not always truth. They aspire to give testimony, and even to teach, as the etymology of the word tells us: *docere*, to teach. But if they are so eager to speak, they are often difficult to hear. Their voices can subside to a whisper in the archives.

Monuments, on the other hand, give the illusion of immediate accessibility; many people are able to give the basic definition of Kant's "categorical imperative" or the plot of *Moby Dick* without having read Kant's *Metaphysic of Morals* or Melville's novel. The more familiar the monument, the greater the space it occupies in the cosmos of culture, amounting finally to a specious familiarity. This space swells into equivalence with the sense of the word *monumental* as huge, overwhelming. It may be that this metaphoric monumentality gives us a clue to the rhythms of remembering and forgetting that traverse work in the humanities, and indeed in culture at large. Writing on the history of philosophy, for example, Randall Collins argues that at any one time, culture can accommodate only a small number of philosophical systems, possibly only three; monumentality crowds out other contenders to the margins or to obscurity.[17] A similar constraint obtains with literature: if Jane Austen achieves monumentality, then Alexander Pope becomes vulnerable to stonification. Again, the duality of the monument/document reveals itself: monuments impose upon any given present, and they are limited in number because they take up so much space. Documents are capable by contrast of infinite accumulation. Even though they are vulnerable to destruction, complete annihilation, and are constantly being destroyed—archivists estimate that only about 5 percent of documents find their way to the safety of the archive—they continue to accumulate, and do so now exponentially in electronic form.[18] As fragile as they are, documents store up power; they hold in reserve the power to alter

17. Randall Collins, *The Sociology of Philosophies: A Global Theory of Intellectual Change* (Cambridge, MA: Harvard University Press, 1998).

18. For the rarity of documents, see John Ridener, *From Polders to Postmodernism: A Concise History of Archival Theory* (Duluth, MN: Littwin Books, 2009).

the order of the monuments themselves. Monuments have the heights, but documents have the numbers.

The relation between monumentality and documentality is always dynamic, which is to say, unstable; documents change our understanding of monuments and sometimes even destroy them, or better, demote them to documental status. The latter effect is an unavoidable consequence of the dynamic inherent in the object, which is always responsive to the present moment, to the ongoingness of historical time. The emergence of "history from below," for example, is itself a historical event, but it has come to possess a certain inevitability in retrospect; we are puzzled that earlier historians failed to see this object. The object called to us, belatedly, from the archive, and in this calling we discovered a new monumentality. The vicissitudes of the object are even more vividly demonstrated in a case such as the Holocaust, which did not appear as a historical object at all until some years after the Second World War. This delay seems almost impossible to believe; it is as though the Holocaust generated a shock wave with a deceptively long period, rising up only when it reached the shallows of memory, the threshold of forgetting, and breaking upon the present with immense but ambiguous impact. This kind of monumentality takes a long time to assimilate and might very well strike our successors differently than it does ourselves. Because objects emerge in time and achieve monumentality by many routes, humanities scholarship progresses without closing on a terminal condition, in a rhythm determined by the duality of its object.

It is always possible to construct a new object of study, but only when the necessary documents survive that would support such a construction. The great question that faces us at the present time is what difference it will make to our conception of documentality that electronic preservation has vastly expanded the archive of documents. At the least we will be compelled to think much harder about the relation between remembering and forgetting and the peculiar gains and costs of both processes. If the object of study in the humanities is indeed characterized by a finite monumentality and a virtually infinite documentality, this condition is being experienced today with a new and challenging intensity. The stakes will be raised for what we choose to remember and what we choose to forget. Those contemporary works of art that seem to refuse monumentality, that are destroyed in their creation and survive only as documents, like Christo's wrapped buildings, struggle with this question. To live in our moment means to be aware of the fact that our culture generates vast quantities of ephemeral artifacts and trivial events; we cannot remember them all, even if we could preserve records of them all. The latter goal is of course suppositional and depends on how really permanent electronic documents are. I raise these questions because it seems to me that they are illuminated by the monument/document concept and that humanities scholars are well positioned to study the problem of ephemeral culture and its correlate, a short-time monumentality. We do not yet know how to understand the constant churning up and under of cultural monuments that seem to command the horizon only to sink quickly into oblivion. We do know, or should, that every decision we make about what to remember, what to save, has very real social effects. But these effects may also require the long term to become apparent. They are unlike the more immediate social benefits claimed for humanities study, but they are equally important. Just as the humanities find their objects in long time, their effects may be disclosed in long time as well.

Memorialization has many sites, but the humanities have an institutional home. As disciplines, their institutional being is characterized not only by a method (or methods), but equally by a curriculum, that is, a constellation of objects. Whatever else we may want to assert about the methods or aims of the humanities, surely the most important fact for us to acknowledge is that by the humanities, we mean the study of a particular kind of object. This object calls to us across the long time of human existence, exceeding by far the duration of any one human life.[19] I believe that most people, even those who have hardened into permanent suspicion of humanities disciplines, will recognize the responsibility that this long time imposes on the short time of individual lives and that this aspect of being human is not trivial. If it elicits in some the kind of lip service given to pieties that always come up short of resources, that is a pity. But those of us who are scholars of the humanities need not borrow our self-understanding from the words of this lip service. Where has that gotten us? The legitimacy of what we do needs in the first instance a better description. A better defense will follow.

19. "Long time" must be distinguished, for this reason, from *geologic time*, extending from the convulsions of planetary formation to the comortality of the sun and the planets. This distinction allows us to avoid the error of anthropomorphizing geologic time, the error we find in metaphysical systems such as Romantic organicism, or the panpsychism embraced by some philosophers today. Geologic time has no *necessary* relation to long time, which is to say that the planet has no need for human beings to exist. Conversely, we might ask: What is the "Anthropocene" if not the result of long time's belated discovery of geologic time? The disavowal of geologic time by human beings is a planetary crisis, one implication of which is the possibility of long time's end. If the human species cannot value long time, which is one way of describing the aim of the humanities, there is little hope for it to understand the dire implications of its interaction with geologic time.

A great and arrogant humanist scholar of the nineteenth century was famously said to remark, "Never apologize, never explain."[20] We scholars can no longer affect the arrogance of a Benjamin Jowett, but perhaps it would be strategic for us at the present moment to stop apologizing and begin explaining what it is that we study.

20. The remark is attributed to Jowett in a novel by Edwin Milton Royle, *Peace and Quiet: A Novel* (New York: Harper and Brothers, 1916), 217.

CHAPTER 5

The Postrhetorical Condition

Yet if we consider that rhetoric—whatever the system's internal variations may have been—has prevailed in the West for two and a half
millennia, from Gorgias to Napoleon III; if we consider all that it has
seen—watching immutable, impassive, and virtually immortal—come
to life, pass, and vanish without itself being moved or changed: Athenian democracy, Egyptian kingdoms, the Roman Republic, the Roman
Empire, the great invasions, feudalism, the Renaissance, the monarchy,
the French Revolution; it has digested regimes, religions, civilizations;
moribund since the Renaissance, it has taken three centuries to die; and
it is not dead for sure even now. Rhetoric grants access to what must be
called a super-civilization: that of the historical and geographical West.

ROLAND BARTHES, "The Old Rhetoric: An Aide-Mémoire"

An art which cannot be specified in detail cannot be transmitted by prescription, since no prescription for it exists. It can be passed on only by
example from master to apprentice. . . . It follows that an art which has
fallen into disuse for the period of a generation is altogether lost.

MICHAEL POLANYI, *Personal Knowledge:*
Towards a Post-Critical Philosophy

THE LONGUE DURÉE OF THE RHETORICAL EMPIRE

Descending from language in use since antiquity, the familiar concepts of
age, period, and *epoch* abstract discrete segments of time from the flux of
events.[1] These concepts also raise difficult questions for historiography.
The narratives of progress or decline that often accompany period con-

---

1. The Latin words *aetas* and *saeculum* denote an individual lifespan, and by figurative extension periods of longer duration. The Greek *epokhê* denotes more poetically
the pause in the circuit of a star, and thus figuratively any large-scale punctuation in the
course of events.

cepts seem empirically dubious, given the vast heterogeneity of the historical record, and the manifest unevenness of change. But if these concepts
tend to be less than persuasive when inflated to Hegelian proportions, or
when burdened with apocalyptic implication, they nonetheless mark out
durable regularities in the historical record without which it would be difficult to conceive of history at all.

The assemblage of tendencies that go by the name of "modernity" constitutes for us an as yet inescapable horizon of historical analysis, even
from the vantage of the "postmodern," which Lyotard famously designated a "condition" rather than an age. It is all the more necessary for that
reason to resist or at least to complicate the dominance of modernity as
perhaps the major organizing principle of historiography. In this chapter, I
propose to examine the relation of this category to the history of rhetoric,
which belongs manifestly to Fernand Braudel's *longue durée*. These long
durational waves interfere with the rapid pulse of short-term events, great
and small, that constitute the more familiar categories of narrative history.[2] Between the *longue durée*, which one traverses according to Braudel
with "seven-league boots," and the singular event, Braudel identifies an
intermediate occurrence in the "episode," related sequences of events taking place over a period of decades, such as the Industrial Revolution.[3] It is
relatively easy to understand this episode in relation to a process of "modernization," but an episode such as the decline of rhetoric in the schools is
more difficult to explain without invoking with Barthes the epochal span
of rhetoric's dominance.

Barthes also reminds us that the demise of rhetoric took three centuries to reach conclusion. The final break involved little more than dispute
between the defenders and the critics of the classical curriculum in the
colleges, the rigorous study of Greek and Latin that formed the backbone
of the curriculum from the grammar schools to the most elite universities. The controversy over the teaching of classical languages was a small
disturbance indeed by comparison to the great episodes of nation formation, imperial conquest, class struggle, and technological transformation.
But the epochal consequence of the classical curriculum's demise is implied by Braudel himself, who cites it as an example of what he means by
a *longue durée*:

2. On periods of historical analysis, see Fernand Braudel, *A History of Civilizations*,
trans. Richard Mayne (New York: Penguin Books, 1993), 24–36; see also Braudel, *On
History*, trans. Sarah Matthews (London: Weidenfeld and Nicolson, 1980), 25–54, 74–
80. I have not attempted to conform precisely to Braudel's distinction, although it will be
evident that this chapter is written in sympathy with his project.

3. Braudel, *A History of Civilizations*, 34–35.

There is the same element of permanence or survival in the vast domain of cultural affairs. Ernst Robert Curtius's magnificent book [*European Literature and the Latin Middle Ages*], which has at long last appeared in a French translation, is a study of a cultural system which prolonged the Latin civilization of the Byzantine Empire, even while it distorted it through selections and omissions. This civilization was itself weighed down by its ponderous inheritance. Right up to the thirteenth and fourteenth centuries, right up to the birth of national literatures, the civilization of the intellectual elite fed on the same subjects, the same comparisons, the same commonplaces and catchwords.[4]

Sustained by the classical languages, rhetoric fell with that curriculum, bringing Barthes's "super-civilization of the West" to an end as well.

The classical languages, including both Greek and Latin (but in comparison with Latin, Greek was a Renaissance newcomer) constituted the infrastructure for that alien system of pedagogy we still know today as "rhetoric," despite the pejorative sense that clings to common uses of that term. By "rhetoric" I refer in this essay not just to texts such as Aristotle's *Techné Rhetoriké* or Cicero's *De oratore* but to the full array of pedagogic techniques for raising language to the level of a formal practice, what in Greek culture was called a *techné* and in Roman an *ars*.[5] I will use the term

---

4. Braudel, *On History*, 31. Max Weber makes this interesting observation about the epoch of humanist rhetorical training, "Politics as a Vocation," in *From Max Weber: Essays in Sociology*, ed. H. H. Gerth and C. Wright Mills (New York: Oxford University Press, 1946): "There was a time when one learned to produce Latin speeches and Greek verses in order to become a political adviser to a prince and, above all things, to become a memorialist. This was the time of the first flowering of the humanist schools and of the princely foundations of professorships for 'poetics.' This was for us a transitory epoch, which has had a quite persistent influence upon our educational system, yet no deeper results politically" (92).

5. There are two words in current English use with which we might reasonably translate *techné*, "art" and "craft," neither of which unfortunately is a precise equivalent. In ordinary language contexts, art connotes a practice that is too narrowly high cultural, while craft is too narrow for the opposite reason. Until the Renaissance, the English "craft" was very close to the meaning of *ars* or *techné* but came to acquire a dominant sense of "hand-made" after the prevalence of industrial manufacture. Since then, the word "craft" has come to mean either amateur production or the possession of rare talent. The latter is closer to the meaning of *techné*, but the former captures the sense of "making" that is an essential component of the Greek concept. For a learned rehabilitation of the Renaissance sense of craft, which responds to the full range of cognitive possibilities, see Scott Newstok, *How to Think like Shakespeare: Lessons from a Renaissance Education* (Princeton, NJ: Princeton University Press, 2020), 25–35. The crucial discussion of *techné* in antiquity is to be found in Aristotle's *Nicomachean Ethics*, 6:5

rhetoric, then, to indicate the orientation of the premodern school to the aim of instructing students in the arts of language, both spoken and written, with the necessary caveat that such pedagogy through the ages varied in its fidelity to the chief exemplars of classical rhetoric.[6] Still, it can safely be asserted that from antiquity down through the nineteenth century, the Western school was organized at every level around the task of imparting the facility to use language well. Learning to speak, read, write, translate, comment, interpret, and dispute defined virtually all of what students did in the premodern and early modern educational systems.[7]

Today we think of the school as dedicated before any other aim to teaching the youngest students how to read. But "literacy," as we call this competence, is very different from the aims of the "old rhetoric." The concept of literacy captures reading and writing as forms of linguistic competence but excludes speaking as a practice equally capable of becoming the object of formal instruction. The epochal break to which I here draw attention is marked by (1) a shift in the systemic relations among speaking, reading, and writing, above all by the gradual exclusion of speaking from the curriculum, and (2) an understanding of reading and writing as *basic skills*; this is what we really mean by "literacy." With the disappearance of rhetoric, a new relation was established between speaking, on the one hand, and reading and writing, on the other. This new relation was by no means correlated with a supposed decline in the language abilities of students, as was sometimes supposed at the time. On the contrary, the programmatic interest of schools and governments in teaching children how to read and write is itself the herald of a new pedagogy that displaced the educational system formerly comprehending speaking, reading, and

----

[1140a1–23], where it appears as one of the intellectual virtues. Aristotle emphasizes the productivity of *techné*, which he demonstrates with examples such as shipbuilding. Aristotle's only treatises on particular arts, however, are the *Rhetoric* and the *Poetics*, where the thing made is a linguistic artifact. In the *Nicomachean Ethics*, *techné* is distinguished on the one hand from "scientific" knowledge or *epistemé*, and on the other from pure action or *praxis*.

6. There are significant differences between classical and medieval rhetoric and again between Renaissance rhetoric and its precursors, but if it makes sense to retain the term "rhetoric" as the name for the language *techné* upon which the very principle of formal education was based in Greek antiquity, then we will be able to assert that the rhetorical *paideia* constitutes a *longue durée*, longer indeed than Latin.

7. For the purposes of this argument, I make no sharp distinction between rhetoric and dialectic, although these were distinct practices in antiquity and the Middle Ages. Along with "grammar," rhetoric and dialectic shared many techniques and were eventually folded into an integrated pedagogy in the medieval trivium.

writing.[8] The end of rhetoric is concurrent with the *extension* of literacy to the populace as a whole.

Nor am I invoking a transition from the presumed cultural supremacy of "orality" to that of "literacy," for the concept of orality—meaning speech *as opposed to writing*—is likewise a symptom of the epochal break, just as much a symptom of rhetoric's demise as its complement, literacy. The epochal transition turns rather on the difference between premodern language "arts" and our modern notion of basic literacy: the former comprehended an "art of speech" for which the latter no longer had a place. Even the famous revival of "elocution" or "oratory" in the eighteenth and nineteenth centuries could not reverse the decline of rhetoric and has to be seen rather as the nova-like efflorescence of a dying system.

The causes of rhetoric's demise have been argued for some time, but the episode is so remote as to evoke little interest today.[9] If, as Barthes suggests, the process took three hundred years, from (approximately) the earlier seventeenth century to the later nineteenth, we can be sure that the causal factors were many and complex. The inertial force of rhetorical pedagogy was such that only sustained pressure, exerted over centuries of challenge and derogation, was sufficient to bring about its expulsion from the curriculum. One causal factor above others can be identified right away, however, and that is the "vernacularization" of literate culture. From

---

8. The concept of literacy was coined in 1885 in the *New England Journal of Education*, this according to Ivan Ilich and Barry Sanders, *ABC: The Alphabetization of the Popular Mind* (New York: Vintage Books, 1989), 85. The bibliography on literacy is vast. Some works of relevance to my argument include Harvey J. Graff, *The Legacies of Literacy: Continuities and Contradictions in Western Culture and Society* (Bloomington: Indiana University Press, 1987); Brian Stock, *The Implications of Literacy: Written Language and Models of Interpretation in the Eleventh and Twelfth Centuries* (Princeton, NJ: Princeton University Press, 1983); M. T. Clancy, *From Memory to Written Record: England, 1066–1307* (Cambridge, MA: Harvard University Press, 1979); David Vincent, *The Rise of Mass Literacy: Reading and Writing in Modern Europe* (Cambridge: Polity Press, 2000); Daniel P. Resnick, ed., *Literacy in Historical Perspective* (Washington, DC: Library of Congress, 1983); R. A. Houston, *Literacy in Early Modern Europe: Culture and Education, 1500–1800* (London: Longman, 1988); Henri-Jean Martin, *The History and Power of Writing*, trans. Lydia G. Cochrane (Chicago: University of Chicago Press, 1994). On the theory of literacy, Brian Street, *Literacy in Theory and Practice* (Cambridge: Cambridge University Press 2015); David R. Olson and Nancy Torrance, eds., *Literacy and Orality* (Cambridge: Cambridge University Press, 1991); Michael Stubbs, *Language and Literacy: The Sociolinguistics of Reading and Writing* (London: Routledge and Kegan Paul, 1980); Stephen Graubard, ed., *Literacy: An Overview by Fourteen Experts* (New York: Hill and Wang, 1991).

9. See my essay, "Mercury's Words: The End of Rhetoric and the Beginning of Prose," *Representations* 13 (2027): 59–86.

the later Middle Ages to the nineteenth century, itself a small epoch, the literature of Roman and Greek antiquity was submitted to a vast project of translation. Vernacularization preserved the works of Greek and Latin antiquity for those without access to those languages, but it was also fatal for the culture about which Curtius, Braudel, and Barthes have written. The consequences of vernacularization were far more widespread than changes in the curriculum and at first had little effect on the school at all. One need only recall here the translation of the Latin Bible, which, even before the printing press, began to act as a solvent on Catholic hegemony.

I will be concerned in this chapter mainly with the latter end of the process, or the moment in which the epochal break is complete. This moment is relatively brief in historical terms, only several decades of the later nineteenth century. This was the moment, very belated in relation to the original impulses of "modernity," in which the universities discarded the Latin and Greek curriculum. Once the elite institutions threw off this regime, its strongholds throughout the educational system quickly surrendered. The "empire of Latin" was long lasting but a fragile structure in the end; it was overthrown much faster than the supposed barbarians dispatched the Roman. To its critics, it was a vast anachronism, a ruin that occupied needed space for new construction. The "rhetorical empire," as Barthes salutes it, collapsed along with classical languages.[10] The two pillars of the curriculum left the school system, and the university in particular, without a clear or coherent successor. Vernacular literary study emerged in the wake of

10. See Roland Barthes's comment on the "rhetorical empire" in his essay "The Old Rhetoric: An Aide-Mémoire," in *The Semiotic Challenge*, trans. Richard Howard (Berkeley: University of California Press, 1988), 14–15. Barthes's notion of rhetoric as the basis of the "super-civilization of the West" is more convincing in my view than Derrida's "metaphysics of presence"; at any rate, the rhetorical system supports considerable philosophical heterogeneity on the basis of its remarkable continuity. On the demise of rhetoric see Gérard Genette, "Rhetoric Restrained," in *Figures of Literary Discourse*, trans. Alan Sheridan (New York: Columbia University Press, 1982), 103–26. Genette focuses on what he calls the "tropological reduction," the reduction of rhetoric to one of its parts, *elocutio*, which is in turn reduced to the theory of tropes. Genette's work is further developed by Paul Ricoeur in his essay "The Decline of Rhetoric: Tropology," in *The Rule of Metaphor: Multidisciplinary Studies in the Creation of Meaning in Language* (Toronto: University of Toronto Press, 1977), 44–64. Also concerned with the problem of figuration is Hayden White, "The Suppression of Rhetoric in the Nineteenth Century," in *The Rhetoric Canon*, ed. Brenda Deen Schildgen (Detroit: Wayne State University Press, 1997), 21–32. On the long-durational history of the Latin language, see Françoise Waquet, *Latin, or The Empire of a Sign: From the Sixteenth to the Twentieth Centuries,* trans. John Howe (London: Verso, 2001), and Jürgen Leonhardt, *Latin: Story of a World Language*, trans. Kenneth Kronenberg (Cambridge, MA: Harvard University Press, 2013).

this decline, as the beneficiary of an epochal break, an artifact of the post-rhetorical condition.

Vernacularization is a condition and a cause of the demise of rhetoric, a force undermining the "dead languages" of antiquity that could not be resisted forever. That they survived as long as they did is a wonder. For my purposes, what matters most about the curricular revolution is the linked fortunes of Latin and rhetoric. But why was rhetoric not capable of vernacularization, of leaving Latin behind? Here it will be necessary for me to offer a strategically functionalist hypothesis, as a spur to further inquiry. The old curriculum suited an older arrangement of society, an established hierarchy of interests and privileges, but less and less efficiently, as the social order evolved into a new complex of fractional interests. When the curriculum of classical languages failed, the institutions sustaining it were immediately captured by a new coalition of interests, a new constituency for the educational system: the professional-managerial class. This coalition set about to reorganize the schools from top to bottom in order to suit its needs and purposes. The "New Class" was the first elite in history to stand wholly *on the other side* of the epochal divide.

If the arrival of a very differently educated class fraction on this undiscovered shore initially provoked widespread concern about the decline of language skills, these skills were from the outset of the new regime narrowly conceived as those of "literacy," the basic ability to read in the vernacular and to write and speak grammatical or "standard" English. And yet, despite the expectation that the schools were to produce speakers of the standard vernacular, formal instruction in speech lost its foundation in rhetoric, and the remnant of rhetoric, still holding a place in the system under the name of "oratory," was increasingly isolated in the curriculum. Oratory, and the related practice of "recitation," survived to some extent in the lower levels of the system for another half century, but these pedagogic forms eventually disappeared too.

The immediate response to a widespread sense of the inadequacy of language pedagogy was a vernacular remedy: freshman English. It is a mistake to imagine that this course was continuous with its rhetorical predecessors, even when the name of rhetoric was sometimes attached to it. The new relation between speaking and writing was institutionalized in the founding assumption of freshman English, that the correction of nonstandard speech could henceforth be accomplished by the correction of nonstandard writing. The perception during the later nineteenth century that the schools were failing to teach standard English, much remarked by historians of education, testifies to a pervasive cultural disorientation following upon a new relation among the educated elite to the practices of speaking, reading, and writing.[11]

What was sometimes still called "rhetoric" in many nineteenth-century classrooms bore ever less resemblance to its premodern versions, not the least in that this course was largely the vehicle for teaching *vernacular grammar*. As late as the seventeenth century in England, "grammar" was thought to be something possessed only by Greek and Latin. It was relatively late in Western schools that speaking, reading, and writing in the vernaculars came to be governed by prescriptive norms sufficiently elaborated to form the basis for the teaching of vernacular grammar in the schools. The system of norms to which we give the name of "grammar" was at first not much more than an analogical extension of Latin grammar.[12] Extending this analogy further, critics of the later seventeenth and earlier eighteenth century derived from the works of antiquity canons of judgment according to which claims were advanced for "classics" of English literature.[13] Literary judgment and grammatical prescription were always very closely allied.

Given the triumph of the vernacular, it is surprising that in the United States the most intense eruption of linguistic anxiety coincided not with the crowding of language pedagogy to a corner of the curriculum but rather with its successful establishment as a common course, a universal requirement. This perplexing circumstance suggests that the overthrow of the classical languages and the establishment of "freshman English" in the curriculum were related in more complex ways than contemporaries were able to see and that the vernacular revolution had unforeseen and unintended

11. For a chronicle of the successive waves of language hysteria in American history, see Dennis Baron, *Grammar and Good Taste: Reforming the American Language* (New Haven, CT: Yale University Press, 1982). For a more sociologically oriented account see Cmiel, *Democratic Eloquence*.

12. A not atypical English grammar of 1624, by John Hewes, spells this out in its title: *A Perfect Survey of the English Tongue, taken according to the Use and Analogie of the Latine*. In fact, the first vernacular grammars were written in Latin, confirming the preeminence of Latin literacy over the vernacular. In the early modern period, the "petty" schools often offered little more than basic instruction in construing written texts phonetically, for the purpose of teaching the catechism. For some more privileged students, alphabetic literacy prepared them for the study of Latin in the grammar schools. On basic alphabetic literacy, see Houston, *Literacy in Early Modern Europe*, 57–61.

13. Classicism eventually came into conflict, however, with the ideological bases for national literatures, a conflict out of which national literatures emerged. For two accounts of the formation of an English literary canon see Trevor Ross, *The Making of the English Canon from the Middle Ages to the Late Eighteenth Century* (Montreal: McGill-Queens University Press, 1998), and Kramnick, *Making the English Canon*.

consequences.[14] In retrospect, the most obvious of these consequences was the fact that in the postrhetorical university, the vernacular literary curriculum was prevented from achieving anything like the dominant position formerly held by the classical languages. The less obvious consequence was that literary study was challenged from the beginning in its effort to establish a coherent pedagogy analogous to that of rhetoric, one that could comprehend both speaking and writing, or both language and literature.

The domain of vernacular language and literature in the curriculum was also limited, as we know, by the increasing proliferation of scientific, technical, and vocational subjects at every level of the school system, but let us acknowledge that vernacular literary study was itself a new, a "modern" subject. It would be more accurate to say, then, that the new scientific and technical disciplines and vernacular language study *together* displaced the classical curriculum.[15] The most interesting question that follows from this recognition is why vernacular literary study failed to convince its constituency that it was a successful vehicle for producing competence in standard English. Public hysteria about the basic language skills of college students only increased after Harvard instituted the elective system in 1869 and abandoned entrance requirements in Greek and Latin. By the 1890s, as Kenneth Cmiel notes in his study of language debates in nineteenth-century America, *Democratic Eloquence*, the supposed deficiency of entering college students was regarded as a "national scandal." The scandal was the occasion for convening the famous Committee of Ten, which sought to address the presumed decline of basic literacy among the college-age population.[16]

---

14. Some of these consequences concern the origins of the "composition" course and its subsequent development, a topic I take up in chapter 11 below, "Composition and the Demand for Writing."

15. It must be recalled that in the decades-long campaign to abolish the classical curriculum, the alternative proposed was most likely to be English literature. See for example, Charles Francis Adams Jr.'s famous polemic against classical study, *A College Fetich: An Address Delivered Before the Harvard Chapter of the Fraternity of the Phi Beta Kappa, in Sanders Theatre, Cambridge, June 28, 1883* (Boston: Lee and Shepherd, 1884): "But in pursuing Greek and Latin we had ignored our mother tongue. We were no more competent to pass a really searching examination in English literature and English composition than in the languages and literature of Greece and Rome" (8). Adams goes on to advocate for the "scientific subjects" as well, but the point is that he saw no conflict or competition between vernacular literary study and the natural sciences. This position agrees with similar arguments by Herbert Spencer and Thomas Huxley in England. See also Waquet, *Latin, or The Empire of a Sign*, 179–206.

16. See Cmiel, *Democratic Eloquence*, 238. In addition to blaming the primary and secondary schools, other causal factors included the increasing ethnic and linguistic

In this context, we can bring into sharper focus the difference between the kinds of social anxiety experienced by the New Class in its relation to language skills (or literacy) and in its relation to literature, as representative of high culture. Although the professional-managerial class came to express considerable nostalgia by the 1920s for what it believed was the easy intimacy of former elites with the great works of Western civilization, it had little enthusiasm for reviving the curriculum on which that intimacy was ultimately based, the study of classical languages. Even when the Greek and Latin classics were featured prominently in "general education" programs of the mid-twentieth century, these works were read almost exclusively in translation. The "classics" were at this time not so much revived as they were assimilated to a new language pedagogy that, as I will argue further in chapter 7, "The Location of Literature," tacitly assumed the identification of "literature" with vernacular writing. The classics were not only translated into the vernacular, they were translated into "literature." Many works in Greek and Latin disappeared on the horizon of this process. Indeed, it is only through the distorting lens of vernacularization that we construe the old classical curriculum as the study of *literature* in antiquity. The old curriculum was oriented on the contrary toward rhetorical aims, a fact that can be confirmed by charting the fortunes of Cicero in the syllabus.[17] It was only after the classics had been assimilated by translation into "literature" that figures such as Cicero ceased to dominate the canon of Latin writing.

When the universities abandoned the classical languages, then, it was not only the study of Greek and Latin that disappeared from nearly every venue except that of the classics department, now one discipline among many; the curricular revolution of the later nineteenth century also decisively shifted the emphasis of higher education away from intensive training in language arts. Rhetoric endured as long as the classical curriculum,

---

diversity of the US population, which presented considerable challenges for teachers in the primary and secondary schools. I want to underscore, however, the significance of the coincidence remarked by Cmiel, that hysteria about grammatical competence was ratcheted up in the decades following Harvard's introduction of the elective system, widely imitated throughout the university system.

17. Already by the time of Quintilian in the first century AD, the name of Cicero was equated with rhetoric. So Quintilian writes in *Institutio Oratoria*: "For posterity the name of Cicero has come to be regarded not as the name of a man, but as the name of eloquence itself" (book 10, chapter 1). Cicero's prestige in the later Middle Ages rested largely on the *Rhetorica ad Herennium*, which he almost certainly did not write. But this misattribution matters less than the fact that his name, after a period in the earlier Middle Ages when many of his works were lost to view, would once again be virtually equated with the name of rhetoric. For Cicero's position in the curriculum, see Martin, *The History and Power of Writing*, 98.

at the same time that it was fatally weakened by its bondage to the corpse of the "dead" languages. The classics at once propped up and undermined rhetorical pedagogy. This paradox is difficult to grasp, because rhetoric, as the art of persuasion, might appear to be so obviously capable of being detached from the study of Greek and Latin languages. To reiterate, the interesting question before us is why rhetoric failed to survive the vernacularization of the educational system, why the old rhetoric could not, in effect, be translated.

This is a question with no simple answer. It is perhaps best approached through the converse question of why the curriculum of classical languages survived for so long, when speaking and writing venues for Greek and Latin had dwindled by the end of the eighteenth century virtually to none. In addition to institutional inertia, which is always a force to be reckoned with, several other conditions can be noted. In early modern England (as also across Europe), for example, the cultural value of the classical languages was temporarily stabilized and even enhanced when the study of Greek and Latin was embraced by the aristocracy, and later by those upwardly mobile members of class fractions seeking to establish their identity as "gentlemen."[18] The ancient languages were given a new lease as a desirable form of cultural capital, however tedious the regimen by means of which this adornment was acquired. In the United States, it must be noted, emulation of aristocratic cultivation was a weaker basis for study of the classics, and defenders of the classical curriculum tended to invoke equally the rationale of "mental discipline" (a value in England as well). Finally, in the later nineteenth century, a much grander rationale for studying the classics emerged: the notion of *culture*, derived from new developments in German philosophy and scholarship and championed by figures such as Matthew Arnold. Even if culture served as the most high-minded of the defenses against vernacularization, however, the aims of culture played little part in the actual teaching of the classics, which required years of dogged training in the minutiae of the "dead languages."[19]

In retrospect it might seem, as it did to many contemporaries, that the

18. See Brian Simon, "Systematization and Segmentation: The Case of England," in *The Rise of the Modern Education System: Structural Change and Social Reproduction, 1870–1920,* ed. Detlef K. Müller, Fritz Ringer, and Brian Simon (Cambridge: Cambridge University Press, 1987), 95–96. Simon cites Gladstone's opinion that study of the classics was a "providential" means of educating English gentlemen.

19. Rudolph, *Curriculum,* 89–90, relates the story of an unfortunate professor at Princeton, Evert M. Topping, who attempted in 1846 to introduce commentary on Greek literature into his courses on the Greek language, in the hope of making the class less tedious for his students. He was forced to resign by the president. Rudolph com-

classical curriculum existed largely to hold at bay the new discourses of knowledge begging entrance to the colleges. And yet it was also the case that this curriculum preserved a residual rhetorical practice that was by no means simply reactionary, or without beneficial effects. Even in its most ossified form, the classical curriculum sustained some part of the old rhetoric's *techné*, and hence a pedagogy comprehending both speaking and writing. At the same time, it was evident that rhetoric as a *curriculum* had no future unless it could be translated into the vernacular.

At first, translation entailed merely rendering into English the rhetoric texts of antiquity, but translation might also be understood as a strategy of modernization. The "old rhetoric" was not simply translated into the vernacular but selectively reoriented, elaborated, and even transformed. In the most well-known example of this process, elements of the old rhetoric were imported in the eighteenth century into the vernacular program of "elocution." The latter term was supposed to mean much the same thing as "oratory," but in fact it represented a severe truncation of the classical practice.[20] Elocution, as the basis of what Gerald Graff has called eighteenth-century "oratorical culture," broke off a piece of the old rhetoric, *delivery* (the last of the traditional five parts of rhetoric in the Roman system), which it developed into an elaborate program for training voice and gesture, in the process discarding other parts of rhetoric.[21] Franklin Court has

---

ments that Professor Topping "was a sacrifice offered on the altar of a dying curriculum and a dying psychology of learning."

20. Oratory was an aspect of the rhetorical system the early modern humanists elected to emphasize in theory, if not in practice. While they enthusiastically resuscitated Cicero's idealized figure of the orator, they were powerless to reproduce the social contexts in which this figure was so important in antiquity. As a consequence, the primary occasion for rhetorical performance in the early modern period was letter writing. For a discussion of orality in Renaissance humanism, see Martin Elsky, *Authorizing Words: Speech, Writing, and Print in the English Renaissance* (Ithaca, NY: Cornell University Press, 1989).

21. See Graff, *Professing Literature*, chapter 3, "Oratorical Culture and the Teaching of English." See also Gregory Clark and S. Michael Halloran, *Oratorical Culture in Nineteenth-Century America: Transformations in the Theory and Practice of Rhetoric* (Carbondale: Southern Illinois University Press, 1993); Franklin Court, *Institutionalizing English Literature: The Culture and Politics of Literary Study, 1750–1900* (Stanford, CA: Stanford University Press, 1992); and Court, *The Scottish Connection: The Rise of English Literary Study in Early America* (Syracuse, NY: Syracuse University Press, 2001). The term "elocution" is of course not to be confused with the old rhetoric's *elocutio*, which is usually translated as "style." The eighteenth-century sense of elocution is still the meaning in common use. Court remarks in *The Scottish Connection* on the move away from classical rhetoric and toward courses that promised to be more "declamatory, practical, and current in scope" (40). Some of the oratorical theorists of the period

recently remarked in his study of oratorical culture that it was "naggingly ill-defined," which is to say that its relation to the classical rhetorical system was far from transparent. Elocution had only a loose connection with the compositional practices of invention, arrangement, and style. The abridgment of the rhetorical system in the practice of elocution contrasted with the large claims of its advocates for its social utility, its supreme importance especially in the civic culture of the new American republic, with its imitation of Roman and Athenian political forms.[22] In the latter context, oratory resonated with the classicism of republican culture without necessarily recapitulating the entirety of classical rhetoric.

The great elocutionary movement of the Republican era failed to translate rhetoric into a permanent basis for the vernacular curriculum. Indeed, as Court points out, early attempts to produce a vernacular oratory were sidetracked by the fact that the "new rhetoric" increasingly drew its examples from English literature, a body of writing that interested students for other reasons than the aim of public speaking. Oratory was overtaken in the classroom by the more inclusive discourse of belles lettres, which was indebted less to the old rhetoric than to the new discourse of "criticism." Belles lettres was a discourse oriented to reading; its correlative oral performance in the schools was the *recitation* of passages from works of literature rather than the composing or delivery of speeches. The aim of belles lettres was the cultivation of the reader's taste, a program espoused by the Scottish rhetoricians—Smith, Blair, Campbell—who passed on to their American followers the practice of incorporating English literature into the "rhetoric" course. This course tended to be called "Rhetoric and Belles Lettres," a hybrid, or transitional subject. While the new rhetoric was dedicated to oratory, its complement, belles lettres, aimed to produce

---

were sensitive to the difference between oratory and rhetoric. Court cites the example of John Ward's *System of Oratory,* published in 1759, and very popular in American schools. Ward drew a sharp distinction between the figure of the orator and the figure of the rhetorician, on the basis of the social context of oratory and the fact of oratory's exclusive orality. For a thorough discussion of the elocutionary movement, see Wilbur Samuel Howell, *Eighteenth-Century British Logic and Rhetoric* (Princeton, NJ: Princeton University Press, 1971), 145–258. The elocution movement is not without interest in its own terms. In its practice of "chironomia," or "chirologia," the study of gesture, it may be said to have produced a real innovation in rhetorical practice, even if it at the same time it greatly diminished the scope of rhetoric.

22. Gregory Clark and S. Michael Halloran offer in their introduction to *Oratorical Culture* an interpretation of its significance which emphasizes the orator's role in articulating "a public moral consensus" (24). They see this role as ultimately subverted in the nineteenth century by the two social developments of "individualism" and "professionalism."

cultivated readers of literature, *polite* rather than public speakers.[23] This contradiction reflected a larger tension within eighteenth-century culture, as Adam Potkay has argued, between a taste-centered norm, based on the literary curriculum and expressed in the practice of polite conversation, and a more civic-minded norm, derived from a stripped-down version of the rhetorical tradition, identified usually as "eloquence."[24]

The different kinds of oral performance practiced in the schools gives us an interesting hint about the complex and changing relation between the new rhetoric and the old. The latter was in a way the very substance of the classical curriculum, where Cicero's treatises on rhetoric and his orations typically headed the syllabus. Although modernizations of the old rhetoric in the vernacular curriculum could diverge considerably from the classical models, they might still express the rhetorical motives of classical rhetoric. The reason these motives endured was of course their nominal orientation to oratory as well as to the classroom rituals of recitation.[25] The recourse to recitation alone guaranteed that no matter how "literary" the content of the syllabus might be, its transmission would express to some degree the rhetorical principle. It is thus a mistake to see the rhetorical system, as I have defined it, as restricted to the study of rhetorical texts as such, whether in classical or modern languages. It was not only the subject of

23. For an account of the complex relation between writing and speech in the eighteenth century, particularly with reference to the elocutionary movement, see Nicholas Hudson, *Writing and European Thought, 1600–1830* (Cambridge: Cambridge University Press, 1994), 92–118. For an illuminating recent study of orality during this period, see the work of Paula McDowell, *The Invention of the Oral: Print Commerce and Fugitive Voices in Eighteenth-Century Britain* (Chicago: University of Chicago Press, 2017).

24. Adam Potkay, *The Fate of Eloquence in the Age of Hume* (Ithaca, NY: Cornell University Press, 1994). For the development of conversation as governed by social norms in the early modern period see Peter Burke, *The Art of Conversation* (Ithaca, NY: Cornell University Press, 1993).

25. See Cmiel, *Democratic Eloquence*: "The new rhetorics, however, spent much time talking about the canons of *written* eloquence" (35). I am emphasizing here only the practice of recitation and not the related form of disputation, which dominated the medieval university. For a comment on the complex situation of disputation in the humanist schools of the Renaissance, see Anthony Grafton and Lisa Jardine, *From Humanism to the Humanities* (Cambridge, MA: Harvard University Press, 1986). The practice of disputation was in decline long before recitation disappeared; it had disappeared from Cambridge, for example, by the mid-eighteenth century. A diminished and anachronistic version of it still survives in such rituals as the oral qualifying exams and dissertation defenses of some graduate programs. Recitation too could be stultifying by the eighteenth century, as Gerald Graff observes in *Professing Literature*, 31–34. At this point the rhetorical system is in decline, and it is becoming increasingly difficult to revive in its moribund rituals the language art that animated Western education for two millennia.

rhetoric that the nineteenth century university would have to overthrow in order to institute a new disciplinary regime but the *rhetorical principle,* as that principle structured rituals of pedagogy.

So long as belles lettres continued to rely upon the recitation of passages from works of vernacular literature, its link with the old rhetoric could become ever more attenuated without actually breaking. But a break with recitation itself, and the correlated practice of oral examination, did come in the nineteenth century with the establishment of the *written examination* as a new and soon to be dominant means of assessment. By the end of the century, the oral rituals of traditional pedagogy were displaced almost entirely by written assignments and examinations.[26] No doubt there are contingent reasons contributing to this development, having to do possibly with the increased size of college classes and the consequent impracticality of recitation beyond the "tutorial" scene. But I suggest that there is a deeper determination of the shift to written evaluation in the later nineteenth century, in that the writing evaluated was no longer primarily valued for its rhetoricity.

I will be concerned later with specifying just what constituted the difference of this writing. In the meanwhile, let us recall that in the rhetorical system, writing did not exactly stand alone, in the sense of bearing no relation to speech. It was rather the case that the possibility of reciting aloud what was written expressed the implicit rhetoricity of writing. This is why the rhetorical system was able to comprehend both speaking and writing within its conception of discourse or *logos.* It was only in the later nineteenth century, when an increasingly writing-based pedagogy converged with the new vernacular curriculum of literary, scientific, technical, and vocational subjects, that the complementary relation between speaking and writing was irrevocably altered and speaking ceased to be a matter of any but the most rudimentary formal instruction, only distantly related to the pedagogy of rhetoric.

The implications of a writing-centered pedagogy, which we are only yet glimpsing on the horizon of the nineteenth-century university, were certainly ominous for the survival of rhetoric, especially given the fact that "elocution" had come to be the strongest explicit link to the rhetorical tradition in the vernacular curriculum. The elocutionary movement was

26. Written examinations were still something of a novelty in the elite institutions of the mid-nineteenth century. When President Woolsey of Yale instituted biennial written examinations for students of the college in 1853, he had to purchase "examination tables" so that students would have a surface to write on. See David L. Barquist, *American Tables and Looking Glasses: In the Mabel Brady Garvan and Other Collections at Yale University* (New Haven, CT: Yale University Art Gallery, 1992), 77.

arguably a *weak* link to the rhetorical system, an inflation of one part of rhetoric, *actio* or *pronuntiatio*, into its entirety. Oratorical culture could pass as the continuation of the old rhetoric because it was a literalization of what had been, since antiquity, the practice of naming rhetoric by reference to the occasion of oratory.[27] Oratory was understood as a metonymy for language *techné* generally, which in its premodern form comprised much more than "oratorical culture" ever succeeded in embodying. This is why the eighteenth-century contraction of rhetoric to "elocution" often degenerated into the mechanical practice that Graff dismisses in *Professing Literature* as "unredeemed drudgery" (50). If the survival of rhetoric no longer depended in the nineteenth century on the classical curriculum, it was a fateful irony that its best chance for "translation" into the vernacular was the program of elocution, which more than ever was dependent on a classroom practice whose days were numbered. The future belonged to writing, to written assignments and written exams. I suspect that very few among us who teach really understand how consequential this shift in pedagogy was, culminating in the conditions that have made possible the ultimate absurdity of our current "testing regime." But that episode has other determinants that cannot be considered here. For the present, we are only observing the immediate effects of the epochal break, the waning of the pedagogy that served the needs of rhetoric. Recitation was the smallest wheel in the great machine that jammed and rusted by the end of the nineteenth century but not the least important. By contrast, belles lettres was much better able to adapt to a writing-centered pedagogy, at least for a while, and for that reason belles lettres was led eventually to sever its relation to oratory, which disappeared from the curriculum over time.[28] Belles

27. It is perhaps the case that the rhetoricians of antiquity may not always have been conscious of the metonymic character of the name for their practice. Rhetoric names the figure of the rhetor, the public speaker. This metonymy betrays a certain theoretical problem, which is never more evident than when delivery is elevated from a part of rhetoric to the whole of it, a reduction already possible in antiquity. Hence Quintilian recollects, in book XI, chapter 3, of his *Institutio Oratoria*, trans. H. E. Butler (London: Harvard University Press, 1922), IV, 245, Demosthenes's famous response to the question of which was the most important part of rhetoric; Demosthenes replied, "pronuntiatio." When asked which was the second most important, he replied the same, and the third, the same.

28. Thomas O. Sloane, in his essay "Never-Ending Dispute: A Proposal for Marriage," in *The Rhetoric Canon*, ed. Schildgen, interestingly speculates that it was the very humanists who apotheosized the figure of the orator "who gradually undercut the importance of orality in education—who in placing a new premium on literacy gave us textbooks, term papers, and in place of disputations, written finals" (209). See also John C.

lettres was from the beginning oriented much more to grammar than to the occasions of orality, and this orientation tended to privilege it in those hybrid courses on "Rhetoric and Belles Lettres" that proliferated in the eighteenth and nineteenth centuries.[29]

Only when we grasp this sequence of events can we go on to characterize the demise of rhetoric in fully epochal terms. The disappearance of the rhetorical system from Western education was much more recent than is generally supposed, and yet when it vanished it seems to have left almost no trace.[30] This circumstance led C. S. Lewis to remark famously, "Rhetoric is the greatest barrier between us and our ancestors . . . an invisible wall." Ernst Robert Curtius goes further when he writes that "in our culture, rhetoric has no place," and that rhetoric "impresses modern man as a gro-

---

Brereton, ed., *The Origins of Composition Studies in the American College, 1875–1925: A Documentary History* (Pittsburgh: University of Pittsburgh Press, 1995), citing the authors of the Harvard 1897 *Report on the Committee on Composition and Rhetoric*, who write that class size has increased to such an extent "as to become wholly unmanageable for oral recitation . . . step by step, the oral method of instruction was then abandoned, and a system of lectures, with periodical written examinations, took its place, so that at last the whole college work was practically done in writing" (112).

29. A good example of the tendency of belles lettres toward a writing pedagogy is provided by President William Samuel Johnson's description of his course in "Rhetoric and Belles Lettres," Columbia College, 1792, cited in Louis Franklin Snow, *The College Curriculum in the United States* (New York: Teachers College, Columbia University, 1907). President Johnson informs his students that he would instruct them in "the grammar and proper pronunciation of the English Language" out of various texts, and in belles lettres "on the plan of Blair's Lectures" (97). His aim, he says, is to convey "the rules and principles of every species of eloquence—the principles of true taste and the rules of just criticism, whereby the students may be enabled to judge properly of each species of composition in every branch of elegant literature, and that they may apply the whole to practice each student is obliged, every Saturday, to deliver him a composition, in which he corrects the errors, either in orthography, grammar, style or sentiment, and makes the necessary observations on them when he returns the composition to the writer" (97). This was a senior-year course, which accounts at least in part for the unusual attention paid to writing. Most teaching would still rely primarily on oral presentation and evaluation. Robert Scholes, *The Rise and Fall of English: Reconstructing English as a Discipline* (New Haven, CT: Yale University Press, 1998) reminds us that standards of spelling and grammar in student writing of the eighteenth century were still extraordinarily lax (5). Examining accounts of student writing at Rhode Island College (the precursor to Brown), he notes that this writing was still largely "script" for oration.

30. For a somewhat different sense of this historical transformation, more cyclical than epochal, see Bruce Kimball, *Orators and Philosophers: A History of the Idea of Liberal Education* (New York: College Entrance Examination Board, 1995). Kimball depicts a perennial conflict between the orators and the philosophers, of which the conflict between the sciences and the humanities is only the latest version.

tesque bogey."[31] Many conditions were necessary for so thorough a revolution as this: the emergence of vernacular literatures, the abandonment of the classical curriculum, the appearance of new discourses of knowledge with claims on the curriculum, and finally a decisive shift from a speech-centered to a writing-centered pedagogy. I would like to explore a little further now the implications of the last of these conditions.

If the rhetorical system comprehended speech and writing within its cognitive program of language *techné*, the epochal break was only fully disclosed when speech lost its formality or character as an art, the supreme art of the educational system. This is the point at which historians will begin to understand (or misunderstand) the aims of Western education with reference to *literacy*, to reading and writing. But literacy is not the same competence as that produced by rhetorical education. If the earliest rhetoricians, the Sophists, can be credited with inventing the school, whose purpose for them was to teach the *technai logon*, the arts of speech, then it is surely a remarkable fact that this art in its oral specificity has so small a place in the vast superstructure of our contemporary educational system. It exists today only in the residual form of "speech" programs, which are only distantly related to the elocutionary tradition.[32] But this fact only returns us to the puzzle of the eponymous relation between oratory and the rhetorical system that comprehended so much more than elocution, narrowly defined as "public speaking."

In his well-known studies of orality and writing in Western culture, Walter J. Ong argues that the decline of rhetoric was correlated with a shift in Western culture away from a dominant focus on orality and toward what he calls a "writing economy." Rhetoric itself was propelled on this wave; it "gradually but inevitably migrated from the oral to the chirographic world."[33] This process was already underway in late antiquity. As George Kennedy reminds us, even as early as the Hellenistic period rhetoric began to "shift its focus from persuasion to narration, from civic to personal contexts, and from discourse to literature," a process of *letteraturizzazi-*

31. C. S. Lewis, *English Literature in the Sixteenth Century Excluding Drama* (Oxford: Clarendon, 1954), 61; Ernst Robert Curtius, *European Literature and the Latin Middle Ages* (Princeton, NJ: Princeton University Press, 1953), 62, 79.

32. Departments of "speech communication" might claim descent from the old oratory course, but there are good reasons to emphasize the discontinuities over the continuities. Speech departments today are a curious catchall of subjects, some of them having to do with problems of pathology, some with media, but few descending from the classical rhetorical tradition.

33. Walter J. Ong, *Orality and Literacy: The Technologizing of the Word* (London: Routledge, 1982), 116.

one.[34] The transition from what Kennedy calls "primary" to "secondary" rhetoric happened again in the later Middle Ages, when many techniques of classical rhetoric were adapted for scriptive purposes such as letter writing (*ars dictaminis*) and poetic composition (*ars poetriae*).[35] The ground of rhetoric's identification with oratory was thus subject recurrently to what the commentators like to call a "shift." It is not so easy to conceptualize this shift in epochal terms, however, if it was in fact *always* occurring. Not surprisingly we are confronted with an uneven development, but I would again point out that this uneven surging of writing to the fore did not succeed in displacing the *technai logon* from the schools completely until the twentieth century. The finality of rhetoric's demise cannot simply be explained as a "shift" from orality to literacy.

This thesis will have to be substantially revised if the rhetorical system is to be understood as a *systemic* arrangement of language arts, within which both speech and writing belong to the *technai logon*—the arts of discourse generally, of linguistic communication. In the postrhetorical epoch, speech comes to mean, as I remarked, *speech as opposed to writing*, and it is this speech that falls outside the formal practice of the school; the new informality of speech thus constitutes its new systemic relation to the competence of literacy. While rhetoric in antiquity was oriented nominally and often practically toward the scene of oral performance, the narrative of a "break" with the rhetorical system does not turn on the distinction between "orality" and "literacy," as these terms are supposed ultimately to define the distinction between societies with and without writing. This distinction was too easily imported into the history of rhetoric, and it is not always clarified by Ong's version of an epochal narrative. It would certainly be misleading to say that the "orality" of rhetoric is a version of the same orality we find in preliterate societies, even if *some* features of that preliterate orality were carried over into the practice of rhetoric.

Whether the rhetoric of the Greeks was at any time a wholly oral practice, the rhetoric that came to dominate the Western school was always a practice of literate persons. We know that the Sophists routinely used writing as a means of composing speeches and of circulating models for imitation among their disciples. Already by the time of Isocrates, oratory was well established as a form of written discourse, and Isocrates himself notoriously never delivered his speeches in public. Although there is no

34. George Kennedy, *Classical Rhetoric and Its Christian and Secular Tradition from Ancient to Modern Times* (Chapel Hill: University of North Carolina Press, 1980), 5.

35. See James Murphy, *Rhetoric in the Middle Ages: A History of Rhetorical Theory from St. Augustine to the Renaissance* (Berkeley: University of California Press, 1974).

question that rhetoric privileged the oral occasion as its *nominal* aim, its orality was characterized by a relation to writing, not a lack of relation. This relation was intimate and complex, not adversarial or mutually exclusive.

It is also worth recalling that in the system of rhetoric, writing was a *compositional* practice, not only a practice of material inscription. The latter belonged to what the ancients called "grammar," a much more capacious array of language arts than its modern successor, and one that was wholly compatible with the rhetorical aims of schooling as a whole.[36] Ancient compositional practice might or might not involve writing in the sense of inscribing a surface.[37] Sometimes composition and inscription were separated, the latter delegated to the "scribe," who produced a text from dictation. In any case, the rhetorical system must be seen as a *total program of cognitive-linguistic training*, whose parts, though conceptually distinct, were thoroughly interconnected in the actual rhetorical practice of the premodern world.[38]

There is also evidence that the very mode of orality that rhetoric made possible depended on the model of the text, as a spatial analogue for the basic cognitive operations of the rhetorical system, composing and remembering. This relation has been explored by Mary Carruthers in her study *The Book of Memory*. Carruthers argues that memory was an art, or "mnemotechnique," that, so far from being perceived as incompatible with the technology of writing, was typically understood by analogy to the physical process of impressing marks upon a wax tablet.[39] To compose or to remember might mean to write on an imaginary surface in the mind. Moreover, if the technology of writing provided a means of modelling the cognitive process, it is not clear that this process could occur *without* such analogies; that is, the very process of imaginarily enacting a procedure of inscription on the mind *constituted* the mnemotechnique.

The ancients had, perhaps, a less rich technical vocabulary for understanding what we call cognition, but they grasped cognitive processes very well in the context of practice. For us, memory is a "natural" process, to be

36. See Martin Irvine, *The Making of Textual Culture: "Grammatica" and Literary Theory, 350–1100* (Cambridge: Cambridge University Press, 1994).

37. Mary Carruthers, *The Book of Memory: A Study of Memory in Medieval Culture* (Cambridge: Cambridge University Press, 1990): "The value of memory training depends more, I think, on the role which rhetoric has in a culture than on whether its texts are presented in oral or written forms, or some combination of the two" (11).

38. See here also Mary Carruthers, *The Craft of Thought: Meditation, Rhetoric, and the Making of Images, 400–1200* (Cambridge: Cambridge University Press, 1998): "*Memoria* is most usefully thought of as a compositional art" (9).

39. Carruthers, *The Book of Memory*, 16.

investigated scientifically, but for the ancients it was "artificial," a practice that could be developed, improved, perfected. This difference provides us with a key to understanding the rhetorical system. Carruthers identifies *memoria* as the "foundation of rhetorical training" (*The Book of Memory*, 9), a proposition that must seem very odd from the vantage of the post-rhetorical condition, but which is closer to the truth of the practice in antiquity than is the modern conflation of rhetoric with the system of tropes. In modernity, we tend to see *elocutio*, style or ornament, as the heart of the rhetorical system, but this is a "reduction" of rhetoric (Genette's famous "tropological reduction"), just as much as the elocutionary movement's equation of rhetoric with *pronuntiatio*.[40]

Memoria compels us to attend to the cognitive functions of the classical rhetorical system, whose contexts were much more diverse than modern constructions of rhetoric have been. This point has been hard to recover from the textual tradition, because *memoria* appears as sometimes the least elaborated of the parts of rhetoric (with the exception of the *Rhetorica ad Herennium*, which came into its own in the later Middle Ages). But Carruthers is right to see this as a distortion produced by the textual transmission of rhetoric. Once *memoria* is recognized as an aspect of cognitive training, it becomes possible to recover its systemic relation to the "parts" of the rhetorical system.

In the light of this analysis, we can introduce a final piece of evidence confirming the epochal significance of the break with the rhetorical system: the fact that the theory and practice of pedagogy turned so decisively against memory in the modern era. The repression of memory as an "art," and its debunking in pedagogic contexts as "rote memorization," is connected at a deep level with the relegation of speech to the extracurricular domain.[41] The coincidence of these two repressions suggests that the epochal break with the rhetorical system was produced by a repudiation of *techné* itself. It was the very conception of a cognitive "art" that became increasingly difficult during the modern era to realize in pedagogy.

40. For the reduction of rhetoric to trope or figures of speech, see Gérard Genette, "Rhetoric Restrained," in *Figures of Literary Discourse*, trans. Alan Sheridan (New York: Columbia University Press, 1982), 103–26.

41. I would underscore here that the epochal break was not so sudden that it had no remainder in pedagogy. Long into the twentieth century, it was still the case that schoolchildren were asked to memorize or recite poems such as Felicia Hemans's "Casabianca." In the later twentieth century, the ventilators sustaining the remnants of oral pedagogy were finally unplugged. For a revelatory study of earlier practices of memorization and recitation, see Catherine Robson, *Heartbeats: Everyday Life and the Memorized Poem* (Princeton, NJ: Princeton University Press, 2012).

In concluding this part of my argument, I glance briefly at several moments in the three centuries of rhetoric's decline, in order to see beyond the usual indictment of rhetoric as the ally of untruth, the charge initiated by Plato and so often repeated when rhetoric is reduced to *elocutio*, or to the taxonomy of tropes. The quotations that follow constitute a catena that links the first early modern repudiations of rhetoric to its fate in the nineteenth century. Together these quotations suggest that what early modern thinkers rejected in rhetoric was indeed its claim to constitute an "art," a foundation for cognitive training.

1. The first item in this catena is drawn from Descartes's autobiographical confession in his *Discourse on Method* of 1637: "I held eloquence in high esteem, and I was in love with poetry; but I thought that both were gifts of the mind, rather than fruits of study. Those who possess the strongest reasoning, and who best order their thoughts in order to render them clear and intelligible, are always best able to persuade one of what they propose, even if they were to speak only Low Breton and had never learned rhetoric."[42] It is already evident from this statement that it is indeed the *art* of rhetoric that is rejected in early modernity, not its truth or untruth. Descartes did not succeed immediately in bringing the reign of rhetoric in the schools to an end, and no doubt he understates here as elsewhere a debt to his rhetorical education by the Jesuits, but his philosophy challenged the old rhetoric in terms so thorough as to demand nothing less than a "new" rhetoric—if anything that might be called rhetorical education was to survive. The philosophers of the Port Royal group, chiefly Bernard Lamy, provided this new Cartesian rhetoric, the first of many.

2. Descartes's rejection of rhetorical pedagogy is echoed toward the end of the century by Locke's *Some Thoughts Concerning Education*, published in 1693:

> Rhetorick and Logick being the Arts, that in ordinary method usually follow immediately after Grammar, it may perhaps be wondered that I have said so little of them. The reason is, because of the little advantage young People receive by them. For I have seldom or never observed any one to get the Skill of reasoning well, or speaking handsomely by studying those Rules, which pretend to teach it. . . . To come therefore to what we have in hand; if you would have your Son Reason well, let him read Chillingworth; and if you would have him speak well, let him be conversant in Tully, to give him the true Idea of Eloquence; and let him read

---

42. René Descartes, *Discourse on Method and Meditations on First Philosophy*, trans. Donald A. Cress (Indianapolis: Hackett Publishing, 1998), 4.

those things that are well writ in English, to perfect his Style in the purity of our Language.[43]

Locke concedes the use of Cicero as a model for speaking well, but expresses elsewhere in the same work doubt about the utility of the classical languages for any constituency but that of gentlemen. In Locke, we can see clearly that the rejection of rhetoric is connected with the long process of vernacularization. What remains of the art of speaking is assigned to a reading of Cicero, while the art of writing is best cultivated by following vernacular models. Locke's pedagogy adumbrates a psychology that, however different from that of Descartes, similarly dismisses the very possibility of a rhetoric that is elaborated, rule-based, and comprehensive. Instead Locke envisions a pedagogic scene in which the effects of rhetorical persuasion are produced by an *intuitive* practice, and that rests upon a theory of human nature rather than a notion of language art or *techné*.

3. The dubious situation of rhetoric in the wake of Cartesian and other challenges was acknowledged by Giambattista Vico in his important debut publication of 1708, *On the Study Methods of Our Time*, a polemic in which he defends the rhetorical system against its critique by the Cartesian philosophers: "As for eloquence, the same men assert that the modern study methods, far from being detrimental, are most useful to it. 'How much preferable it is,' they say, 'to induce persuasion by solid arguments based on truth, to produce such an effect on the mind that, once that truth coalesces with reason, it can never again be separated from it, rather than to coerce the listener's soul by meretriciously eloquent allurements, by blazes of oratorical fire which, as soon as they are extinguished, cause him to revert to his original disposition!'"[44] This version of the debate between the ancients and the moderns might look like a repetition of the old dispute between philosophy and rhetoric, but further examination of Vico's argument reveals that the issue for him is not so much the supposed conflict between new knowledge (what we would call "natural sciences") and rhetoric but rather what he announces in his title as "study methods" (*studiorium ratione*). In that pedagogic context, Vico adopts a measured position rather than simply taking sides with the ancients against the moderns: "Even if you know more than the Ancients in some fields, you should not accept

43. John Locke, *Some Thoughts Concerning Education* (Oxford: Clarendon, 1989), 240.

44. Giambattista Vico, *On the Study Methods of Our Time*, trans. Elio Gianturco (Ithaca, NY: Cornell University Press, 1990), 38. The *Port-Royal Logic*, which translated Descartes's "method" into a pedagogic program, is the more proximate target of Vico's polemic.

knowing less in others" (5). Vico suggests that some kinds of knowledge can be lost, and he is specific about where that knowledge resides in the rhetorical system. For him this still recoverable cognitive training is to be found not so much in *memoria*, which had probably faded away as a developed mnemotechnique, but in the *topics*, the technique for the finding of arguments. These, he laments, are "utterly disregarded" in the universities of his time (14).

Even in the eighteenth century, rhetoric might still have been recognized for what it once was, a system for the training of cognition, if only it had been able to retain its topical logic, its method of finding arguments. In retrospect, the reduction of rhetoric to *elocutio*, such as we find in Ramus and other figures in the early modern period, weakened rhetoric not so much because figures of speech could be regarded as deviations from the correspondence of language to reality, but because the identity of rhetoric as a kind of knowledge—a *techné*—was dependent on the integration of its parts into a total system. The knowledge claims of the rhetorical system inhered less in *elocutio* than in the topical logic of *inventio*, where argument emerged. In an important study, *The Sixth Canon*, Barbara Warnick has convincingly demonstrated that the rhetorical system was undermined most seriously by the rejection of *inventio*, the topical logic that supported rhetoric as a mode of reasoning.[45] One might hypothesize in retrospect that the coherence of the rhetorical system depended on the binding together of its compositional and performative functions. These were not so much operations that can be distributed to different fields, as Ramus argued, as they were the parts of the rhetorical system that closed the whole, establishing thereby a coherent relation between its cognitive functions and its final product, a formal or "artificial" use of language for a range of specified purposes or occasions.[46]

45. Barbara Warnick, *The Sixth Canon: Belletristic Rhetorical Theory and Its French Antecedents* (Columbia: University of South Carolina Press, 1993), chapter 1, "Lamy's *L'Art de parler* and the Eclipse of Invention." For Lamy's dismissal of the topics, see John T. Harwood, ed., *The Rhetorics of Thomas Hobbes and Bernard Lamy* (Carbondale: Southern Illinois University Press, 1986): "That to persuade, we need but one Argument, if it be solid and strong, and that Eloquence consists in clearing of that, and making it perspicuous. All those feeble Arguments (proper as well to the accused, as the accuser, and as useful to repel as affirm) deriv'd from Common-places, are like ill Weeds that choke the Corn" (350).

46. Ramus famously reduces rhetoric to two of its parts, *elocutio* and *pronuntiatio*. The other parts, *inventio*, *dispositio*, and *memoria*, were assigned to dialectic. For this distribution of the parts of rhetoric, see Peter Ramus, *Peter Ramus's Attack on Cicero: Text and Translation of Ramus's* Brutinae Quaestiones, trans. Carole Newlands (Ann Arbor: Hermagoras, 1992), 17.

4. This closure of rhetoric as a practice governs what otherwise might appear to be its uncontrolled profusion of terms, particularly in the part denominated as *elocutio*, the figures of speech. It was just in response to what Barthes called the "taxonomic frenzy" of the tropes that Adam Smith, in his lectures titled "Rhetoric and Belles Lettres" delivered in 1748, would dismiss the handbook tradition, and in effect, start over: "'Tis however from the consideration of these figures, and the divisions and subdivisions of them, that so many systems of rhetoric both ancient and modern have been formed. They are generally a very silly set of Books and not at all instructive."[47] Smith's rhetoric was grounded on a principle of economy, of adequating expression to "sentiment." For this purpose, the "art" of rhetoric was rather an impediment than an aid. It was too late by the time he wrote to recover the cognitive function or coherent *techné* of the rhetorical system (though other commentators tried); as we have seen, rhetorical *techné* survived largely in the rituals of pedagogy, which were ever more attenuated in the schools of the eighteenth and nineteenth centuries.

5. Having glanced at Descartes, Locke, Vico, and Smith, we turn finally to perhaps the most sweeping critique of rhetoric to be found at the end of the early modern period, issued by Kant in a footnote of his *Critique of Judgment* (1790). In this text we see once again that the rejection of rhetoric meant above all the rejection of its *techné*:

> Eloquence and well-spokenness (together, rhetoric) belong to beautiful art; but the art of the orator (*ars oratoria*), as the art of using the weakness of people for one's own purposes (however well-intentioned or even really good these may be) is not worthy of any respect at all. . . . He who has at his command, along with clear insight into the facts, language in all its richness and purity, and who, along with a fruitful imagination capable of presenting his ideas, feels a lively sympathy for the true good, is the *vir bonus dicendi peritus*, the speaker without art but full of vigor, as Cicero would have him, though he did not himself always remain true to this ideal.[48]

In the phrase "without art but full of vigor" Kant seems to allude to the ancient debate at the origins of Greek rhetoric about whether rhetoric was an art (*techné*) or an intuitive ability, a power (*dynamis*). The rhetoricians

---

47. Adam Smith, *Lectures on Rhetoric and Belles Lettres* (Indianapolis: Liberty Classics, 1985), 26.

48. Immanuel Kant, *Critique of the Power of Judgment*, ed. Paul Guyer (Cambridge: Cambridge University Press, 2000), 205.

won this argument, and in doing so they invented the Western school; they defined its reason, its *ratio studiorum*, for over two millennia, a rhetorical epoch. If the Western school *was* rhetoric, what is it now? Can there be *bene dicendi* after rhetoric? Speaking well is today understood as the effect of a *dynamis*, a power that is possessed by some and that cannot finally be taught. But speech is not the only stake in the demise of rhetoric, as I have tried to demonstrate. What is at stake is rather *the systemic arrangement of the language arts*: speaking, reading, and writing. If these cognitive arts can lay claim to a foundational role in pedagogy, the demise of rhetoric must mean that a new pedagogy, a new way of forming minds, has been established following the suppression of the old. Rhetoric today is only a rumor, an Atlantis sunk beneath the waves.[49] It remains for us now to name and to describe the system of cognitive training that has arisen in its place.

INFORMATION SOCIETY AND THE ARTS OF LANGUAGE

Ars est celare artem.
OVID (erroneously attributed)

The notion that we live in an "information society" is a commonplace of social theory.[50] I propose to consider the idea of information here in a context that is not usual for discussions of the subject, namely the end of rhetorical education. I concede, however, that the demise of rhetoric is probably easier to set in relation to the scientific revolution than to the idea of information as such. Indeed, it would be surprising if the end of rhetoric did not have some relation to the triumph of modern science. Is rhetoric not the art of the lie? Was it not toppled by a new epistemic order that established a rigorous test of truth for all arguments? I want to suggest, on the contrary, that the juxtaposition of science and rhetoric yields a

49. Many in the "rhet-comp" field point to lively attempts to devise new rhetorics for the modern era. Rhetoric today, however, is a highly specialized subject; it is not taught as the foundation of the cognitive arts. Rhetoric also had a role to play in literary theory in its deconstructive mode, which follows Nietzsche in identifying rhetoric as the undoing of metaphysical truth by the tropological deviations. The rhetoric that was nowhere is now said to be everywhere, in the ubiquitous motive of persuasion, in the will to power of every speech act. This conception of rhetoric deserves separate treatment, but it is not identical to what I am calling *techné*.

50. The idea of information is now the basis for grand theory in sociology, such as Manuel Castells, *The Information Age: Economy, Society, and Culture*, 3 vols (Oxford: Blackwell, 1996–98). For the idea of information and a reliable account of information society as a sociological concept, see Schement and Curtis, *Tendencies and Tensions of the Information Age*.

mistaken picture of the epochal break, an error of the same type one finds in assumptions about the conflict between science and religion in the early modern period.

We do not lack theories that relegate rhetoric and science peaceably to their separate kingdoms.[51] But, as the quotations above exhibit, the mutual antipathy between rhetoric and science could only arise when the knowledge inhering in rhetorical *techné* itself was called into question. Until that point (indeed, for a good part of the early modern period), it was usual for natural philosophers to defend the use of rhetoric as a means of persuading others of the truths discovered by natural philosophy. This was essentially Bacon's position and that of the later Hobbes.[52] In order to put science and rhetoric on all fours with respect to each other, then, we must proceed on the assumption that science and rhetoric represent different forms of knowledge.

To bring the challenge to rhetorical *techné* as a form of knowledge into sharper historical focus, we must go behind the monolith of science in order to discriminate the components embedded in the category of knowledge itself. Only when we specify one of these—the idea of *information*—does it become possible to identify the principle of antagonism undermining over the long term the status of rhetoric as the embodiment of real knowledge. While this undermining resulted in part from the routinization of rhetoric's *techné* in early modernity, its degeneration into mechanical rituals, the final expulsion of rhetoric from the Western school coincided with the assertion of a principle of knowledge in which the component of informa-

---

51. The most interesting of these defenses in the modern era is in my view that of Hans Blumenberg, "An Anthropological Approach to the Contemporary Significance of Rhetoric," in *After Philosophy: End or Transformation?*, ed. Kenneth Baynes, James Bohman, and Thomas McCarthy (Cambridge, MA: MIT Press, 1996), 429–58. Blumenberg bases his defense on a "principle of insufficient reason," which inverts Leibniz's famous "principle of sufficient reason." Blumenberg's principle roughly corresponds to what the ancients called "probability" as opposed to the certainty they attributed to other kinds of demonstrative argument to be found in physical or metaphysical discourses. Modern notions of certainty, apart from the domain of formal logic, are not usually based on demonstration. More often certainty means to us an extremely high degree of mathematical probability. Scientific certainty does not, and Blumenberg argues, never will, erase the margin of the probable (in the older sense) in human affairs, where rhetoric finds its application.

52. Bacon's position on rhetoric can be found in *The Proficience and Advancement of Learning*. Hobbes works out his final position in *Leviathan*, which takes a somewhat less hostile view of rhetoric than his earlier *De cive*. On this subject, see Quentin Skinner, *Reason and Rhetoric in the Philosophy of Hobbes* (Cambridge: Cambridge University Press, 1996).

tion was of chief importance. This component traversed all the knowledge fields that developed into "disciplines" in the modern university, whether or not these fields were what we would now call "sciences." Although the curriculum of the new university often proclaimed its basis in science, it was in fact founded on the much broader epistemic principle of "expert knowledge," which I shall identify in the argument to follow with the process of generating and manipulating particular kinds of information. The significance of information for the educational system is succinctly indicated by Alain Touraine in his study *The Academic System in American Society*: "American society at the end of the nineteenth century was one of industry, entrepreneurs, manual labor, the market, and the conquest of the frontier. In the second half of the twentieth century, it is a society of computers, programs and planning, management, and white-collar workers. In a civilization of energy, the academic system cannot have the same importance as in a civilization of information."[53] That is, the academic system in America discovered a mission it did not formerly possess, and in realizing this mission, the American university leapt ahead of other systems of higher education in the Western world, leaving rhetorical pedagogy behind. At the same time, as I will demonstrate here, the great success of the new university in transforming discourses and practices of knowledge produced a blind spot in the new system of disciplines, after which it was difficult to recognize the art of rhetoric *as* knowledge, as something other than "mere words."

It is necessary to begin, then, with the concept of information, and its difference from the conception of knowledge. Knowledge is a concept of great generality; it includes not only science but many nonscientific discourses as well, including rhetoric itself. Information is a component of many distinct types of knowledge, but knowledge is not merely an accumulation of information. The sciences, for example, consist also of the organizing principles and operational practices by which a particular kind of information, *scientific data*, is produced and utilized. In the same way, the knowledge of law implies the production and use of *legal data* and so on, for all types of professionalized knowledge in the modern world, including humanities disciplines. The distinctive nature of information is already visible in the early modern period, when information became a desideratum in many venues, not only the scientific. Governments became interested in finding out about the governed, how many they were, how long they lived, when they married, and how many children they had. This is information. Merchants needed to know what happened to money and goods in their

53. Touraine, *The Academic System in American Society*, 56.

far-flung transits, what environmental conditions, political interventions, rates of exchange, or vagaries of taste would affect the course from investment to profit. This too is information.[54]

In the argument to follow, I adopt the definition of Michael Hobart and Zachary Schiffman in their historical study *Information Ages*: information is any "knowledge that can be stored apart from the knower."[55] Or, to be more precise, information is that aspect or component of knowledge that can be stored or transmitted in symbolic form—writing, numbers, algorithms, images, graphs, etc. Information is defined by its formal properties, not by its content or validity. If information is distinguishable from knowledge in general, as a component of its disciplinary form, this component is conversely distinguishable from the notion of fact. In common usage, information and fact are often interchangeable, but fact is characterized by a certain informality; it is only what is said to be the case, such as whether it is raining at this moment. Facts circulate in the most casual contexts of news or gossip; as such, facts are insufficient in themselves to constitute information or data in a disciplinary context without an act of curation, a recontextualization in the terms of a formal knowledge practice.[56] This recontextualization means putting facts into the *form* of information, which can be stored, correlated, transmitted, and manipulated.

This conception of information is a choice among competing possibilities, two of which can be acknowledged here. First, I have rejected the notion of information that some commentators now advance, the notion that everything that exists is information. This metaphysical definition might be useful for some purposes, but not for constructing a history of infor-

54. For a historical account of information in this sense, see Theodore M. Porter, *Trust in Numbers: The Pursuit of Objectivity in Science and Public Life* (Princeton, NJ: Princeton University Press, 1995).

55. Michael E. Hobart and Zachary S. Schiffman, in *Information Ages: Literacy, Numeracy, and the Computer Revolution* (Baltimore: Johns Hopkins University Press, 1998), 5. Hobart and Schiffman speak of distinct information ages, beginning with the invention of writing. The signal value of their study is to relate literacy and numeracy to each other as information technologies and to bring to light the emergence of the "idea of information" in the modern sense. See also John Seely Brown and Paul Duguid, *The Social Life of Information* (Boston: Harvard Business School Press, 2000), 119–20, who also argue that the distinction between knowledge and information corresponds to the distinction between the knower and the kind of knowledge that is detachable from the knower. I am indebted in this area to the work of Alan Liu in his inexhaustible websites, *Palinurus* and *The Voice of the Shuttle*.

56. For an important study of the idea of the fact in history, see Mary Poovey, *A History of the Modern Fact: Problems of Knowledge in the Sciences of Wealth and Society* (Chicago: University of Chicago Press, 1998).

mational modes.[57] The formal properties of information make it possible
to construct this history and to distinguish information within the broader
domain of human communication. The second definition I have rejected is
as narrow as the first is broad, although these two definitions have a certain sympathetic relation. According to the second definition, information
consists of what can be represented by information technology, or even
more narrowly, what can be reduced to the computer's binary language.[58]
This definition understands "information society" in the immediate context of current technology, at the expense, as with the first, of a deeper
historical insight.

While there are obvious reasons for the ubiquitous association of computer technology with the idea of information, Hobart and Schiffman argue for a long-durational history of information in which two major technologies are dominant: the system of writing and the system of numbers.[59]
Computer technology, and the algorithms that operate their programs,
together constitute a development of the numerical coding of information, albeit one with far-reaching implications, perhaps even inaugurating

57. For a conception of information that tends toward the universal cybernetic
view, with some qualification, see Albert Borgmann, *Holding on to Reality: The Nature of
Information at the Turn of the Millennium* (Chicago: University of Chicago Press, 1999).

58. This is the sense of information one finds in much discussion of information society, for example, Michael Detourzos, *What Will Be: How the New World of Information
Will Change Our Lives* (San Francisco: Harper Edge, 1997). There is a deep metaphysical
question that arises from current views of information as at once what everything consists of, and at the same time capable of being expressed without remainder in binary
code. This metaphysics supports the theory of "the singularity," which refuses to see the
body as anything but one repository among many of information. The notion of the singularity is evidence of how far we have moved away from acknowledging embodied art.

59. Is there information in an "oral" society? This question is rather difficult to answer, because what we call writing is defined too narrowly to capture the possible means
of storing information by altering the external world. It would be difficult to find a human society with no graphic representation of any kind, as any such marking of the
body or the environment might function as a technology for storing information. It is
doubtful that there are any human societies without "writing" in this sense of symbolic
inscription. Some scholars, such as Eric Havelock, regard the epic as a vehicle of "informational storage" in preliterate society. See "The Oral-Literate Equation: A Formula
for the Modern Mind," in *Literacy and Orality*, ed. Olson and Torrance (Cambridge:
Cambridge University Press, 1991), 24. Havelock argues that meter and narrative are
means by which knowledge can be stored in the epic. But in oral poetry, the knowledge
recalled by means of it is embodied in the knower and can only be "stored" in another
knower. Nonetheless, I do not think that this question is so clear cut as to permit an easy
resolution. Perhaps the rhapsode might be construed as an "information storage system"
by other members of the culture. In that case, the rhapsode would be rather like a book
or a computer is to us.

a third information age.[60] In any case, information can be distinguished by its materially encoded form, which permits in all cases transmission and manipulation.

This definition specifies the relation between information and the identity of the class fraction of "professionals" or "experts," the class that has made a distinct claim to possess a highly valued sort knowledge. Professional "knowledge workers" labor not upon matter directly but *information in its symbolic form*, a form that we recognize instantly as "book knowledge." Words and numbers are the chief forms of information by means of which knowledge is detached from individual knowers and transmitted as information. The concept of symbolic transmission permits us to aggregate "knowledge workers" as a social group distinct from myriad other workers whose work, typically and unjustly, has been devalued in modern society. These other kinds of labor usually involve knowledge too, but by and large this knowledge is transmitted in the mode of *techné* from master to apprentice. Often this knowledge is demoted to the form of "craft," a term that, as we have noted, names a kind of work of supposedly lesser social value, but this perception betrays a misunderstanding of *techné* generally, wherever its social location. Although the difference between "craft" knowledge and professional knowledge divides the world of labor between them, this notion of craft is marked by contradiction. Modern society has set aside a domain of work in which craft is highly valued but as an *exception* to its ordinary status; this is the domain of the "fine arts." There is no real contradiction, however, as every instance of *techné* or craft, whatever the social value attached, exhibits the same underlying principle of transmission from one body to another, teacher to disciple.

The modern survival of a highly valued *techné* in the case of the "fine arts" raises an interesting question about the relative status of teaching in the various situations of knowledge transmission. No one expects that learning to play the piano is easy to do without a teacher or that this process is any different for the other arts. The embodied nature of this kind of knowledge is even the basis of its claim to value, if also the occasion of a certain mystification of aesthetic accomplishment. In the case of professional expertise, the position of the teacher is troubled by the availability of symbolic modes of transmission that increasingly stand on their own—or at least claim to do so. If the teacher survives in the modern school, this fact suggests the survival of *techné*. And yet the "art" that goes into the acquisition of professional knowledge is much more difficult to see. We know

60. See Stephen Wolfram, *A New Kind of Science* (Champaign, IL: Wolfram Media, 2002).

it is there, but it eludes us, because information is so much more visible. Information is what exists in the book or in computer files or in the multitude of vehicles that engage learners in the process of becoming knowledge workers. Yet this problem is much easier to solve than its neglect would indicate: the art that is embodied in knowledge workers is nothing other than the art of *working upon information*, everything that is involved in generating, storing, transmitting or manipulating information, building it up into a "body of knowledge."

Once we recognize the nature of this art, we also recognize that it is not new. There are prototypes in the premodern world for the modern knowledge worker, a fact that complicates the self-identification of this worker as modern. "Book knowledge," as we know, defined the three "ancient" professions: the clergy, the law, and medicine. Why should we not consider these professions "modern"? Even more interestingly, the book knowledge of these premodern professionals was wholly compatible with the rhetorical system, with its performative *techné*. How was this possible? Rhetoric in the premodern world embraced without contradiction the embodied mode of transmission as an art and its symbolic transmission as book knowledge. This duality puzzles us today because it is difficult to see from our vantage how different the relation of the premodern professional was to the symbolic encoding of knowledge in the form of writing. The relation of these premodern professionals to books was much closer to what is meant by art or craft than we can conceive; the book still possessed for them the properties of a material substance that called forth an art, an art of *reading*. The ability to read was understood in the premodern professions as a fully embodied knowledge, responsive first of all to the resistant materiality of symbolically encoded information, to the physical resistances of the book itself, as real to these serious readers as stone to the sculptor. Our sense of "book knowledge" is very different, and is premised on the reduction of information to an abstract utility, only temporarily materialized in the form of the book (or analogous electronic vehicle). The book as repository of information in modernity is infinitely fungible and can be discarded when its information is absorbed or outdated. In this "postrhetorical condition," information briefly inhabits the material form of its encoding before it is extracted for use. It is only the information that matters. The abstract utility of information has made a new world, recasting the social identity of the modern knower, the modern professional type. And yet, in the very process of extracting information from its material encodings, the modern expert falls into a blind spot; our knowledge worker fails to see that the very practice by which information is generated, transmitted, and manipulated is *itself an art* which, by definition, *cannot be reduced to information*.

The art hides behind the abstraction of information. This art is genuinely embodied, like all arts, and therefore like its precursors in the premodern world. But for some reason, we cannot see it for what it truly is, nor can we find the terms to value it. We know where this art resides, of course: *in our bodies*, and we also know where it is *learned*—where else than in the school?

In the remainder of this essay, I consider three principal ways in which the postrhetorical condition can be contrasted with its long-durational precursor. The purpose of this analysis is to explore further the distinction between *techné* and information but also to demonstrate the coexistence of these component forms of knowledge in any context of learning or of labor. More particularly, in relation to the larger argument of this chapter and the others, a better understanding of this complexity of learning will tell us why the arts of *speaking, reading*, and *writing* have been devalued in modernity, why they tend to be relegated to basic competencies or, in the case of speaking, to fall outside the domain of formal instruction. This too defines the postrhetorical condition.

1. Techné versus Method. As the argument above implies, the art of rhetoric is not equivalent to the stored information that descends to us in textual form. The full significance of this fact is difficult to register because the rhetoricians compiled a huge store of *information about language*, such as the topics and tropes. This body of knowledge is loosely organized by competing taxonomies, and as a consequence the terms that descend to us can seem bafflingly recondite or even, as Adam Smith thought, useless. That is not always the fate for the arts of antiquity. The art of "grammar," for example, bequeathed a taxonomy, the "parts of speech," that remains of enormous utility to linguists, even though many primary schools no longer transmit this information to students. The accumulation of knowledge in the discourses of grammar and rhetoric is valuable, but these forms of knowledge have long since been deracinated, which is to say that they have been detached from the arts they were supposed to support. In the process, it has been possible to forget their composite nature as both art and information.

In contemporary philosophical discourse, *techné* is usually acknowledged in the distinction between "knowing *that*" and "knowing *how*" (*savoir faire*); Michael Polanyi has famously analyzed the latter in his study of what he calls "personal knowledge."[61] These terms roughly convey the

61. Michael Polanyi, *Personal Knowledge: Towards a Post-Critical Philosophy* (Chicago: University of Chicago Press, 1958), 53. The distinction between *techné* and information is roughly analogous to the distinction drawn by David Hollinger in his essay

distinction between information and art. No textbook can overcome this duality, because no textbook can produce the effect of "knowing how." Mistaking the "handbook" or "knowing that" for the art itself might also be described as a misconstruction of the relation between theory (or method) and practice. A *techné* may give rise to a "theory of practice"—handbook rhetoric or piano theory—but theory/method does not become practice in the same way that knowledge is encoded and stored as information. What we call "method" in this context is an attempt to *translate practice into information*. To render an art as information would be to reduce it to a set of precise instructions, rather like those for assembling a piece of furniture. But even that humble example discloses how actually difficult it is to translate practice into information. Anyone who has ever assembled furniture knows how confounding and useless the instructions can be. We can assume that the art of furniture making will be exponentially more difficult to translate into information. In all but the most extraordinary circumstances, an art requires transmission by a teacher—someone who embodies the art—in direct relation to the student, someone who desires to embody it.[62] Reading even the best book on piano theory will never produce the ability to play the piano; though the information might be useful, it will require a teacher to show one how to use the information.

Let me emphasize here that I am *not* saying that art has simply disappeared from our world. On the contrary, it can be shown that *techné* survives everywhere in our information society, just because teaching goes on everywhere; the embodiment of knowledge happens all the time. If that is so, then where is the epochal break? This break occurs, I suggest, in an altered *social relation* to the practice of transmission, as a result of which *techné* has been relegated to an epistemological and pedagogical limbo. Its status as knowledge has become difficult to credit just because it cannot be expressed fully in the form of information. Always in our society, there is

"The Knower and the Artificer," *American Quarterly* 39 (1987): 37–55. Hollinger's "knower" is identified with the scientist and his "artificer" with the artist, a delimitation that permits him to explore the ideological messages that arise with conflict between these two groups. My argument tries to bring out the underlying distinction between information and *techné*, which operates more broadly to separate categories of production but within categories as essential to all productive labor.

62. The ancient rhetoric texts usually acknowledge this fact. So the author of the *Ad Herennium*, trans. Harry Caplan (Cambridge, MA: Harvard University Press, 1919) tells us that the "faculties" of rhetoric can be acquired "by three means: Theory, Imitation, and Practice [*arte, imitatione, exercitatione*] (7)." *Theory* is in my view not a happy translation of *ars*, but the context makes plain enough the process invoked. *Imitation* stimulates us to attain, in accordance with a studied method, the effectiveness of certain models in speaking. *Practice* is assiduous exercise and experience in speaking.

an effort to reduce the transmission of an art to the transmission of information. Our textbooks grow ever larger as our trust in the embodiment of art declines.

No doubt the modern relation between *techné* and information arises from the circumstance that the *effect* of certain cognitive functions previously (and still) operative in *techné* can be reproduced prosthetically by various kinds of information technology. Even the most sophisticated mnemotechnique is easily overwhelmed, for example, by the volume of knowledge that can be stored as information (that is, outside the body) in most modern contexts of knowledge use. It is a great advantage to all of us that so much information can be translated into material forms, from Post-It notes to computer files, and also that methods for gaining access to this knowledge can be externalized, as with internet "search engines" and other such devices. In fact, these techniques, as many scholars have pointed out, have their precursors—book indexes, catalogs, cross-references, and the like—which confirms that the volume of knowledge available in the form of information long ago overwhelmed human memory.

Nonetheless, the development of prosthetic cognition comes up against certain limits in the potential of these technologies to enable the use of information. "Natural" cognitive functions must continue to be exercised, improved, perfected, made "artificial" (in the ancient's sense of a deliberate and formal practice). Information technology may change the location, type, and threshold of cognitive arts, but it does not remove the necessity for cognitive training in arts. Our information society is stubbornly reluctant to recognize this embodied knowledge, which it tends either to mystify as talent or genius or to relegate to the dreary domain of that theory of practice we know as "pedagogy."

The theory of pedagogy has sometimes fallen to the lowest level of discourse about *techné*, often a mix of inspirational blather and pseudoscience, and it is easy to see why. It is precisely the difficulty of translating an art or craft into information which has produced the peculiar blind spot of our educational system, its mistrust of any knowledge that cannot be produced directly in the form of information. In the lower levels of our school system, this mistrust is expressed as the domination of theory over the practice of teaching, the manic prescription of its procedure, down to the last minute of classroom time. This overprescription is sustained by a vast production of educational theory, always chasing the receding horizon of embodied knowledge. Information society has developed what I shall call, following Gouldner, an "invisible pedagogy," in which the very aim that supremely defined premodern education—the transmission of cognitive arts—has been relegated to the margin of the modern school. Gouldner is concerned with the "culture of critical discourse" (discussed above in chapter 1), which it is easy to see describes generally an art of thinking and communicating that seems to have no location or assigned pedagogy in the school. There, knowledge continues somehow to be embodied in various arts, as ever before, even while educational theory turns away from the recognition of embodiment as interpersonal engagement or attempts to reduce teaching to a rigid prescription. Theory sets itself against *techné*, against the transmission of knowledge from one body to another, in a face-to-face relation. From the vantage of theory, the teacher is rather an impediment to the transmission of knowledge and might perhaps be replaced eventually by a sequence of programs, that is, by what I have been calling information.

Since the sixteenth century, pedagogy has sought a *method*, or a theory of practice, that would economize and streamline the árduous task of teaching, even behind the back of the teacher. This project of modernity, which continues today in many forms, depends on the idea of information as disembodied knowledge. Early modern thinkers were acutely aware of the accumulation of information, overwhelming cognitive faculties such as memory, and they hoped to solve this problem by a new means of transmission, which they called *method*. Method emerged in the Renaissance as a "short form of art," a kind of shortcut to the effect of *techné*.[63] This is the context in which we might see a phenomenon such as Ramism: as a forerunner of the information system. Ramus's aim was not to transmit new knowledge but to reduce the massive accumulation in the traditional arts—grammar, rhetoric, and dialectic—to an easily transmissible form. The distinction of his pedagogy was its method, the *via certa* or exact procedure by which knowledge could be externalized as instantly accessible information.[64] In diagrammatic form, the famous Ramistic dichotomies worked like a slide rule, as one traced terms from the general to the particular through their branching subdivisions. The significance of Ramus's system was its attempt to supersede the old pedagogy in favor of an easier, faster way to accomplish an effect of *techné*—finding the right argument,

63. For an introduction to the discourse of method in the early modern period, see Neal W. Gilbert, *Renaissance Concepts of Method* (New York: Columbia University Press, 1960). Method was originally a means of shortening and simplifying the arduous program of medieval "terministic" logic. For a general account of method in the French tradition, see Phillippe Desan, *Naissance de la méthode: Machiavel, La Ramée, Bodin, Montaigne, Descartes* (Paris: Nizet, 1987).

64. On Ramist method, see Walter J. Ong, *Ramus, Method, and the Decay of Dialogue: From the Art of Discourse to the Art of Reason* (Cambridge, MA: Harvard University Press, 1958).

or the right figure, to make one's case. Was this pedagogy successful? With good reason, its critics thought it was shallow, a means not of embodying an art but of pretending knowledge of it.

If Ramus's innovation was as consequential as Walter Ong hypothesized in *Ramus, Method, and the Decay of Dialogue*, this consequence was not in my view based on a shift from "oral" to "visual" culture. The diagram was simply a more "methodic" device of writing than its precursors, that is to say, easier to read than older graphic conventions of writing, which demanded a more involved and complex interaction between mind and visual symbol, or student and teacher. Lisa Jardine and Anthony Grafton accurately summarize the significance of method in their discussion of Ramus's teaching: "Ramus offered an *all-purpose* technique for transmitting knowledge (the infamous *unica methodicus*) in place of the detail and complexity of traditional teaching. His 'one and only method' was a suitable vehicle, he claimed, for transmitting the content of any discipline. . . . It opened the prospect that the purpose of education was to purvey information and skills, not to be morally improving."[65] For the humanists, moral improvement was mixed like a secret ingredient into the transmission of the arts, an ancient topos of teaching, and Jardine and Grafton note its absence from Ramus's teaching. But just as important from my perspective is the connection they assert between method and the transmission of information. Ramus presages a good deal of modern pedagogy, in its attempt to make teaching "methodic" and thus to bypass as much as possible the "personal" relation between teacher and student.[66]

To put my argument summarily, then, the epochal break I am attempting to describe was not a transition from oral to written culture but from the arduous system of embodying knowledge as *techné* to one in which access to knowledge was "methodized." Method constituted a procedure for

65. Grafton and Jardine, *From Humanism to the Humanities*, 169–70.

66. Grafton and Jardine are direct about the extent to which humanist teaching fell short of its grander, ethical aims; they point out that classroom practice could be a dismal routine of note-taking and memorization. There was no guarantee that the educational experience was edifying or even pleasurable, even if it succeeded in producing graduates who were skilled speakers and writers in classical languages (and often, the vernacular as well), very marketable abilities in the early modern period. In that context, the emergence of method responded realistically to an increased demand for education. Reformist educational theory in the later sixteenth and seventeenth century (such as that of Comenius) strongly emphasized method, which became an increasingly important theme in educational writing. For a comment on this subject, see David Hamilton, "Notes from Nowhere (On the Beginning of Modern Schooling)," in *Cultural History and Education: Critical Essays on Knowledge and Schooling,* ed. Thomas S. Popkewitz, Barry M. Franklin, and Miguel A. Pereyra (New York: Routledge, 2001), 187–206.

transmitting information in disembodied form, but, as I will acknowledge below, its role in the future was to be more interesting than merely as the antagonist of art. For as I have already pointed out, embodied knowledge is not extinguished in modernity so much as relocated, flourishing where its identity as art is, so to speak, hidden or, as Gouldner says, "invisible."

2. *Comprehension versus Differentiation.* I have already observed that the rhetorical system comprehended both speech and writing, but there is another, larger sense in which it may be said to be comprehensive. While language *techné* managed the information technology of writing, it also managed or comprehended whatever knowledge was expressed in language, about any subject. The rhetorical system functioned as the cognitive support for all intellectual discourses, even those not immediately concerned with the classical "occasions" of rhetoric. The rhetorical system thus comprehended, in this larger sense, the philosophical discourses proper, both natural philosophy and moral philosophy, along with potentially all other discourses.

In the information system, knowledge is organized by a very different principle, which responds to certain inherent limitations in the rhetorical system as a means of managing and producing information. This alternative principle is "differentiation." According to this principle, knowledge must be produced on the basis of methodologies specific to different kinds of object.[67] These methods were no longer tied to the universal *techné* of the rhetorical system, which was concerned ubiquitously with mastering *linguistic* information. The emergence of new sciences in the early modern period was contingent on the differentiation of knowledge discourses and the development of new information technologies, such as the algebraic geometry described by Hobart and Schiffman in *Information Ages*, the inaugural technology of a second information age, the age of "numeracy." The initial differentiation of words and numbers occasioned in turn the development of new

---

67. Differentiation, it might be noted, bears a superficial resemblance to Aristotle's principle asserting different methodologies for determining truth about different objects. In Aristotle's system, for example, truths about the translunary and sublunary worlds were established by different procedures, because for him these were ontologically different objects. Nonetheless the underlying "logics" of demonstration were much less different than Aristotle's differentiation principle would seem to imply, and certainly nothing like the difference between discourses of knowledge in modernity. The bundling of Aristotle's texts on logic in the medieval *Organon* confirms the tendency in premodern culture toward a unified logic underlying the arts and sciences. As Hobart and Schiffman point out in *Information Ages*, this logic was essentially linguistic and based on the principle of classification; this principle would prove inadequate for the system of numeracy.

symbolic representations of information. Beginning modestly enough with the kinds of schemas we find in Ramus and his contemporaries, the graphic representation of information has become a massively elaborated alternative to the representation of information in words. Or more commonly, words and numbers tend to be integrated in these new graphic modes.[68]

The symbolic representation of numbers, of course, was older than rhetoric, and the first kind of writing may well have been nothing other than arithmetic notation, but what Hobart and Schiffman mean by "numeracy" is something different, a new information system, the transformation of mathematics into a language for representing and intervening substantially into *this* world, not an ideal or Platonic realm of numbers and shapes. The system of numeracy operated by a rigorous "abstraction" of experience, a form of encoding experience that seemed to be farther away from it even than natural language.[69] In the end this new system could not be "comprehended" by the principles of rhetoric or the kind of logic governing the verbal arts. Numeracy gave rise to new kinds of logic, wholly distinct from the language-based syllogistic logics of the premodern era. The probability theories of Pascal, Laplace, Bayes, Peirce, and Boole, to name only major examples, conformed very little either to the old formal logic of the syllogism or the informal principle of rhetorical "probability" known from antiquity.[70] The in-

68. For an invaluable account of this phenomenon, see Edward Tufte, *The Visual Display of Quantitative Information* (Cheshire, CT: Graphics Press, 2001).

69. This subject is too complex to treat adequately in this context. For a fuller discussion I refer readers to Hobart and Schiffman, *Information Ages,* chapter 5, "Numeracy, Analysis, and the Reintegration of Knowledge." They argue that "'modern' mathematics provided a new symbolic language whose principal advantages in mastering information lay in its greater abstraction from the universe of words and things, from experience, and in its unprecedented capabilities of analysis" (115), and they associate this breakthrough with Descartes's algebraic geometry. How writing changed with the inception of numeracy is a more difficult problem to address. For an account of numeracy in the range of its contexts, see Lynn Arthur Steen, "Numeracy," in *Literacy: An Overview by Fourteen Experts,* ed. Graubard, 211–31.

70. The rhetorics of Port Royal, *La Logique ou l'art de penser* (1662), and of Bernard Lamy, *De L'Art de parler* (1675), derived from Cartesian conceptions of "method" and can be read as transitional, no longer satisfied with the argumentation of the "old rhetoric" but not yet capable of articulating a "logic of discovery." A more definitive break with the old logic can be found in Pascal's "Art of Persuasion," in *Pensées and Other Writings,* trans. Honor Levi (Oxford: Oxford University Press, 1995): "It is not *barbara* and *baralipton* which make up the argument. The mind must not be blinkered" (204). Pascal is referring in the italicized terms to the mnemonic verses composed by William of Sherwood and used for remembering the permutations of syllogism in the medieval system of formal logic. Pascal's "art of persuasion" on the other hand, generalizes from "mathematical" rules to a new logic of argumentation.

formation system would require not the latter but new "logics of discovery" in order to develop numeracy as a productive new information technology.

The principle of differentiation is easiest to see where the mathematized sciences depart from the language-centered rhetorical system, but this is by no means the only site of differentiation. Different fields of knowledge developed most rapidly in the modern world by emphasizing their difference from one another, a process that eventuated later in what we recognize as the "division of the disciplines." By contrast, rhetoric comprehended all knowledge by means of language, and in a certain sense, *as* language; even natural philosophy saw its object as "the book of nature."[71] The emergence of the twin systems of literacy (as a modern concept) and numeracy offers us perhaps the most conspicuous evidence for the reorganization of knowledge discourses according to the principle of differentiation. For literacy represented a new conception of language, just as numeracy represented a new conception of numbers. Henceforth there could be no tacit subordination of numbers to words, as there had been in the "liberal arts" of the medieval university, the trivium and the quadrivium. The rise of numeracy would have important consequences in turn for the conceptualization of language skills in modernity.

It might be tempting at this point to assimilate the distinction between comprehension and differentiation to our notion of "general" versus "specialized" knowledge, but this would be a mistake. The rhetorical system was not in our sense a kind of general knowledge. By that term, we mean that one knows some of the information produced across a variety of knowledge discourses, without necessarily knowing how to produce such knowledge. But rhetoric was not general in this sense, which tends to attract the stigma of the shallow. The rhetorical system was founded on a rigorous cognitive practice, which comprehended knowledge in potentially many areas quite thoroughly and deeply, because the discourse of these diverse knowledges was never far removed from the infrastructure of the rhetorical system. Consequently, many discourses we now think of as distinct disciplines, such as psychology or poetics or political science, could be grasped within and through rhetoric, as belonging to its *techné*.

Differentiation is obviously related to what I have considered elsewhere in these essays as "specialization," but it is not quite the same process.

---

71. It must be noted that this new principle of numerical representation immediately produced the same claim to the status of a universal dialectic as its predecessor. The Cartesian *mathesis universalis* or *more geometrico* was perhaps the most important ideologeme of early modern philosophy. It was not until this ideologeme had been superseded that a distinction between the natural sciences and the social sciences could be developed, grounded on a distinction of methodologies.

Specialization, as we have seen, underlies all forms of labored practice inasmuch as such practice addresses repeatedly a particular object or purpose. But differentiation projects this primal specialization of action into the realm of knowledge discourses. Differentiation creates new objects of epistemic specialization, the ramifying system of the disciplines and subdisciplines. As differentiation creates disciplines, the process of distinction makes it difficult to see what is *common* to different knowledge discourses. In addition to Gouldner's identification of a certain style of speech and argument, the lingua franca of the professional class fraction, there is yet another commonality that subtends the disciplines, and that is *the art by which knowledge is transmitted*, or more simply, the fact of teaching.

3. *Generativity versus Accumulation*. The rhetorical system was rigorous and comprehensive, but it was limited as a means of developing new knowledge. Its *techné* was oriented toward the productivity of language, and its orientation to language was not perceived as a limitation so long as it was unnecessary and even difficult to distinguish knowledge *about language* from knowledge about the world. The rhetorical system in antiquity acknowledged the distinction between *verba* (words) and *res* (matter) but managed this distinction as a challenge for decorum rather than an epistemological dilemma. But in the early modern period these terms spelled very big trouble indeed, the catastrophe in which rhetoric came to be denounced as *mere words*.[72] More matter and less art! This trouble arose at a particular moment, the knowledge crisis of the early modern period, which, as we have seen, was a crisis of accumulation. It was provoked in part by the immense increase in the volume of stored information created by print technology. In this crisis, it became possible to draw a distinction between knowledge *of opinion*, mere words, and knowledge of "matter" or the world, *res*.[73] The skeptical crisis of the early modern period responded to the sense that the accumulation of knowledge about what the ancients *said* did not represent the growth of knowledge so much as it did the piling up of mere words. Many thinkers began to challenge the knowledge handed down from antiquity as not, after all, so great an accumulation.

Bacon famously argued that knowledge must be "augmented," a new kind of accumulation because it is the accumulation of new knowledge. This kind of accumulation can be contrasted with what might be called the

---

72. For a subtle account of the *res/verba* distinction in the Renaissance, see Terence Cave, *The Cornucopian Text: Problems of Writing in the French Renaissance* (Oxford: Clarendon, 1979).

73. For a provocative interpretation of the knowledge crisis of early modernity, see Stephen Toulmin, *Cosmopolis: The Hidden Agenda of Modernity* (Chicago: University of Chicago Press, 1990).

generativity of the rhetorical system. This generativity was far from empty, mere words. Erasmus's celebrated *De utraque verborum ac rerum copia* (*On Copia of Words and Ideas*), one of the most frequently reprinted rhetorical texts of the Renaissance, demonstrated a *techné* for generating words, hundreds of ways to say, for example, "Your letter pleased me greatly." His fecund variations on this statement constituted a *copia* of both words and matter. But the credibility of this double *copia*, the command of rhetoric over both domains, was coming into question. This is not to deny the linguistic generativity of the rhetorical system and its manifold uses: it was a superb technique for training in communication, for personal relations and advancement, for negotiation, for settling disputes and avoiding violence, and of course for the particular motive of persuasion. It rested on a very real knowledge, an *art*, and on a substantial body of knowledge about language. But it could not be said that the knowledge base of the "old rhetoric" continued to increase in the early modern period. The rhetorical system was concerned by definition with the reproduction of its *techné* through an arduous pedagogy and not necessarily with producing *new* knowledge about objects, not even the object of language.

In the difference between the principles of *generativity* and *accumulation* we can discern again the shadowy type of information, though not yet the "information age" in our current sense. Nor yet the birth of science. Information is a component form of knowledge that scientific methods were able to increase, to accumulate, and this accumulation validated that method at the same time it could be invoked to discredit the knowledge represented by the old rhetoric.[74] This scenario provides us with a basis for understanding how new arts might arise, which answered to the need for manipulating information, but which at the same time ceased to be regarded as arts at all.

The person who knows how to produce or use information is one whose ability is no longer defined chiefly as a cognitive art or *techné*, even if in

74. The development of the notion that knowledge can be indefinitely accumulated, Bacon's "augmentation" of knowledge, is beyond the scope of this essay. But it might be noted that Bacon developed this notion by drawing a distinction between the older sense of *inventio* and his own innovative definition, in *The Advancement of Learning*, ed. Michael Kiernan (Oxford: Clarendon, 2000): "The *Inuention* of speech or argument is not properly an *Inuention*, for to *Inuent* is to discouer that, we know not, & not to recouer or resummon that which wee alreadie knowe." Jardine remarks on this "misunderstanding" in *Francis Bacon: Discovery and the Art of Discourse* (Cambridge: Cambridge University Press, 1975): "It was never the intention of the humanist reformers to offer a logic of discovery; for them dialectic was the key to teaching, and clear and eloquent expression in all fields of knowledge" (6).

practice the mastery of knowledge continued to assume its embodiment in the knower. The accumulation of knowledge in increasingly diverse fields now obscures the relation between the transmission of particular bodies of knowledge and the body of the knower. Knowledge in the form of accumulated information seems to stand outside the body, as a "body of knowledge." The production and use of particular bodies of knowledge requires a different kind of knower, of which the scientist is only one type. This knower is the *expert*. We may define this expert, in the context of the *longue durée*, as the knower who is no longer concerned mainly with how knowing can be embodied but rather with how it might be *disembodied* in order to be manipulated in a new way, ultimately with the purpose of producing new knowledge. The art of the new expert is in the first place the art of disembodying information, putting it into symbolic form, and in the second, the art of manipulating that stored information. Let us call this *the art of devising methods*. And yet this art of disembodying information appears to be a kind of epiphenomenon of information itself; *techné* becomes the unconscious of knowing. The postrhetorical expert sees only a body of knowledge, a towering accumulation that must be assimilated as efficiently as possible, by means of a "method."

The growing cadres of experts in the manipulation of information evolved in the nineteenth century into a recognizable collectivity, the professional-managerial or New Class. As I have remarked, this group did not initially exhibit anything like a class consciousness. The epochal concept of "information society" is the belated annunciator of that consciousness, but the idea of information was capable only partially of bringing knowledge workers to an understanding of themselves as a class fraction. The self-consciousness of this new historical agent was curiously impaired as a result of the epochal break that plunged the rhetorical system into oblivion, at the same time that it brought the educational system within the control of these new agents. The new class of knowers was in possession of greater knowledge than all the generations of its predecessors, but at the price of understanding less well than ever the process of learning, the relation between art and information. Nowhere is this perplexity more evident or consequential than in the knowledge worker's relation to the arts of language, so often marked by inarticulate speech and an alienated relation to writing. These ancient arts stretch beneath and across all the fields of knowledge as their common cognitive foundation. Every other cognitive art is built on these foundations, and yet no other social group in history has exhibited a less knowing relation to the arts by which it communicates its knowledge than our contemporary knowledge workers.

CHAPTER 6

Two Failed Disciplines

Belles Lettres and Philology

"English" has never really defined itself as a discipline.
WILLIAM RILEY PARKER, "Where Do
English Departments Come From?"

FROM ARTS TO DISCIPLINES

The title of this chapter might appear to be misleading, as both belles lettres and philology were thriving subjects of study in the Anglo-American university for more than a century. Yet belles lettres is usually dismissed today as a discourse of mere "appreciation," while philology is acknowledged as a ghostly practice that still somehow informs literary scholarship without defining it. By naming these two discourses "failed disciplines," I mean to call attention to the fact that neither succeeded in establishing a permanent institutional form in the university; neither is recognized today as a *discipline*, if by that we mean a subject in which one might take a degree, and which has a bureaucratic base of operations, the *department*.[1]

What features of belles lettres and philology prevented their evolution into permanent disciplines or their institutionalization as departments? This is a question that has yet to be asked about the two discourses *together*, although much has been written about them separately. As they are in many ways the antecedents of vernacular literary study in its current form, it would be useful to consider their relations both to each other and to their successor. This is a question, fundamentally, about the formation of disciplines, the conditions of their emergence. Before the nineteenth century, there were no disciplines in the modern sense; the curriculum consisted of a sequence of *arts*, which dated from antiquity. These were formalized in the medieval trivium of "grammar, rhetoric, and dialectic," although the

---

1. Departments arrived earlier in the American university than in the British, but eventually this institutional form came to dominate both systems and has slowly displaced the European "professorial" structure as well.

number of recognized arts was much larger and included many different kinds of skill or craft. Over the course of the eighteenth century, the concept of "art" was radically revised and restricted to the usage common today, as in the phrase "fine arts."[2] The older sense of the arts survives as an anachronism, in notions such as "liberal arts," "bachelor of arts," or "arts and sciences." The curriculum of the arts had to disappear before it was possible for the curriculum of disciplines to replace it.

The formation of a new conception of art in the specialized sense of "fine art" can be dated precisely in France (though it was not without some precedents) by the publication in 1746 of Charles Batteux's *The Fine Arts Reduced to a Single Principle*. For Batteux, the "fine arts" are five in number—poetry, painting, sculpture, music, and dance—and they have in common the intention to give pleasure.[3] They are distinguished on the one hand from the "mechanical arts," such as carpentry or agriculture, which are based on utility, and on the other hand from those arts that mix pleasure and utility. Among the latter Batteux numbers rhetoric and architecture. The oddity of relegating rhetoric and architecture to the same category is a corollary of this early attempt to segregate what we would call "creative" arts from the multitude of arts in antiquity. Batteux's influential aggregation of the "fine arts" was taken over in Hegel's monumental philosophy of fine art, with the difference only that Hegel substituted architecture for dance; his "system of the arts" remains in force today, as a given that is difficult to think without or around.[4] It is worth recalling how recently this notion of art was devised, as well as the conceptual revolution implied by the exclusion of rhetoric, the highest and most paradigmatic art of antiquity.

I will not discuss further here the decline of the older system of arts, which I have treated in the preceding chapter, "The Postrhetorical Condition." My point of departure in this inquiry is the fact that belles lettres and philology belong neither to the older curriculum of the arts nor to the

---

2. This is a great theme of Raymond Williams's work. For instance, see *Culture and Society, 1870–1950* (London: Chatto and Windus, 1958): "An *art* had formerly been any human skill; but *Art*, now, signified a particular group of skills, the 'imaginative' or 'creative' art" (xv).

3. Charles Batteux, *The Fine Arts Reduced to a Single Principle*, trans. James O. Young (Oxford: Oxford University Press, 2015). See especially chapter 6, "Why Eloquence and Architecture Differ from the Other Arts," 22–25.

4. Paul Oskar Kristeller, "The Modern System of the Arts: A Study in the History of Aesthetics," *Journal of the History of Ideas* 12 (1951): 496–527; and Kristeller, "The Modern System of the Arts: A Study in the History of Aesthetics (II)," *Journal of the History of Ideas* 13 (1952): 17–46. D'Alembert's *Encyclopédie, ou dictionnaire raisonné des sciences, des arts, et des métiers* (1751–72) effectively archives many of the older arts at the moment of their reconceptualization as what we now call "technology."

current system of disciplines. Belles lettres does, however, have a certain relation to the concept of "fine art" signaled in the qualifier "belles," which, as we shall see, underlies the concerns of philology too, if more obliquely. In retrospect, belles lettres and philology look like transitional discourses, emerging in the gap between the university of arts and the university of disciplines; their main point of commonality, despite the differences between them, is their transitional status, which only discloses its meaning fully when vernacular literary study crystallizes in the twentieth century as a discipline.

I propose to open an inquiry into the problem of these transitional or protodisciplinary forms of study by way of a small philological exercise, drawn from a moment in Hugh Blair's famous work of the later eighteenth century, *Lectures on Rhetoric and Belles Lettres*, published in 1783.[5] Blair drew heavily on lectures of the same title given by Adam Smith two decades earlier, one iteration of which Blair attended. Those lectures were not published until the twentieth century, but Blair's book was an instant success and widely used as a teaching text through the nineteenth century, running to more than one hundred editions. The coupling of rhetoric with belles lettres is a strong hint as to the transitional nature of this subject in both Smith and Blair. Rhetoric was a legacy of immense prestige, still a dominant university subject in the eighteenth century. Belles lettres, on the other hand, was a new subject, and it leaned on the authority of rhetoric for its introduction into the curriculum. Initially, it is not the difference between them but their common features that Blair emphasizes; he tells us in the opening pages of his *Lectures* that "the study of Rhetoric and Belles Lettres supposes and requires a proper acquaintance with the rest of the liberal arts" (4). The inclusive note seems to look backward to the university of arts rather than forward to the university of disciplines. Rhetoric knows no boundaries such as establish the disciplines as distinct and sovereign domains of knowledge; its freedom to range over all the fields of learning is restrained only by its dedication to the singular task of forming the orator. Yet the making of an orator could not really serve as the mission of eighteenth-century education as it did for education in antiquity. Blair's society was too far along in the development of specialized fields of knowledge, most of them remote from the scene of oratory, if not yet organized as university disciplines.

Blair praises the orator as a figure of consummate learning, that is, *not a specialist*: "Hence, among the ancients, it was a fundamental principle,

5. Hugh Blair, *Lectures on Rhetoric and Belles Lettres*, ed. Linda Ferreira-Buckley and S. Michael Halloran (Carbondale: Southern Illinois University Press, 2005).

and frequently inculcated, 'Quod omnibus disciplinis et artibus debet esse instructus orator,'" which Blair translates in the next clause as "that the orator ought to be an accomplished scholar, and conversant in every part of learning" (4). The Latin phrase is drawn from Quintilian's *Institutio oratoria*, but Blair's loose translation raises a question about the extent to which Quintilian *can* be translated. Blair renders *artibus instructus* as "accomplished scholar" and *omnibus disciplina* as "conversant in every part of learning." The disappearance of Quintilian's term, *ars*, is one moment in the long history of relegating the older system of arts to oblivion. *Disciplina* too resists its straightforward English equivalent. Quintilian's words are hard to recover through the filter of Blair's translation, yet the history of Western education can be summed up with these two words: *from arts to disciplines*. When disciplines finally colonized the institutional space of the university, they established the "parts of learning" as sovereign territories, permanent specializations. The disciplines made it possible for the university to maintain its historical mission of credentialing professions, but no longer restricted to the "ancient" professions of law, medicine, and theology. Disciplinarization became the requisite for new forms of expertise to advance to the status of professions, with all the advantages attached to that title. By means of this strategy, the disciplines remade education and remade the world.[6]

In this new world, as we saw in chapter 5, the situation of rhetoric was uncertain, despite many efforts to translate it into vernacular terms. If the fate of the arts themselves, in the older sense of that word, was caught up in that failure, then Blair's effort to translate Quintilian was sure to encounter the same cultural headwinds facing other rhetoricians of the period. The "parts of learning" were in flux; many new fields of study were unrepresented in the university curriculum, which was still dominated by Greek and Latin. As the study of belles lettres gained momentum, it effectively reorganized the field of "letters," but the qualifier "beautiful," as we shall see, was in the end too narrow to characterize the variety of genres comprehended by belles lettres. In the narrative that I shall offer here, the effort to "reduce" the field of writing to a single principle, as Batteux hoped to reduce the "fine arts," was frustrated by the irreducible diversity of the forms

6. For a comment on the word *discipline* and its history, see James Turner, *Philology: The Forgotten Origins of the Modern Humanities* ((Princeton, NJ: Princeton University Press, 2014). Turner notes that the sense of "branch of learning" comes into English in the later Middle Ages but that this fact "obscures the novelty of the new kind of disciplinary specialization that appeared in the nineteenth century" (232). He also observes rightly that this development was connected with the emergence of a "professionalizing ethos" (232).

of writing. Still, the effort itself had consequences for the development of the disciplines down to the twentieth century for as long as belles lettres continued to have a presence of some sort in university teaching.

In the context of the history of the disciplines, or rather their prehistory, the compound title of the lectures by Smith and Blair begins to speak volumes. What lack in rhetoric is being supplemented by belles lettres? What lack in belles lettres is being compensated by the invocation of rhetoric? In light of these questions, the enterprise of belles lettres looks more interesting than the discourse we dismiss today as mere effusion; it is more revelatory of eighteenth-century conditions of knowledge than we might have supposed. The moment of this discourse needs to be understood, above all, in the context of vernacularization, the translation of antiquity's art of rhetoric into a modern equivalent—or better, a *nonequivalent*. The name for this nonequivalent is the hybrid "rhetoric and belles lettres," a popular subject for more than a century but never achieving the institutional status of a discipline.

BELLES LETTRES

As a borrowing from French, belles lettres confirms that the progress of vernacularization in England followed a path laid down across the channel, and generally, this precedence is characteristic of Restoration culture until the later eighteenth century.[7] The bigram "belles lettres" can be found occasionally in the seventeenth century, but its most influential deployment was by Charles Rollin, who published between 1726 and 1728 the four volumes of *De la Manière d'enseigner et d'étudier les belles lettres, pour rapport à l'esprit et au coeur*. Rollin's study was translated anonymously into English in 1734 as *The Method of Teaching and Studying the Belles Lettres, or An Introduction to Languages, Poetry, Rhetoric, History, Moral Philosophy, Physicks, etc.* Although other importations of the term occur, it is Rollin and his translator who established the idea of belles lettres as a course of study in England. Commenting on this episode in his *Eighteenth-Century British Logic and Rhetoric*, Wilbur Samuel Howell observes that the reception of Rollin's work made belles lettres into an "English term," adding that "English vocabulary had no single native word or phrase for that particular

---

7. For an exhaustive lexicographical account of the term "*belles lettres*" in France, see Philippe Caron, *Des "Belles lettres" à la "littérature": une archéologie des signes du savoir profane en langue française (1680–1760)* (Paris: Diffusion Peeters, 1992). In Carron's account, the stabilization of the term "literature" in a more restricted signification was achieved by 1780, a little sooner than was the case in England.

entity" (533). Samuel Johnson accepted the term into his dictionary, where he defined it as "polite literature." Blair embraced the concept of belles lettres in the title for his appointment as "Regius Professor of Rhetoric and Belles Lettres" at the University of Edinburgh. By the time he published his lectures in 1783, the notion of belles lettres was thoroughly anglicized and appeared in the title of an increasing number of courses in educational institutions.

If the coupling of rhetoric with belles lettres marks a transitional moment in the history of vernacular education, the point I would like first to emphasize is the way in which belles lettres gathers together so many genres of writing under the qualifier "belles." This epithet seems only roughly to characterize the discourses in Rollin's treatise or the English translation. In French culture, "belles lettres" makes a distinction within the broader field of learning, or "letters," between writing of greater and lesser value.[8] In English, Johnson's "polite" is perhaps closer to an accurate descriptor for the forms of writing comprehended, stretching from the study of classical and vernacular "languages" to "moral philosophy," the former seeking to impose standards for speaking and writing, the latter attempting to establish standards for behavior. These concerns resist reduction to a notion of the "beautiful." This qualification is equally true for Rollin's French; in his treatise, the pages allotted to poetry, which we might expect to anchor an aesthetic conception of the field of belles lettres, are relatively few. The larger part of the treatise is devoted to *history* (Rollin was a historian), reminding us that belles lettres is more or less equivalent to the genres of literature judged to be serious in the eighteenth century: poetry, history, eloquence (orations), and moral philosophy. The qualifier "belles" seems to function as a placeholder for what these discourses have in common.

Belles lettres does exclude some kinds of writing: medical and legal treatises, theological and devotional writing, most of the writing we would now call "scientific," as well as the vast profusion of periodical writing such as newspaper reportage. These exclusions establish belles lettres as a domain that is more restricted than the sense of "literature" as any writing whatsoever, but at the same time larger and more heterogenous than the kinds of writing that later came to shelter under this term. Johnson's "polite literature" suggests an effort to correlate values that span a continuum from correctness in speech and writing at one end to manners and morals at the

---

8. See Rémy G. Saisselin, *The Literary Enterprise in Eighteenth-Century France* (Detroit: Wayne State University Press, 1979): "'Letters' was understood to include all activities of the mind from poetry through the sciences (meaning bodies of knowledge) and theology, a broad view which obtained well into the eighteenth century" (18).

opposite end. The more obviously aesthetic forms of writing (to us, any-
way), such as poetry, bridge these terminal poles, which fold back on each
other in a cryptic reliance on the *policing* of both language and behavior.
"Polite literature" hints at a gentler mode of persuasion than either grammar or morality. Blair captures succinctly this fusion of aesthetic and ethical values when he notes that anyone who elects to study belles lettres "has
always at hand an innocent and irreproachable amusement for his leisure
hours, to save him from the danger of many a pernicious passion" (*Lectures
on Rhetoric and Belles Lettres*, 6). And further: "How then shall these vacant
spaces, these unemployed intervals, which, more or less, occur in the life
of every one, be filled up? How can we contrive to dispose of them in any
way that shall be more agreeable in itself, or more consonant to the dignity
of the human mind, than in the entertainments of taste, and the study of
polite literature?" (8).

A polite society is entitled, then, to exercise judgment upon literary
works according to a principle that only *appears* to be restricted to the
value of beauty: "The public ear is become refined. It will not easily accept
what is slovenly and incorrect. Every author must aspire to some merit in
expression, as well as in sentiment, if he would not incur the danger of being neglected and despised" (6). The last clause of Blair's sentence reveals
what is at stake in these values for authors: their survival. For the writers
of antiquity, selection was accomplished by time itself, but for eighteenth-
century culture, the accumulation of writing in the vernacular was far too
rapid to await the judgment of time. Selection had to be undertaken force-
fully and in the present. Here another concept emerges from behind the
placeholder notion of beauty: *taste*. It is only on the basis of "taste" that
a selection of the best examples of vernacular writing can be made. Taste
inheres in the selection of writing, but it is also the *effect* of belles lettres as
a program of study; the person of taste, or the "man of letters," is the figure
in eighteenth-century society who corresponds to the orator in antiquity.
Rhetoric itself is infused with the value of taste, which was virtually unknown to the rhetoricians of antiquity. Latin had no word corresponding to
the metaphorized sense of English "taste" or French "*goût*." The coupling of
belles lettres with rhetoric permits Blair and his contemporaries to *transmit*
rhetoric by translating it into these vernacular values and so redeeming it
from the aspersions against it that had been circulating for more than a century. Nothing confirms this strategy more strikingly than the ubiquity with
which the notion of taste was promoted in the "rhetoric and belles lettres"
courses of the period.

The subject of taste has been of perennial interest to scholars, and for
that reason, I intend here only to underscore its fundamental role in belles

lettres. The program of belles lettres transformed rhetoric in the process of translating it. In recognizing taste as a value, we must also recognize its filiation with a discourse that is at once adjacent to belles lettres but also a condition of possibility for the aestheticization of manners and morals in notions such as "taste" or the "polite." This discourse is "moral philosophy." Moral philosophy is increasingly distinct from natural philosophy during this period, a development reflected in the fact that the topics engaging eighteenth-century philosophers were relatively more specialized than those of the previous century. Figures such as Bacon or Descartes straddled both domains of natural and moral philosophy, but that scope is becoming less possible. Belles lettres itself is a driver of this separation (or its effect?), as Philippe Caron argues in Des "Belles lettres" à la "littérature." Despite the tendency of moral philosophy and natural philosophy to drift apart, they were recognized as *equally* modern ways of thinking about the kinds of knowledge, equally empirical in their orientation, and indeed, these two discourses became the seedbed of future disciplines.[9] Looking back on this long durational tendency of the organization of knowledge, the close relation between belles lettres and moral philosophy seems obvious enough. It was not surprising that belles lettres received such a strong impetus from Adam Smith, who can best be described as a moral philosopher, though his works ranged widely across fields that later solidified into distinct disciplines. Belles lettres looks less marginal from this perspective, as Smith's interest in the subject resonates with his strategy of invoking aesthetic categories in making social or ethical arguments.[10]

The notion of taste was also closely allied to a genre of writing that had been circulating in the sphere of periodical publication: "criticism." This

9. Thomas P. Miller, *The Formation of College English: Rhetoric and Belles Lettres in the British Cultural Provinces* (Pittsburgh: Pittsburgh University Press, 1997), 230, notes that Blair chose "belles lettres" for its "modern sound."

10. I have made an argument about the importance of the aesthetic in Smith's work in *Cultural Capital: The Problem of Literary Canon Formation* (Chicago: University of Chicago Press, 1993). Recent work on rhetoric in the eighteenth century tends to see the movement from rhetoric to belles lettres as a turn from an engaged political discourse to a less engaged investment in the aesthetic. My sense of this question is that we are seeing in the eighteenth century, as Marx understood, a transition from a status society in which all social relations have a "directly political" character to one in which the domains of the political and the aesthetic begin to appear as distinct. For views of rhetoric and belles lettres in recent scholarship, see Court, *Institutionalizing English Literature*; Court, *The Scottish Connection*; Miller, *The Formation of College English*; Miller, *Literacy Studies from the Puritans to the Postmoderns* (Pittsburgh, PA: Pittsburgh University Press, 2010); Robert Crawford, ed., *The Scottish Invention of Literature* (Cambridge: Cambridge University Press, 1998).

discourse was itself little more than a century old; it originated in the lively culture of Restoration theater, not surprisingly in imitation of the French court.[11] Beginning as nothing more than conversation among the elite auditors of Restoration plays, criticism was ushered into print by Dryden with his "Essay of Dramatic Poesy" and with the prologues and epilogues to his own and others' plays. It was primarily concerned with the judgment of *new* works, although the standards applied to these new works were commonly supposed to be derived from the model of the ancients.

Throughout the eighteenth century, a close relation obtained between the practice of criticism and moral philosophy.[12] Most conspicuously, criticism gave rise to the problem of judgment associated with the famous debate between "the ancients and the moderns." The judgment of new work in vernacular literature became the occasion for the development of principles of judgment that extended to the whole of society, as though a society could be judged like a poem or a play. The criticism of the period can seem shallow to us today, egregiously prescriptive, but its problems crossed over into important debates on social and political themes among philosophers such as Shaftesbury, Hutcheson, Hume, and Smith. Their systemic reflections on "human nature" in turn provided criticism with increasingly sophisticated terms for describing the process of judgment. This two-way exchange was enabled by the fact that belles lettres and moral philosophy were alike dedicated to the end of refining conduct or of disseminating "polite" manners.[13]

Belles lettres, then, insofar as it was a discourse of taste, was at the same time a version of criticism; it was an attempt to return criticism to the very "philosophy" Addison brought out of the schools. Belles lettres was a way of systematizing judgment across a range of writing genres. If criticism mainly took the form of the periodical essay, belles lettres was instituted in the university as a course of lectures, often in association with moral philosophy. Such lectures were typically offered as a culminating recreative experience

11. On the origins of criticism in the theater milieu of the Restoration, see Michael Gavin, *The Invention of English Criticism, 1650–1760* (Cambridge: Cambridge University Press, 2015).

12. This is evident even for the discourse of criticism, as in Henry Home, Lord Kames's contention in *Elements of Criticism (London: G. Cowie ,1824)* that the fundamental principles of criticism are "drawn from human nature" (15).

13. On this continuity, see Rudolph, *Curriculum*: "Beginning in the 1760s the idea of the 'man of letters' as a proper definition of the college graduate intruded into the curriculum the study of belles lettres—orations, history, poetry, literature. An emphasis on reason and observation, on rational moral behavior, replaced a reliance on divine law in the study of ethics" (53).

for students in their last year or term of study.[14] Even though belles lettres was a university subject, it was in fact a much smaller enterprise than criticism in the periodical sphere. There, criticism was a burgeoning discourse, filling the newspapers and journals that proliferated through the century with reviews of new publications and excerpts from these works. By contrast, the study of vernacular writing remained marginal in the university, a situation that obtained until the later nineteenth century.

If we return again to Rollin, we can see what it means for belles lettres to be on the cusp of a reorganization of knowledge. In Rollin's treatise, belles lettres swallows philosophy whole, both moral philosophy and natural philosophy. Belles lettres at this inaugural moment includes rhetoric, classical languages, philosophy, poetry, and sundry other subjects; it aspires to be a comprehensive system of education. But this ambition is at the same time contradicted by its self-nomination as the field of "beautiful letters." It is obviously not limited by the aesthetic category of the beautiful, but the foregrounding of an aesthetic concept had unintended effects down the line. Eventually, the domain of belles lettres contracted to correspond more closely to the aesthetic genres. By the time that Blair composed his lectures, the field of belles lettres had settled into an aggregation of genres closer to what we mean by "literature" today, though still not quite there. These genres included poetry, drama, essay, sermons, orations, and history. Blair devotes only one lecture to philosophical writing, mainly addressed to genres such as dialogue. His discussion is oddly perfunctory and deviates in the end to a consideration of "fictitious history" (meaning romances and novels) that betrays his real interest in forms of writing closer to the literary. Both Smith and Blair struggled with the novel, for reasons that are highly interesting and related to the instability and anachronism of the generic categories available to them. New forms of writing such as the novel were resistant to the categories of the genre system of antiquity, which endured long beyond its utility. Belles lettres opened the door, ever so slightly, to the novel under the guise of "fictitious history," but it would take another turn of the screw (or several such turns) to grasp the diversity of vernacular writing in any way systematically. In the meantime, the default setting for judgment was always Greek and Latin writing, from which belles lettres attempted to derive principles for judgment of the vernacular.

14. See Rudolph, *Curriculum*, on the development of moral philosophy into the culminating senior course in the American university: "Developing into a kind of capstone course that was wonderfully reassuring in its insistence on the unity of knowledge and the benevolence of God, moral philosophy by the mid-eighteenth century had achieved a dominance over logic, divinity and metaphysics in the course of study" (39).

If belles lettres dropped away from the march to the disciplines, it left behind the category of "literature," as writing potentially defining a new aggregation of writing. Belles lettres was a bridge between the older sense of literature, meaning *all forms of writing*, and its new aggregation as *aesthetic forms of writing*—poetry, drama, essay, and, later, Blair's "fictitious history."

Beneath the mutations of these categories is always the steady pressure of the vernacular. In this context, we can recognize a second agenda of belles lettres in addition to the cultivation of taste. This is its orientation toward vernacular writing *as such*. We might think of belles lettres as one side of a kind of seesaw of emphases. As the burden of rhetoric lightened, along with its notional orality, belles lettres could press down on the practice of writing. The signature of this emphasis is the emergence of another dominant concept in belles lettres: *style*. This concept was imported from the old rhetoric, with some substantive changes: the word "style" was the favored translation of *elocutio*, that part of rhetoric constituting an archive of techniques—the figures of speech—by means of which language could be ornamented and infused with passion. But the concept of "style" emergent in Smith, Blair, and their contemporaries was, as we would expect, as much transformation as translation. Style was the counterweight on the balance of values to the notion of *eloquence* as a notionally oral practice. Although ambiguously a genre of both speech and writing, the *oration* was the premier genre of rhetoric, always imagined as spoken, even when only encountered as a text. The oration, however, was not the genre in reference to which belles lettres developed its conception of style. What we see in Smith and Blair, despite their dutiful discussion of orations, is their much greater interest in a new genre: the *essay*. This genre, not the oration, became the vehicle for developing norms of style; again, belles lettres effected a transformation of rhetoric.

As we know, Addison and Steele were frequently invoked as models for fine writing or style in the later eighteenth century. This turn to vernacular models of writing is conspicuous in belles lettres and helps to make sense of the enormous publishing success of Addison and Steele in the later eighteenth century—far greater success, in fact than *The Tatler* and *The Spectator* achieved in their moment. Addison and Steele's periodical essays expressed and disseminated the values of both taste and style at the same time that they also projected these values into social life. It would be fair to say that the essay continued to be dedicated to these values throughout the century. The essay did the boundary work of belles lettres, moderating the enforcement of polite values by submitting them to a gentle aestheticization. Insofar as the essay accomplished this task, it began to redraw the boundaries of literature too. It is one of the great ironies of literary history that the essay, as a literary form, later fell out of the domain of canonical transmission.[15] The essay form survives into the present, but for the most part as the signature genre of belletrism, a form of "light" literature.

Both belles lettres and the essay genre must be seen in retrospect as powerful agents of vernacularization, encroaching upon the seniority of Latin and Greek writers in the curriculum. With the essay, a pedagogy emerged that was specific to writing in the vernacular. This pedagogy of course recycled much from the program of the old rhetoric, but within it, writing began to supplant the notional orality of eloquence. A good example of how this writing pedagogy worked can be seen in President William Samuel Johnson's description of his course on "Rhetoric and Belles Lettres," given in 1792 in Columbia College. President Johnson set out to instruct students in "the grammar and proper pronunciation of the English Language" out of various texts, and in belles lettres "on the plan of Blair's Lectures." His aim was to convey "the rules and principles of every species of eloquence—the principles of true taste and the rules of just criticism, whereby the students may be enabled to judge properly of each species of composition in every branch of elegant literature, and that they may apply the whole to practice each student is obliged, every Saturday, to deliver him a composition, in which he corrects the errors, either in orthography, grammar, style or sentiment, and makes the necessary observations on them when he returns the composition to the writer."[16] This was a final-year course, which accounts in part for the unusual attention paid to writing. Most teaching still relied primarily on oral "recitation" and evaluation; the use of writing in this course was forward-looking. Unfortunately, what the course anticipated in the next century was a narrower focus on "grammar" than was ever intended by the concept of style. At the end of this road was "freshman English."

If belles lettres failed to achieve disciplinary status, this outcome was in part the result of a resurgent investment in the classical curriculum in the latter half of the nineteenth century, something that would have been hard to anticipate in Blair's day. But even taking account of this later reversion to Greek and Latin, it is striking that belles lettres itself never established more than a marginal place in the curriculum. Its broad mix of writing genres prevented it from achieving the focus necessary for a discipline. The rhythm of expansion and contraction that characterized its history did not settle down on the one candidate for disciplinary object to which it seemed

15. See the important study by Brian McCrea, *Addison and Steele Are Dead.*
16. Louis Franklin Snow, citing Johnson, *The College Curriculum in the United States,* 97.

to gesture: *literature*. The future belonged to other new disciplines, which succeeded by trading scope of study for intensity of focus. And yet the practice described in President Johnson's senior course also tells us why the aims of belles lettres never disappeared entirely from literary study. It is still the case that literary education is widely seen by the "laity" as tasked with upholding English grammar and imparting an appreciation of great works of literature. This is not wrong, but it is not adequate as a conception of literary education. For this very reason, belles lettres remains a repressed antecedent to literary study as we know it.

PHILOLOGY

The trajectory of belles lettres in Britain was determined to a great extent by its French provenance. Its decline in the nineteenth century was exacerbated by a concurrent scholarly development, which emerged in Germany and was unrelated to the conditions of the French discourse. This was the apparent success of a new discipline—philology—along with the important concept of "culture" correlated with this study. The notion of culture, which requires preliminary consideration before turning to philology, ought to have converged with the aims of belles lettres, but by the later nineteenth century, the reputation of belles lettres had fallen too far to sustain such an alliance. Championing the concept of culture, Matthew Arnold was forced to confront this problem when one of his antagonists, Frederic Harrison, remarked in print that talk of "culture" was "the silliest cant of the day" and "sits well on a possessor of belles lettres."[17] In truth, belles lettres differed from the program of culture in falling short of the socially transformative claims so often made by its German idealist advocates, of reconciling the division of the head from the heart in modern civilization. Nor did culture succeed in establishing an extrapolitical basis for social harmony as Arnold hoped.

The difficulty of integrating the ideal of culture into British (and also American) education requires that we acknowledge a large divergence in the developmental trajectories of the German and Anglo-American universities. For figures such as Humboldt, Schiller, Schleiermacher, and Fichte, culture, in the pedagogic form of *Bildung*, was to be concretely realized in a new kind of university. The program of culture had state approval in Humboldt's famous plan for the University of Berlin. As there was no

---

17. Matthew Arnold, *Culture and Anarchy and Other Writings*, ed. Stefan Collini (Cambridge: Cambridge University Press, 1993), 55. Harrison is quoted from the preface by Collini.

analogous institutional project in England, Arnold transplanted culture, as it were, into the air. Neither in Britain nor America did the university adopt the rationale of culture or translate its program into curricular form. Even in the German university, the ideal of culture far exceeded the social possibilities of that institution, as Habermas observes in an important essay on the reformers of the German university: "Taking the perspective of an idealist philosophy of reconciliation, they attributed to the university a power of totalization that necessarily overburdened this institution from the beginning."[18] The attempt at a top-down reformation of the national culture was doomed to fail, whatever the merits of *Bildung*, because the reformers did not understand the limits of the university as an institution, nor could they predict its turn to other aims in the future.[19]

Habermas's comment on the idealist origins of the German university reminds us that the project of culture was always linked to the development of the nation-state and that culture, despite its invocation of universalist values, was to be realized in the form of *national* culture. The ideal of culture emerged in Prussia in part because the German principalities lagged behind other European nations in their consolidation into a nation-state. The university provided an opportunity to promote this goal, and so to establish a national culture in preference to the importation of French *civilité*. While supporters of the German *Kulturstaat* may have been eager to sponsor the university for this reason, nothing like such a project was called for in either Britain or the United States; in neither country was the university seen as the agent for producing national culture.[20] In addition to its longstanding function of training the ministry, the Anglo-American university was primarily devoted to investing a ruling elite of the aristocracy and the *haute bourgeoisie* with a distinct cultural capital. The concept of culture as

18. Jürgen Habermas, *The New Conservatism: Cultural Criticism and the Historians' Debate*, ed. and trans. Shierry Weber Nicholsen (Cambridge: MIT Press, 1989), 108.

19. On this subject, see Ringer, *Decline of the German Mandarins*.

20. This question complicates the otherwise valuable argument made by Bill Readings in his *The University in Ruins* (Cambridge, MA: Harvard University Press, 1996). Readings supposes that the old university of "culture" descends from Humboldt to recent times and that the Humboldtian university has been demolished (ruined) by the emergence of the new university of "excellence," whose normative principles derive from corporate managerialism. Already in the first decades of the twentieth century, however, Thorstein Veblen complained that the imposition of corporate values and practices on the American university was pervasive. See *The Higher Learning in America: A Memorandum on the Conduct of Universities by Business Men* (New York: B. W. Huebsch, 1918). The notion of "excellence" has been recurrently popular in public statements of the university's mission. Touraine, in *The Academic System in American Society*, remarks on its prevalence in the 1920s (71).

a national project did not successfully penetrate discourse about the university until much later. In America, this did not happen until after the first world war, with the emergence of "general education."

If the concept of *Kultur* was only marginally important in the development of the Anglo-American university, the German university successfully transmitted a much more powerful ideal to its Anglo-American counterparts: *research*. In the German system, state sponsorship of scholarly research was justified because the ideal of culture was supposed to be realized through the teaching of the most distinguished scholars. Culture was linked from the first with the production of new knowledge, and not with the acquisition of taste, as in Britain or France. In this one respect, the German university was more forward-looking than its Anglo-American counterparts, which by no means combined at this time the two functions of teaching and producing new knowledge. As I have argued, we should speak of "disciplines" in the modern sense as the institutional form uniting teaching and research functions in the university. Previously university professors may not have pursued scholarship at all, and if they did, their scholarship might be unrelated to their university teaching. Thomas Warton, for example, professor of poetry at Oxford in the eighteenth century and author of the first major history of poetry in England, lectured on Greek and Latin literature. The unity of teaching and research in the German university, on the other hand, implied that teaching could translate new knowledge into culture: *Bildung durch Wissenschaft*.

Belief in the necessity of new knowledge and the cultural effects of disseminating this knowledge sustained a powerful if temporary rapprochement between what Wilhelm Dilthey later posited as the distinct metadisciplinary templates of *Naturwissenschaft* and *Geisteswissenschaft*. Knowledge of nature and knowledge of humankind were enclosed within the overarching program of culture, as defined by the philosophers. By the later nineteenth century, however, as Habermas further notes, "The empirical sciences that sprang from the womb of the philosophical faculty pursued a methodological ideal of procedural rationality that doomed to failure any effort to situate their contents encyclopedically within an all-encompassing philosophical interpretation" (113). The ideal of scientific research thus overtook and displaced the pedagogic aims of culture when the "empirical sciences" came to represent that ideal exclusively. This displacement was all the more striking, given the fact that prior to the nineteenth century very little research in what we would now call "natural science" was pursued in the university. On the other hand, all the scholarly discourses that developed into what we now call the "humanities" were just as likely as the natural sciences to consider themselves empirical, but to call these disciplines "humanities" is of course anachronistic, as our understanding of the disciplines presupposes the distinction between the humanities and the sciences emergent in the twentieth century.[21] At the moment in which the disciplines were born, they were still comprehended within philosophy, with its two wings, moral and natural.

One of the protohumanistic empirical sciences within this faculty can in retrospect be identified as crucially mediating the relation between *Naturwissenschaft* and *Geisteswissenschaft*. This science was philology.[22] As we know, something called philology existed in antiquity, in the etymological sense of the love and study of language. There was also a long tradition of classical philology extending from the "textual criticism" of the Renaissance humanists to Vico and thence to Friedrich August Wolf's famous seminar on Homer in the later eighteenth century, which established the very form in which disciplines would unite teaching and research. This innovation supported the scope of philology, which was initially no less broad than belles lettres. At this moment, the primacy of research compensated for the breadth of subjects in philology, which might otherwise have prevented philology from achieving disciplinary status. In the event, philology became the *first discipline*, the model for all subsequent disciplines in the university. The fact that there is no autonomous discipline of philology in the university today is all the more surprising, then, especially in the context of the relation between philology and the "modern language" disciplines that were established in the later nineteenth-century American university.

Although one might date the academic inauguration of philology to Wolf's seminar and the publication in 1795 of his *Prolegomena to Homer*, what has come to be called "modern philology" emerged with the extension of language research to vernacular languages and their origins in the East, in Sanskrit and the hypothetical Indo-European. The pivot to the East was made in the 1780s by Sir William Jones, but the development of this version of vernacular philology into a disciplinary form was accom-

21. For a commentary on the sense of *Wissenschaft*, see David Hollinger, "The Knower and the Artificer," in *Modernist Impulses in the Human Sciences*, ed. Ross, 88.

22. Philology in the sense of the "study (or love) of language" is of course an old concept, appearing in both Greek and Latin texts, and importantly in medieval works as well (Martianus Capella's *The Marriage of Mercury and Philology*, for example). In the Renaissance, the humanists developed a "philological" method for the study of classical literature and the Bible. Philology developed new techniques for determining authorship and establishing reliable texts. The most important point to recall about this earlier history is the orientation of philology to texts. This was to change with modern philology, which undertook to recover the history of living, spoken language, and in which documents had a different role to play.

plished by Bopp, Rask, and the brothers Grimm—to name only the most prominent figures. Philology's status as a discourse of knowledge was further solidified by Wilhelm von Humboldt, who produced major works of comparative philology, as well as the famous plan for the University of Berlin. By giving nations a cultural origin in a common language, philology effectively fused the philosophical concept of culture with that of *ethnos*. As capacious as this notion seems, it exerted a pressure on philology that resulted in its increasing specialization over the course of the nineteenth century to the history of particular languages. In the case of "English" philology, the discipline crystallized into a narrow set of concerns by the end of the century, with consequences we will note.

The grounding of philology in the connection between language and *ethnos* translated the German idealist program into an empirical discipline, which grew rapidly and endured for more than a hundred years.[23] Insofar as the philological method strongly affected research protocols in the other disciplines we now call the "humanities"—classics, history, philosophy, literature—it brought these courses of study into a close relation to current standards of scientific knowledge at the same time that it unified scholarly enterprises within a total view of the history of civilization.[24] One might invoke in this context Johann Gottfried Herder's work on folk cultures, or Hegel's philosophy of "universal history" in which the development of "spirit" is embodied in the *Volksgeist* of particular nations, to confirm the paradigmatic status of philology among the disciplines.

In his account of the rise of philology, Hans Aarsleff remarks its status as "the model humanistic discipline" which was also "factual, descriptive, classificatory, empirical, and comparative."[25] Further, its identity as an em-

23. See Hans Aarsleff, *The Study of Language in England, 1780–1860* (Minneapolis: University of Minnesota Press, 1967), 171, for a comment on the relation between language study and ethnos in the context of the recovery of Anglo-Saxon.

24. I believe that James Turner is correct when he asserts that philology is the origin of the humanities, the thesis stated in the subtitle of *Philology*. I differ somewhat from his enumeration of the humanities, as I would not exclude philosophy from their number. It seems to me that the influence of philology on philosophers from Hegel to Nietzsche to Heidegger is immense, and justifies the inclusion of both in the humanities.

25. Hans Aarsleff, *From Locke to Saussure: Essays on the Study of Language and Intellectual History* (Minneapolis: University of Minnesota Press, 1982), 32. It is well known that philology was beaten back as the dominant faction of English departments during the first decades of the twentieth century, a fate that was sealed in the United States by the hostility of New Criticism. René Wellek and Austin Warren deliver a death blow in their *Theory of Literature*, 3rd ed. (New York: Harcourt, Brace, 1968), complaining somewhat disingenuously that philology's scope was too great to constitute a discipline, and that, since "the term has so many and divergent meanings, it is best to abandon it"

pirical discipline was never perceived as incompatible with its reliance on archival or textual evidence. On the contrary, philology and related historical discourses arguably advanced a more plausible claim to empirical standards of verification than earlier arguments in moral philosophy, which often seemed speculative by comparison.[26] Historical research did not necessarily require the kind of epistemological defense against skeptical questioning that Kant sought to provide for morality or aesthetics. Throughout the nineteenth century, in fact, historical discourses made empirical claims equal in strength to those of natural science. History, in the view of Leopold von Ranke and his followers, established *facts*. It was also on the basis of facts that philology sought to establish *laws* governing linguistic change. In retrospect, however, this mode of argument deferred certain theoretical questions raised by the interpretation of textual evidence.

These textual questions—which were articulated under the rubric of the "hermeneutic"—arose most urgently at the juncture between interpretation of the Bible and rigorous research into the history behind biblical narrative, but the truth of literary or "fictional" texts troubled philology even more acutely.[27] Philology might be said to combine the study of language and literature, but in a manner very different from belles lettres. If philology studied the textual traces that constituted evidence for hypotheses about language, the true object of study was the living language that loomed behind the textual evidence. This object was different from the use of language in both works of literature and in oral performances of rhetoric. The new philologists wanted to capture the living language as it was

---

(38). But this charge misses first, philology's entitlement to the status of a discipline, its empirical methodology, and second, the steadily narrowing focus of philology in the latter half of the nineteenth century, up to the 1920s. By this point, philology had long ceased to be the universal discipline it appeared to be at the time of Humboldt. Wellek repeats his complaint about philology in a review of Erich Auerbach's *Mimesis*, "Auerbach's Special Realism," *Kenyon Review* 16 (1954), 299–307. See also Lee Patterson's negotiation of the two tendencies of philology, "The Return to Philology," in *The Past and Future of Medieval Studies*, ed. John V. Engen (Notre Dame, IN: University of Notre Dame Press, 1994), 231–44. See also Sean Gurd, ed., *Philology and Its Histories* (Columbus: Ohio State University Press, 2010).

26. Note here the difference between the eighteenth-century debate about the "origin of language," which was a major topos for moral philosophy, and the very different arguments in philology about the origins of European languages.

27. Hermeneutics, as the formal practice of determining a text's meaning, is conventionally said to originate in the writing of Friedrich Schleiermacher. For an argument tracing the major questions of literary theory to hermeneutics, see Andrew Bowie, *From Romanticism to Critical Theory: The Philosophy of German Literary Theory* (London: Routledge, 1997).

really spoken, *without art*. This language had its own history, developing internally as well as by interaction with other languages (hence the necessity of "comparative" research). The living language was above all *spoken*. When philology broke free of the textualism inherited from its humanist precursors, the whole noisy world of language came into view, articulate sounds with a history. The relation between language and literature was thereby unsettled. "Modern philology" came into its own by relegating literature to a subordinate object; the containment of literature was part of philology's boundary work.

With its object so defined, philology was able to defend its claim to scientific status through the end of the nineteenth century and beyond, and even to erect its theories alongside the powerful monument of Darwinian biology, as in the work of Max Müller. In *The Order of Things*, Michel Foucault presents this fact as nothing other than an expression of the "episteme." Philology, biology, and economics rose to dominance together as the "sciences of man" by developing analogous techniques of historical interpretation, the object of which might be the traces of Indo-European in modern languages, the fossil record, or the genealogy of the concept of "value" (Foucault sees Marx's *Capital*, for example, as a historical "exegesis" of the value concept.)[28] Darwin's invocation of linguistic evolution as an analogue for natural selection, and Müller's echoing of the analogy in reverse, supports this argument to some extent. But unlike philology, neither biology nor economics disappeared in the twentieth century, an outcome Foucault does not go on to explain. The decline of philology is a puzzling fact, given its former status as a science. Aarsleff calls philology "an aberration" in the history of language study.

This decline is all the more surprising because philology's esteem among the *Geisteswissenschaften* was instrumental in establishing the ideal of research in the university. The humanistic disciplines roused the university from its dogmatic slumber by calling upon it to take up the production of new knowledge and by attracting state sponsorship for this task.[29] The humanists themselves undertook to bring the natural philosophers into the university. The association was at first to their advantage, but it also meant that humanistic scholarship had to sustain its identification with empirical science at a time of rapid advances in the natural sciences and in techno-

28. Michel Foucault, *The Order of Things: An Archaeology of the Human Sciences* (New York: Random House, 1970), 294.

29. Immanuel Wallerstein, *Open the Social Sciences: Report of the Gulbenkian Commission on the Restructuring of the Social Sciences* (Stanford, CA: Stanford University Press, 1997), 8.

logical applications that threw into relief the difference between natural science and the humanistic disciplines.

The convergence of *Kultur* with an inclusive concept of *Wissenschaft* was consequential, if ultimately unstable. In the later decades of the nineteenth century, philology began to move away from the biological analogy popularized by Müller or the alternatively Hegelian version of evolutionist philology espoused by August Schleicher.[30] The earlier version of philology, strongly linked to the program of *Kultur*, came to be regarded as dubious in the light of the "positivist" turn in nineteenth-century science and the rise of more restrictive specifications of scientific method. A second phase of scientific philology, perhaps best represented by the German "neo-grammarians," attempted to set philology on more solidly scientific grounds by focusing strongly on the problem of phonetic change, which could be treated by positing laws; these laws no longer implied any overarching destiny of humankind, or a mission of *Bildung*. The task of "culture" could always be reclaimed by philosophy, but making such large claims came under increasing challenge from the positivistic disciplines.[31]

In England and the United States, the philologists who trained in the German universities of the later nineteenth century returned to their home institutions with a conception of their discipline more than ever prescribed by norms of scientific investigation, as well as by the turn to vernacular languages. When universities and colleges began to organize language disciplines into departments, beginning in the 1870s (Harvard created its language departments in 1872), it was the philologists who determined the direction and orientation of these departments. But the necessity of this development is not so obvious in retrospect, given the fact that "rhetoric and belles lettres" probably numbered a larger cadre of teachers than the philologists. (This cadre is hard to count, however, as most university teachers taught several subjects.) On the other hand, if the growing prestige of science enhanced the position of the philologists, this advantage was really the effect only of a brief conjuncture, the coincidence of a bureaucratic reorganization with the turn to positivistic science.

The dominance of philology in the formation of the new departments of vernacular language study created a peculiar clash of agendas, as well as tension between the highly credentialed professoriate of philologists (often

30. For a brief account of August Schleicher's Hegelianism, see April M. S. Mc-Mahon, *Understanding Language Change* (Cambridge: Cambridge University Press, 1994), 319–21.

31. Ringer, *Decline of the German Mandarins*, on the new meaning of *Bildung*, 296; see also Ringer, *Fields of Knowledge: French Academic Culture in Comparative Perspective, 1890–1920* (Cambridge: Cambridge University Press, 1992), 196–98.

with doctorates from German institutions) and the less credentialed professors teaching classical languages along with rhetoric and belles lettres. This moment has been well documented by Michael Warner, Gerald Graff, and others. As the university relaxed its requirements in Greek and Latin, many of these teachers switched to teaching "English," which meant rhetoric and composition, usually taught through Blair, or other rhetorical theorists, such as George Campbell or Richard Whately. But sometimes English also meant English literature. As we know, the philologists, who embraced the new departmental structure of the American university (in Britain, this would come later), elevated language over literature as a disciplinary object. Because their research could be pursued by means of what was regarded as a scientific method, the moment of departmental organization advantaged the philologists. Why, then, did language and literature not split into different disciplines? This outcome was prevented by the fact that both objects were held together within the unity of language and nation. It was the unity (or ambiguity) of "English" that permitted it ultimately to become the successor to Greek and Latin in the Anglo-American university and thus to advance the horizon of vernacularization.[32] In retrospect, belles lettres and philology competed to drive this process, pitting language and literature in opposition to each other as alternatives to the classical curriculum. There were even sporadic attempts to separate language from literature bureaucratically (the University of Wisconsin, for example, instituted separate departments of rhetoric and philology in 1876), but these proved unsatisfactory, despite the philologists' insistence on the distinction between the science of philology and the (belletristic) study of literature.[33]

The continuity of the early "modern language" departments with the discipline of literary study in its current form is belied by the marginalization of literature in the nineteenth-century disciplinary field. One need only return to the first volumes of the *Transactions of the Modern Language Association* to confirm how thoroughly the public self-presentation of the language departments, and the protocols of research in these departments, assumed the superiority of language to literature as object of study.[34] As we

32. Relieved of the burden of upholding "English," comparative literature and foreign language departments were able to engage with European linguistics after the Second World War, which paved the way for the assimilation first of structuralist linguistics and eventually of "theory" in all its forms.

33. See Cmiel, *Democratic Eloquence*, 179, on the ambivalent relation of the philologists to the study of literature.

34. Perhaps the most telling document in the very first volume of the MLA Transactions is the essay by H. C. G. Brandt, "How Far Should Our Teaching and Text-Books

have already established, belles lettres was underdeveloped as a discipline in the nineteenth century, as a consequence of the fact that the empiricism it borrowed from moral philosophy had been displaced by the stronger "positivist" model, and by virtue also of the fact that it lacked the focus of the new disciplines. Some of the subjects in its field, such as history, were themselves on the way to becoming autonomous disciplines. This under-development disadvantaged belles lettres and thus literature itself when the moment arrived for the organization of disciplines into departments. English departments continued to employ lecturers to teach literature and composition (the latter still usually called rhetoric) to undergraduates.[35] At the same time, philology commanded the higher reaches of graduate education, where the prestige of doctoral credentials was sought. As we are now able to show, philology's advantage was short lived, paradoxically because it had moved *too far* along the path of disciplinary specialization.

Despite the confident assertion of philologists such as Francis March that "English should be studied like Greek," it was obviously impractical for "English" at the undergraduate level to be organized entirely as the study of the English language.[36] Yet the coexistence of language and literature

---

Have a Scientific Basis?," *Transactions of the Modern Language Association* 1 (1884): 57–63. Brandt's essay is a kind of manifesto for the new discipline. He complains that there are still "teachers of modern languages, who do not realize, that their department is a science." But among the philologists, Brandt adds, to demonstrate this fact "will hardly be necessary. I need only recall here such names as ten Brink, Sweet, Skeat, Scherer, the father of the 'Jung grammatiker,' though Saturn-like he would now devour his own children, Sievers, Paul, Verner, Braune, Kluge, Grober, Tobler, Forster, Neumann. We recognize these men as the foremost among those who have developed within the last fifteen years the old humdrum empirical treatment of living languages into the scientific study of them of to-day" (58–59).

35. Cmiel, *Democratic Eloquence*, makes the point that the philologists did not intro-duce English studies, which, as we have seen, existed in the form of the rhetoric and belles lettres course but that they successfully territorialized the departmental form (178).

36. Francis March's comment is cited from his report on the program in English at Lafayette College, in William Morton Payne, ed., *English in American Universities* (Bos-ton: D. C. Heath, 1895), 75. This volume brings together descriptions by professors at twenty universities and colleges of their undergraduate and graduate programs. The es-says were commissioned originally for an 1895 issue of *The Dial*, and they constitute an invaluable snapshot of literary study as it existed at the time. Lafayette College's program is slightly atypical for the degree of its emphasis on language, which can be attributed to the influence of March. For the philologist March, literary study means "the study of the language as it is found in masterpieces of literature" (76). But the question of why the study of language requires the reading of "masterpieces" has obviously not yet been fully considered and reveals a weakness in the rationale for the "English" department. Another very useful view of the early state of the discipline is provided by the first vol-ume of *The Transactions of the Modern Language Association*, which prints several essays

within the same departmental structure soon opened the possibility for what might have seemed like a fusion of belles lettres and philology, that is, for a *philological study of literature*, at least at the graduate level. In a discussion at the 1887 MLA convention, James Morgan Hart went so far as to suggest that future professors of literature "will make it their business to lay down for us laws for the critical study of literature which will do for us what the laws of Grimm and others have done for language."[37] The invocation of Grimm's law was no doubt reassuring for the neogrammarians, who revered it as a precedent to their own scientific approach to language. Nonetheless, one wonders how the philologists planned to subject literature to the rule of such laws. If "the critical study of literature" for the philologists had little to do with "criticism," as the belletrists conceived it, neither did this new scientific approach to literature remain strictly philological. It was another discourse—*literary history*—that enabled the professoriate to extend empirical research methods to literature, although these methods conspicuously failed to eventuate in "laws." (An analogous effort in France, pioneered by Hippolyte Taine, had somewhat greater success.) Literary history provided even those who were not trained in philology with topics for "research": discovering the sources and analogues for literary works, reconstructing the historical transformation of forms and genres, establishing the canons of major authors. To what extent could these tasks claim the status of science, however empirical or even "positivist" they often were?[38]

---

on the teaching of language and literature. Typical of these essays is a comment by James Garnett, "English and Its Value as a Discipline": "The teaching of language is as strictly *scientific* as that of any of the natural sciences" (68). For a fine-grained study of the progress of departmentalization in America, see Elizabeth Renker, *The Origins of American Literature Studies: An Institutional History* (Cambridge: Cambridge University Press, 2007).

37. Quoted in Michael Warner, "Professionalization and the Rewards of Literature," *Criticism* 26 (1985): 4. The quotation is drawn from the proceedings of the 1887 MLA convention. Similar views were expressed by Francis March in his *Method of Philological Study of the English Language* (New York: Harper and Brothers, 1865); and by Theodore Hunt, *Studies in Literature and Style* (New York: A. C. Armstrong, 1890). In "The Place of English in the College Curriculum," *Transactions of the Modern Language Association* 1 (1887), 118–32, Hunt recommends the application "of Professor March's Philological method to the study of Shakespeare" (127).

38. James Morgan Hart, in "The College Course in English Literature, and How It May Be Improved," *Transactions of the Modern Language Association* 1 (1884–1885): 84–95, stretches the claim for the scientific status of literary history when he asserts, for example, that the hypothesis for the influence of Boccaccio's *Filostrato* on Chaucer's *Troilus* had recently been given a "mathematical demonstration" (89). One can see in Hart's recommendation for research on such topics such as "the evolution of blank verse" that the concept of "evolution" here is not a casual metaphor but a deliberate extension from

The extension of the philological method to literature entailed a certain risk to the very scientific status of that method.

By the 1890s, the curricular structure of literary study in the university was organized according to the period concepts of literary history, the same period concepts that organize the discipline today.[39] By contrast, the study of rhetoric and belles lettres had been organized according to categories of genre, with the aim of inculcating skills: speaking, reading, and writing.[40] The textbooks that anthologized literary works for rhetoric and belles lettres mixed older and recent works together, in no historical order, but with an emphasis on the use of recent literary works as models for imitation. Literary history abolished this anthological principle, along with its presentist bias, when it came to function as the matrix for both research and teaching.[41] Its own anthological principle was skewed heavily in favor of older work, with Anglo-Saxon as both the oldest and the most prestigious field of specialization. This skewing of literary history was determined by the necessity of fusing literary history with the research protocols of philology. But this new hybrid standard struggled to extend the curriculum beyond the period of Shakespeare. The philologists were in the end more comfortable with earlier medieval and especially Anglo-Saxon literature, which could be held up as an origin both for the English language and for English literature. In this way, philology could associate its discipline with the general aims of national culture, but this rationale was attenuated when competing with the more accessible works of later literature in English. The relation between language and literature was an unresolved conflict

---

the domain of philology. Hart advocates such scholarly projects in strong preference to more vacuous pronouncements of literary merit. The philological treatment of literary history also privileged older literature and established Anglo-Saxon in a premier position it was to have for some time to come.

39. Hart, "The College Course in English Literature," stresses "the importance of teaching literature by *periods*" (88).

40. It should be recalled here that Hugh Blair's *Lectures on Rhetoric and Belles Lettres* was used as a textbook through the nineteenth century. The very first "Professor of English Language and Literature" (so-called), the Rev. Thomas Dale, appointed at the new University of London in 1828, delivered several sets of lectures, on dramatic poetry, epic poetry, divinity, the history of romantic fiction, and finally, the history of English literature. Literary history was by no means the necessary organizing category for the study of English literature. For a discussion of Thomas Dale, see D. J. Palmer, *The Rise of English Studies: An Account of the Study of the English Language and Literature from Its Origins to the Making of the Oxford English School* (London: Oxford University Press, 1965), 18–22.

41. Much had to change in order for a professor of literature such as Melvin B. Anderson, "English at Stanford University," in Payne, *English in American Universities*, to describe one of the chief functions of literary study as "to impart a scientific knowledge of the English language and of literary history" (50).

within the discipline inhabiting the department of English. This conflict has of course remained with us, as the residue of our precursor, philology.

Literary history was not a solution for this problem, as it descended from a mode of scholarship that preceded modern philology and all the other university disciplines, a form of scholarship once known without prejudice as *antiquarian*. This scholarship circulated in a kind of satellite relation to the university. It was scholarly without being institutionalized as a discipline or as the basis for a curriculum. Its empirical credentials were established for the scholars of the later nineteenth century by virtue of its status as a *historical* discourse; to do literary history was not necessarily to do "criticism."[42] Literary history was concerned with establishing facts, for example, whether and to what extent Chaucer's *Troilus* was influenced by Boccaccio's *Filostrato*. The proper understanding of older texts might depend upon these facts, but literary history did not necessarily offer interpretations of literary texts, and its judgments of quality were usually merely assumed. The antiquarian project was often sufficiently absorbing in its own right to defer questions of meaning and value indefinitely. At the undergraduate level, the convergence of philological method with literary history reinforced a tendency already present in undergraduate pedagogy to overemphasize memorization of historical facts.[43] This is not to say that literary history was merely trivial in its concerns or results but that it was difficult to devise an engaging undergraduate pedagogy based on this discourse.

For this reason, the belletrists continued to practice a version of their established pedagogy, even within the new curricular matrix of literary history. Nor did the new disciplinary mode exclude "criticism," even among the philologists who taught undergraduates, but the place of judgment within such a quasi-scientific discipline was uncertain. The professors typically transmitted received judgments about the great works of literature *along with* the facts of literary history, and as a consequence, value judgments were often reduced to a peculiar sort of fact. These judgments were

42. For the history of literary history, see René Wellek, *The Rise of English Literary History* (Chapel Hill: University of North Carolina Press, 1941). See also Kramnick, *Making the English Canon*. Kramnick draws our attention to the largely forgotten debate between the public sphere critics and the literary historians of the eighteenth century over the judgment of vernacular literature. The modernist and even presentist bias of the critics was contested by midcentury literary historians, who sought to establish scholarly standards for the reading of older works and in the process sometimes came to value the vernacular "ancients" over the moderns. Kramnick thus backdates Graff's conflict between the scholars and the critics to the eighteenth century.

43. Palmer, *The Rise of English Studies*, 23.

not usually accompanied by an account of how they were determined, much less any inquiry into aesthetic questions generally. Supported by an examination system strongly oriented to the faculty of recall, this arrangement prevailed in Anglo-American universities, at least until the inception of "practical criticism," which was conceived by reformers such as I. A. Richards as an attempt to reinvent a discourse of criticism neither positivist nor belletrist.[44]

Within the matrix of the literary historical curriculum, belles lettres continued to be represented, then, by a cadre of lecturers who saw their function as communicating an appreciation of literature but were as incapable of making their discourse scientific as they were disinclined. The cultivation of a refined or humanistic sensibility through the teaching of literature could be claimed as the special province of these lecturers (the "generalists," as Gerald Graff calls them), but this task was only weakly connected to the program of *Kultur* in its grand idealist form. In addition, the practical difference between cultivating appreciation and the assimilation of facts divided literature itself from literary history.

Already discontent with their lot in the 1890s, the "generalists" began to struggle with their philological colleagues over the aims and methods of literary pedagogy.[45] Graff has made this episode familiar to us as the recurrent conflict between the "scholars and the critics," but the point I would wish to emphasize here is that the discourse of the "generalists" was too *undisciplined* to offer a serious intellectual challenge to the "scholars" (the

44. Post-Kantian aesthetics undermined the discourse of judgment based on criteria, redirecting it toward inquiry into the nature of aesthetic response. Aesthetics after Kant thus remained essentially Romantic and subject also to a certain marginalization within philosophy. Aesthetic response was difficult to teach, a fact that can be confirmed interestingly by Hiram Corson's poetry classes at Cornell, in which he mainly recited passages to his students. See Hiram Corson, "English at Cornell University," in Payne, *English in American Universities*, 60–65. Professor Corson was also a noted philologist. He exemplifies the split between philology and belles lettres by embodying it, which should remind us that this split is a disciplinary phenomenon and not only the result of individual career choices.

45. In Britain the opposition was led by John Churton Collins, who published the most famous of the diatribes against philology, *The Study of English Literature: A Plea for Its Recognition and Reorganization in the Universities* (London: Macmillan, 1891). For a discussion of Collins, see Palmer, *The Rise of English Studies*. James Turner expresses doubt about the reality of this struggle (*Philology*, 422), but it seems very evident to me in my reading of the antiphilological polemics of the early years of the twentieth century that although this conflict was not universal, it was consequential. It should be acknowledged, however, that the contenders in the later postwar debate between the "scholars and the critics" were different, as the "scholars" were no longer philologists but literary historians.

philologists and literary historians). At the same time the belletristically oriented professoriate saw clearly that the extension of philological methods from language to literature often failed in the classroom to rise above a boring recitation of facts. This weakness of the scholars as teachers energized the belletrists, despite their marginal institutional status, and enabled them in the first decades of the new century to enlist the aid of critics in the journalistic sphere in a polemic against the scientized mode of literary study.[46]

The institutional shape of literary study at the turn of the century strikes us today as both familiar and very unlike what we do now. Literary history held together within an unstable departmental structure the two discourses of philology and belles lettres. At the same time, the belletristic professoriate was being rapidly absorbed into the new enterprise of "freshman English."[47] This course was nominally the heir to the great tradition of rhetoric, though diminished in scope and authority by the other courses crowding the new departments of English. This least prestigious of the English department's tasks would nonetheless go on to secure the department's future in the American university; "expository writing" or "composition" expanded to fill some of the space formerly occupied by rhetoric, strengthening the bureaucratic position of the English department in the process.[48]

A question must be confronted here regarding the emergence of this incoherent institutional arrangement in the 1890s, when four different practices vied for disciplinary dominance: philology, literary history, belles lettres, and rhetoric, the latter redefined now as the course in composition. This question is the demise of philology. The formation of the modern disciplines, as we have seen, was driven by the development of a principle of

46. See Gerald Graff, "The Generalist Opposition," in *Professing Literature*, 81–97. It is worth clarifying here a point of terminology: I have by and large avoided referring to the "belletrists" as a group, meaning a cadre that identified itself by invoking this term; that was never the case. I mean by "the belletrists" all of those teachers who were engaged in teaching Latin and Greek, though later in the nineteenth century increasingly in teaching rhetoric, composition, and literature. This group only achieved something close to a corporate identity in the first decades of the twentieth century, in response to the dominance of the philologists over language and literature teaching in the vernacular.

47. The contraction of rhetoric is evident in comments such as that of George E. Maclean, "English at the University of Minnesota," in Payne, *English in American Universities*, asserting that the "first duty of rhetoric [is] that of teaching students to speak and write the English language correctly" (159).

48. This is essentially the account given by William Riley Parker, in "Where Do English Departments Come From," *College English* 28 (1967): 339–51.

scientific knowledge. The "humanistic" disciplines in the eighteenth and nineteenth centuries assimilated versions of this principle into their disciplinary practices. But this arrangement did not prevail over the long term.

The strength of philology must have concealed a weakness, after all, since it did not survive as a discipline. If belles lettres was underdeveloped as a discipline, philology was, I suggest, *overdeveloped*. Müller's claim that philology held "the highest place among the Physical Sciences" points in this direction.[49] We might speculate that the disciplinary claims of philology were in part enabled by philology's capacity to distinguish itself from the nonscience of belles lettres. The distinction between science and nonscience was then mapped onto the distinction between language and literature.[50] Philology might have survived if it had been able to heal this breach, but its notion of language was too narrowly focused and yielded diminishing returns when applied to literature. Moreover, a discipline that constructed literature *for the sake of philology* had less and less to say about literature the closer this literature came to the present moment.

In the problematic relation between language and literature, literary study might be said to have internalized the fault line between the sciences and the humanities; that line crossed the center of its discipline, and indeed it became in some fashion constitutive of the discipline. In drawing so severe a distinction between the study of language and the study of literature, the philologists confirmed the positioning of literature already explicit in the public discourse of criticism, as represented, for example, by Matthew Arnold. Precisely because it resisted scientific treatment, literature could be positioned in opposition to science, to industrial civilization, even to modernity itself. We have come a long way from the eighteenth century, when literature, in the curricular form of belles lettres, was a modern category for organizing discourse. By the end of the nineteenth century, literature came to be identified with the fictional speech act and then with "nonliteral" language. Literature became the repository of whatever in language was *resistant* to scientific explanation, to modernity, and ultimately even to the goal of communication. Foucault saw the importance of this development, which he noted cryptically in *The Order of Things*: "Literature is the contestation of philology (of which it is nevertheless the twin figure)" (300).[51]

49. Cited in Aarsleff, *From Locke to Saussure*, 35.

50. Hart, in "The College Course in English Literature," typically emphasizes the "two radically distinct matters, viz. language and literature" (85).

51. Kenneth Cmiel, *Democratic Eloquence*, 165, also notes the specification of literature in the dictionaries of the nineteenth century as it ceases to denote "*all* learning" and

If the philologists overextended their claim to scientific status, the extremity of this claim became apparent when empirically based historical discourses came to be sorted out from the "natural" sciences and a generalized epistemological crisis of the disciplines drove a wedge between different discourses of the human world. It was during the period between 1880 and 1920 that "human sciences" such as sociology were effectively distinguished from the natural sciences on the one hand and from the "cultural" disciplines on the other.[52] Philology was ultimately disadvantaged by this reorganization of the disciplines, because it straddled these divisions in the new system of the disciplines. It attempted first to claim language as its scientific object, and then, in the form of a positivistic "literary history," it claimed literature as well, the object that seemed to resist science by its very nature.

In the end, the failure of philology to establish the study of literature on scientific grounds weakened its institutional status, at the same time opening space for a new science of language: *linguistics*. This discipline took up some of the methods of the neogrammarians, but it was no longer oriented chiefly toward the problem of linguistic change, much less to literature. The emergence of a new science of language did not prevent philologists from producing interesting and even major works of scholarship, but it did prevent philology from maintaining its hold on language as its special or exclusive object.[53] The philologists in the end could not sustain "English

---

comes to signify the imaginative genres. Cmiel notes especially the exclusion of oratory and history from the domain of literature so redefined.

52. The discourse of criticism was also disadvantaged by this new division of the disciplines—it existed as yet only in the quasi-disciplinary form of belles lettres—because the emergent social sciences began to take over the "criticism of society," which for these new sciences could be grounded in empirical study. The contention between criticism and sociology has been magisterially surveyed by Wolf Lepenies in *Between Literature and Science: The Rise of Sociology* (Cambridge: Cambridge University Press, 1988). The decades preceding the First World War saw the occurrence of the German *Methodenstreit*, the struggle against positivism. Analogous conflicts of method can be discovered in the Anglo-American universities, though they are less well defined than in the German system. There, as Fritz Ringer has shown, a powerful reaction set in against the positivism that triumphed in the Anglo-American and French systems. See *The Decline of the German Mandarins: The German Academic Community 1890–1933* (Hanover, NH: Wesleyan University Press, 1990), 305–16. See here also Fritz Ringer's reexamination of Weber's intervention into this controversy on behalf of affirming the nonpositivistic scientificity of the interpretive method, in *Max Weber's Methodology: The Unification of the Cultural and Social Sciences* (Cambridge, MA: Harvard University Press, 1997).

53. For a concise account of this story, see Haruko Momma, *From Philology to English Studies: Language and Culture in the Nineteenth Century* (Cambridge: Cambridge University Press, 2013). Momma comments shrewdly on the scientific ambition of

studies" as a discipline, much less the "comparative" approach that nour-
ished it at its origin. Even as linguistics emerged in the first decades of the
twentieth century, literature began to displace language as the primary object of study in the "language" departments.[54] After the First World War,
the question of the relation between language and literature was reformulated by a transit through linguistics rather than philology. Anglo-American
theorists such as Richards and continental linguists such as Jakobson raised
the "contestation" between philology and literature to a new level of universality by positing a profound contradiction in language between a "referential" function and an antithetical "emotive" or "poetic" function. The
problem of the relation of language to literature was transformed into the
problem of "literary language." Language was divided against itself, and literature became the name of its internal contestation.

The fate of philology may no doubt be read in the complex relation between language and literature as disciplinary objects. Nevertheless, we
cannot say that philology disappeared because its research program was
exhausted. Although literature pushed philology to the same margin literature itself once occupied in the modern language departments, the repu-

---

philology as a factor in its decline: "In other words, philology contains a paradox in
that it loses its very quality when it is placed in a position of prestige: the fire of its
inspiration will be smothered by its own ambition to produce knowledge, to construct
a scientific paradigm, to outclass other schools, to become orthodox. Philology then
becomes grammar" (161). The trajectory of philology in the Anglo-American university
was very different in this respect from its course in continental venues. This difference
corresponds roughly to the different trajectories of "Teutonic" and "romance" philology.
The great philological works of Curtius and Auerbach, for example, have few parallels in
Anglo-American philology, because Auerbach and Curtius did not experience the *disciplinary* segregation of language and literature that characterized departments in Britain
and America. This is not to say that criticism and philology were seamlessly wedded in
the Romance tradition but that this relation played out in response to large questions
about European culture. Hence, although Curtius claims in *European Literature and the
Latin Middle Ages* that "philology" is the "scientific technique which is the foundation of
all historical investigation" (x), this statement does not express the "scientism" that was
associated with Anglo-American philology.

    54. The heyday of philology as a discipline in the American university was relatively
brief, from perhaps 1870 to 1900, with 1920 as a terminal date. Already by 1904, the
essays in *Transactions of the Modern Language Association* are almost all on literary historical subjects. Although these essays are by and large still on relatively older and more
obscure texts, by several decades later the preponderance of essays address major works
of literature from all periods. My argument is close here to James Turner's diagnosis of
philology's demise, though he tends to see philology's weakness as its lingering identification with "humanistic scholarship" at the same time that the new discipline of linguistics was establishing a more decisively scientific paradigm for the study of language
(*Philology*, 253).

diation of philology by the new discipline of linguistics is a more mysterious event. Linguistics today has traveled very far indeed from philology.
It is a very different "science of language," affiliated with psychology and
neurophysiology rather than literary study, with which it has almost no
exchange. We might speculate that philology suffered such a precipitous
decline in the new arrangement of disciplines in part because its relation
to literature was never as distinct as it might have wished; it remained the
"twin" of literature but also, perhaps a hidden reserve. Looking back on
this history we are compelled to acknowledge that literature has been
made to play a kind of allegorical role in the development of the disciplines,
as the name of the principle antithetical to the scientific norm governing
early discipline formation. Despite its institutional weakness in the later
nineteenth century, belles lettres successfully contested the "positivism"
of its departmental associate, philology, on behalf of literature. The decline
of philology yielded space for linguistics but also for a successor to belles
lettres, "literary criticism." This complex disciplinary byplay transmitted
to the new discipline of literary criticism a notion of "literature" intricately
crossed by the contradictions of its history.

CHAPTER 7

The Location of Literature

Rhetoric and Oratory were taught everywhere, but literature, even classical literature, seems not to have been an important subject.

DON CAMERON ALLEN, *The Ph.D. in*
English and American Literature

... All the rest is literature.

PAUL VERLAINE, "L'Art Poetique"

Few scholars today need to be persuaded that the term *literature* is a complex historical abstraction and not simply or obviously the category of writing to which poems, novels, and plays belong.[1] Foucault's assertion that literature in the nineteenth century was both the "contestation of philology," and its "twin figure" reminds us that despite the many venues for literary study, it remained difficult in the nineteenth century to conceive of literature as the object of its own discipline. If the concept of literature entered the curriculum usually by a kind of side entrance—in the course on rhetoric and belles lettres—the disappearance of this course by the end of the nineteenth century would seem to have doomed the candidacy of literature for the status of disciplinary object. Yet literature acquired during the same period an ever more important role in the sphere of print culture, which comprehended a much larger world of writing and reading than the one occupied by the professors. In that domain the concept of literature passed through several phases of what I will call *delimitation*, a progressive accumulation and correlative disaccumulation of meanings, the effect of which was steadily to magnify literature's social importance. This sequence of delimitations charts a great excursus of literature: its movement out

1. For a strenuous attempt to argue for a conception of literature originating in ancient Greece and retaining a core meaning throughout its history down to the modern era, see Adrian Marino, *The Biography of "The Idea of Literature" from Antiquity to the Baroque* (Albany: State University of New York Press, 1996). Marino's book reads at moments like special pleading for the ancients, yet its encyclopedic survey testifies on my reading much more to the shifting significations of *litterae* than it does to a fixed transhistorical concept.

from the lower schools where literature was the vehicle for producing basic literacy, its widespread dissemination in the sphere of print culture, and finally its return in the twentieth century to the schools with the institution of "literary criticism" as a university discipline. These phases of delimitation sometimes overlap but tend toward a contraction in the system of genres comprising literature. From the vantage of the terminal phase of disciplinarization, we can look back on the progressive delimitation of literature as a sequence of historically determined predicates. Literature is

1. equated in premodern usage with *writing* (according to its etymology, *litterae*), and with the attainment of *learning* or "letters," a notion ubiquitous in European culture and circulating as the precursor term for the later (and narrower) conception of "literacy," the basic capacity to read and write;[2]
2. identified increasingly in the later seventeenth and eighteenth centuries with *vernacular* writing and thus implicitly opposed to writing in Greek or Latin, which only became "Greek literature" or "Latin literature" after the fact of vernacular delimitation and largely as a result of translation into modern languages;
3. associated in the eighteenth century with the development *of new generic forms*—such as the periodical essay, the familiar letter, and the novel—and with growing awareness of the transformative effects of print media in both the controversial public sphere and the private sphere of consumption;[3]
4. assimilated during the same period into the educational system as a repository of vernacular grammatical and stylistic norms, and deployed from the curricular base of the "rhetoric and belles lettres" course in a campaign (conducted simultaneously in print media) to establish and disseminate a *standard of taste* in reading and writing and a *standard*

2. The concept of *literacy* was coined, according to Ivan Illich and Barry Sanders, *ABC: The Alphabetization of the Popular Mind* (New York: Vintage Books, 1989), 85, in the *New England Journal of Education* of 1885. In chapter 5 I take up the question of why the term *literacy* was needed to replace the precedent conception of "letters" or "literature," but it will be evident already here that the new significations assigned to literature in the later nineteenth century rendered its use to mean what we mean by "literacy" confusing.

3. Into this note one would like to insert all of the best work on the emergence of new generic forms such as the novel, works too numerous at this date even to sample. A minor point of qualification of the analysis above: although the "familiar letter" is not necessarily a genre of print, its intimate relation both to the periodical essay and to the novel is confirmed by the frequent doubling of both novels and essays as letters, one of the more conspicuous features of the genre system during this period.

English dialect for speaking, the latter enabling and eliciting corollary politico-ethnic projections of a "national literature" back onto the field of writing;[4]

5. restricted between the later eighteenth and the twentieth century to the *imaginative genres of poetry, novels, and plays,* thus permanently retiring from usage the precedent generalized sense of "poetry"—a term that included fictional genres in verse or prose but after the Renaissance could no longer be stretched to include nonverse writing—and thereby clearing discursive space for new conceptualizations of scientific and informational genres of writing as "nonliterary";[5]

4. Raymond Williams, *Keywords: A Vocabulary of Culture and Society* (New York: Oxford University Press, 1976), dates the appearance of "national literature" to as early as 1767 with the publication of Herder's *Über die neuere deutsche Litteratur,* followed shortly thereafter by similar treatises in the other European languages (185). I have drawn freely on Williams's entry on "literature," still the most concise and insightful account available, in my view. The concept of "national literature" was succeeded after only several decades by the concept of "world literature," first articulated by Goethe, who connected the appearance of "*Weltliteratur*" with the emergence of a "world market of intellectual goods" or "general intellectual commerce." See David Damrosch, *What Is World Literature* (Princeton: Princeton University Press, 2003), 1–36. Pascale Casanova, in her important *The World Republic of Letters* (Cambridge, MA: Harvard University Press, 2004), sets out from Goethe's concept of *Weltmarkt* to outline a Bourdieuvian theory of how this market works. Casanova does not identify this *Weltmarkt* directly with the fact of imperialism, the study of which is the dominant tendency in literary study today, but with the capacity of the market to transcend national boundaries and to establish an autonomous world literary space (10).

5. This delimitation was anticipated in a note of Thomas De Quincey's "The Poetry of Pope," first published in the *North British Review,* 1848; reprinted in *The Collected Writings of Thomas De Quincey,* ed. Thomas Masson, 12 vols. (London: Adam and Charles Black, 1897): "What are called *The Blue Books,*—by which title are understood the folio Reports issued every session of Parliament by committees of the two Houses, and stitched into blue covers,—though often sneered at by the ignorant as so much waste paper, will be acknowledged gratefully by those who have used them diligently as the main wellheads of all accurate information as to the Great Britain of this day. As an immense depository of faithful (*and not superannuated*) statistics, they are indispensable to the honest student. But no man would therefore class the *Blue Books* as literature" (11:88). In this essay, it will be recalled, De Quincey makes his famous distinction between the "Literature of Knowledge" and the "Literature of Power," the former exemplified in the essay by Newton, the latter by Milton—a familiar distinction indeed, but for us a distinction between science *and literature.* This delimitation was sufficiently established for Matthew Arnold to stumble over it in his dispute with Huxley. When it suits his purpose Arnold reverts to the most general conception of literature in order not to have to make this distinction. See *The Portable Matthew Arnold,* ed. Lionel Trilling (Harmondsworth: Penguin, 1980): "Literature is a large word; it may mean everything written with letters or a printed in a book. Euclid's *Elements* and Newton's *Principia* are thus

6. restricted further in the twentieth century as a result of an increasingly sharp distinction between the epistemic claims of scientific, informational, and literary genres of writing, claims that in turn lay the conceptual groundwork for a *linguistic* delimitation of literature as the expression of *literariness* or *literary language*, instances of which might even, paradoxically, be identified in "nonliterary" specimens of writing;[6]

7. distinguished by the mid-twentieth century from the poetic or narrative productions of mass or popular literacy, which were relegated thereafter to the status of the subliterary—or "genre" writing—at the same time that literature was restrictively identified with a countermodern *high culture* exemplified above all by the works of High Modernism.[7]

In this chapter I argue that the serial delimitation of the *literature* concept in its earlier phases is correlated to its systemically eccentric location, its absence altogether from the most prestigious institutions such as Oxford and Cambridge, its presence for the most part in marginal niches of the cur-

---

literature. All knowledge that reaches us through books is literature" (405). De Quincey has already moved beyond Arnold's sticking point when he writes that "the very highest work [Newton's *Principia*] that has ever existed in the Literature of Knowledge is but a *provisional* work: a book upon trial and sufferance" (11:88). Future scientific work in De Quincey's view might well render Newton's *book* supernumerary. His ideas will then have "transmigrated into other forms." Part of the puzzle of De Quincey's distinction between the two kinds of literature, between Newton and Milton, circles around the relation between information and knowledge, both terms De Quincey uses but does not distinguish.

6. Another turn of the screw thus liberates literature from the literary work itself, and returns it to language, as the ground of a literary effect not restricted to literary genres. I. A. Richards in the Anglo-American tradition and Roman Jakobson in the continental institute nearly simultaneous new conceptions of literary language—for Richards the distinction between "emotive" and "referential" language, for Jakobson, the notion of the poetic as language oriented to the "message," by which he means oriented to the *language* of the message rather than the referent. For Richards, see *The Principles of Literary Criticism* (London: Routledge and Kegan Paul, 1924); for Jakobson, see "Linguistics and Poetics," in *Selected Writings*, 3 vols. (London: Harvard University Press, 1987), 3: 18–51. These later delimitations presuppose the distinction between science and literature even as they liberate literature from the concept of the "book," the material form that troubles De Quincey's distinction between two kinds of literature.

7. This sense of literature subsumes the qualifiers "belles" in belles lettres, and "fine" in "fine writing," but the important point is that the category of "literature" now excludes the very possibility of "bad literature" as a contradiction in terms. Journalistic writing is also excluded henceforth from consideration as literature. See, for example, Professor Martin Sampson's comment on the syllabus of the English department in Indiana University, "English at Indiana University," in Payne, *English in American Universities*: "Current magazine writing is not held up as ideal literature" (93).

riculum of other institutions, in lower-level institutions, in nonconformist schools, or in provincial or colonial colleges and universities. The systemic eccentricity of vernacular literature to the "central" sites of the educational system is a condition for its peculiar semantic plasticity, its susceptibility to redefinition or delimitation. Literature lacked semantic fixity until very late in its career, not until after it became the exclusive object of the discipline we know as literary criticism.

The multiple phases of delimitation argue against identifying a single *moment* in which literature came to mean what it does to us today, in which, as is often said, literature was "invented."[8] I want to argue, however, that it is better to understand the category of literature as the result of a historical *process* rather than a historical *event* or *moment*. The notion of an originating event possesses the capacity to surprise by virtue of its radical contingency and local specificity. Trevor Ross, for example, writes not atypically that "on 22 February 1774 literature in its modern sense began" (297). He refers here to the legislative defeat of the perpetual copyright, which resulted in the vastly wider availability of English literary works than ever before. But Ross's scrupulous and everywhere illuminating reconstruction of canon formation over several centuries belies the precision of his claim and testifies rather to a process as such. Is the literature that began in 1774 the same literature that circulates in 1874? Does that difference make a difference? Others might say that literature began earlier or later or elsewhere, even very far elsewhere, in Scotland or India, but certainly not with an act of the English House of Lords. The preference for the colonial origin makes no better argument for *the* originating moment. Indeed, the process of literature's delimitation is a pan-European. To the French we owe the concept of belles lettres. Germany gave us aesthetics, Romanticism, and, arguably, the delimitation of literature as "imaginative" writing. Can literature have so many places and times of origin? Perhaps it is less exciting to think of literature as a concept "in process," with many locations and moments, but the multiplicity of sites compels us to attend to the *systemic* features of literature and of literary culture.

Only after the last phase of delimitation does the meaning of literature become relatively fixed and thus available to *curricular* stabilization. Literature is for us today essentially what it came to mean during the inter-

---

8. The motif of the "invention of literature" is pervasive in histories of literary study. See Gauri Viswanathan, *Masks of Conquest: Literary Study and British Rule in India* (New York: Columbia University Press, 1989); Crawford, *The Scottish Invention of English Literature*; Miller, *The Formation of College English*; Court, *The Scottish Connection*; Court, *Institutionalizing English Literature*; Ross, *The Making of the English Canon from the Middle Ages to the Late Eighteenth Century.*

war period, and if literary critics are often now restless with that delimited object, redefining the discipline remains extremely difficult for the very reason that delimiting the meaning of literature was a condition in the first place for constituting literary criticism as a discipline. Literature departments entered late but not entirely *post festum* into the process of delimitation. Literary criticism inherited a concept of literature both freighted with significations accumulated over its long history but also considerably lightened by the divestment of its oldest, most general sense. The works of Newton and Blackstone, it need hardly be said, are by definition no longer "literature" for us as they were for their contemporaries. The object of literature is a given and cannot easily be taken away, but the possibility of literature as object of a discipline was still uncertain as late as 1895, when William Morton Payne speculated not atypically in his introduction to *English in American Universities*, "The question may be raised whether it would not be well to set an official seal upon the separation of literature from its allied subjects by making of it a separate department of university work, just as some of our more progressive institutions have erected sociology into a distinct department, thus definitely marking it off from the allied departments of political and economic science."[9] Departments of English, Payne concedes, were still disposed to study literature as "material for minute philological and historical analysis" rather than for itself, however that essence might be defined (19).[10] The problem of disciplining literature was

9. Payne, *English in American Universities*, 26. The accounts in Payne's collection are virtually unanimous in describing the discipline of English as consisting of three "distinct natural groups," named by Martin Sampson in his essay "English at The University of Indiana": "language, composition, and literature." (92). The curricular balance between these subjects, however, varied considerably among institutions, but few departments offered anything recognizably like the English major of our day, structured as a sequence of literature courses, often organized by periods. Composition was a larger part of the curriculum, as was philological study, even at the undergraduate level. See Fred Newton Scott's statement in "English at the University of Michigan," Payne, *English in American Universities*, on the importance of language study (116), and L. A. Sherman, "The University of Nebraska," on the desirability of reading Chaucer as an example of "Teutonic poetry" (124). Philology of course still claimed the larger share of the graduate curriculum. The general impression one receives from the reports in Payne is of a discipline in which "rhetoric and belles lettres" had been almost completely diffused in the triad of language, composition, and literature.

10. As Francis. A. March remarks, in "English at Lafayette College," in Payne *English in American Universities*, "English should be studied like Greek" (75). David B. Frankenburger reports in "English at the University of Wisconsin" that in his department, "the method of instruction is scientific" (139). Melvin B. Anderson writes in "English at Stanford University," that the purpose of literary study is "to impart a scientific knowledge

well understood by Payne: "It is doubtless much easier to treat literature by the method of science than by the method of aesthetics; but does not literature, thus treated, cease to assert its peculiar and indispensable function? (*English in American Universities*, 26)." The study of literature in the "aesthetic" form of belles lettres was displaced by the century's end with a version of literary history bound to the mere fact, in which the question of judgment or taste that energized the founders of belles lettres had more or less disappeared. The *terminus ad quem* of this tendency was expressed widely and prosaically in the observation, repeated by many, that *there can be no examination in taste*, an opinion that curtly discloses the nonnegotiable condition of disciplinarity—that it produce a testable knowledge.[11]

The successful establishment of scientific disciplines in the university of the later nineteenth century throws into relief the resistance of literature to disciplinarization, which I understand as an expression of its systemic eccentricity to the official curriculum, both the classical curriculum of the earlier nineteenth century and the scientific disciplines of the later. However, if literature suffered a kind of internal exile in the new language departments dominated by philology, where it lingered on as the subject of the increasingly moribund pedagogy of belles lettres, it would be easy to demonstrate that its social importance outside the university was at this

---

of the English language and of literary history" (50). Albert H. Tolman avers contrarily in "English at the University of Chicago," that "literary masterpieces should be studied chiefly, it seems to me, for their beauty" (89). Bliss Perry of Williams and Hiram Corson of Cornell also emphasized appreciation rather than scientific philology. On this question, see Applebee, *Tradition and Reform in the Teaching of English*, 28.

11. For a discussion of the importance of the examination system in this context, see Stephen Potter, *The Muse in Chains: A Study in Education* (London: Jonathan Cape, 1937). It was well known and much lamented that the study of literature in its incarnation as "literary history" was disciplined by reduction to facts, which could easily be tested but at the same time permitted the essence of literature to escape, leaving only the facts behind. The belletrists endured this disciplinarization effect uneasily, without necessarily being able to offer at first an alternative program for a literary discipline. Margaret Mathieson, *The Preachers of Culture: A Study of English and Its Teachers* (Totowa, NJ: Rowman and Littlefield, 1975), notes the alternative view in the later nineteenth century that English was less a "subject" and more a "way of life"—not a promising basis for a discipline (12). For a study of the examination system in the nineteenth century, see Cathy Shuman, *Pedagogical Economies: The Examination and the Victorian Literary Man* (Stanford, CA: Stanford University Press, 2000). E. M. W. Tillyard, *The Muse Unchained: An Intimate Account of the Revolution in English Studies at Cambridge* (London: Bowes and Bowes, 1958), points to the incorporation of a practical criticism paper into the Cambridge Tripos as an innovation that moved the study of English literature there beyond mere recollection of facts (103–9).

moment no less than immense. There, vernacular writing circulated as the major form of mass entertainment, as a means of self-improvement and self-information and as a vehicle for the expression of opinion, for public debate on all subjects: political, social, and cultural.

The cultural importance of vernacular literature is surely why the belletristic professors who languished in the backwaters of the "modern language" departments revolted in the first decades of the twentieth century against the hegemony of the philologists and the literary historians. As we saw in chapter 2, the belletrists joined the public exponents of the *Kulturkritik* tradition in advancing the literary curriculum as a defense against the dominance of the sciences and as a means of institutionalizing opposition to the cultural depredations of modern industrial society. It was by following this path of *greatest resistance* that the concept of literature entered into the system of the disciplines as the name not only of a disciplinary object but of a truth antithetical to the truth of science, deeply at odds with the tendency of modernity. The assertion of literature as *Kulturkritik* was signaled by the preeminence of figures such as Carlyle in lower-level and introductory literature courses of the time, a preeminence almost impossible to imagine now because its traces have been so thoroughly obliterated by the supersession of the high modernists in the curriculum and by the emergence of subtler versions of cultural criticism no longer fixated on industrial society.

The emergence of this "social mission" of criticism (to invoke Chris Baldick's formulation) in the later nineteenth and early twentieth century tells us why the vernacular curriculum then was dominated by nonfictional prose. During this period, it was possible to construct the literature course as the vehicle for a straightforward, culturally conservative critique of modern industrial society by stringing together the work of writers such as Coleridge, Carlyle, Arnold, and Ruskin. Professor Felix Shelling of the University of Pennsylvania writes not atypically in Payne's *English in American Universities* that literature is to be valued for its "enormous weight against utilitarianism" ("English at the University of Pennsylvania," 131). Another of the contributors to Payne, Melville B. Anderson of Stanford, describes the *first* course students are required to take after composition as "a careful study of some of the prose writers of the nineteenth century: such as Macaulay, De Quincey, Carlyle, Savage Landor, Cardinal Newman, Matthew Arnold" ("English at Stanford University," 53). Martin W. Sampson of Indiana describes a similar introductory course on English prose style, including "Macaulay, De Quincey, Carlyle, Ruskin, and Arnold" ("English at the University of Indiana," 94). This kind of syllabus would never be

found in a standard introductory course today, only perhaps in a specialized graduate seminar.[12]

These early organizations of the vernacular literary curriculum diverged
scarcely at all from the agenda of the "Victorian sages" in their response
to industrial society. For some time, the popular novel developed along a
parallel track, a convergence of critical and fictional prose that filled the
space of reading and writing. I propose to name this eccentric and largely
extracurricular world of reading and writing *literary culture*, a term already
current but which I here give a technical signification. I do not refer, then,
simply to the readers of literature, nor to the literate populace, but to a historically bounded set of systemic relations constituting the practices and
institutions of reading, writing, and speaking. The system of literary culture
emerged in the eighteenth century, became dominant in the nineteenth,
and began to wane in the twentieth. The culture was founded on much
more than the mere possibility of vernacular literacy; its enabling condition was the *massification* of literacy, the extension of reading practices to
large numbers of the populace.[13] I posit three major abstractions—an *extra-*

12. On this subject, see the important essay by Stefan Collini, "From 'Non-Fiction
Prose' to Cultural Criticism: Genre and Disciplinarity in Victorian Studies," in Juliet
John and Alice Jenkins, *Rethinking Victorian Culture*, (Basingstoke: Macmillan, 2000),
13–28. Collini is interested in how "non-fiction prose" of the nineteenth century was
relegated to the "dustbin category" (17). He sees nonfiction prose as toggling between
"context" and "literature," which ultimately disadvantaged it in a discipline that wanted
a clear demarcation of literary texts. See also Oscar James Campbell, *The Teaching of College English* (New York: D. Appleton, 1934); Potter, *The Muse in Chains*; Jo McMurtry,
English Language, English Literature: The Creation of an Academic Discipline (Hamden,
CT: Archon Books, 1985); Tillyard, *The Muse Unchained*; Chris Baldick, *The Social Mission of English Criticism*; Mathieson, *The Preachers of Culture*; Palmer, *The Rise of English
Studies*.

13. For a general account of this process, see Vincent, *The Rise of Mass Literacy*.
See also Clifford Siskin, "More Is Different: Literary Change in the Mid and Late Eigh-
teenth Century," in *The Cambridge History of English Literature, 1660–1780*, ed. John
Richetti (Cambridge: Cambridge University Press, 2005), 795–823. For three essential
eighteenth-century studies of the reading public, see Alvin Kernan, *Printing Technology,
Letters, and Samuel Johnson* ((Princeton, NJ: Princeton University Press, 1987); Robert
DeMaria Jr., *Samuel Johnson and the Life of Reading* (Baltimore: Johns Hopkins Uni-
versity Press, 1997); and William B. Warner, *Licensing Entertainment: The Elevation of
Novel Reading in Britain, 1684–1750* (Berkeley: University of California Press, 1998). For
a study of the earlier formation of a reading public, with an emphasis on its stratification
into high and low strata, see Barbara M. Benedict, *Making the Modern Reader: Cultural
Mediation in Early Modern Literary Anthologies* (Princeton, NJ: Princeton University
Press, 1996).

curricular trivium—constituting literary culture as a system of vernacular reading, writing, and speaking practices. These abstractions are

1. *Grammar*, the prescriptive principles of pronunciation, diction, syntax, spelling, and usage comprising the linguistic norm of standard English.[14] Analogous developments prevailed in Europe, but I will continue here to use the English-speaking nations as the model. The normative function of grammar, which was early expressed by the concept of "correctness," was rapidly enlarged by the nineteenth century to include numerous and complex canons of "usage," very different from the "accidence" of early modernity. These canons could be elaborated into supersubtle refinements designed to bring language into conformity either with logic or with established precedent and governing both syntax and orthography. Grammar was supported in the lower schools by an extensive vernacular pedagogy, and in print media by an astounding proliferation of guides to every aspect of pronunciation, diction, syntax, spelling, and usage. The prominence in nineteenth-century periodical venues of self-styled "grammarians" continually stimulated linguistic anxiety in the populace, often correlated with other anxieties about upward mobility, gender inequality, or ethnic assimilation.[15] The command of correct speech thus constituted the first and most important form of cul-

---

14. Grammar in the prescriptive sense is very late; this is not what grammar meant in antiquity—when it belonged to a comprehensive *paideia* and included, for example, "interpretation of the poets", nor is its meaning in literary culture identical to what linguists now often mean by the term. Grammar has been and still is used in both restrictive and inclusive senses. The former is exemplified by the early modern use, in which grammar referred mainly to inflection—hence English could be described in early modernity as a language without grammar. At the inclusive end is the twentieth-century linguist's use, which is descriptive of structural regularities in language, and which eschews prescription. The concept of grammar as a *historical* abstraction in the above account will seem from the linguist's point of view merely uninformed, but the social importance of this abstraction in connection with the project of standardizing vernacular language is undeniably immense. For a discussion of the different conceptions of grammar, see Dick Leith, *A Social History of English* (New York: Routledge, 1983), 86–111. See also Sterling Andrus Leonard, *The Doctrine of Correctness in English Usage* (New York: Russell and Russell, 1962); Tony Crowley, *Standard English and the Politics of Language* (Urbana: University of Illinois Press, 1989); Laura Wright, ed., *The Development of Standard English, 1300–1800* (Cambridge: Cambridge University Press, 2000); Tony Bex and Richard J. Watts, *Standard English: The Widening Debate* (London: Routledge, 1999).

15. See Cmiel, *Democratic Eloquence*, 123–24; also Barron, *Grammar and Good Taste*.

tural capital circulating in modern society.[16] As a prescriptive practice, grammar must be distinguished from the descriptive science of the nineteenth-century philologists, who often dismissed the grammarians for lacking a scientific understanding of language.[17] Grammar belongs to literary culture, then, not to the sciences of language in the university. In this cultural contradiction, two versions of modernization clashed and remained unreconciled.

2. *Literature*, in the second through the seventh stages of delimitation, the chief source of mass entertainment in the nineteenth century, an instrument for self-improvement and self-instruction, and the curricular basis for the teaching of standard English in the schools.[18] Because literature—especially in the delimited sense of poetic and narrative forms—was disseminated on a mass scale through print media, these narrative forms could also become the screen for myth-like projections of a "national culture." The development of the nation-state as a cultural formation was always intimately related to the development of a literary culture and a national literature.[19] If the linguistic substratum of standard English was a condition for recognizing a canon of national literature, it also permitted the vernacular canon to assume supplemental ideological functions as the carrier of traditions and values, often projected as expressions of "Englishness." The concept of literature thus came to possess a density and complexity that far exceeded its later delimitation as the supergeneric category comprehending the forms of

16. See Pierre Bourdieu, "The Production and Reproduction of Legitimate Language," in *Language and Symbolic Power*, ed. John B. Thompson (Cambridge, MA: Harvard University Press, 1991). For the long history behind the idea of standard English, beginning with the standardization of Chancery English, see John H. Fisher, *The Emergence of Standard English* (Lexington: University Press of Kentucky, 1996).

17. See Kenneth Cmiel's discussion of the conflict between the scholars and the "verbal critics" in the journalistic media in *Democratic Eloquence*, 148–52.

18. By "mass entertainment" I refer to those modes of cultural consumption that were nonlocal but connected consumers across regional, class, and other divides. Jane Austen was a favorite of the Prince of Wales, but she might also be read by the shopkeeper or the servant, by anyone who could read and anywhere it was possible to purchase or borrow her novels. By this definition, printed matter provided the major and almost the only forms of mass entertainment before the introduction of massified visual media.

19. Though much controverted, still the most important attempt to explain this relation is Benedict Anderson, *Imagined Communities: Reflections on the Origin and Spread of Nationalism* (London: New Left Books, 1983). I will address the relation of the category of literature to the category of the nation further in the conclusion.

poetry, novel, and drama. It may seem to us now that literature in this later sense belongs to literary culture as its most central—because most enduring (or canonical)—exhibit, but literature so delimited always circulated in a crowded universe of periodical writing (reviews, journals, magazines, newspapers) which was also regarded as a form of literature, at the same time that it functioned as the ambient medium of literature in its later, most delimited sense, imaginative or fictional writing. Works of literature in this narrower sense were mediated by the vast machinery of reviewing that supported and sustained literary culture beyond the school. This complementarity began to decay in the twentieth century, when journalism and literature diverged and journalists and "creative" writers ceased to be the same persons.

3. *Criticism*, the discourse of judgment or taste, the purpose of which at the time of its inception in the seventeenth century was to discriminate between good and bad writing, between the "beauties" and "faults" in works, and at the time of its disciplinarization in the twentieth century to discriminate between literature and its mass cultural other, popular or "generic" writing. In between these two points lies the "Age of Criticism," as Kant dubbed it, which I name here more broadly by the concept of literary culture. The discriminations generated by the discourse of criticism presupposed the widespread possession of vernacular literacy, its implantation in diverse social groups. The critic emerged in the seventeenth century, as we saw in the introductory chapters, as a new kind expert, the "organic intellectual" of a relatively large and diverse literary culture, very large indeed by comparison to the tiny fraction of those literate in Greek or Latin. The critic was an expert very close to the vernacular reader, removed from that group only distant enough to produce the theory of its reading practice, to instruct the mass reader as one of them. The ancien régime of the critic lasted a surprisingly long time, all the while driving the delimitation of literature in concert with the reflexive theorizations of the poets, playwrights, novelists, and essayists themselves—from whom, after all, the critics were seldom wholly distinct.

If criticism in its twentieth-century incarnation aimed to restrict the name of literature to those imaginative works of a quality high enough to constitute an elite or high culture (whole genres such as detective fiction or science fiction would henceforth be excluded as mere "genre" work, in contradistinction to the supergenre of literature), the paradoxical effect of this final delimitation was to demote criticism itself in relation to the supergenre of literature.[20] For the age of belles lettres, critical

20. See Williams, *Keywords*, 186.

prose belonged equally with poetry and drama to the field of literature and was even in some ways more exemplary for literary culture, more useful in transmitting its norms of grammar and style. We can cite here the key function of the *Spectator* essays in the belletristic pedagogy of Hugh Blair and his many successors. Criticism between Dryden and Eliot still belonged in some necessary way to the category of literature, as largely though not exclusively the work of *littérateurs* or "men of letters," but thereafter criticism would stand over against literature in a new relation. The status of criticism as literature was sacrificed for the power to determine which texts *belonged* to the category of literature. Literature ceased once and for all to refer to writing generally, and its subsequent delimitations were locked into place. This fixing of the category of literature coincided with the redefinition of criticism itself as a *professional* discourse, that is, with the institutionalization of literary criticism as an academic discipline. The determination of the category of literature from within the university's system of disciplines marks the waning of literary culture, which we must understand as a rearrangement of the systemic relations constituting the practices of reading and writing. With this new arrangement, literary culture ceased to be the most dominant feature of public sphere communication, or of private consumption.

The relation between literary culture and the university in the eighteenth and nineteenth centuries was characterized above all by the exteriority of literature to the university, the fact that the university curriculum overlapped so little with the productions of literary culture. This condition paradoxically encouraged the rapid development of literary culture, because that culture responded not immediately to the aims of the school, which were by definition conservative, but rather to the market, to readers as consumers.[21] Nonetheless, we cannot describe literary culture as exterior in the sense of being *wholly* absent from the universities and colleges. A space was cleared for a belles lettres course in some institutions, and the popularity of this course testified to the demand for vernacular writing even within the university. The fading reputation of belles lettres at the time of

21. On the emergence of the market for literature, see John Brewer, *The Pleasures of the Imagination: English Culture in the Eighteenth Century* (New York: Farrar Strauss Giroux, 1997). Lawrence Veysey, "The Plural Organized World of the Humanities," in Oleson and Voss, *The Organization of Knowledge in Modern America, 1860–1920*, remarks on the indifference of the Modern Language Association in its early years to what I call literary culture, its dedication to the "internal academic goals" of university departments (74–76).

the institution of modern language departments in the 1870s suggests that what I am calling the eccentricity of literary culture must be understood as *systemic*: even when literature was admitted into the universities and colleges, as it was in the later eighteenth century with the course on "rhetoric and belles lettres" in the Scottish universities, it occupied a marginal or supplemental place. This supplementarity was evident in the version of belles lettres sometimes offered as a "culminating course" in American universities, a more relaxed offering for seniors fatigued by their years of study in the official curriculum of Latin, Greek, mathematics, and theology.[22]

In the later eighteenth and early nineteenth centuries, the intensity of the social demand for literature was confirmed by the emergence of numerous extracurricular literary societies. Students who toiled grudgingly at their Greek and Latin enthusiastically patronized these societies, which were dedicated to the sophistication of vernacular literacy.[23] In one of the few studies of these reading and debating clubs, historian of education

22. For an interesting discussion of an earlier mode of belles lettres, see David S. Shields, *Civil Tongues and Polite Letters in British America* (Chapel Hill: University of North Carolina Press, 1997). Shields describes belles lettres as a form of casual and occasional writing that need not published but supported an elevated conversational practice and forms of sociability centered on clubs and societies. The emergence of a "republic of letters" in the late colonial and federal periods was both continuous and discontinuous with this early culture and no doubt predisposed university students to welcome the formalization of belles lettres in the work of Blair and his successors.

23. See James McLachlan, "The *Choice of Hercules*: American Student Societies in the Early 19th Century," in *The University in Society*, 2 vols., ed. Lawrence Stone (Princeton, NJ: Princeton University Press, 1974), 2:472; see also Rudolph, *Curriculum*, 95–97. Rudolph notes the disparity between the level of student interest in belles lettres and its modest curricular position. See also Wilbur W. Hatfield, "General and Specialized Literary Clubs," *English Journal* 15, no. 16 (1926): 450–56. McLachlan observes that student reading habits in the societies were very inclusive—they included works in Greek, Latin, and modern foreign languages, in addition to English (478–79). The most important consequence of this inclusiveness, however, was to provide an opening for the reading of vernacular work in an intense and quasi-formal setting, thus countering the exclusiveness of the official curriculum. McLachlan also notes that despite curricular innovations in the eighteenth century—the introduction of belles lettres, for example—the universities of the earlier nineteenth century tended to lapse into uninspired routines. McLachan's case study is the College of New Jersey (later known as Princeton), where even belles lettres "amounted to little more than basic English grammar" (468). Much the same was true in many other institutions. The relative lack of student interest in the official curriculum had the unintended effect of permitting literary culture to thrive unobstructed in the unofficial student societies: "What was true of Yale seems to have been true of almost every other American college from, very roughly, the last third of the 18th century through the middle of the 19th. The student literary societies engrossed more of the interests and activities of the students than any other aspect of college life" (472).

James McLachlan observes that they were highly structured organizations, in effect, colleges within colleges. They enrolled students, conducted classes, and granted diplomas, but they were not part of the official university: "The surprising—and, at the moment, inexplicable—thing about the relation of the faculty to the student societies . . . is that it was almost nonexistent" (485). The existence of these shadow colleges, amounting to what McLachlan calls an "extracurriculum," is compelling evidence for the social importance of literary culture, as well as for its systemically eccentric location. The course in rhetoric and belles lettres was by comparison perhaps a weaker echo of contemporary literary culture. The more robust student societies were closer to the thing itself, to literary culture speaking in its native tongue.

The reading societies might also be seen as part of a network of communalized reading practices complementing the private reading that sustained literary culture in its atomized mass. The societies were similar in their social aims, if not in the degree of their formality, to other, later sites of communalized reading, such as the Browning society and the Shakespeare society, down to the "Janeites" of our own day.[24] Such reading groups continue to thrive today outside the university, a circumstance that betrays their origin in the literary culture of the nineteenth century and highlights the difference between literature as a disciplinary object and as the object of a mass reading practice. To the professors, of course, the Janeites and their like can only seem "undisciplined."

It will not be possible to do more than glance at the phenomenon of "lay reading," which I have considered more fully in chapter 12 below. I propose instead now to examine literature's systemic eccentricity to the classical university. The puzzling absence of literature from the curriculum of that university, remarked by Don Cameron Allen in the first epigraph to this chapter, has provoked scholars to search elsewhere for what is absent there: the invention of English literature, a founding moment of literary study. But the systemic eccentricity of literary culture confirms the operation of a process occurring at many different sites over a relatively long period of time. A notion such as the "Scottish invention of English literature" discovers a time and place of origin by mapping time and place onto the colonized globe, but is that kind of mapping the only possible way of understanding the location of literature? To be sure, there is a rich historical

24. See Veysey's discussion of the Shakespeare and Browning societies, "Plural and Organized Worlds of the Humanities," in Oleson and Voss, *The Organization of Knowledge in Modern America 1890–1920*, 75–76. See also Deidre Lynch, ed., *The Janeites: Austen's Disciples and Devotees* (Princeton, NJ: Princeton University Press, 2000).

irony in the discovery that English literature was invented by those who were not English. But the pleasure of this irony must yield to the humbler recognition that the English are after all very hard to locate themselves, that many of them inhabit various elsewheres, diverse cultural suburbs and provinces. Was it not the case, for example, that the metropole itself was an elsewhere from the perspective of the educational centers, that the first systematic study of English literature by the English themselves at University College London was in some way occasioned by literature's exclusion from Oxford and Cambridge?[25] London was eccentric too. If Scotland, Wales, and Ireland are eccentric to England, as also India and Africa, the Caribbean and the American colonies, these spatial peripheries have to be systemically related to the eccentricity of education for women, of adult education or "extension" programs, of the schools for Dissenters excluded from Anglican schools and from Oxford and Cambridge—all of the sites of eccentricity where vernacular literary study first found a hearing and a home.[26] The relegation of literature to the lower levels of the school system and to its marginal institutions—socially, geographically, politically, religiously—is so manifestly a systemic feature of the educational system before the twentieth century as to defeat any attempt to explain this eccentricity by taking any one of its sites as representative of all.

All of these sites nevertheless have something in common, a historical tendency, a force rising up from below and from the margin. This force pressing in from the various peripheries of the educational system was vernacularization, the name not only the leading edge of an irresistible social

25. Even when Oxford introduced an English examination in 1873, it was only for a Pass. Honors were still reserved for the classics. In much recent work Adam Smith and Hugh Blair have displaced the Reverend Thomas Dale, first professor of English language and literature at University College London, for the honor of being the first professors of English literature. The famously dreary Dale might just as well have been teaching in the colonies, so far as Oxford and Cambridge were concerned. For the story of Dale, see Palmer, *The Rise of English Studies*, 15–28.

26. For the introduction of English literature into the curriculum of the dissenting academies, see my *Cultural Capital*, 100–107. In the same chapter, I cite a passage from a letter of Hume's to Gilbert Elliot, which I resurrect here for its pertinence: "Is it not strange that, at a time when we have lost our princes, our parliaments, our independent government,—even the presence of our chief nobility; are unhappy, in our accent and pronunciation; speak a very corrupt dialect of the tongue we make use of,—is it not strange, I say, that, in these circumstances we should really be the people most distinguished for literature in Europe?" (122). Here is perhaps another Scottish invention of English literature. Interestingly, Hume understands very well the claim he is making, which is not a claim for invention but for "distinction," a distinction that *writing* and *print* make possible in the face of political domination by the English and in spite of the disadvantage of the Scottish dialect.

storm but also, conversely, testimony to the fact of inertia in classical education, the effect of immense accumulated distinction or cultural capital.[27] Like a great store of gold, too heavy to move, the classics were a form of wealth that had to compete with the *currency* of periodical writing, with the unimpeded circulation of books in English. And yet the classical languages remained all the while the canonical standard, ensuring the value of vernacular paper, at least for as long as the true force of vernacularization failed to be understood.

One consequence of vernacular education was the emergence of a "high culture" alternative to the classics, an alternative site for the accumulation of cultural prestige, an alternative procedure for the making and marking of distinction. Vernacular high culture was very different from what we might be tempted to call "Latin literacy"—a dubious concept constructed by analogy to vernacular literacy. Knowledge of Latin was linked most strongly to an occupational group with very particular status claims: the clergy, physicians, and lawyers of the old university, the traditional "learned professions." The operative premodern distinction was not between those who were literate or illiterate *in the vernacular* but between the clergy and the laity, the latter defined as those ignorant *of Latin*. What we now call "literacy" means the ability to read and write *one's own* language, whatever dialect of that language one speaks, and that knowledge is very different in its cultural implications from knowing Greek or Latin. The concept of "literacy" is itself a vernacular concept, an effect of the process of vernacularization.

Nor do I mean by vernacularization only the dissemination of a minimal linguistic knowledge—basic literacy—a supplement to the knowledge one already possesses as a speaker of one's own language. Vernacularization

---

27. For an exemplary midcentury statement of the argument for vernacular education in preference to the classics, see Henry Sidgwick, "The Theory of Classical Education," in *Essays on a Liberal Education*, ed. F. W. Farrar (London: Macmillan, 1868), 81–143. The campaign for vernacularization can be traced at least as far back as to Locke and includes too many figures along the way to list. I cite Sidgwick for the economy of his statement, and its timeliness, delivered on the threshold of victory. For a study of early American anticlassical arguments, see Meyer Reinhold, "Opponents of Classical Learning during the Revolutionary Period," *Proceedings of the American Philosophical Society* 112 (1968), 221–34. It should be recalled that despite the apparently unidirectional force of vernacularization, the later triumph of vernacular literature in the university represented a complicated fold in this linear narrative. The most ardent advocates on behalf of vernacular literature—such as John Churton Collins and Irving Babbitt—were also ardent classicists. By this point, as we saw in chapter 6, Collins and Babbitt were fighting not with the classicists but with the advocates of another kind of vernacular study: English philology, with its focus on Old English.

was much more than the dissemination of basic literacy: it was also the *systematic alienation* of speakers from their own language, a turning of the vernacular to the end of social distinction. Hence the absurd multiplication of rules for "usage," more numerous than ever bedeviled the students of Latin or Greek. The strategies for producing that alienation effect swelled into a stream of grammatical imperatives addressed especially to the middle classes, stimulating both their social ambition and their anxiety. Vernacular literary culture was not, then, just superimposed on the preexistent culture of "letters," on classical education. Located outside the institutions of that monumentalized classical culture, literary culture disseminated a normative cultural ideal premised on the possibility of rising through linguistic emulation (or falling through a failure to measure up to the vernacular standard). Literary culture held out to those seeking to rise a continuous ladder for reaching the higher rungs of that culture, from the most rudimentary literacy to the most cultivated taste in literature. This vertical continuum was uninterrupted by the necessity for acquiring a dead language along the way, however difficult it was to achieve the higher levels of skill and taste in the vernacular. Literary culture thus brought into being a high culture more complex, widely disseminated, and internally stratified than the old high culture founded on training in the classical languages and in performative rhetorical skills.[28]

Vernacularization can be seen as one strand in a bundle of tendencies belonging to the collective or summary tendency of *modernization*. Vernacularization was perhaps not as conspicuous a modernizing tendency to contemporaries as the explosion of new scientific knowledge; it was a process hundreds of years old.[29] Yet our analysis suggests that the tendency of vernacularization was *equally expressed* in literary culture and in science: in the former as the progressive delimitation of vernacular literature, and in the latter as the displacement of the classical curriculum by an influx

28. A typical expression of the motives for literary culture is offered by the Rev. H. G. Robinson, "On the Use of English Classical literature in the Work of Education," in the October 1860 issue of *Macmillan's Magazine*, quoted in Palmer, *The Rise of English Studies*: "It is, however, in connection with what is called 'middle-class education' that the claims of English literature may be most effectively urged. In that literature, properly handled, we have a most valuable agency for the moral and intellectual culture of the professional classes" (45).

29. For the long history of Latin, see Françoise Wacquet, *Latin or the Empire of the Sign: From the Sixteenth to the Twentieth Centuries*, trans. John Howe (London: Verso, 2001). For a discussion of the complex and multiple strategies of vernacular writing, see Ruth Evans et al., "The Notion of Vernacular Theory," in *The Idea of the Vernacular: An Anthology of Middle English Literary Theory, 1280–1520*, ed. Jocelyn Wogan-Browne et al., eds., (University Park, PA: Pennsylvania State University Press, 1999), 314–30.

of new scientific disciplines, henceforth disseminated in vernacular prose. The fact that vernacularization was a precondition for modernizing and de-limiting the categories of both literature and science complicates the pic-ture we inherit of their epistemic opposition, the "two cultures." If there is an underlying linguistic identity of scientific and literary culture, this common linguistic ground supports a common social identity, that of the *expert*. As soon as this term of analysis is introduced, however, it becomes evident that the epistemic distinction between science and literature—expressed earlier as De Quincey's distinction *within literature* between the "Literature of Knowledge" and the "Literature of Power"—splits the figure of the expert into two kinds and stands these two figures in opposite cor-ners of their common linguistic ground. The vernacularization of expertise was followed almost immediately by this division between the epistemic modes of expertise.

We have already seen that the critic functioned as an expert for literary culture and that this mode of expertise could be very close in its origins to a "lay" practice of reading. In the seventeenth century in England, the size of the reading public was still small enough—though growing—to sustain a common social identification between critic and reader based on the as-sumption that reading, and the correlative practice of judgment, required both "letters" and leisure, skills and opportunities still unavailable to most persons. The massification and concurrent stratification of literary culture in the later eighteenth century removed the critic to an ever-greater dis-tance from the instructed mass. I invoke again here the genealogy of the authoritarian cultural critic discussed in part 1, the figure who sets up as the judge of literature but in the end submits the whole of society to judgment. In the nineteenth century the figure of the scientist was also rising in the estimation of society, now as an increasingly distinct social type, less a fig-ure of literary culture than before. If the "natural philosophers" were once indistinguishable as producers of "literature" from other learned figures, the perception was gradually sinking in that their enterprise of knowledge production required new categories to describe their writing—the kind of generic concept toward which De Quincey gestures with his "Literature of Knowledge."[30] The corresponding increase in social esteem for the scien-tific enterprise was confirmed by the opening of the university to scientific

30. A comment of Felix F. Shelling, in "English in University of Pennsylvania," in Payne, *English in American Universities*, confirms the tendency of the delimitation of literature by the end of the century: "The study of English literature, except for a brief estimate of the historical values of other products, is confined entirely to the range of what is known as 'the literature of power'" (131).

discourses and by the establishment of new disciplines founded on the criterion of scientificity.

As we know, the critics and the scientists began to clash in the later nineteenth century—the Arnold-Huxley debate is the most familiar relic of that conflict—but it would be an error to suppose that the stakes of this conflict were exclusively epistemological or that the conflict between criticism and science was only another version of the low-intensity conflict between the "scholars and the critics" waged in the eighteenth century. It has been convenient in histories of literary criticism to epitomize its conflictual relations with other discourses of knowledge by invoking the opposition of literature and science, but the opposition to which I draw attention here is also between the two institutional *sites*—the periodical sphere and the university—and between the two kinds of *expert* specific to those sites. This is not a question of epistemology so much as it is of institutional history, the social organization of expert cultures. A conflict between science and literature characterizes only the later phase of literary culture's history, the period of discipline formation in the later nineteenth and early twentieth century. During that period, it was not only the natural scientists who came into conflict with the sages of literary culture but also the scholars dominating the new language departments, the philologists.[31]

On the American side of the Atlantic especially, the epistemic conflict between natural scientists and the figures of literary culture was not typically expressed in versions of the Huxley-Arnold debate; it was most likely to be found in the struggle between philologists and self-styled *grammarians* over issues of usage, that is, over the standardization of English, a project of immense importance in a country populated by waves of immigration. The grammarians, or "verbal critics," were figures of literary culture; they belonged to the world of periodical writing. Kenneth Cmiel describes their conflict with the philologists in his *Democratic Eloquence* as one in which the "scholars stressed the importance of learning over breeding. They called themselves 'experts' and 'specialists' whose command of the English language must be bowed to. To write verbal criticism, the linguists argued, would take a degree of specialized knowledge the critics did not possess. Refined sensibilities and broad acquaintance with English letters no longer were sufficient to settle questions of usage. . . . Knowledge was

31. On the early history of the debate between the scholars and the critics, see Joseph M. Levine, *The Autonomy of History: Truth and Method from Erasmus to Gibbon* (Chicago: University of Chicago Press, 1999), 109–26.

pitted against taste."[32] Our interest here is not in the debate itself—which did not in any case have quite the outcome portended by the severe antithesis of "knowledge" and "taste"—but in its significance for the evolution of expertise in modernity. The figures called "verbal critics," who abounded in the print media of nineteenth-century America, were just as exemplary of literary culture in the United States as Carlyle and Arnold were in England. In the dispute between the philologists and the grammarians, we can see that the epistemic stakes were not simply those implied by the categories of science and literature but that all three components of literary culture entered into this dispute—grammar, literature, and criticism.

Neither the philological scholar nor the verbal critic was able to stand against the other on purely epistemological grounds without drawing strength from the *institutional* bases of their respective modes of expertise. Regarded in this light, the conflict between the philologists and the verbal critics confirms the exterior location of literary culture, even as it reminds us of the great social prestige of the men of letters. The philologists were by no means successful in toppling the verbal critics from their positions of authority over language and "grammar." It is also highly significant for the timing of this debate that the philologists who represented themselves as scientists launched their attacks on the critics from *recently* acquired departmental bases in the university. As we have had occasion to observe before, most scientific inquiry before the later nineteenth century took place outside the university, and there was no necessary contradiction then between the "amateur" and the "expert." The opening of the university to new sciences (not just mathematics and astronomy, as in the old college), along with the reformation of older disciplines according to scientific paradigms, gave the philologists an institutional advantage the critics lacked, but the institutional authority of the philologists was not yet sufficient to win the debate over grammar.

When advocates for new kinds of knowledge—both scholarly and what we now call scientific—campaigned for the accommodation of these new discourses in the university curriculum, this campaign was ipso facto a campaign for vernacularization, which quickly developed into a powerful centripetal social force. The vernacular pressed in upon the centers of the educational system from every periphery, including the ambient literary

---

32. Cmiel, *Democratic Eloquence*, 162. Cmiel includes an appendix listing the many dozens of works of verbal criticism along with the contending works of scientific philology. This debate is more or less forgotten today, but its importance at the time is an index of the preeminence of literary culture in the nineteenth century.

culture.[33] The pressure on the classical university did not cease with the partial opening of the curriculum to new courses, such as the "rhetoric and belles lettres" course in the eighteenth century or a few new sciences in the earlier nineteenth; this pressure did not cease until it forced the collapse of the classical curriculum altogether just as though it were an overstressed dam. (A more detailed account of this transition is offered in chapter 5, "The Postrhetorical Condition.") The effect of the collapse was to make possible the rapid multiplication and diversification of professional fields, now liberated more or less from the prerequisite study of Latin. The tendency of vernacularization was in this way fused with another social tendency, which we can name *professionalization*, or the redefinition of occupational fields by analogy to the ancient learned professions. And yet the occupations associated with literary culture were not immediately served by the opening of new professions in the university. It was above all the technical and scientific discourses (engineering, physics, and biology) that rushed into the curricular vacuum and were established as disciplines and then new professions. The scientific study of the modern languages also followed this path, but vernacular literature remained eccentric to the new curriculum, just as it had been eccentric to the old.

What would constitute the writing of literature (including criticism) during this period as a profession, in the absence of university credentials?[34]

33. For the status of Latin and Greek in the early modern university, see Joseph Levine, *The Battle of the Books: History and Literature in the Augustan Age* (Ithaca, NY: Cornell University Press, 1991): "Already under Queen Elizabeth the curriculum is determined that will govern English education for two or three centuries. And it is deliberately restricted to the literature of classical Greece and Rome, with everything else set intentionally to one side" (5). The "everything else" defines the large domain of "eccentricity" from which emanates the centripetal force of the vernacular, a domain that includes much that has been understood as the "origin" of literature or literary study. These peripheries include, of course, the Indian Civil Service, the education of whose members, both English and Indian, is determined from the imperial center according to principles set out in the famous 1854 *Report on the Indian Civil Service*, which mandated study of English rather than classics.

34. An early and extremely important instance of this negotiation occurs in the famous chapter on "productive and unproductive labor" in Adam Smith's *An Inquiry into the Nature and Causes of the Wealth of Nations*. I quote here from the edition of R. H. Campbell and A. S. Skinner, 2 vols. (Indianapolis: Liberty Classics, 1981): "The labour of some of the most respectable orders of society is, like that of menial servants, unproductive of any value. . . . In the same class must be ranked, some both of the gravest and most important, and some of the most frivolous professions: churchmen, lawyers, physicians, men of letters of all kinds; players, buffoons, musicians, opera-singers, opera-dancers, &c. . . . Like the declamation of the actor, the harangue of the orator, or the tune of the musician, the work of all of them perishes in the very instant of its production" (1:330–

Our sense of a "profession of letters" wavers uncertainly between signifying the social prestige of the published writer and the other sense of "professional," writing for money. But it was just as likely that the social prestige of a writer in the earlier eighteenth century was enhanced by gentlemanly status, by *not* having to write for money and, therefore, the tendency to regard writing for money as *proof* of professional status is anachronistic. It was still possible well into the nineteenth century for the man of letters who wrote for money to be regarded as engaged in something closer to a trade than a profession.[35] The taint of trade clinging to the career of writing for money might also be contrasted with the more favorable association between the traditional "learned professions" and the status of gentleman, at least in England.[36]

In any case it was not until the British census of 1861 that authors, editors, and journalists were categorized in any official usage as professionals.[37] Until such confirmation of rising social status, the "profession of letters"

---

31). The juxtaposition of the grave and the frivolous surveys the ground that must be traversed in asserting the profession of letters as more than an analogy. A. S. Collins, in *The Profession of Letters, 1780–1832* (New York: E. P. Dutton, 1929), notes that several pamphlet writers in the 1750s and 1760s refer to "authors by profession" (21). This locution too confirms what I mean by the negotiation of a social identity. It is not yet the case that the "profession" of author goes without saying; therefore it must be said, or professed. For a judicious analysis of the complex relation between the claims to professional status and the social prestige of occupations such as "men of letters," see Penelope J. Corfeld, *Power and the Professions in Britain, 1700–1850* (London: Routledge, 115), 174–99.

35. Zachary Leader, "Coleridge and the Uses of Information," in *Grub Street and the Ivory Tower: Literary Journalism and Literary Scholarship from Fielding to the Internet,* ed. Jeremy Treglown and Bridget Bennet (Oxford: Clarendon, 1998), reminds us that Coleridge advises "youthful literati" in his *Biographia Literaria* that they should "never pursue literature to a trade" (26). Of course, most literati of the nineteenth century were in some sense "journalists," even the novelists who published serially. On this question in eighteenth-century literary culture, see Douglas Lane Patey, "The Institution of Criticism in the Eighteenth Century," in *The Cambridge History of Literary Criticism,* ed. H. B. Nisbet and Claude Rawson (Cambridge: Cambridge University Press, 1997), 3–31. See also W. J. Reader, *Professional Men: The Rise of the Professional Classes in Nineteenth-Century England* (New York: Basic Books, 1966), 148, for a comment on the association between professionals and gentlemen.

36. See Frank Donoghue, "Colonizing Readers: Review Criticism and the Formation of a Reading Public," in *The Consumption of Culture, 1600–1800: Image, Object, Text,* ed. Ann Bermingham and John Brewer (London, Routledge, 1995), 62–63. Donoghue argues that although the term was never mentioned with reference to periodical writers of the eighteenth century, something like a "rhetoric of professionalism" emerged at that time in the debates between rival editors and reviewers of the period.

37. See W. J. Reader, *Professional Men,* 146–66, for a discussion of the census and other signs of recognition for new professions.

had to be a kind of mimetic performance of professionalism, successful for some—the so-called Victorian sages—but not for others, the mere hacks of journalism, of Grub Street. The increasing stratification of the journalistic sphere in the nineteenth century into high and low venues, high-status and low-status writers, did not necessarily clarify the social identity or status of writers in the print media. Because their social status was still somewhat ambiguous in the later nineteenth century, many of them actively sought out the more formal recognition bestowed by academic credentials. For the "preachers of culture" especially, recognition by the university was a surer path to unequivocal professional status than any honor afforded by literary culture. Many of these figures actively sought out university professorships, and sometimes achieved them, as did Matthew Arnold, John Churton Collins, and Sir Walter Raleigh. Nevertheless, these crossover scholar-critics coexisted uneasily with their philological peers, with whom they often competed for the same university positions.[38] There was thus no resolution in the nineteenth century of the underlying conflict between the two kinds of expertise, a conflict that could always be played out in the struggle over the disciplinary status of literature itself, as Foucault rightly saw in naming literature as both the contestation and twin of philology.

What does this account tell us about the history of literary study? What we call "literature" today was defined before the twentieth century by its location in vernacular culture, by its exteriority to the educational system, and even by its resistance to the form of the discipline. This resistance did not characterize *language* as an object, nor the works of Greek and Roman antiquity, which only became "literature" by virtue of translation into the vernacular. Outside the school, on the other hand, literature was exploding in social significance at the same time that it was gradually contracting as an assemblage of genres. Can such a moving target be arrested for the purpose of serving as the object of discipline? My conclusion is that literature does not need to be defined, nor should it be defined, by its *stasis* as an object; its object status is rather determined by the forces, at any historical

---

38. Although I have emphasized the exteriority of literary culture to the official curriculum of the university, it was possible for a figure such as Matthew Arnold to be appointed to a professorship. See Jeremy Treglown and Bridget Bennet, eds., *Grub Street and the Ivory Tower: Literary Journalism and Literary Scholarship from Fielding to the Internet* (Oxford: Clarendon Press, 1998). However, relations between the philologists and the "men of letters" remained contentious. The competition for the Oxford professorship of English coveted by John Churton Collins exhibits the conflict at its most intense. The appointment of a philologist, Arthur Sampson Napier, provoked Collins to write his blast, *The Study of English Literature.*

moment, organizing writing under this name. A simpler way to put this point is that literature is a *historical* object. Much of what has passed in the discipline as a "theory of literature" has mistaken this object for something like a natural kind.

The literary object seems nonetheless more fixed at the end of the delimitation process than ever before—yet literature is possibly on the move again. When I teach the introductory course for the English major, some of my students express surprise when they find poems on the syllabus as well as works of fiction. They tell me, "But I thought this was a course in literature!" Poetry is something else for them. The conflation of literature with the form of the novel possibly inaugurates an eighth phase in the delimitation of literature. Poetry is becoming for many readers something *different* from literature, a mode of verbal expression that is conspicuous for its nonacademic social venues. If we cannot define literature as a stable object for all times and places, however, we can at least chart its complex delimitations. I will return to this question in the conclusion to this book, which considers some of the implications for our discipline of literature's generative determinations.

CHAPTER 8

The Contradictions of Global English

It is only from the interconnection of all the events (συμπλοκῆς) one with another and from their comparison, and from their resemblances and differences, that a man can obtain his object and, thanks to a clear view of these matters, can derive both profit and pleasure from history.

POLYBIUS, *The Histories*

My reflections on global English in this chapter are prompted by two occasions, the first dating from some years ago when I was chair of the department of English at NYU. At that time, the department had no faculty cohort in postcolonial studies—already in the first decade of the twenty-first century a conspicuous lack. We proposed hiring such a cohort, first one senior scholar and then two junior scholars. The deans approved, and at the end of the hiring process we had established a new cohort in this field. Since that time, the faculty has expanded in other directions beyond the curriculum of British and American literature and even postcolonial, with many new offerings in global and contemporary literature. As we discovered, however, we did not fully comprehend the demands these new courses would make on our majors. Most students are familiar only in general terms with the history of European imperialism, which they tend to encounter through a handful of canonical texts, such as Conrad's *Heart of Darkness*. Many are even less familiar with the long, complicated, and still ongoing process of decolonization. Consequently, some new courses in postcolonial topics were at first underenrolled. For some students, the appeal of reading works by familiar British and American authors outweighed the appeal of unfamiliar works of contemporary or global literature.

The second occasion for reflection occurred several years ago, when my department conducted a review of the curriculum in the major, focused especially on the three-course literary historical sequence in British and American literature. At the end of the review, we added a fourth course in World Anglophone as well as other minority literatures, largely contemporary. The purpose of the fourth course was to extend the core curriculum in time to the present and in geopolitical space to the world, thus matching the scope of upper-level courses. By this means we hoped to level the pedagogic terrain between British and American writers and their global contemporaries and to interest students in writers of whom they may not even have heard. Although I believe that this revision of the major was the best resolution of our review, it was more controversial than we thought it would be. The controversy did not arise from advocates for retaining the British and American curriculum as it was—there were no such advocates—but from those who felt that not enough space had been ceded in the core sequence to literatures that were contemporary or that represented the writing of minorities here and Anglophone writers abroad.

In our (sometimes tense) discussions of curricular reform, I had occasion to repeat some arguments I made in *Cultural Capital* about identifying authors in the curriculum with currently defined social identities. These arguments proved less than effective, however, in response to a new sense of urgency about curricular reform, which has developed since into a movement with a new signature agenda, "decolonizing the curriculum." This notion constructs the curriculum ambiguously both as colony and as instrument of colonization, but in either case, the rhetorical force of the trope is very great. Decolonization as an agenda for literature programs in the United Kingdom and the United States raises many questions, beginning with the displacement of decolonization from its geopolitical timeline to the present and from the colonized world to the colonial powers or "the West." Equally importantly, decolonization is transposed to the cultural sphere, according to the precedent established by Ngugi wa Thiong'o's seminal work, *Decolonising the Mind*.[1] These displacements are not uncomplicated and require some conceptual work in order to be understood in the context of curricular revision.

The movement to "decolonize the curriculum" converges on the disciplinary project of postcolonial studies, although this meme arrived late in the development of the field. Robert J. C. Young anticipated the motif of cultural decolonization in his study, *Postcolonialism: An Historical Introduction*, published in 2001, some years in advance of the curricular movement: "For postcolonial theory is designed to undo the ideological heritage of colonialism not only in the decolonized countries, but also in the west itself. Once the process of political decolonization has taken place, then a cultural decolonization must follow: decolonize the west, deconstruct it."[2]

1. Ngugi wa Thiong'o, *Decolonising the Mind: The Politics of Language in African Literature* (Nairobi: James Currey, 1981).

2. Robert J. C. Young, *Postcolonialism: An Historical Introduction* (Chichester: Blackwell, 2001), 65. For the geopolitical process of decolonization, see Martin Thomas, *Fight or Flight: Britain, France, and Their Roads from Empire* (Oxford: Oxford University

This process has a potentially much broader field of action than the university curriculum, as wide as Western culture itself, which constitutes a vast system of global circulation, inclusive of film, television, art, and music, as well as mass-produced commodities like T-shirts, jeans, and Coca-Cola. These artifacts of culture have effects both within the colonizing nations of their production and globally, but their assimilation in the formerly colonized world is by no means passive. Even those commodities that are coercively marketed are integrated into local cultures in ways unimagined by multinational corporations. Taking this wide view of the cultural impact of the West, including both high and low cultural products, the university curriculum seems a relatively small domain of action. But in recent years, the point of greatest pressure in the decolonization project has been nothing other than the curriculum, exemplified chiefly by a canon of philosophical and literary figures. In the Western metropoles, diversifying the curriculum has proven to be easier than diversifying the student population and very much easier than making university faculties and student bodies truly inclusive.

The focus of decolonization on the curriculum is worth remarking for its intrainstitutional limits as well. It would be hard to deny that the force of decolonization falls off rapidly beyond the humanities curriculum, despite efforts to target even the most resistant disciplines, such as mathematics or physics. These efforts have also made little headway in the business and technical disciplines that occupy the vastly larger terrain of the university curriculum. One ironic consequence of this process is that Western "high culture" has become the low-hanging fruit for the decolonial project. Figures who are no longer much read, who have already suffered from cultural divestment, have been roused from their dormancy to serve as representatives of Western culture, the face of imperial domination. In that context, the decolonial project is difficult even to describe without engaging passions that are entirely understandable, given the staggering depredations of Western imperialism, for which "Rhodes Must Fall" came to circulate as a shorthand in the British and the South African university systems. Although the name of Cecil Rhodes is linked to the university because of his eponymous fellowship, his career implies nothing about the relation of *literature* to the global system of cultural production today.

It cannot be forgotten, however, that literature had its role to play in the colonial enterprise, an impressively large one, as we know, in India, South Africa, and other sites of British colonization. Nonetheless, it is an

---

Press, 2014). Thomas offers an exhaustive account of the very different paths to decolonization for Britain and France, depending on the individual colonies and their history.

open question today what role the cultural form of literature, in English or other languages, continues to play in a world of ramifying and competing cultural forms. It does not seem to me, in the current situation, that literature has so great a role to play as it once had. At the same time, its less central position in the global circulation of culture contrasts strikingly with the fact of its exponential growth in the form of works written in English, or translated into English. This is the real-world condition in which curricular reform for English departments must be situated, a contradiction: literature occupies a smaller place among cultural forms, while at the same time literature *in English* has proliferated far beyond its accumulation in the nations of its earlier writers. We have long since arrived at the moment when literature in English no longer means British and American literature but "world literature." There is no question that English departments must accommodate themselves in some way to global literary production in the English language. Changes in the curriculum will be necessary in order to achieve this goal. The question I want to put before us is whether we want to conceptualize this accommodation as a process of decolonization.[3]

It is a safe assumption that decolonization must mean something different in Kenya, South Africa, and India than it could mean in the United Kingdom or the United States. Insofar as the curriculum is in question, it matters in Britain and America that we have been here before. Decolonization of the curriculum in the United Kingdom and the United States appears to rehearse many of the same arguments for canonical revision undertaken decades earlier in the "culture wars." When decolonization is invoked today, it does not necessarily refer directly to colonialism but more generally to the exclusion of people of color, women, and other minorities from representation in the curriculum. Although it is true that cultural decolonization is a real and ongoing process for former colonies, it is my sense that the movement to decolonize the curriculum in the United Kingdom and the

3. For a more detailed critique of the relation between decolonization and the curriculum than will be possible to offer here, see Jonathan Jansen, *Decolonisation in Universities: The Politics of Knowledge*, ed. Jonathan Jansen (Johannesburg: WITS University Press, 2019). Writing in the introduction to this volume with reference to South Africa, Jansen raises a number of questions about "the uncritical adoption of the language of decolonisation 20 years into South Africa's democratic transition" (5). He argues that the "reduction of curricular problems . . . to one particular kind of regime, colonialism, is to deny the many ways in which knowledge has been propagated, contested, nullified, subverted, and transformed across more than three centuries stretching from the pre-colonial society to post-apartheid governance" (5). He also reminds us of the "misrepresentation of Western knowledge as unitary when, in fact, the West itself has experienced considerable epistemological turmoil" over the last century (10).

United States is indeed a rehearsal of the agenda advanced in the culture wars of the 1980s and '90s. Revision of the canon then was oriented around the concept of "multiculturalism" but with somewhat greater emphasis at the time on gender than on race or ethnicity. The shift in emphasis to the latter categories corresponds to the extended scope for canonical revision, from the national to the transnational or global. Complicating but also reinforcing this recycling of arguments from the canon wars is the fact that the term "decolonization" today circulates as a name for all efforts to undo injustice, of whatever kind. The question before us here is not the necessity of decolonization as an ongoing geopolitical struggle with many sites of engagement but whether this concept is the best frame for the task of curricular revision. Not surprisingly, some who advocate strongly for decolonization as a political exigency are uncomfortable with its metaphoric extension to all instances of resistance or opposition. [4]

In my department, the urgency of curricular reform was also expressed in an idiom analogous to that of pastoral care, as in the notion that students need to "see themselves in the curriculum." This notion, which has become a commonplace, raises interesting questions about how *identification* enters into the transmission of literature. Identification in this context refers chiefly to the category of the *author*, with whom readers are assumed to identify according to gender, race, or other concepts of identity. Problematically, works of earlier literature do not lend themselves easily to these identifications, both because literacy was rare in earlier societies and because categories of identity change over time. Identification also describes the response of readers to characters in stories, though this is precluded for some forms of literature, mainly poetry, which often does not have characters as such. Most importantly, the senses in which works of literature function as a kind of mirror for readers or groups of readers is greatly complicated by the changing demographic constitution of society

---

4. The metaphoric extension of the decolonizing project has provoked resistance from scholars who want to insist on the literal sense of the term and the full political implications of that agenda. Eve Tuck and K. Wayne Yang, for example, in "Decolonization Is Not a Metaphor," *Decolonization: Indigeneity, Education & Society* 1 (2012): 1–40, make the case for taking the term literally in the context of Native American society and settler colonialism. They assert that decolonization "is a distinct project from other civil and human rights–based social justice projects" (2). Further, "There are parts of the decolonization project that are not easily absorbed by human rights or civil rights based approaches to educational equity" (3). In 2019, Tuck later retreated from the rigor of this position, conceding some space for the metaphoric conception of decolonization. See Scott Challener, "Introduction: Not Only a Metaphor," *Post45* (2021), https://post45.org/2021/07/introduction-not-only-a-metaphor/.

itself, which at any historical moment does not correspond to the subset of the reading public, or of college students. These are conditions that need to be acknowledged before we can begin to think about the relation between identity categories and the process of identification in readers.[5]

The language of pastoral care implicit in the notion that students should "see themselves" in the curriculum echoes our students' own idiom of judgment, especially the notion that works of literature should be "relatable." This sense of the word appeared in colloquial English only a few decades ago; it betrays the extent to which reading belongs to the domain of commodity consumption. Embedded in this tangle of desires and expectations is a discrepancy between what students see as relatable and what my colleagues see as their demand for representation. For my colleagues, it is principally underserved or excluded minorities who want to "see themselves" in the canon, and curricular reform should proceed accordingly. But in addition to the fact that many students belong to "majority" categories of identity, the very fact of the diversity of minority students vexes the aim of constructing the curriculum in a mirror relation to demographics. Only contemporary literature has any chance of representing real-world diversity, with obvious implications for the distribution in the curriculum between older and contemporary works. Even if this problem of representation were solvable, it would still be doubtful that the desire of our students to see themselves in what we ask them to read would be gratified. Most of our students (and many minority students as well?) express desires in their reading that connect most immediately with their cultural formation as young people, "American" by birth, with adolescent issues and uncertain job prospects. These identities are most likely to be reflected in the genre of "young adult fiction" (or "YA," as publishers know it), which makes up a large part of their pleasure reading and increasingly a large part of the secondary school curriculum. In the fall of 2016, I had the interesting experience of teaching several of these novels in a freshman seminar on dystopian fictions, a subgenre of YA that dominates our literary and film culture. The ideological message of this subgenre is questionable by any progressive standard, as it endorses, wittingly or not, the antigovernment

5. To put this point in the clearest possible terms, although it is very important that people "see themselves"—their identity or identities—in the representative political sphere, this desire is not transferable to the context of reading literature. But it is important also to understand why this is the case. What we see in the history of all cultural works is the result of historical forces that are often repugnant to our current morality and politics. At the same time, we find in these works the record of struggle with these forces as they were defined at the time, condensed in the form of artifacts—literature, art, music, and other cultural works. I return to this question below, in the conclusion.

attitude that drives right-wing political discourse. In my classes, I tried to prod my students into a critical relation to dystopian narratives, to distance themselves somewhat from what they saw as their relatable correspondents in YA stories, even the heroic Katniss of *The Hunger Games*.[6]

Whether or not I was successful in my advocacy of these basic critical techniques, I continue to believe that teaching students how to read literature that is *not* immediately relatable to their self-identification is one of the most important things we do. The balance between identification and critical distance is hard to maintain, a high-wire act. We want our students to become engaged by what is *other*, including persons who are different from themselves, but more than that, we want them to become engaged by whole worlds of otherness and irreducible difference. If the works of non-European or non-American authors can look forbiddingly unrelatable to some of our students, as we discovered in my department when we began to offer courses in postcolonial and world Anglophone subjects, so also do the works of earlier literature, coming from, as the historians like to remind us, a country as foreign as any currently to be found on the planet. There is no lack of difference in the literature of the past; figures who offer themselves for identification are harder to find there, however, and sometimes only seem to be like us.

In the struggle with anachronism, I am not yet ready to concede defeat. But I can easily see the English major in the future breaking into two tracks across the spine of World War II, because it will be increasingly difficult to establish a common curriculum for a major that runs from Anglo-Saxon works to the present. In the first track, students would study "English and American" literature, culminating in modernism. In the second track, students would study literature in English written largely if not exclusively after the Second World War, with an orientation toward issues of social identity. The English major is, for better or worse, unlikely to sustain for much longer a common core of courses, even after such a strategy as that adopted by my department of offering a fourth survey course in postwar and world literature in English. It seems very probable that the study of prewar literature in English will become like the classics, in ways that we can hope will be as interesting as classics are today. With the global accu-

---

6. In this course I also taught a much better novel, Lois Lowry, *The Giver* (1993), sometimes regarded as the first true YA novel. Its eerie premise, as fantastic as that of *The Hunger Games*, meditates on the forgetting of history, which is the premise of its totalitarian system. Setting aside the historical interest of the YA genre, it is worth remarking that much pleasure reading has a legitimately narcissistic motivation. The question for me in relation to the pastoral framing of the curriculum is whether we have gotten this motive right for young adults.

mulation of literature in English, the discipline of English literature will be at once enlarged and diminished. But in truth, this is not the future of the discipline but its present, and that is what I would like to examine in this chapter.

What I have predicted as the "second track" in the English major will be dominated, as it is now, by topics of identity and social justice, for mainly historical reasons. These include not only the history of imperial conquest and anticolonial struggles but also the "new social movements," as they were once known, which inaugurated a new phase of political struggle, along with new disciplinary projects in the academy, discussed in chapter 2 above. These new movements were diverse, but they had their greatest (if uneven) success in the larger project of remedying the long-standing oppression of groups for whom social identity could be sharply defined or marked. This identity thematic dominates the study of contemporary literature, but it is also difficult not to interpret the literature of the past without the lens of these concerns. The farther back we travel, however, the more this lens falls out of focus, and needs constantly to be corrected for anachronism. It becomes ever more difficult to understand the past in its own terms, in order then to understand it in ours. Those who teach older literature know that for many students, this is the deep end of the curriculum. As literature recedes into the past, the familiar categories of identity become attenuated; they can only be recovered by a careful labor of historical contextualization. Confronted with this strangeness, our students understandably want to translate it into what is "relatable" and, failing that, literature itself sometimes seems to fail them, or rather, our teaching fails them. We can promise our students what is relatable *ultimately*, but not at first. What we should not do, I suggest, is permit our students to study only those works in which they "see themselves," as experience tells us that choice will almost always skew to the present.

The curriculum is in any case not about choice, despite the measure of choice we build into it at the margin, with our electives. The element of choice in the curriculum is modern, of course, and reflects the enormous explosion of knowledge in modernity. There is no one curriculum that works for everyone, as there was in premodern Europe, which relied on the Latin language and Catholic theology for making the curriculum cohere. Still, a curriculum in which there is no coercion is not a curriculum at all. The curriculum is a site of contention because it exerts force, bureaucratically recognized in the notion of "requirements." This force in turn measures our responsibility for the transmission of a valued knowledge. If we don't exert force in the curriculum, we are disclaiming that responsibility. Yet in the fact of choice, of the "elective," a counterforce is manifest as well, which cannot simply be denied. This countervailing force arises above all from the absolute accumulation of writing, one of many vast accumulations of modernity. We cannot require it all, nor can we leave all choice to the student.

This contradiction is greatly exacerbated in English departments when world Anglophone literature enters the curriculum. The amount of literary writing in the postwar period has increased almost exponentially, a consequence of the fact that as many as fifty-eight countries now use English as an official language. Wherever English is taught, it can also become a literary language. This accumulation is far greater than the amount of writing that already in antiquity provoked a complaint about "too much to read." In our own age of *far too much to read*, scholars such as Franco Moretti have responded by proposing new techniques of reading, such as the "distant reading" he first broached in an essay on world literature.[7] I don't intend to take that detour on this occasion, but I do want to underscore how increasingly problematic the volume of literature will become for the discipline in the future. What will this accumulation look like in thirty, forty, or fifty years? World Anglophone studies will soon acquire, and probably has already, a sufficient literature and history to constitute the knowledge base for a new discipline altogether, distinct from British and American. In the event of the curricular division I am contemplating, British and American literature of earlier periods will likely contract further. There is no point in bemoaning this eventuality, if only we can manage the transition without debasing both the historical and contemporary fields of study.[8] That will not be easy to do.

At least part of the struggle over the curriculum, then, is the result of the massive accumulation of works. It will only become more difficult to determine the right balance of authors, works, genres, periods, or nations represented in the curriculum. It seems to be the case already that the world Anglophone curriculum has become what David Damrosch calls "postcanonical," in the sense that world literature is divided into a very small number of "hypercanonical" figures (Achebe, Rushdie, Walcott, and a few others) and a great many figures who circulate globally but with far

---

7. Franco Moretti, "Conjectures on World Literature," *New Left Review*, second series, 1 (2000): 1–15.

8. I am not proposing here that the two tracks of English "go their separate ways." There are many research projects, and many possible courses as well, that will straddle both tracks. Methodologies such as digital humanities will likely range freely over both tracks, along with many other projects. The problem I address, rather, is the difficulty of establishing a curriculum that is common for all English majors or that constitutes the common knowledge base for literary study at the graduate level.

less fame.[9] Damrosch calls the latter a "shadow canon," the casualty of a complex interaction between literary markets, schools, and the dominance of the English language in literary production. Interestingly, the canon of British and American literature seems to be following the same path, as minor writers steadily disappear from courses. The mechanism of contraction presses upon both past and present, driving the curriculum toward extreme selectivity and militating against representation of the real-world diversity of literary production. In order to preserve Wordsworth in an ever-expanding English curriculum, Hazlitt or Hunt or Clare might have to be sacrificed, along with many other minor writers. Among these minor writers, there might be room for Dorothy Wordsworth, for the purpose of gender representation, but for this inclusion, too, a price must be paid. Just as Anglophone writing is being organized into "hypercanonical" forms, so is the canon of historical British and American literature, *for the same reason.*[10] This ineluctable tendency calls for new thinking about the concept and form of curriculum. Yet the contest for representational space has not given rise to such a theoretical project.

We might begin to address the need for such a theory by reframing curricular revision with reference to all the sites of literary production and circulation and all the possibilities of their interaction. I propose that curricular revision need not be motivated specifically or only by the aim of decolonization, which is a limited frame for capturing the relations of literary works to local cultural environments or their external relations to global sites. These relations are enormously complex; they are interactions that cannot be reduced to unilateral acts of domination or appropriation. A version of this thought occurred many centuries ago to the Greek historian Polybius, whom I would like to awaken from his canonical slumber for a moment in order to make my point. Polybius tried to discern in the vast complexity of the Roman Empire an ideal of "interconnection" (*symploké*) that transcended the empire's brutal reality. This condition of interconnection was not orchestrated from the imperial center, which was only a *part* of the total system. Whether or not this ideal was sufficiently realized in the time of Polybius to mitigate the effects of Roman imperialism, the transcendence of the "world system" over its parts is a reality for us today. The

9. See David Damrosch, "World Literature in a Postcanonical, Hypercanonical Age," in Haun Saussy, ed., *Comparative Literature in an Age of Globalization* (Johns Hopkins University Press, 2006), 43–53.

10. Let me stress again that the best outcome for English will be a division of labor. One possible consequence of a future for English as two tracks or even two disciplines is that the "shadow canon" might be recovered for serious study.

circulation of global culture can be understood as a process very like what Polybius called "interconnection" or, more literally, "interweaving."

More recently, Kwame Anthony Appiah makes the case for something similar to Polybius's notion in his study *The Lies That Bind: Rethinking Identity*, which carries forward his career-long advocacy of a "cosmopolitan" perspective on matters such as the global circulation of culture. Discussing the possible interconnections between the supposed essence of "the West" and its projected others, such as the Islamic world, he writes: "No Muslim essence stops individual inhabitants of Dar al-Islam from taking up anything from the Western Civ. Syllabus, including democracy. No Western essence is there to stop a New Yorker of any ancestry taking up Islam. Wherever you live in the world, Li Po can be one of your favorite poets, even if you've never been anywhere near China."[11] Before Appiah, we might invoke C. L. R. James, who "connected" cricket and the novels of Thackery in his memoir, *Beyond a Boundary*, expressing his love for both, but without yielding a jot in his radical critique of British imperialism.[12] And most famously, W. E. B. Du Bois insisted before James, in *The Souls of Black Folk*, "I sit with Shakespeare, and he winces not. Across the color line, I walk arm in arm with Balzac and Dumas."[13] These are precedents that we should not set aside lightly.[14]

The notion of *symploké* might be a good concept for reframing curricular reform, which is troubled by strategic puzzles. It has become a commonplace in curricular debates, for example, to dismiss the "additive" solution to curricular revision as "tokenism." But the obverse strategy of segregating literatures according to social identity and in service to the decolonizing motive has equal disadvantages, most importantly sacrificing interconnection for the sake of assembling a politically coherent phalanx of writers. It might be better to approach the curriculum without worrying too much about whom to add or whom to subtract, and consider instead how to present literature in relation to its real conditions of production and circulation. This would entail, for any work of literature whatsoever, an honest accounting of those conditions, and more than that, the scrupulous recognition of how those conditions enter into the fabric of a literary work.

11. Kwame Anthony Appiah, *The Lies That Bind: Rethinking Identity* (London: W. W. Norton, 2018), 207.

12. C. L. R. James, *Beyond a Boundary* (Durham, NC: Duke University Press, 2013).

13. W. E. B. Du Bois, *The Souls of Black Folk* (Mineola, NY: Dover, 1994), 67.

14. For a different view, see Jesse Alemán, "The End of English," *PMLA* 136 (2021): "We should all come to the position that our long-standing investments in the literary and cultural values of the standard English curriculum must go the same way as the Confederate and conquistador statues that are falling across the south and southwest" (472).

For contemporary works, it is again, in my view, a question less of who best represents the depredations of colonialism or the anticolonial struggle than of the use to which writers on the global scene have put the English language, as an agent of global interconnection. Global English is not dominated from the center, nor is it merely an echo of the center sounding in the periphery. It is a proliferating network that covers the world and makes possible literary expressions that are relatively autonomous in relation to imperial metropoles, as well as literary expressions within the metropoles that are relatively autonomous in relation to the formerly colonized world. This is to say in the latter case that the works of British and American writers (or more generally, of "the West") can be seen as belonging to this network without being reduced to standard-bearers of imperial power. Let us widen the frame for reconstructing the curriculum, then, to include all of these possibilities.

One entailment of this reframing is that those who read literature in the formerly colonized world have a right of access to the literature of the "West," just as those who read literature in the metropoles have a right of access to the literature produced by writers of the former colonies. Only on the basis of a global cultural commons can literary works be situated accurately in different aesthetic, social, political, or geopolitical contexts. Is it possible to imagine a curriculum that preserves this possibility of universal access? I suggest a new slogan for this effort: Democratize the curriculum! This is the real task we face in curricular revision, a different matter than the question of whom to include or exclude. The latter decisions are more properly made at the moment in which a teacher constructs a *syllabus*, where the subject of any particular course directs attention to some works rather than others. The notion that there are works that can be permanently retired from the curriculum (or its fantasmatic double, the "canon") for any other reason than that scholars are no longer interested in reading or writing about them is unnecessary.

At the present time, in my view, the most important occasion for curricular revision in the discipline of English is the emergence of global English—which, though it is a long-term consequence of imperialism, exceeds that origin in countless ways. (Analogous occasions, of course, would govern curricular reform in other European languages and literatures.) The English language interconnects populations in ways that exceed the effects of Britain's colonial projects, however gruesome they were, or damaging they continue to be. Our understanding of the globalization of English is only at the beginning. At the moment, we experience this climacteric in literary study as curricular incoherence, the simultaneous contraction of the curriculum (in some parts) and its growth (in other parts). The globalization of English resulted in the most important systemic contradiction we need to acknowledge in the project of curricular revision: between the global and the local. Every literary work in English springs from the soil of a local culture at the same time that it potentially circulates globally. There is no possibility of mastering this global accumulation by canonical summation, much less by a singular curricular arrangement. It might be possible to construct a stable "canon" for what Kafka called a "small" language—his term has been translated unfortunately as "minor"—like that of Czech or Yiddish, but even this seems to me a dubious prospect over the long term. Of the "major" languages, none is more major than English, and none is so generative of literature. For those of us who teach English literature, this is both a blessing and a curse—another contradiction.

I would like to draw out now some further consequences of global English, as it shapes the mission of the English department and its curriculum. I want to take a moment first, however, to explain why I insist in these remarks on the term "global." I am aware that the terms in circulation are alternatively "postcolonial" or "world literature," of which literature in English or world Anglophone is a subset. Derrida made the turn from globe to world (*mondiale*) fashionable in these contexts, and some of the notable scholars of world literature, such as Pheng Cheah and David Damrosch, have followed in this choice of term.[15] World literature has also developed as a competitor to comparative literature, and perhaps its successor, because programs in world literature so often rely on translated texts. Strenuous objections have been registered by comparatists such as Gayatri Chakravorty Spivak and Emily Apter to dependence on translation in curricula of world literature. In her manifesto, *Death of a Discipline*, Spivak argues for a return to a comparative literature based on close reading of texts in their original languages.[16] Emily Apter makes an analogous argument for the political value of "untranslatability" in a work provocatively titled *Against World Literature*.[17] The stakes in these arguments are high, especially as "world literature" seems to be acquiring a disciplinary form more closely aligned with English departments than with modern foreign languages or comparative literature. I am very mindful of these stakes, but

15. Pheng Cheah, *What Is a World? Post-Colonial Literature as World Literature* (Durham, NC: Duke University Press, 2016).

16. Gayatri Chakravorty Spivak, *Death of a Discipline* (New York: Columbia University Press, 2003).

17. Emily Apter, *Against World Literature: On the Politics of Translatability* (London: Verso, 2013).

I want to focus more narrowly on the situation of works either written in English or translated into English, as these are the works that will be taught in the English department to come.

The concept of the "global" compels us to acknowledge the dominant position of English in relation to other languages and to foreground the relation of English to globalization—that is, the network, still under construction, of political, commercial, scientific, and military apparatuses, all of which are correlated with global capitalism. I do not think it is possible to understand English without acknowledging its global projection. This projection is very different from the notion of "world," which might be identified with the planet but is more richly tied philologically to territories, kingdoms, or empires. According to linguist David Crystal, English is arguably the first global language.[18] Before global English, there were two "world" languages in the European West: Latin and French. (In the Asian world, of course, there were others.) Global English shares with Latin and French many institutions and practices supporting these languages' dissemination beyond the kingdoms or states of their origin, but the difference of the global marks an epochal break.

The cultural institution we call "literature" is at once a projection of national identity—the supposed coincidence of language and nation—and a store of transferable cultural artifacts, always capable of transnational dissemination. Both Latin and French literature were propagated by empires but endured and thrived for cultural purposes beyond national boundaries. In the case of French, as Pascale Casanova has argued in her book, *The World Republic of Letters*, the cultural domination of French literary elites over the institutions of judgment transformed Paris into the capital of a "world republic" of literature, nearly global in extent.[19] I have some reservations about this argument, but Casanova makes a persuasive case for acknowledging the centrality of Parisian literary elites in consecrating many works, often those written in languages other than French. I am doubtful that the Parisian hegemony constituted either a world or a republic, though its extent was certainly very great, at the least "Western." In the case of English, the issue is not consecration, the bestowal of literary prestige, but the *production* of literature, largely narrative in form. More than the French cultural hegemony, global English is inextricable from the economics of globalization, exemplified in a worldwide market for literary goods in the

18. David Crystal, *English as a Global Language* (Cambridge: Cambridge University Press, 1997).

19. Casanova, *The World Republic of Letters*.

English language. For better or worse, this is a market largely for novels; every novel is also a book for sale.[20]

The generic contraction of "literature" to its most commodifiable form is a point of no small interest or consequence. Some of the problems that scholars have noted with global English literature arise from the intimate relation of English literary production to commerce, stimulating the production of standardized "world literature" novels that can have much the same superficial relation to the local as tourism. But setting that particular problem aside as beyond the scope of my remarks, I note that global English is distinguished by the fact that writing in English often takes place where England itself never held imperial sway. For Anglophone writers, English might be a second or third language but a first *literary* language. English can suppress the motive to write in one's native, non-English tongue, a situation lamented by writers as diverse as Vladimir Nabokov and Ngugi wa Thiong'o.[21] The worst that can be said of English, as an agent of globalization, is that it has undermined the literary vitality of other languages, and has probably contributed to the disappearance of some of the world's languages. This worst is very bad indeed.

At the same time, it must be said again that global Anglophone is a force that does not answer simply to the demands of the West, much less to the imperial authority of Britain or America. This is a point stressed by Casanova about literature generally, and it is only truer of English. Works in global English can return to the English homelands as expressions of resistance to political or cultural hegemony. This resistant thematic is both to be expected and to be welcomed, but it has contributed to a certain malaise afflicting the discipline of English literature in the Anglo-American university. This too is a contradiction. It underlies the tacit assumption that teaching world Anglophone is more politically progressive than the transmission of the national or imperial—or let us say, "traditional"—canon. In curricular discussions, the notion of the "traditional" imparts a stigma that may be unavoidable, but is not actually merited. The stigma in turn fuels "root and branch" movements for curricular revision, motivated by the implicit charge that English and American literature are objectionably "national-

20. For a comment on this matter, see Alexander Beecroft, *An Ecology of World Literature: From Antiquity to the Present Day* (London: Verso, 2015). Beecroft notes the "increasing need for sales in translation to sustain a literary career" as one of the factors "pushing towards an increasingly homogeneous literary world," resulting in "the emergence of a sort of standardized 'world-novel,' designed for easy translation and consumption abroad" (249).

21. See Ngugi wa Thiong'o's well-known argument for composition in one's native language, "The Language of African Literature," in *Decolonising the Mind*, 4–33.

ist." The curriculum is thus divided into two antithetical components, the one supposedly nationalist and imperialist, embodied in historical British and American literature, the other transnational and postcolonial, embodied in global Anglophone.

It would be good to clear the air on this subject, as I do not believe that this allegorization of the curriculum can survive historical inspection. (I have commented further on the matter of "national literature" in the conclusion to this volume.) Currently, the division of the curriculum into political opposites exacerbates a certain mood of pessimism in the discipline. For some scholars, world Anglophone, along with related minority literatures in the contemporary English homelands, is the real site of vitality and progress in the discipline. These scholars' sense that they have been prevented from advancing the discipline by those who specialize in traditional fields such as medieval or Victorian studies and who unfairly dominate the curriculum. The malaise that inhibits the professoriate from honestly negotiating its curricular problem also dovetails now with a certain exaggerated response to the decline in the number of majors since the financial crisis of 2008. The statement I cited earlier, to the effect that students fail to "see themselves" in the curriculum, was offered in the context of my department's curricular discussion as an explanation for why enrollments in the major fell in recent years. I believe it can be shown empirically that tendencies in enrollment have nothing to do with the curriculum and everything to do with externalities of the economy. To the question some of my colleagues have been asking, "What have we done wrong?"—I would answer, "nothing" or, rather, "nothing new." Nonetheless it has been difficult for the professoriate to resist the temptation to blame the curriculum for a decline in enrollments. This mistaken hypothesis has been reinforced by the generally beleaguered state of the humanities in general, for which there is in fact considerable evidence.

The pessimism that pervades English as a discipline in the British and American university systems makes for a puzzling contradiction when juxtaposed to the advance of global English. In a recent work that confronts directly the professoriate's pessimism, *The Global Future of English Studies*, James English vehemently rejects the narratives of decline pervading the discipline. Looking at the study of English literature from the global perspective, what he sees everywhere is proof of "its institutional health and fair prospects for the future."[22] So far from yielding to various incursions from cultural studies, media studies, composition, business English, and so

22. James F. English, *The Global Future of English Studies* (London: Wiley-Blackwell), 5.

forth, the discipline in his view has maintained a relatively stable core commitment to literature. The rival disciplinary forms mentioned have for the most part tended to hive off into separate programs.

English supports his argument with an impressive marshalling of statistics, but his strategic move is to look at the discipline in the global aggregate. This involves a certain risk, because we need to be persuaded that a global discipline of English literature exists, with enough common elements to justify aggregating statistics from all the sites of global education. English's optimism is the result of this aggregation, which minimizes the differences between the study of English in native-speaking homelands and its study in global Anglophone settings. I have some reservations about the strategy of aggregation, but I also want to credit the global perspective as a way to look at the future of English studies.

Addressing the condition of the discipline in the Anglo-American scene, English acknowledges the contraction of the English major but argues that these relative declines must be understood in relation to the total or absolute numbers of majors over the long term. These sums have remained relatively stable or even increased. The argument for decline, he rightly points out, all too often sets out from a baseline dating from the late 1960s and early 1970s, after the discipline had grown rapidly to keep pace with an equally rapid growth in the undergraduate population, at the same time that many students responded to the cultural upheaval of the sixties decade by moving into humanities majors. The spike in enrollments turned out to be temporary and anomalous; the size of the discipline and the major subsided thereafter to nearer its postwar mean.

The one development that troubles this picture is the declining ratio of tenure-track to adjunct or contract faculty. Taking a longer view of this tendency, English rightly argues that the growth of university education worldwide transformed the university into a relatively more democratic institution serving a mass public. The democratized global university, however, was unable to replicate the postwar model of a tenure-track faculty, which would have had to sustain its rate of growth at ever greater cost in order to service a swelling population of undergraduates. The casualization of a large segment of the professoriate was thus the cost of democratization, the global drive to credentialize an expanding class of professional and technical experts. English concludes: "The point is simply that the growth of higher education was never a promise of comparable growth of the traditional professoriate" (56). In the Anglo-American system, we experienced early on the costs of democratization and massification that soon came to characterize the global system.

If there is a global system of education that aims to democratize university education, this system does not seem to be developing to the benefit of humanities fields generally, despite the importance of global English—meaning the English *language*—to the global economy. English suffers alongside other humanities disciplines from reductions in support. The study of English is lucky only in that literature is still regarded as a useful means of producing literacy, and departments of English are not likely to disappear for that reason. But this is a condition that obtains only in the global setting. The same necessity does not govern the future of departments of English in the United Kingdom or the United States. It is not obvious that humanities fields in the Anglo-American university will be the beneficiaries of the global university system as it converges on a set of common goals, largely serving the competitive economic agendas of nation-states and multinational corporations. Nor, on the other hand, is it inevitable that the study of English literature across the global system will follow the model of the Anglo-American English department, with its orientation toward research and its emphasis on graduate education. That may be just as well if the employment situation is globally convergent. But the comparatively good fortune of English seems more ambiguous to me in the context of global tendencies.

Even if there is a bright future for the global study of literature in English, Anglophone studies in the Anglo-American university tend to play out in the context of conflicts internal to that system. In our discussions at NYU, my colleagues complained that the teaching of older British and American literature has been framed as a story about the Western nation-state and its triumphant emergence and destiny. Historical literatures look complicit with a nationalism that is questionable—especially now, when the ugliest forms of ethnic nationalism are resurgent, both here and in Europe. In response clearly to the exigency of the current situation, some of my colleagues argued that the older historical literatures, if they are to be retained, ought to be presented in a different way, suggested by the concept of the *transnational*. British works might be taught, for example, alongside American works or other non-European works. The pedagogic difficulties raised by this tandem approach were finally too great to solve, however, and this plan was abandoned. But it was a strong signal of the anathema aimed at what is perceived to be "national" literature. The stigma of nationalism slides easily from the curricular allegory to a judgment upon literary works themselves, regardless of the politics expressed in those works. Blake may write with scorn about priest and king, but teaching Blake as a British writer transforms his fierce dissent into an expression of the very nationalism he despised.

Now, in my experience, I do not know any colleagues who teach in the historical literatures before 1900 who celebrate a nationalist conception of English literature, either British or American. This allegorization of the curriculum went into default long ago, discredited by the very process of decolonization that broke up the old empires. Conversely, the non-Western works that make up the postcolonial curriculum often express the nationalist sentiment that motivated anticolonial struggles (with some exceptions, such as Tagore and Fanon). If a work of literature in English circulates transnationally, it does not do so by severing its relation to the nation-state of its origin. That relation defines the "local" pole of the contradiction between the global and the local. Finally, the way in which the curriculum has been used in the school system can and ought to be distinguished from the positions embodied in any given literary work, as in the example of Blake, just mentioned.

I have one final point to make about global English and its contradictions. If scholars have learned to resist the nationalist agenda of national literature, I would suggest conversely that the study of world Anglophone must learn to resist analogous effects of global transmission. Here I would agree with Emily Apter's stand "against world literature." Global English may seem like the answer to our prayers for the future of the discipline, but it is also a problem for the world. Cultural systems are healthier when they are diversified, a condition that has the advantage of preserving differences that can be banked for resistance to pressure for conformity. The substance of what I mean by difference here is *language*, or rather *languages*. Global English is a systemic phenomenon, but it should be resisted on behalf of preserving the languages occluded or destroyed by the system's convergent tendencies. To put this more bluntly, it would impoverish humanity if the net effect of global English and global English education would be to crowd out writing in non-English tongues. Aamir Mufti stages the radical response to this possibility when he titles his book on world literature *Forget English!*[23] The preservation of linguistic diversity is important in much the same way that the preservation of biological diversity is important. The systemic effect of "interconnectedness" can be seen in this context as the preservation of the openness of the system, resistance to the *convergence* of its multiple strands of interaction.

The solution to this problem is by necessity another expression of the problem: *translation*, which all too often means translation into English. Here is a final contradiction of global English. Translation into English has become the means to save and circulate literature in vernacular languages

23. Aamir R. Mufti, *Forget English! Orientalisms and World Literatures* (Cambridge, MA: Harvard University Press, 2016).

throughout the world, but translation also buries the source language even as it transmits new literature. It is even the case, again unavoidably, that some works translated *into* vernacular languages today take English translations as their source text, burying the original text even more deeply in the local. I have no solution to these problems, which have become the occasion for much important and urgent work in the expanding field of translation studies. I only want to affirm here, in conclusion, the proposition that global English should be both welcomed and resisted. Global English is a problem for our discipline, not just the solution to its desire for relevance. English has many purposes in the world system, among them to preserve at least mediated access to thousands of languages. Literature in English will continue to maintain an advantage globally for as long as English is a global language. In this interim, let us hope that the future of global English will be to help preserve linguistic diversity rather than destroy it. A careful reframing of the curriculum in recognition of this problem will perhaps enable us to envision a future for the study of English literature, in all of its times and places.

[PART THREE]

*Professionalization
and Its Discontents*

CHAPTER 9

On the Permanent Crisis
of Graduate Education

What form does science [*Wissenschaft*] take as a profession [*Beruf*] in the
material sense of the word? In practical terms this amounts nowadays to
the question: What is the situation of a graduate student who is intent on
an academic career in the university?

MAX WEBER, "Science as Vocation"

Back where I come from we have universities, seats of great learning—
where men go to become great thinkers. And when they come out, they
think deep thoughts—and with no more brains than you have. . . . But!
They have one thing you haven't got! A diploma!

The Wizard of Oz (1939)

MARKETS

In 1996, I published the first of two essays on graduate education, "Preprofessionalism: What Graduate Students Want," followed in 2000 by "The
System of Graduate Education."[1] In those essays I set out to analyze the way
in which graduate education was transformed by the collapse of the job
market for new PhDs. At the time, there were far fewer analyses of the job
situation in print than today, and the field of "critical university studies" did
not yet exist. Further, the realization that the job crisis was permanent was
only slowly sinking in. The market for new PhDs had improved in the later
1980s but crashed again in the '90s. After a temporary rise with the turn of
the century yielded to another slump, it was apparent that the decline was
permanent. My essays were controversial, chiefly because they were taken

---

1. John Guillory, "Preprofessionalism: What Graduate Students Want," *Profession*
(1996): 169–78; "The System of Graduate Education," *PMLA* 115 (2000): 1154–63. The
reader should note that the present chapter is concerned with the condition of permanent crisis in the job market and the effects of that market on the culture of graduate
education. There are many other problems confronting graduate education that will not
be treated here.

(incorrectly) as expressing an "antiprofessional" view of doctoral training.[2] My argument seemed to contradict the common wisdom that pressed upon new PhDs and their advisors as they approached the season of applying for jobs. To them, the obvious response to a buyer's market was to improve the quality of the product, to make it more attractive. In addition to having a completed dissertation that looked like a book, candidates were advised to have publications, to be able to demonstrate their professional activity with conference presentations, and to have a record of excellence in teaching. From this perspective, the notion that graduate students might be professionalized too early or too much was counterintuitive, even absurd; a job candidate needed *more professional achievement* in order to stand out from the mass of candidates.[3]

From the vantage of the system as a whole, the common wisdom resulted in unintended consequences. Every demand upon individual job candidates was a demand upon graduate education as a whole. Unfortunately, ramping up the professionalization of graduate students did nothing to increase the number of jobs, only to intensify the competition for those jobs. The result was untold anguish, generations of young people who worked very hard to achieve a goal that from the beginning was only marginally within their grasp, who lost years of their lives and years of earning power and who had to reinvent themselves professionally when the academic job did not materialize. This is the situation we inherited from the collapse of the job market and live with today, a permanent crisis.

And yet, looking back on graduate education of earlier decades, from the 1960s and before, it is indisputable that the system that emerged in the 1970s was fairer than its predecessor. The process of admission to graduate school was democratized with the creation of new and larger graduate programs. The "old boy" network was dismantled, and students encountered a job market that was a more level playing field, where merit would suppos-

---

2. A sampling: Cary Nelson, "No Wine before Its Time: The Panic over Early Professionalization," *Profession* (2000): 157–63; Gregg Lambert, "What [Does] Do [Woman] Graduate Students Want? John Guillory and That Obscure Object of English Desire," *Minnesota Review* 52–53 (2001): 249–62; Paul Eisenstein and Ken Petri, "Working through Professional Fantasy: Changing the Myths We Live By," *Journal of the Midwest Modern Language Association* 31 (1998): 45–64; Jeffrey Williams, "Career Choices," *Works and Days* 41–42 (2003): 283–300.

3. The question of what actually succeeds in the job market is more complex than is implied by the list of professional achievements above. Walter Broughton and William Conlogue, "What Search Committees Want," *Profession* (2001): 39–51, conducted a survey of hiring committees and found that the desire most often expressed is for a "fit" between the candidate and the department. What goes into the notion of "fit" is not obvious but probably involves desiderata very specific to individual departments.

edly determine the outcome. For women especially, the new order was a revolution; the gender distribution of the professoriate was transformed. Academic careers became more accessible for people of color as well, although at a painfully slower pace. Unfortunately, there were problems with the job market that undermined the equity conditions upon which the meritocratic principle depended. The old hierarchy of schools continued to dominate the hiring cycle, sorting candidates before their files were even read. Worse, universities took advantage of what looked in those early years like a temporary downturn in the economy and a disequilibrium in the job market in order to impose a harsh economy on hiring, capping tenure-track positions by employing MAs and "surplus" PhDs as adjunct or contingent faculty to fill curricular needs.[4] The ratio of contingent to tenure-line employment began steadily to increase.[5] When the number of PhDs produced by the graduate schools reached a plateau from which it did not appreciably decline thereafter, the buyer's market was able to

4. There were two components to the crisis: a turn to part-time labor by university administrations and a run of years in which the production of PhDs overshot the number of advertised tenure-track positions. The precise relation between these two developments is difficult to reconstruct. Alain Touraine, *The Academic System in American Society*, has an interesting account of graduate education written in the early 1970s, setting out from the observation that "economic stagnation" and "reductions in government support for scientific research resulted in unemployment among science Ph.D.'s in 1970–71" (150). He conjectures that "over a long period, the demand for Ph.D.'s will probably be on the decrease after an initial period of rapid growth in the university population. As a result, the country will experience a considerable overproduction of the Ph.D.'s." (151) This is exactly what did happen, while William G. Bowen and Julie Ann Sosa's famous prediction in *Prospects for Faculty in the Arts and Sciences: A Study of Factors Affecting Demand and Supply, 1987 to 2012* (Princeton, NJ: Princeton University Press, 1989) of expanded tenure-track hiring in the 1990s proved disastrously wrong. For a more recent account of what we know about the origins of the crisis, to which I am indebted throughout this essay, see David Laurence, "The Humanities: What Now? What Next?," http://blc.berkeley.edu/wp-content/uploads/2021/02/The-Humanities_What_Now_What_Next.pdf. Laurence demonstrates that despite what we may think from the vantage of doctoral programs, the growth of the non-tenure-track work force was not driven by overproduction of PhDs. The contingent corps consisted mostly of those holding MAs. Reducing the size of the PhD-holding population won't have much of an effect on contingent hiring, and arguments for reducing the size of the graduate cohort will therefore have to be based on other considerations. For a longitudinal study of the job market, see David Laurence, "Demand for New Faculty Members, 1995–2016," *Profession 2019*, http://profession.mla.org/demand-for-new-faculty-members-1995-2016/.

5. In order to avoid the awkwardness of "tenure/tenure track," I will refer to both categories inclusively as "tenure-line" or "tenure track."

reproduce itself indefinitely. This is what I meant by the "system of graduate education."

Certain externalities drove the cyclical operation of this system—the defunding of higher education by the states, the growth of administration and ongoing "corporatization" of the university, and a redirection of resources toward competition between schools—but these externalities came to mesh like a smooth set of gears with the internal tendency of graduate education itself. The growth of the doctoral student population provided desirable graduate teaching for many faculty, even while the surplus labor pool of PhDs fed the ranks of "casualized" faculty. At the same time, doctoral students were driven to compete ever more fiercely in the zero-sum market. "Professionalization" became an increasingly prevalent agenda in graduate programs, with effects that far exceeded preparation for the job market.[6] The first of my two essays attempted to describe those effects, inasmuch as they transformed graduate education into what I will describe as a semiautonomous professional sphere. This was the phenomenon I called "preprofessionalism."

In this chapter, I recover some hypotheses from my earlier work as a point of departure for exploring the structural determinations that resulted in the paralysis of the graduate system, its inability to move beyond its crisis. This paralysis, of course, is not restricted to literary study, which makes its remedy all the more difficult to imagine. The concept of "permanent crisis" names the situation with seeming accuracy—but this is not altogether helpful. If we are to understand why the disparity between the numbers of job applicants and the number of jobs has become a permanent dysfunction, we need a theory of how professional fields *should* reproduce themselves. If the reproduction of the professoriate is *not* the purpose of doctoral education, then we should have a notion of an alternative purpose. Many scholars have been working on this problem and have proposed many reasonable and practical courses of action to ameliorate the situation. Still, it is my impression that very little has changed in how we manage graduate education since the time in which I first addressed this subject. I do not mean here to slight the efforts that go by the name of "alt-ac" or "public humanities" or any number of such measures. What I mean is that the basic structure and components of graduate education are for the most part the same as they

---

6. The turn of the professoriate to professionalization was remarked as a desideratum by Don Cameron Allen in *The Ph.D. in English and American Literature* (New York: Holt, Rhinehart, and Winston, 1968): "We should, consequently, stop thinking of the Ph.D. in American and English Literature as a person with a cultural degree. They are as professional professionals as physicians, engineers, and public accountants" (104).

were four decades ago. So far as I can tell, there have been only two ma-jor structural changes in the system of graduate education. The first is the growth of the predoctoral MA, a reanimation of the MA degree after being abandoned by its earlier constituencies, as a result of which many students now seek the MA chiefly in order to improve their chances of admission to a doctoral program. The second is the emergence of the "postdoc" for hu-manities PhDs, which extends the period of the job search and sometimes does lead to a job. These new structural features of graduate education have systemic consequences I will consider later in this chapter.

It will not be my aim, let me underscore, to consider in any detail recent work on what Leonard Cassuto aptly calls "the graduate school mess." I have great regard for the work that has been done in recent years on the problem of graduate education, including that of Cassuto in his earlier book (with the title just quoted), and his more recent study coauthored with Robert Weisbuch, *The New PhD: How to Build a Better Graduate Edu-cation.*[7] In addition to these and many other book-length studies, the last two decades have seen hundreds of articles and blogs. My sense in survey-ing this work is that something close to a consensus has emerged about courses of action that are within the authority of the professoriate. These include mentoring students with a view toward the diversity of career pos-sibilities; career counseling that makes information about alternative ca-reers available to doctoral students; establishing a "public humanities" cur-ricular option that makes connections with nonacademic institutions such as libraries, foundations, and publishing houses; and reducing the time to

---

7. Some major statements: Leonard Cassuto, *The Graduate School Mess: What Caused It and How We Can Fix It* (Cambridge, MA: Harvard University Press, 2015); Leonard Cassuto and Robert Weisbuch, *The New PhD: How to Build a Better Graduate Education* (Baltimore: Johns Hopkins University Press, 2021); Leanne M. Horinko, Jor-dan M. Reed, and James M. Van Wyck, eds., *The Reimagined PhD: Navigating 21ˢᵗ Cen-tury Humanities Education* (New Brunswick, NJ: Rutgers University Press, 2021); Ka-tina L. Rogers, *Putting the Humanities PhD to Work: Thriving in and beyond the Classroom* (Durham, NC: Duke University Press, 2020); Gordon Hutner and Feisal G. Mohamed, *A New Deal for the Humanities: Liberal Arts and the Future of Public Higher Education* (New Brunswick, NJ: Rutgers University Press, 2015); Kathleen Fitzpatrick, *Generous Thinking: A Radical Approach to Saving the University* (Baltimore: Johns Hopkins Uni-versity Press, 2019); Ronald G. Ehrenberg et al., *Educating Scholars: Doctoral Education in the Humanities* (Princeton, NJ: Princeton University Press, 2010); Chris M. Golde and George E. Walker, eds., *Envisioning the Future of Doctoral Education: Preparing Stew-ards of the Discipline* (Stanford, CA: Jossey-Bass, 2006); Sidonie Smith, *Manifesto for the Humanities: Transforming Doctoral Education in Good Enough Times* (Ann Arbor: University of Michigan Press, 2015); George E. Walker et al., *The Formation of Scholars: Rethinking Doctoral Education for the Twenty-First Century* (San Francisco: Jossey-Bass, 2008).

degree by revising the form of the dissertation, usually by substituting a collection of articles for the traditional protomonograph. Other proposals aim to enforce ethical standards, such as pressuring administrations to offer full funding for doctoral students at the level of a living wage, with teaching limited to what does not impede progress toward the degree. The tactic that seemed most urgent in earlier decades—reducing the size of graduate programs—has become much less so, for reasons to be considered later.

These proposals seem reasonable to me, and yet they somehow falter when departments are faced with the task of implementation. The idea of a more streamlined dissertation, for example, has been discussed for decades, but it does not seem ever to advance beyond discussion. Why is this the case? On the one hand, it is obvious that professors have not given graduate students either models for an alternative to the monograph or encouragement to adopt this form. On the other hand, one wonders whether most graduate students continue to hold out hope for a tenure-track job and perhaps believe that an "alternative" dissertation will damage their prospects.[8] Very powerful structural determinants must be at work, if reasonable courses of action seem in every case to falter. Cassuto and Weisbuch puzzle over this situation: "Once we review the current attempts at doctoral reforms, it's difficult not to be discouraged. The defects of doctoral education have remained constant and have resisted any number of solutions" (91).[9] I suggest that we have arrived at a moment in which solutions to the "mess" of graduate education address problems but not *the* problem. There have to be underlying conditions that account for the permanence of the crisis, for the inability of the academy to take actions that have been so long considered and so generally approved. This is the question I would like to explore in this chapter. I should say, however, that greater clarity about these structural conditions will not guarantee resolution of the crisis. My purpose in this chapter is rather clarity itself, as a condition for estab-

8. Both the Ford Foundation and the Mellon Foundation funded experimental programs, in which grants to individual graduate students were used to encourage shorter time to degree. Both experiments yielded disappointing results. On the Ford and Mellon experiments, see Cassuto, *The Graduate School Mess*, 170–76, and Cassuto and Weisbuch, *The New PhD*, 32–43. A shorter dissertation was already proposed by Don Cameron Allen in *The Ph.D. in English and American Literature* as a means of speeding up the production of PhDs in response to the "crisis" of underproduction in the 1960s (115).

9. In addition to the question of the dissertation, Cassuto and Weisbuch note that the problem of time to degree has fallen into the same rabbit hole: "We have been having the same arguments about time to degree for more than 60 years" (*The New PhD*, 274). See also Robert Weisbuch, "The Liberal Arts at Work," in Leanne M. Horinko et al., eds., *The Reimagined PhD*, quoting a comment by David Damrosch: "If everybody knows what needs to be done, why isn't anyone doing it?" (14).

lishing *honesty* and *transparency* in graduate education. These are values that can hardly be contested, but their absence immerses the professoriate in a miasma of bad faith.

We can point to an example of this bad faith in the emergence of the term "job system" in preference to "job market." This circumlocution is typical of a certain failure of analysis that offers itself as ideological unmasking. I have and will continue to refer to a "job market" for professional occupations, on the assumption that when jobs are advertised and candidates apply for those jobs, we are in fact looking at a job market. Why is it difficult for academics to accept this fact? We have been instructed by Marc Bousquet in *How the University Works*, and by Cary Nelson and Stephen Watt in *Academic Keywords*, that the notion of a "job market" is a fraud, because the ratio of tenure-track jobs to the number of applicants for these jobs is "artificially" skewed.[10] As Nelson and Watt assert, "The supply of candidates has been artificially increased and the demand for full-time employees artificially depressed" (157). Such a notion implies that the relation between supply and demand in the labor market gravitates to a "natural" state of equilibrium; if there is a disequilibrium, it is no longer an economic matter but (as Nelson and Watt argue) "cultural and institutional" (157). Since when, however, has a disequilibrium of supply and demand ceased to be an *economic* problem? Are not such deviations from hypothetical norms what economists study? The notion that there is a natural state of equilibrium between supply and demand in any market whatsoever is as mystified as the medieval notion of the "natural price" for a commodity, which political economy in the early modern period dismissed in one of its inaugural moves.

We do not need to reinstate the labor theory of value (in the tradition of Smith and Marx) in order to acknowledge that all kinds of labor, including professional labor, enter a market in which labor is exchanged for compensation—a wage or a salary. It is unfortunate that the notion of the "job system" has taken hold in literary study, if not elsewhere in the academy, because it blinds us to a certain reality.[11] "Job market" is objectionable to

10. Marc Bousquet, *How the University Works: Higher Education and the Low-Wage Nation* (New York: New York University Press, 2008); Cary Nelson and Stephen Watt, *Academic Keywords: A Devil's Dictionary for Higher Education* (New York: Routledge, 1999).

11. The notion of a "job *system*" is not incorrect, in the sense that every social process has systemic aspects; what is problematic is rather the rejection of the concept of a job *market*. The job market belongs to the system of graduate education and to the system of professional employment. My argument in "The System of Graduate Education" set out from the observation that the systemic features of graduate education were the result in

academics who are anxious about their professional status because the very concept is a *status insult*. As I noted in chapter 1, professions aim to control as much as possible the market for their labor, and one way in which they do this is to present this labor as transcending market conditions and values. Professionals have never conceded that their services have a "price" in the same sense that a commodity has a price, but let us admit that this claim to transcend the market is an ideological gambit and that it does not always succeed.[12]

Bousquet, Nelson, and Watt also reject the idea that graduate schools "overproduce" PhDs, along with the notion that the equilibrium of the market can be restored by restricting the labor supply—a strategy that is in fact how many professions historically have controlled the market for their labor. Bousquet calls this a "supply-side fantasy" and counters that universities "underproduce jobs." In the early years of the job crisis, departments were not yet schooled in this higher wisdom, and some did reduce the size of their incoming classes. It is difficult to tell at this distance what result those efforts had, but they were certainly not enough to bring the market into equilibrium for those seeking tenure-track jobs. This disequilibrium, however, is itself an effect of our point of view; if we were to aggregate all of the teaching jobs perennially available in the job market, something closer to an equilibrium of supply and demand comes into focus: of the total number of positions in any given year, some offer terms of *professional* employment, as defined by the tenure-track, academic freedom, and the concept of the "career." The remaining positions—the majority of positions—are defined by *contingent* terms. These are jobs, but not careers. They offer meager compensation and little hope of security or advancement. As administrators and departments discovered, both kinds of positions were readily filled by drawing from the *same* corps of job seekers, who possessed MAs or PhDs. By virtue of contingent hiring, it must be admitted, universities were able to continue raising compensation for ladder faculty, which had traditionally been very low, as well as to reduce teaching loads further—both features the tenure-line professoriate welcomed,

---

part of the decentralized organization of graduate education in the United States. This system has no executive level, but it reproduces itself by the mechanism of mutual imitation, described in chapter 2 above as "institutional isomorphism."

12. Louis Menand, *The Marketplace of Ideas: Reform and Resistance in the American University* (New York: W. W. Norton, 2010), notes "the belief, central to the academic's professional self-conception, that the university does not operate like a marketplace" (16). For an account of the strategies professions have adopted to oppose the market, see Larson, *The Rise of Professionalism*, 40–63.

just as it welcomed an influx of graduate students into its seminars.[13] All of these "systemic" aspects of university employment work together in such a way as to make it difficult to alter any one aspect of the system, thus ensuring its perpetuation.

The notion that universities "underproduce" jobs, as the counterthesis to overproduction, tells us nothing about how the academic job market actually operates. Employers do not "produce" jobs in the same way that professional schools produce degree holders or that factories produce commodities. No employer is obliged to create jobs for all those who might wish to have them—except perhaps in Utopia. The sorting of jobs into two very different categories of employment exposes the threat implicit in the status insult of the "job market," the prospect of what has sometimes been called "deprofessionalization," or less accurately, "proletarianization." The widespread embrace of the latter term makes the status insult apparent, but it does not identify the actual class position of contingent academic labor or the reality of its economic conditions.[14] We know that in fact most PhDs who do not attain tenure-track positions go on to get jobs in professional and managerial fields.[15] These PhDs possess symbolic and cultural capital

---

13. Richard Lewinton, "The Cold War and the Transformation of the Academy," in *The Cold War and the University: Toward an Intellectual History of the Post-War Years*, ed. Richard Lewinton et al. (New York: New Press, 1997).

14. See, for example, Heather Steffen, "Intellectual Proletarians in the Twentieth Century," *Chronicle of Higher Education*, November 28, 2010, https://www.chronicle.com/article/intellectual-proletarians-in-the-20th-century/. I too have described contingent academics as "proletarianized" in "The System of Graduate Education," and my reservation applies to that use as well. I have generally preferred the term "contingent" to "adjunct," partly in order to temper the rhetoric attached to the latter term, but also because the composition of the adjunct professoriate is extremely heterogenous, a fact that complicates devising measures to address casualization. On this subject, see Jeremy C. Young and Robert B. Townsend, "The Adjunct Problem Is a Data Problem," *Chronicle of Higher Education*, August 30, 2021, https://www.chronicle.com/article/the-adjunct-problem-is-a-data-problem.

15. See Ehrenberg et al., *Educating Scholars*: "The employment experience of those who leave graduate school departs substantially from the stereotype of the unemployed or taxi-driving graduate-school dropout. Three years after leaving school, their employment rate topped 96 percent, and most had professional or managerial jobs" (18). See also Merisi Nerad, Rebecca Aanerud, and Joseph Cerny, "So You Want to Become a Professor: Lessons from the PhDs—Ten Years Later Study," in *Paths to the Professoriate: Strategies for Enriching the Preparation of Future Faculty*, ed. Donald H. Wulff and Ann E. Austin (San Francisco: Jossey-Bass, 2004); and Merisi Nerad and Joseph Cerni, "From Rumors to Facts: Career Outcomes of English Ph.D.s—Results from the Ph.D.s Ten Years Later Study" (1999), cited in Cassuto and Weisbuch, *The New PhD*, 117–18.

that members of the noncredentialed working class do not and better prospects accordingly. To say this is not to diminish the conditions of precarity suffered by doctoral students in the event of an unsuccessful search for a tenure-track position; it is rather to insist on the difference between the kinds of poverty and social disruption our neoliberal order occasions.[16] The job crisis of the university is a development in the history of *professional labor*; its relation to other sites of labor in the economy is more complex than is expressed by the concept of "proletarianization."

CREDENTIALS

Here we begin to touch ground, after a sea of confusion. The issue before us is not just another calamity of neoliberalism but the specific question of *how teaching and scholarship in the humanities are valued*, what constitutes the basis for the classification of this labor as professional. In this context, it is telling that the job crisis is worst in the humanities, though hardly confined to that division of the university system. Nor is the problem of valuing knowledge work confined to the university, which is one site of a much larger social struggle. There is an ongoing crisis of expertise in our society that parallels what is happening in higher education. The "death of expertise" manifested in climate change denial or vaccine skepticism has national and even global consequences, vastly more disruptive than the job crisis for PhDs.[17] I want to insist, however, that the decline in the credibility of expertise in our society is related to the collapse of professional employment for our doctoral students in the humanities. These are two sites of the same struggle. The difference of the latter site is that the challenge to credentials in the humanities is coming from the university itself, as the main employer of humanities PhDs.

If the repudiation of expertise in general seems to emanate from an amorphous coalition of groups in contemporary society, what is happening in the university can be localized as a conflict between managerial and professional elites. This conflict has been underway for a very long time, less visible to the public by virtue of the fact that managerial elites also

---

The "Ten Years Later" survey found that job satisfaction among those who left academia was actually higher than among those who got academic jobs.

16. It seems to me morally imperative to acknowledge the difference between the conditions of precarity inflicted upon the adjunct professoriate and upon the many millions of people who work for less than a living wage in the United States and have little means to improve the conditions of their labor.

17. See Tom Nichols, *The Death of Expertise: The Campaign against Established Knowledge and Why It Matters* (New York: Oxford University Press, 2017).

present themselves as professionals.[18] Over the course of the university's development in the twentieth century, a managerial cadre—the university administration (specifically, its upper stratum)—has successfully wrested control over the conditions of work from the faculty, the corps of professional knowledge workers.[19] The orientation of these two cadres diverges: the upper administration operates more like the managers of a business enterprise—hence the notion of "corporatization." Rather than privatize profits from incomes, however, universities redirect resources in order to compete with each other for students and for prestige. Income streams for institutions of this sort have nowhere to go except back into the institution, as the means to further its growth and reputation; these become the *aims* of quasi-corporate management. University managers take advantage of whatever helps to accomplish these aims, including divisions within the faculty itself, such as that between the humanities and the sciences. (The other professional schools, such as law, business, engineering, and medicine do not enter into this conflictual situation in the same way, and indeed, they are closer to the interests of the professional managers who run the university today.) The casualization of labor is more severe in the humanities disciplines because of the historical weakness of the humanities in relation to the sciences, but this weakness does not explain casualization, which occurs in the sciences as well.

The most portentous fact about the job situation in the humanities is that the PhDs who have been relegated to contingent positions possess the *same credentials* as those who have attained tenure-track jobs. The *meaning* of the job crisis is simply this: the credentials of humanities teachers and scholars have been devalued. But on what basis? It is not that administrators are judging the value of humanities scholarship adversely or that they are judging its content at all. They typically assess scholarship only with reference to the reputation of individual scholars and departments, in competition with other universities. The basis for devaluation of the credential is rather the connection between humanities disciplines and lower division teaching, such as composition, general education, language instruction, and introductory-level courses. By and large, the contract professoriate (whether full time or part time) has been relegated to this level of teach-

18. For the earlier history of the rise of managerial elites in business enterprise, see Alfred Chandler, *The Visible Hand: The Managerial Revolution in American Business* (Cambridge, MA: Harvard University Press, 1977); and Adolf A. Berle and Gardiner C. Means, *The Modern Corporation and Private Property* (New York: Harcourt, Brace and World, 1968).

19. See Benjamin Ginsberg, *The Fall of the Faculty: The Rise of the All-Administrative University and Why It Matters* (Oxford: Oxford University Press, 2011).

ing, while upper-level and graduate teaching is ceded to ladder faculty. The underlying determinant in the comparative valuation of the disciplines is the relation between teaching and research. Those disciplines more closely identified with the teaching function are at a disadvantage, which has been impossible thus far to overcome.

One result of this legacy is that humanities disciplines have welcomed opportunities to assert their identity as research professions by distancing themselves from lower-division teaching. The growth of the contingent faculty has an upside for the tenure-line professoriate in relief from this teaching, an arrangement that risks moral hazard. Ultimately, the relegation of contingent faculty to the first two years of the undergraduate curriculum has been a devil's bargain for humanities faculty, because it undermines the PhD as a credential. The university administration discounts the value of the PhD whenever it offers postdoctoral job seekers terms of contingent or adjunct employment. These terms make no distinction between MAs and PhDs, thus reducing the higher credential to the lower. Arguably, the MA too is devalued by these terms of employment, which fall below what can reasonably be demanded for university teachers. These terms of employment have only successfully been upgraded by means of collective bargaining. Yet this highly trained professoriate has to bargain from the baseline of an absurdly minimal valuation of the credential.

The devaluation of credentials in the humanities is evident in the weakened position of humanities departments, which have lost the right to make tenure-track appointments that would cover lower-division teaching.[20] Teaching in the lower division falls to the level of "essential services," which in our society are poorly compensated. The tenure-line humanities faculty is compensated on the assumption of parity with other disciplines, because it is a research faculty. At the same time, it cannot simply disown the lower division, in relation to which it expresses an ambivalent sense of responsibility. In this way, the ladder faculty slips into a tacit relation of exploitation to the contingent corps. Often the adjunct or part-time sector of this corps is hired and fired without the collective participation of the tenure-line faculty, further derogating the disciplinary work that is essential to the mission of the humanities and of the university.

The status of humanities departments is not wholly determined by its relation to lower-division teaching, which continues to define the job descriptions of tenure-track hires, though not their number. These appoint-

20. The English department is a somewhat exceptional case in the arrangement I describe, because its responsibilities for lower-division courses are usually greater than other departments.

ments are the expensive ones, always measured by administrators against the economy of hiring contingent faculty. Not surprisingly, new categories of contingency have been introduced into faculty hiring, which now encroach upon the upper division, including contract faculty with the status of "lecturer" or (at my institution) "clinical professor." Sometimes temporary appointments for new PhDs are structured as "visiting professorships." These innovations give administrators the ability to deliver the curriculum at all levels while constraining the ranks of tenure-line faculty. Although it does not seem likely that tenure will disappear in the near future, the contraction of the tenured faculty is without question *ongoing*. It is only a question of the rate at which this contraction takes place, and whether there will in the future be a tipping point that fatally undermines departmental control over the constitution of its own faculty. What is at stake in this process ultimately is the question of who controls the reproduction of the professoriate.

Faculties in the sciences might seem to be insulated from the devaluation of their credentials, but this is not entirely so. They suffer from a less extreme version of the employment crisis: many of their graduates have been relegated to adjunct teaching as well or sentenced to a purgatory of serial "postdoc" appointments. The status of the sciences is not my concern in this chapter, but it is worth acknowledging the fact that all the core fields of the university—all of the "liberal arts"—suffer from the crisis of expertise that extends to the horizon of American society. Here I would only point out the ambiguous results of the relatively recent introduction of postdocs into the humanities, on the analogy of the sciences, as a way of improving the chances of new PhDs to secure a tenure-track position. Despite the good intentions of the strategy, the postdoc itself has come to function as a kind of contingent labor, helping humanities departments to deliver the curriculum, often upper-level courses, and thus exerting a downward pressure on tenure-track hiring. The very fact of the humanities postdoc is an artifact of the job crisis. If the decline in the value of the PhD degree for the humanities is a front in the much larger conflict over expertise, all university disciplines have a stake in a better resolution of this conflict than appears to be in the offing. The humanities, the social sciences, and the natural sciences are all in the situation of having to defend the social value of their knowledge and the credentials that certify their identity as professional knowledge workers.

Taking in the full scope of the problem, we see that the conditions I have remarked are nested within each other. The extramural "death of expertise" encloses the intramural crisis of the liberal arts disciplines, and within that corps, the humanities disciplines. The social value of these disciplines, as opposed to the professional and technical fields, is openly questioned by political operatives on the right and repudiated by large sectors of the public. The humanities survive precariously in this environment, but even the sciences struggle in comparison to the business, professional, and technical schools that deliver reliable income streams in the form both of enrollments (consider the undergraduate business degree!) and of donor contributions.[21] Given the true scope of the problem, the intransigence of the employment crisis in literature departments is not surprising, even before we factor in the weaker inherited position of humanities disciplines in relation to the sciences. I present this situation in its daunting complexity not in order to discourage the literary professoriate from attempting to address the employment issue, much less to excuse inaction. The point is rather to have an accurate picture of the problem in its true dimensions.

The causes and occasions of the repudiation of expertise are too complex to follow up here in detail. This social problem has a long timeline as well as a broad effect in our society.[22] I want to look more closely now at the concept of *credentials*, with reference specifically to the PhD. Once this credential is awarded, no one can take it away (unless there has been fraud in its acquisition), but neither can anyone guarantee that it will result in professional employment. Like all credentials, the PhD is a reservoir of *credit*, of belief in its value, even though this value cannot be expressed precisely in the way that currency announces its value on its face. Professions have always understood that the value of the credential is established in part because it is difficult to acquire and that this fact establishes a baseline for assessing the credential's value. Indeed, professions sometimes make the credential more difficult to acquire than the tasks that are later performed with it.

A further assumption inheres in educational credentials: the limited social need for credentialed occupations. This condition obtains for all

21. On the contraction of the liberal arts core and the rise of "business, engineering, computer science" and related subjects, see Steven Brint, "The Rise of the 'Practical Arts,'" in *The Future of the City of Intellect: The Changing American University* (Stanford, CA: Stanford University Press, 2002), 232–35.

22. It is customary in this context to invoke Richard Hofstadter, *Anti-Intellectualism in American Life* (New York: Vintage Books, 1962). I take away from Hofstadter's famous treatise his observation that education does not in itself protect a society from anti-intellectualism: "Here no doubt the American educational creed itself needs further scrutiny. The belief in mass education was not founded primarily upon a passion for the development of mind, or upon pride in learning and culture for their own sakes, but rather upon the supposed political and economic benefits of education" (305). One implication of this observation is that mass education defined exclusively by credentialism will inevitably drive toward an inflationary crisis.

highly skilled or professional employment where credentials are required. In every society that we know of, there is a compression of personnel at the higher strata of skilled or professional jobs. The tasks performed by persons in these positions might be crucial for the society, but the number necessary for these tasks will always be limited. This fact has been difficult to accept in American society, where anyone can become president, but it makes obvious sense. How many lawyers does a society need? How many heart surgeons? How many aeronautical engineers? How many museum curators? How many teachers of literature? No profession is founded on the principle that a society can absorb an unlimited number of such professionals.[23] Conversely, there are far more jobs in this and every other world human beings have created that are tedious, painful, and poorly compensated. Societies might never solve this problem, but let us acknowledge that *the distribution of work* is as much a matter of concern in a hypothetically just society as the distribution of resources.[24] Our society favors an opposing principle, however, that seems to deny the real-world conditions of labor. This notion is expressed as "equality of opportunity," which does not describe a real-world condition but nonetheless has enormous effects in that world.

The number of those who seek the "opportunity" to succeed in highly skilled or professional jobs will in the ordinary course of things exceed the number of positions available. This fact is not tragic but an inevitable consequence of the hierarchical division of labor. At the upper end of the hierarchy, there is always a disequilibrium of supply and demand in the job market—a permanent crisis, although we always hope that the effects of this crisis will not be ruinous. The educational system exists in part for the purpose of preparing aspirants to compete for places in a hierarchy of labor. The job of college professor is one such place for which aspirants compete; like most other higher-end occupations, to be a college professor requires considerable knowledge in a disciplinary field, along with the credential that certifies possession of this knowledge.

The life of the professor of literature is regarded by many of our undergraduates as well worth the expenditure of effort, time, and money it takes to acquire the doctoral degree. This fact is confirmed whenever we speak to our students about applying for graduate school. They want to study lit-

---

23. For a discussion of this point, see Freidson, *Professionalism Reborn*, 160–61.

24. Those of us still committed to socialism might ask why tedious and unpleasant work might not be shared, with appropriate compensation for the exaction of pain and tedium. On the same principle, we might ask why pleasant and interesting work might not be similarly shared.

erature, to be sure, but they also want the life of the college professor. In my experience, they are disinclined to regard, for example, teaching in the secondary school system as an alternative to their *professional* aspiration—despite the fact that there is a shortage of secondary school teachers. Raising this option at all requires considerable delicacy.[25] As we know from every admissions season in living memory, the demand for the PhD remains very high. Doctoral programs still receive dozens or hundreds of applications for every class, a fact that occasions pride but also bewilderment. If the credential is such a risk, like those mortgages that led to the financial crash of 2008, what is the meaning of the demand? There is a puzzling contradiction here between the persistent demand for the credential and its falling value.

Social scientists speak of the phenomenon of "credentialism" in this context, by which they refer in the most general sense to the increasing importance and proliferation of credentials in society. In a narrower context, credentialism refers to the phenomenon of "credential inflation," the correlation between the proliferation of credentials and their falling value. Credentials are like those kinds of luxury commodities that are in high demand but lose value the more people come to possess them. Demand explains only part of the price for these commodities; rarity is the other part.

There is considerable evidence that the BA became subject to "credentials inflation" in the half century following World War II. Over the course of the twentieth century, university enrollment among those of college age expanded from 4 percent of the population in 1900 to nearly 50 percent by the end of the century. We marvel at the fact that the jobs for which a high school diploma was once sufficient now require a college degree, but there is no mystery here: as the number of students entering universities and colleges rose spectacularly in the decades after World War II, the proliferation of BAs depressed the value of the credential in the job market, its vaunted "wage premium." Randall Collins, in *The Credential Society*, writes of a "credential crisis" beginning in the later twentieth century. This crisis was driven in part by pent-up demand for college degrees, especially among minorities, who saw these credentials as their best chance for upward mobility.[26] Collins points to some striking results of the crisis, most

25. See Michael Bérubé, *The Employment of English: Theory, Jobs, and the Future of Literary Studies* (New York: New York University Press, 1998): "In my experience, suggesting to students that they might teach in secondary schools has been a little like nominating one's colleagues for early retirement" (84).

26. Randall Collins, *The Credential Society: An Historical Sociology of Education and Stratification* (New York: Columbia University Press, 2019), 191. See also the important follow-up essay, "Credential Inflation and the Future of Universities," in *The Future of*

conspicuously the fact that the implications of credential inflation were different for men and women. College enrollment for men declined, but women more than made up for this decline. Today, women are the majority of undergraduates. In the last several decades, the university has exploded with many new degrees and certificate programs, evidence perhaps of how urgently credentials are being sought that might function like the BA once did, as an indicator of *distinction*.[27] Yet the demand for the BA itself remains strong, despite the manifest decline in the credential's value.

This fact alerts us to the curious dialectic between access to credentials and the value of credentials, their tendency to move simultaneously in opposite directions. This complication makes intervening into the system's operation very difficult, though it helps us to understand why the professoriate eventually rejected attempts to resolve the job market crisis by reducing the size of graduate classes. Whether or not the professoriate understood the consequences of this decision, it chose the risk of credential inflation in preference to limiting access. In this choice, the professoriate acted to reinforce a long-standing historical tendency, which can be described as the *democratization* of the educational system. This unidirectionality of the system contrasts with higher education in Europe, which always has, and still does, restrict access to higher degrees with a sequence of examinations. Given the tendency of democratization, we might wonder if there is a terminus at some point in the future. Can we imagine a society in which everyone has a BA? What would the credential mean in that event? As the Dodo says in *Alice in Wonderland*, "Everybody has won,

---

the City of Intellect: The Changing American University, ed. Stephen Brint, 23–46. Steven Brint, *In an Age of Experts: The Changing Role of Professionals in Politics and Public Life* (Princeton, NJ: Princeton University Press, 1994), 42, remarks on the "glut" of "college-educated labor" beginning in 1969 that resulted in falling pay, especially for those with humanities and social science degrees. The failure of the wage premium for BAs presaged a decline in the wage premium of the PhD, *but mainly for those who were not hired to the tenure-track*. It is difficult not to see the compensation of tenure-line faculty as sustained in part by a transfer of savings from the hiring of contingent faculty. The complication here would be explaining compensation for faculty in the four-year colleges, where there is little or less reliance on contingent faculty. On the always tricky finances of universities, see the studies by Christopher Newfield, *The Great Mistake: How We Wrecked Public Universities and How We Can Fix Them* (Baltimore: Johns Hopkins University Press, 2016), and *Unmaking the Public University: The Forty Year Assault on the Middle Class* (Cambridge, MA: Harvard University Press, 2008). Newfield's account of how money is transferred from humanities disciplines to other sectors of the university is relevant here.

27. On the subject of degree proliferation, see John Marx and Mark Garett Cooper, "Curricular Innovation and the Degree-Program Explosion," *Profession 2020*, https://profession.mla.org/curricular-innovation-and-the-degree-program-explosion/.

and all must have prizes." This is a fantasy scenario, of course, as the attrition rate in the colleges and universities confirms. If we ever did achieve universal postsecondary education, it would have to have other purposes than credentialization.

Although access to undergraduate education was expanded slowly in the first half of the twentieth century, and very rapidly after World War II, the expansion of access to graduate education did not get underway seriously until the 1960s. This expansion was motivated less by an affirmation of access as a democratic principle than in response to a severe disequilibrium of supply and demand in the professoriate: There were not enough professors to teach the mass of college students. The rapid expansion of the undergraduate population forced the graduate schools to open their doors to new aspirants and to mint new professors as fast as they could. In fact, the graduate population expanded at a greater rate proportionally than the undergraduate population. It is difficult to register today how utterly transformed the system of higher education was, in consequence. Before the 1960s, nearly everyone who applied to graduate school was accepted. Nearly everyone looking for a tenure-track job found one. The notion of a "job crisis" meant the opposite of what it means today.

Nostalgia for these halcyon days is neither necessary nor warranted, because that system was in fact as selective as its successor. But it was a system of *self-selection*, an internalization of cultural values that held down to a very small number those persons who regarded the career of college professor as desirable at all. Let us remember that at the time, the job of college professor was characterized by high prestige and low pay, a combination that, along with other cultural factors, gave us a professoriate that was largely white, male, and upper middle class or higher.[28] The growth of the undergraduate population and the response of the graduate schools transformed the social conditions for the reproduction of the professoriate. Graduate education would be very different in the future, beginning with a new relation between the BA and the PhD. As the BA came within reach of half the American population, it was inevitable that more undergraduates would find postgraduate degrees desirable, including the PhD in literature.

In the meantime, the credentials crisis remarked by Collins did not depress the desire for the BA. On the contrary, the BA came to seem all the more necessary for acceptable employment, the marker of a threshold below which no one wanted to fall. This fact may explain by a perverse logic why our undergraduates are not put off by our cautions about the job

28. When I was an assistant professor at Yale in the 1980s, there were still "dollar-a-year" men on the faculty, professors who were too wealthy to bother taking a salary.

market for new PhDs; a postgraduate degree must seem to them like the aspirational goal the BA once embodied. If this speculation has any validity, there may be more rationality in the desire for the PhD than is generally supposed, given that compression at the top for professional-managerial positions is universal, generating intense competition at every point of access to the next level, including the job search for those with a BA. Some students no doubt worry that even though their BA might gain them a remunerative job, it would be unexciting at best. Why not try, instead, for something more interesting: the career of college professor, a lifetime of reading, writing, and teaching about literature? They might be wrong in the calculation of their chances, but the possibility of a better working life than they would have with a BA makes the risk of graduate school seem worth taking.

Of course, this is speculation, because the train of thought I have been trying to follow is not necessarily something that is elicited in our conversations with students. They only tell us how much they want to study literature and, further, that *they know all about* the job market for new PhDs. Understanding the psychology of decision-making at this moment in their lives is not easy. We can only be sure of the fact that the BA is no longer enough for these students, that it no longer promises the career that most appeals to them. This failure of the BA in turn makes the PhD desirable and drives multitudes of students in quest of it. The fact that the job market at the end of this quest will function like a lottery, in which only a fraction of those who buy the ticket will win the prize, is a truth that for these students can be conceived abstractly but not internalized.

The inability of students to penetrate the weakness of the PhD is the result of their position in relation to their possible futures, a position in which probability is easily overruled by desire. I want to underscore here that the appeal of the PhD is a consequence of the decline in the value of the BA. Students do not see the PhD from the perspective of the professoriate, which has to contend with the fact that the proliferation of PhDs has driven the value of that credential down too. The PhD would ordinarily be sustained by the immemorial professional strategy of limiting its proliferation, but these are extraordinary times, and there are several reasons why the professoriate is ambivalent about reducing admission to graduate school. First, as I have suggested, the professoriate sees graduate school as an instrument of access, of opportunity. The professoriate would like to extend access to the PhD more or less for the same reason that drove the democratization of the BA. We tend to name this reason now by the term "diversity," a concept that condenses a long history of oppression and exploitation and gestures toward the redress of that history. But there is a second, more self-interested motive, which I have also noted, the desire to teach graduate students, to use graduate seminars as vehicles for research, and in this way to create a public for one's work. This is not an insignificant desire, when scholarship has so limited a field of dissemination. Given this tangle of mixed motives, it is hardly surprising that the professoriate is disinclined to limit admission to graduate school as a means of propping up the value of the PhD as a credential.

Credentials inflation is the cost of increasing access, a price that might once have seemed deferred to the future for payment. The graduate students one admits today will not arrive at the job market for years to come. Perhaps this lag is what caught the professoriate by surprise in the 1970s, producing the overhang of new PhDs that was increasingly difficult to reduce with each passing year. When the timeline for confronting the consequences of one's decisions extends out for six to ten years, these decisions yield to shorter-term desires; they are less subject to rational planning. In the absence of governing agencies in our decentralized system of higher education that might undertake adjustments of a systemic nature, local decision-making is inevitably reactive and chaotic.

Once again, it will be helpful to step back from the site of local decision-making to look at a systemic aspect of the job market at the upper end of the hierarchy. We know that the most conspicuous feature of this market is the fact that there are many more competitors for the highest positions than there are positions. This constitutive disequilibrium has been justified by a notion that does not so much describe the actual operation of the system as its reflection in ideology. I refer here to the concept of "meritocracy," the complex of ideas and assumptions that justifies the American educational system by positing "equality of opportunity" as its foundational principle and "merit" as the guarantor of fair outcomes. When the university opened its doors in the twentieth century to so many young people, its aim was to bring them to this starting line of equal opportunity. (I set to one side here the other principal reason for mass education, the cultivation of an educated citizenry.) Meritocracy is supposedly blind to all difference, whether defined by wealth, race, gender, religion, ancestry, etc. The history of college and university admissions, however, reveals how far this ideal is from the reality.

Meritocracy has recently come under severe critique by two scholars, Daniel Markovits, in *The Meritocracy Trap*, and Michael Sandel, in *The Tyranny of Merit*, both eminent scholars perched at the top of the educational system, Yale and Harvard, respectively.[29] The argument of these books is

---

29. Daniel Markovits, *The Meritocracy Trap: How America's Foundational Myth Feeds Inequality, Dismantles the Middle Class, and Devours the Elite* (New York: Penguin,

very similar, and I will not attempt to reprise them here in any detail. Markovits and Sandel develop the earlier critique of meritocracy by the inventor of the term, Michael Young, in his satiric treatise, *The Rise of the Meritocracy*.[30] Young summed up the object of his critique in the formula IQ + Effort = Genius. This was a mock Einsteinian formula for *producing* Einsteins. What Markovits and Sandel demonstrate with abundant evidence is that the American educational system has been, so to speak, thoroughly rigged by the efforts of the wealthy to ensure that their children are the ones who are passed on from one level to the next. "Equality of opportunity" is something that does not exist in the real world. Here is Markovits's summary statement: "American meritocracy has become precisely what it was invented to combat: a mechanism for the concentration and dynastic transmission of wealth, privilege, and caste across generations" (72). The distinguishing feature of this system is that its mode of transmission is no longer the inheritance of wealth but the intense preparation of the children of the wealthy for entry into the "best" schools, from preschool to the graduate and professional schools. The strategy for subverting meritocracy has been hugely successful, even though the educational system is nominally committed to establishing equality of opportunity. Among many statistical measures of the subversion of equity conditions is the fact that, as Markovits reports, "at Harvard and Yale, more students come from households in the top 1 percent of the income distribution than from the entire bottom half" (25).

I forgo here further summary of this thesis, which I take to be persuasively presented by Markovits and Sandel. The pertinence of the thesis for my argument is that it permits us to understand better the interaction between democratization of access and the judgment of merit that determines ultimately who enters the higher ranks of the professions. To put this simply, the educational system is organized by the antinomies of *access* and *merit*. What is called "meritocracy" is a spurious reconciliation of these two antinomic principles. Unfortunately, there is no moral algorithm of which I am aware that reconciles access and merit; there is no set of procedures that adjusts these principles to one another in such a way as to guarantee that access is not subverted or that merit is not a false honorific for the winners of a rigged game.

Markovits and Sandel confidently identify the cause of subversion as income and wealth inequality. There is no point in the course of anyone's

2019), and Michael Sandel, *The Tyranny of Merit: What's Become of the Common Good?* (New York: Farrar, Straus and Giroux, 2020).

30. Michael Young, *The Rise of the Meritocracy* (London: Thames and Hudson, 1958; reprint, London: Routledge, 2017).

educational experience when there is actual equality of opportunity. The reality of our meritocratic system is that some children begin to compete for admission to "good" schools from the very first schools they attend and never stop competing thereafter. My concern is with the system at its upper end, but my larger point is worth reiterating: the job crisis in the humanities is enmeshed in the contradictions that afflict the educational system as a whole. Democratization of education and the acquisition of credentials presuppose conflicting principles. The conflict of these principles is always on the point of becoming a "crisis" in the oldest sense of the term, a moment in the narrative of an individual's life suspended between better or worse outcomes. In the trajectory that aims at the job of college professor, these moments are (1) admission to a college or university, (2) admission to graduate school, and (3) application for a tenure-track position. Very rigorous procedures of judgment are exercised at these portals of entry, the purpose of which is both to deny access (to some) and to grant it (to others). Great numbers of students stand on the near side of these portals; only a fraction will be admitted to the far side.

The ineluctable fact of the necessity for judgment is troubling for those who want to affirm the nobler purpose of education as an agency of access, of democratization. The professoriate typically oscillates between the two principles of merit and access, depending on where it stands in relation to the portal of access. On the near side, professors want to make the best case for as many of their students as possible. The temptation on this near side of judgment is to inflate the performance of students, a pressure that is hard to resist. The result is "grade inflation," which is nothing other than credentials inflation writ small. On the far side of judgment, admissions committees try to discern the reality behind inflated credentials, not always an easy task. What is the meaning of this game? We are looking here directly at the contradiction between access and merit, the collision of opposing values. The same ritual is repeated for students applying to graduate school and for candidates approaching the job market. For students doing graduate course work, grades are inflated so as to position them advantageously for the market. On the other side of the portal, inside hiring committees, faculty members try to penetrate the illusory equality of candidates, their seemingly uniform excellence. For the candidates, paradoxically, the effort of their teachers to multiply access by inflating credentials creates an additional burden: they must work very hard to overcome the illusory equality of grades, as well as the seeming uniformity of their teachers' letters of recommendation. Their task is to demonstrate merit, which is only minimally certified by a slate of perfect grades or enthusiastic recommendations. Merit means distinction, not uniformity.

The incoherence and irrationality of this situation is worth remarking only in passing. What is more important is to recognize the ramifying effects of this systemic feature, beyond its immediate precincts. Students will always be driven by the need to demonstrate merit to seek new ways to do so. In the context of admission to doctoral programs, for example, one wonders whether those seeking admission have been compelled more and more to acquire an MA as a means of improving their chances. I have not been able to confirm empirically that this is so, but my experience of the last several decades is that almost all of the applicants to the doctoral program at my institution now hold an MA.[31] These students do in fact have an advantage over those who do not have this degree: they know how graduate school works and can present themselves as *already professionalized*. They have recommendations that testify to their performance in graduate seminars. The systemic effects of this effort to demonstrate merit, however, are unintended: another layer of time, expense, and credentialization is interposed between the BA and the PhD. One might observe here a symmetry with the humanities postdoc, as an item that brings additional merit to the job market. The "time to degree" increases with these additional layers, which also multiply points of application and multiply committees whose task it is to make judgments at these points. These structural innovations in graduate education would seem to be an instance of the "mess" into which it has fallen. Behind these and the other local deformations to which I have drawn attention is the ultimate fact of the compression of personnel at the top end of the professional hierarchy, the structural feature that is the condition for permanent crisis.

PROFESSIONS

The question of *numbers* has been at the center of this analysis, most conspicuously greater numbers of graduate students and job applicants and lesser numbers of jobs. The disparity between these numbers constitutes the condition of "crisis." If we were to look at graduate education in the

---

31. On the earlier decline of the MA, see Cassuto, *The Graduate School Mess*, 44. Cassuto and Weisbuch, *The New PhD*, 148, condemn the use of the MA as an "audition" for doctoral study; they point out that, as MA programs are seldom supported, students who take the MA are adding a lot of educational debt in advance of the PhD. Later in their study Cassuto and Weisbuch argue for a rehabilitated terminal MA, which would have a broad spectrum of uses (284). Recently, the master's degree has come in for a good deal of criticism because of its use as a "cash cow" by universities. See Kevin Carrey, "The Great Master's-Degree Swindle," *Chronicle of Higher Education*, August 5, 2021, https://www.chronicle.com/article/the-great-masters-degree-swindle.

period before the 1970s, numbers tell a different story: we would see a very much smaller aggregate number of doctoral students than today. Students in one graduate program would be relatively isolated from students in others. There was no email, texting, social media, or internet blogging to establish lines of communication between students in far-flung institutions. The experience of being a graduate student was highly variable, more or less determined by the distinguishing features of one's graduate program, the chance constitution of one's student cohort, and above all, the interests and idiosyncrasies of one's teachers. By contrast, the reality of graduate education today is that the population of students constitutes a national and even international corps. Students are connected with each other by all the technical means just enumerated but also by new associational forms, such as the graduate student conference. These new forms have transformed the aggregate population of graduate students into a distinct *culture*, which I described at the beginning of this essay as a "semiautonomous professional sphere."

In "Preprofessionalism," I attempted to describe this culture, though with limited success.[32] I did not at the time have a sense of the difference technology would make in the cultural life of graduate students, as this technology was only just coming into common use. None of us could foresee in the 1990s how transformative the technology would be, both for social life generally and for graduate school in particular. I have no desire to celebrate or lament the technology itself, which is by many orders too complex and too diverse in its effects to characterize as good or bad. I return here to some of the questions raised by my earlier essays on graduate education in order to attempt again a description of the culture of graduate education in the wake of the collapsed job market and the emergence of a transinstitutional corps of graduate students.

The members of this corps are "preprofessional" in the simple sense of not yet being hired to tenure-track jobs, whether or not the term "preprofessionalism" still applies in any other sense. From our later vantage, the question of whether or not graduate students should or will engage in activities that are identical to those of their professors is moot. Most incoming doctoral students already know quite a lot about professional activity in

---

32. At the time I composed my earlier essays, I was most struck by what I saw as the mutual intensification of professionalization and politicization in graduate education. Today, it seems to me that "politicization" can be taken for granted for both the graduate corps and the professoriate. As this theme is discussed at length in chapters above, I have focused in this chapter on the issue of professionalization.

literary study and want to engage immediately in these activities.[33] In fact, undergraduates were becoming much more informed about the professional aspects of graduate study already by the early 2000s. One graduate student commentator on my earlier essay, Craig Ferhman, writing in 2009, called attention to what he termed "pre-preprofessionalism," by which he meant that many seniors applying to graduate school had thoroughly internalized the norms of professionalism and approached the application process with the design of presenting themselves in this light.[34] Graduate school today, I suggest, involves a process of *continuous* professionalization. This continuity of focus on professional life creates what I will call a "culture of professionalization."[35] The graduate seminar is only one site of this cultural activity and perhaps not the most important one. Professionalization is different from "apprenticeship," a concept that graduate students have vehemently rejected in recent years, partly in the context of unionization, but more fundamentally, I suggest, because it does not capture their sense of themselves as *already* professionals. Unlike apprenticeship, professionalization is not a means to the end of the degree or even of employment; it is an end in itself. Or rather, every moment of professional activity implies the possibility of further "professional development."

Professionalization as an end in itself brings us back to the state of graduate education since the 1970s and the collapse of the job market. Graduate education takes place under the sign of this collapse, the possibility or probability that the years a student spends in graduate study will not culminate in a tenure-track appointment. The professional life of the graduate student, however, cannot wait for a job that may never happen; it begins with the first day of graduate school. It has a minimum duration in the number of years students spend in the ecosphere of graduate study. This is currently anywhere from six to twelve years, but on average around nine. These are years in which students live and act as professional scholars and teachers. As I observed in "Preprofessionalism," students have an abbreviated form of the professional career, which can be experienced as passing through phases, having high points and low, and offering considerable satisfactions

33. Erik D. Curren, "No Openings at This Time: Job Market Collapse and Graduate Education," *Profession 1994*, 67–61. Curren was writing as a graduate student at the time.

34. Craig T. Fehrman, "Pre-Preprofessionalism: Rankings, Rewards, and the Graduate Admissions Process," *College Literature* 36 (2009): 184–201. See also Jonathan Mulrooney, "Acting like a Graduate Student," *Profession 1999*: 258–67.

35. This phrase is intended to invoke Burton Bledstein's *The Culture of Professionalism: The Middle Class and the Development of Higher Education in America*, acknowledging the cultural force of "professional development."

along the way. This career defers the crisis of the market that will determine whether professional life will continue indefinitely or will end. The satisfactions of professional life as a graduate student are for this reason a disincentive to finishing the degree—this, even though the longer students take to finish, the less likely they will find tenure-track employment.[36]

The temporary career of the graduate student is shaped in many ways by the nature of the job market, with its temporal precipice. I suspect that the career narrative would lose some of its cultural force if graduate students were assured of attaining a job; it might even lapse into a version of "apprenticeship," for better or worse. Graduate students must hold two incompatible thoughts in mind during their temporary careers, first that "I" am the one who will succeed in getting the job, and second, that graduate school will very likely constitute all there is to "my" career in literary study. These contradictory thoughts are suppositional, of course. They are extrapolated from the *conditions* of graduate study, not from assumptions about individual students. The larger point I want to make is this: that when confronted with the precipice of the job market, generations of graduate students made a *world* out of the temporary career, a semiautonomous professional sphere. Students enter into and eventually leave this professional sphere, which is built out enough, and rewarding enough, to survive the coming and going of these generations. By virtue of the graduate population's size, the years committed to graduate study, and the ease of communications between programs, this semiautonomous professional sphere evolved new institutional forms like workshops and reading groups and the student-organized conferences that draw students from different schools into collaborative relations. Unionization is another site of this collective consciousness, a site in which the contingent form of academic labor is resisted, usually with sympathetic support from neighboring populations of students. These collaborative actions are made possible to some extent by the transformation of communication technology, but the technology is not the cause.

In this concluding section of the chapter, I want to consider briefly what the emergence of the semiautonomous professional sphere means, what it might portend. Taking the risk here of prematurely broaching my hypothesis, I put some pressure on the fact that this sphere of intellectual activity is

36. See Ehrenberg et al., *Educating Scholars*: "Students who finish their degrees in five or six years do no better in the job market, and are no more likely to get tenure-track jobs, than those who finish in seven years. However, PhDs in the humanities (unlike good wine, apparently) do not improve after seven years: those who finished in more than seven years were less likely than faster completers to obtain tenure-track positions" (18).

transinstitutional, that it escapes the control of the graduate faculty of any one institution; hence my qualifier, "semiautonomous." Further, I want to suggest that this semiautonomous professional sphere might model a version of literary study beyond the career of college professor. Currently, the graduate professional sphere is self-reproducing, but only within the confines of graduate programs, of individual institutions. Can we imagine such a sphere liberated from these institutions? Or perhaps, fostered and supported by the university but existing in its own space, self-reproducing in a *public* sphere. Graduate education in its semiautonomous form might then model a literary and intellectual culture that no longer needs the career of college professor as its only home, its only way to exist. It would no longer need a job market for its reproduction. Literary study would be dispersed *among the professions.*

Now, I am more than willing to admit that this is a view of graduate education that is, for the present, counterfactual, even fantastic. I am speaking only as yet of a *model.* But I would like to use this model as a frame of reference in order to advance our understanding of what has happened in consequence of the collapse of the job market, even to see in what I once regarded as a simulacrum of the literary profession something more like its transcendence. Or, I should add by way of qualification, its *ideal* transcendence. In order to assert the bigger claim, it will be necessary first, however, to make a very brief survey of what the culture of graduate education looks like now.

By any standard of comparison, graduate education is far more complexly organized than before its transformation in the 1970s. In addition to seminars—the foundational practice for reproducing the discipline—graduate school entails teaching, giving papers at conferences, participating in workshops, and writing for publication. In the end, there is the dissertation, but this is the task that is the most challenging, where students often founder, because it is the most solitary. Publication promises at least an indeterminate number of readers, and essays are often "workshopped" in advance of submission. Most dissertations will be read by only a handful of professors. Communal activity is dominant in graduate education over the scene of individual reading and writing, a fact that is not unproblematic and that possibly contributes to the long time to degree of graduate study. The sociability characterizing graduate school, it is worth adding, disappears when a candidate for a job accepts a tenure-track appointment. As busy as the professor's life can be, the occasions of communal activity are actually fewer.

Efforts have been made to compensate for the solitariness of thesis writing by the use of dissertation workshops, though I do not know how effective this has been for students. Progress toward the degree is still often halted at this stage. I come away from my very brief overview of the components of graduate school life with the impression that among the array of sociable activities, the graduate seminar has declined in importance. Giving conference papers and participating in reading workshops are more important. Publishing articles falls somewhere in between—crucial for the job market but not as difficult or alienating a labor as the dissertation. Finally, let us recall that conferences and publication were conspicuously absent from graduate education before the 1970s. At that time, graduate study centered around the dyad of dissertation advisor and advisee, a relationship that could be generative but that had no exit if it failed.

From the perspective of the faculty, the seminar remains the central practice of graduate education, at least equal to, and possibly greater in importance than directing the doctoral thesis. Seminars involve far more time than dissertation advising. The divergence between the experience here of students and faculty is important, but it is difficult to determine the degree of its importance. My sense is that this divergence is a measure of the "semiautonomy" of the graduate sphere. Students are advised well or badly by their professors, but with conferences, workshops, and publication, students are much more in their own social space than in seminars, much more dependent on their peers for affirmation and intellectual exchange. Their interactions with their peers are the condition, and indeed the point, of these alternative forms of exchange. At its most complex and interinstitutional, this collaborative realm of activity functions as a niche public sphere. Although these associational forms are often supported by department funds, their organization seldom requires direction or even much involvement on the part of the faculty.

Professors are often asked to give plenary lectures at graduate student conferences, but this site of participation again looks different from the faculty point of view. For the professors, the graduate student corps functions as a public *for* the professoriate. This is also their role in the seminar, as the scene of a kind of beta testing for faculty research. In lectures and seminars, graduate students are a *first public* for professors, in advance of publication. Students also disseminate recent faculty research, in which they are keenly interested. Their engagement with new work is wider than that of the faculty, who are comparatively more specialized and who are likely to read more narrowly in their fields. The conditions of intellectual work for faculty are cluttered with tasks that constrain reading that ventures too far from subjects of research. Much of this reading, of course, is work by graduate students themselves: seminar papers, dissertation chapters, essays for submission to journals. I need not detail how much other reading of a bureaucratic nature faculty members do in the course of their days and nights or how little of it is of intellectual interest.

The narrowness of specializations is an old complaint about the academic professions, and it is more or less true, depending upon the intellectual habits of individual scholars. I am less interested in repeating the complaint than I am in observing the difference between the conditions of reading and writing for faculty and for graduate students. This difference is what makes it possible for the aggregate corps of graduate students to constitute a niche public for itself and a reading public for the professoriate and, further, to exercise a feedback function in the dissemination of scholarship. This function is quite important and explains, in my experience, the shrewdness graduate students demonstrate in their judgment of new scholarship. Their understanding of new work is often well ahead of their ability to bring their own writing to fruition and sometimes inhibits their writing by holding it to the high standard of recent publication. Their judgment can only be faulted on the grounds that it has too short a timeline, that it is too attuned to the moment. The feedback loop between the faculty and graduate students is an ambiguous benefit for literary study. This loop tends to accelerate the turnover of movements and tendencies in the discipline, submitting scholarship to the demands of fashion. As a result, even scholarship that is relatively recent by historical standards gets retired very quickly and is largely forgotten.

The engagement of graduate students with what is current in literary criticism is strongly determined by the culture of professionalization; the temporary career is one that is necessarily speeded up. The desire to be current, to be of the moment, is retroactively determined by the job market, which will cut many students off from further participation in the semi-autonomous public sphere. This should trouble us greatly, because underneath the enthusiasm for professional practices and rituals is genuine intellectuality. The question I would like to raise here is whether the culture of professionalization encourages this intellectuality to develop outside or beyond the professional sphere of the graduate school or, rather, whether the graduate faculty has succeeded in showing how these engagements might become permanent, even if graduate students do not go on to careers in the professoriate. It seems to me that a permanent engagement with literary study can only be achieved on the condition of an unqualified *freedom of inquiry*, by which I mean freedom from anxiety about what will look acceptable or desirable from the vantage of the job market (or more crudely, what is fashionable). For the faculty, unfortunately, the interest students express in their dissertations tends to be overly monitored, with one eye on the market. I would like to think that the devastation of the job market might liberate students to pursue whatever most interests them, whether or not their interest is responsive to the perceived demands of the market. I have touched on this question in chapter 2 above, but I want to advance it seriously here as a proposition. There are two ways to relate to the job market: to submit everything to its Sauron-like surveillance or to ignore it.

My suspicion is that in the latter case, better dissertations would result, but that is not my main point. And in any case, I do not expect that my recommendation will be taken seriously. What I want to propose more urgently is a way of relating the temporary career of graduate students to the lives they will most likely have after graduate school, if circumstances do not favor their getting a tenure-track job. I argued in another venue (at the MLA conference of 2020) that graduate students need to be apprised of market conditions and of alternatives to the career of college professor as soon as they arrive on campus.[37] Only such honesty and transparency, instated at the very beginning of the first semester, has any chance of preventing or mitigating the bitterness of disappointed expectations, so vividly represented in the protagonist of Christine Smallwood's recent novel, *The Life of the Mind*. The novel offers a powerfully disillusioned account of graduate school, and of its grim companion, adjunct teaching. Its protagonist, Dorothy, struggles mightily to sustain "the life of the mind," but the novel does not hold out much hope for her success.[38]

I argued further in my MLA paper that the best way to accomplish this goal is to introduce graduate students to as many alumni of the system as are willing and able to speak to them about their careers after graduate school. Many of these alumni, we know, did not get tenure-track jobs but escaped the trap of adjunct labor; many are now employed in nonacademic professions. Let us invite them to return and tell us what they got from their experience in graduate school. Many of these former students do not regret having spent time working on a doctorate, whatever the benefit of the credential in their later working life. But to the graduate schools they have left behind, it is as though they disappeared from the face of the earth once they entered new professions. This is a waste, the loss of considerable talent and passion to a diaspora.[39]

Can these former students maintain a relation to literary study with-

37. For a reprise of this unpublished essay, see Leonard Cassuto and Robert Weisbuch, *The New PhD*, 229–30.

38. Christine Smallwood, *The Life of the Mind* (London: Hogarth, 2021).

39. To say that these graduate students are unknown to us is not to deny that many have gone on to success in other fields. But to the literary professoriate, they are like Dorothea at the end of *Middlemarch*, whose fine spirit "spent itself in channels which had no great name on the earth."

out the organization of the profession, without the structure of graduate school? To ask this question is to put the intellectual seriousness of the literary disciplines to the test. Literary study in its disciplinary form obviously cannot be separated from the organizational structures of the university and the departments of which it is composed. But it is surely within the power of these departments to reconnect with former students and bring them into contact with graduate students currently in the system. To do so would be to enlarge, in small increments, the sphere of intellectuality by tapping the intellectual sociability in the corps of former graduate students. There is no reason why intellectual engagement with literature has to exist *only* in the form of a profession, however gratifying professional life may be, however abundantly scholarship has thrived within the academy. I gesture here to the realm of what Merve Emre calls the "paraliterary," all those sites where literary study is cultivated outside the purview of graduate education.[40] At these sites one might find long-standing projects such as the "medical humanities," but the more promising locations in this context are less disciplinarily organized. These are sites (for the most part) of intellectual exchange on the internet, new versions of "little magazines," such as *n+1*, or of journals such as *The Point*, as well as the now vast proliferation of blogs on cultural matters, some of which host high-level exchanges.[41] Such sites disclose the widespread desire for an engagement with literature and culture that is more serious than the habits of mass consumption and that demands new genres and forms of discourse.

My gesture of support for outreach to our former graduate students—

40. Merve Emre, *Paraliterary: The Making of Bad Readers in Postwar America* (Chicago: University of Chicago Press, 2017). For comments on humanities study outside the university in the postwar period, see Reiter and Wellmon, *The Permanent Crisis*, 247–49. Similar to the public constituted by our former graduate students is the one served by adult education (sometimes conducted under the rubric of "continuing studies"). This public includes former undergraduate majors but probably many others besides. My sense is that if we really care about the future of the discipline, adult education should be a *much* larger part of what we do. But this is a subject for another venue. My point here, which I would hope reinforces the arguments of other chapters in this book, is that the literary disciplines must figure out how to *create a public* that does not consist only of professors and graduate students.

41. I do not mention here "reading groups," which have been around since the nineteenth century, but which are less organized and less "public" than internet venues. What is important for my purposes is the level of organization that is achieved in the niche public sphere: less than professional, but more than amateur. For a relevant discussion of the aims of *The Point*, see Len Gutkin's interview with its editors, Jon Baskin and Rachel Wiseman, "The New Intellectuals and the Academy: A Conversation with *The Point*," chronicle.com/newsletter/chroniclereview/2021-08-30. The editors discuss the origins of their journal in their unhappiness with graduate study.

some graduate programs have already been making efforts of this kind—is not offered as a solution to the crisis of the job market, only a reminder of the fact that our former students are everywhere and that they are certainly still interested in literature and in intellectual life broadly. The collapse of the job market has deformed graduate education by burdening students with enormous anxiety and by constraining their freedom of intellectual inquiry in response to the market. But it has also established the conditions for the transformation of graduate school into a semiautonomous professional sphere. Insofar as this sphere transcends the organization of individual graduate programs, it has moved graduate education closer to a niche public sphere. Reconnecting our former students with our current students will strengthen the autonomy of this sphere, and if it does not resolve the calamity of the job market, it will at least reassure our students that the life of the mind can survive the crisis of the profession.

CHAPTER 10

Evaluating Scholarship in the Humanities

It is my personal opinion that Mr Wittgenstein's thesis is a work of genius; but, be that as it may, it is certainly well up to the standard required for the Cambridge degree of Doctor of Philosophy.

G. E. MOORE, READER'S REPORT ON
WITTGENSTEIN'S *Tractatus Logico-Philosophicus*

SCENES OF EVALUATION

The evaluation of scholarship is a difficult subject to discuss as a matter of general principle or procedure. At this level of abstraction, discourse about evaluation becomes awkward, uneasy, inarticulate. The chronic institutional disadvantage of humanities disciplines in relation to the natural and social sciences exacerbates this difficulty.[1] In recent decades, we have also had to acknowledge a very real crisis in scholarly publishing, evidenced by the collapse of some university presses and the reduction or elimination of the humanities line in others. In a widely cited letter to the literary professoriate of 2002, Stephen Greenblatt delivered a warning about the possibly dire consequences of this development for the future promotion or tenure of younger scholars.[2] Although there does not seem to have been

---

1. Commentary on this subject is so extensive now as to require an annotated bibliography that would far exceed the length of this essay. For a representative statement see Alvin B. Kernan, ed., *What's Happened to the Humanities?* (Princeton, NJ: Princeton University Press, 1997). For an account of the formation and development of humanities disciplines, see Lawrence Veysey, "The Plural, Organized World of the Humanities," in Oleson and Voss, *The Organization of Knowledge in Modern America, 1860–1920.* I wish to express my debt here to my colleagues Edward Sullivan, Robin Kelley, Mary Poovey, and Mary Louise Pratt, with whom I collaborated on a memorandum entitled "Assessing Achievement in the Humanities," for use internally by New York University administrators in the context of tenure and promotion.

2. Stephen Greenblatt. "A Special Letter." May 28, 2002, April 27, 2005, http://www .mla.org/scholarly_pub. See also MLA Ad Hoc Committee on the Future of Scholarly

a decline in the tenure rate as a result of retrenchment in university presses, the damage has been registered in other ways; monographs are expected to be shorter and press runs are smaller.

The humanities disciplines emerged over the last century and a half as a division of the disciplines nominally at parity with the natural and social sciences. Despite the parallel development of the three disciplinary divisions, there seems to be an ever-worsening problem with the integration of humanities scholarship into the system of the disciplines, a problem attested by the greater toll of financial cutbacks on the humanities but also, and equally disturbingly, by the difficulty academics in other disciplines attest they have in understanding what scholarship in the humanities is about. (I have addressed some of these issues in chapter 4 above.) Those who have prepared cases for tenure and promotion committees know that this problem exists, and we all recognize it in the larger context of public suspicion or incomprehension of what we do. In this chapter I focus on the scene of evaluation. My assumption, which I don't believe will strike anyone as controversial, is that the practice of evaluating individual works of scholarship is also a practice through which the value of scholarship is expressed to ourselves, to those in nonhumanities disciplines, and ultimately to those who fund the university, whether by donation, tuition, or through the taxes they pay.

To begin this conversation, I offer two preliminary observations concerning the ways in which the nature of humanities scholarship is misunderstood.

First, I observe that scholarship is generally identified in the university with the form of publication, an identification that must seem obvious but that is questionable on several grounds. Books and articles are understood as the product of humanities scholars and so as the most appropriate measure of their productivity. But if scholarship can be distinguished as a practice from the fact of publication as product—as I argue it must be—then it is possible to demonstrate that scholarship as publication counts in the university's system of rewards at the cost of distorting scholarship as *practice* and of limiting its range of expression.

Second, I observe that the concept of scholarship is generally understood in the academy as synonymous with the concept of research. Again, this understanding of scholarship is so universal as to be nearly beyond question. This identification of scholarship is problematic too for the hu-

Publishing, "The Future of Scholarly Publishing," in *Profession 2002* (New York: Modern Language Association, 2002), 172–86.

manities disciplines because it skews the understanding of scholarship toward a concept that is too closely identified with the natural sciences.[3] Both these common identifications of scholarship—with publication and with research—prevent humanities scholars as well as those outside our disciplines from *recognizing* scholarship, that is, understanding what it really is. The prevalent misrecognition prevents the humanities professoriate from conveying the value of scholarship within and without the university.

In questioning these commonplace identifications, I hope I will not be mistaken as saying that scholarship is in any way opposed to publication or research. The point of opening a conversation on the evaluation of scholarship by disentangling it from these two allied concepts is not to claim for humanities scholarship a difference that would distance it from the site of its cultivation in the university or deny its modern character as the discourse of professional academics who do research and properly desire to publish their writing. It is rather to grasp the specificity of humanities scholarship in such a way as to cast some light on the trouble in which it perennially finds itself, as the poor relation among the disciplines, as the first to suffer when presses cut back on publication or libraries on acquisition or administrations on budget lines. It will not suffice, then, to despair of scholarship's survival before one attempts to convey a better sense of what it is or why it has social value. I offer this argument, then, not to bury scholarship but to praise it.

If the evaluation of individual scholarly works makes implicit claims about the value of scholarship, it would be highly advisable when we undertake to evaluate individual works that we be able to say what makes a given essay or book a contribution to scholarship. I do not mean to suggest that it will be possible to achieve a kind of Cartesian clarity about this matter. Evaluative discourse constitutes a mode of argument different from demonstration. Evaluation entails offering what I will call an *account*. This account must function in its appropriate institutional setting as an expression of *accountability*; evaluative discourse gives an enriched description of scholarly work by answering to it and for it. Evaluation is not just a simple gesture of thumbs up or down, a *non disputandum est*. The foreclosure of discourse implied by that inarticulate gesture serves no one particularly well, but, on the other hand, let us not underestimate the difficulty of devising a language and mode of discourse specific to the task of evaluation and to establishing the condition of accountability or answerability—the capac-

3. For a version of this point, see Robert Scholes in "Learning and Teaching," *ADE Bulletin* 134–35 (2003): 11–16.

ity of the evaluator to elaborate on her account of the work when requested to do so. Answerability, or more generally still, responsibility, is built into the discursive scenario of evaluation as its condition of possibility.

Nonetheless this preliminary hypothesis is also a gesture toward a set of normative conditions and not an observation about how evaluation actually proceeds institutionally. When we look at scenes of evaluation in the university, the ideality of the formulation proposed above is immediately evident. The institutional scene is complicated by a tendency in the process of evaluation toward a flattening or thinning of accountable discourse, an emptying out of the very information richness toward which evaluative discourse aims. To put this point in more familiar terms, institutional conditions militate against what I call accountability and in favor of its eventual negation in the recourse to *counting*, the quantification of judgment.

So let me turn now to these real-world conditions of evaluation in the humanities. In the university today, evaluation of scholarship takes place in several linked scenes, which can be described as a continuum from the most internal to the most external. By an internal scene, I refer to the fact that disciplines and subfields within disciplines are very different from one another—hence works of scholarship must be judged first by other scholars within the field or subfield. Internality might be understood alternatively as the necessary immanence of judgment in any field of expert knowledge. Taking as exemplary now the most fraught scene of evaluation—tenure and promotion—we observe that once evaluations have been produced by scholars within a field, they are relayed to sites progressively more distant from that sheltered space of immanence. Evaluations proceed first from experts in the field, from thence to the department as representative of the discipline, from thence to promotion and tenure committees (sometimes these are divisional, sometimes they represent all the arts and sciences, and sometimes they represent all university units), and finally to provosts and presidents (these figures may be far indeed in their own expertise from the field of candidates for tenure). I describe this process as one of *externalization*, a highly formalized procession from the most internal scene to the most external. This procession is nothing other than the process of tenuring, or tenuring as *trial* (to activate the etymological pun in "process"). It is an unavoidable feature of the tenure process—as the most fraught and consequential scene of evaluation in the academy—that evaluation moves from the most internal site to the most external.

A moment's further consideration confirms the tendency of this process, as the descriptive language of evaluation loses its density with each relay, as the cumulative record of publication and other numerable measures substitute for the information-rich accounts or descriptions of scholarly work by experts in the field. I have no doubt that members of tenure and promotion committees make abundant good-faith efforts along the way to counter this flattening effect, to recover the density of evaluative language, but some loss in the subtlety and richness of this language is inevitable, even a necessary consequence of the procession from internal to external scene.

The distinction between the two scenes or poles of the evaluative process can be correlated with a distinction in more common use, between *subjective* and *objective* measures of scholarly accomplishment. The terms "subjective" and "objective" have conventional senses that refer to the presence or absence of bias or interest, but that is not chiefly what I mean by these terms. Rather, I am noting that the end point of externalization in the evaluative process converges with the sense of an achieved objectivity in the process itself. At the most external site of evaluation, no reading of a candidate's work need be done at all and would even in some ways be undesirable. At these sites a computer scientist who happens to be dean or provost justly refrains from assessing directly the work of a scholar in Chinese music or Victorian poetry. The dean or provost must defer to the immanence of the field, and confidence in objectivity is gained in the end by a summing of the majority opinion of scholars in the field, books or articles published, fellowships and grants awarded, honors or prizes won, invited lectures, conference presentations, and frequency of citation. At the limit of externality, evaluation would appear to be capable of being reduced entirely to a numerical tally, and, indeed, some institutions already regularize evaluative procedures by just these quantitative means, which promise by virtue of their objectivity also to be the fairest, the most devoid of bias.

The quantifying of achievement is a policy that arouses concern in the humanities, for very good reasons, if one can demonstrate in some (or any) cases a disparity between objective measures and contradictory but persuasively argued subjective judgments about the quality of a scholar's work. The possibility of this disparity is opened up by the very diversity of professional strategies for claiming distinction, strategies that sometimes (though certainly not always) bypass or neutralize the most thoughtful individual exercises in evaluation. Here I would point to the familiar circumstance of scholars whose volume of publication does not necessarily confirm the high quality of the scholarship, leaving us uneasy about how to explain a disparity between quantity and quality.

I take it as simply a matter of historical wisdom that objective or quantified measures of achievement cannot be regarded as infallible indicators of the enduring significance of scholarly work. Their status as measures is likely to be just as fallible in the long run as any act of judgment in any area of human enterprise. History tells us that the judgment of contemporaries not infrequently proves to be erroneous or misguided from the perspective of the long run (granting that even the long run is not the last word, as no one has the last word in the sphere of evaluation). We know that much work in the creative arts, for example, does not reveal its significance except in the long run, even posthumously. Likewise, some scholarly projects take time to be acknowledged for their significance—although posthumous recognition is too late for those with academic careers. Some of these unfortunates will probably fall by the wayside altogether, as mute inglorious Auerbachs.

THE BLACK BOX EFFECT

In the context of promotion and tenure, the final scene of evaluation is the one that is practiced at an institutional site most remote from the discipline itself—the promotion and tenure committee or the provost's or president's office. Only when the process of evaluation is expressed by "objective" measures does it become fully available to those outside the discipline, who may have no easy way into the discipline. Yet the scene of evaluation I describe as external or objective is always preceded by, and based on, acts of evaluation that must be internal to the discipline. Conversely, those at the higher institutional level whose role is to acknowledge scholarly achievement without necessarily understanding its content must assume that those who do understand it have done the work of evaluation that they themselves cannot do. The objective measures that reach the scene of external judgment are thus always the result of the multiple acts of judgment performed by the appropriate subjects of judgment, those immanent to the field.

   In the course of most tenure proceedings today a department's evaluation of a tenure candidate by its own field experts (if the department has any) is submitted to an initial strategy of externalization by soliciting "external" letters of reference. These letters are at once immanent to the field and yet external to the department scene, a crucial moment of duality. If external letters arrive at the department's door with the assumption of greater objectivity than the department's own evaluation, each such letter is still the expression of an intersubjective relation, an encounter between minds through the medium of scholarly work. It is important, then, not to confuse the externality of the external letter with the effect of objectivity, in the other sense of disinterest or lack of bias. The confusion of peer review with absence of bias or objectivity is an error—the point of peer review is to acknowledge the immanence of field expertise. Though we may hope for disinterested referees, disinterest is neither necessary nor inevitable in peer review.

But perhaps this confusion is a necessary error from the vantage of the institutional process, a moment in which evaluation hovers ambiguously on the threshold of externalization. This ambiguity is resolved when the perlocutionary force of the external letter is registered—that is, when the letter can be labeled positive or negative and added to the sum of positive or negative letters. Objectivity here means not that bias has been avoided or transcended but rather that immanent judgments have been rendered objective, laundered, as it were, by a simple procedure of summing, of tallying the positives and negatives. In this process, the subjectivity of evaluation fades like invisible ink from the page and becomes thereby objective. The process of externalization thus relegates acts of evaluation to a version of the philosopher's black box. The effect of objectivity, misrecognized as the transcendence of bias, is a result of this black-boxing of judgment— which again, let us underscore, is a necessary and inevitable effect of the institutional process.

The paradox of institutional objectivity—an *objectivity effect*—is something we would probably all concede because we know that when we look into the black box, when we look on the immanent scene of evaluation (not just in the context of tenure but in any context of evaluation), we discover that there is considerably more disagreement among experts within disciplines and fields than is recognized from the external perspective, from the perspective of summing opinions. Further, at the level of individual evaluative arguments, some disagreements will remain irresolvable for indefinite periods of time, because they have their source deep in the complexities of disciplinary knowledge, complexities that are the result of the immanent development of disciplines, the fact that they change. On occasion these deep disagreements might actually be indicators that a scholarly project is ahead of its time, that it will one day, if not today, prove its worth. Conversely, on occasion, unanimity about the value of a project may indicate that it is behind its time, that it is only telling us what we already know, or think we know. And finally, a caveat to cover all cases: disagreement about the value of a scholarly work is no guarantor of its worth, any more than consensus is a sure indicator of mediocrity.

Here we can remark a difference specific to the humanities, which often troubles understanding of scholarship in the context of promotion and tenure. In that context, natural scientists are likely to see an irremediable weakness in humanities scholarship, the evidence of which is just the difficulty of resolving in due time disagreements about the value of certain scholarly work. Although historians and sociologists of science have taught us to see in the history of science itself much more disagreement than is easily visible from outside looking in, scientists nonetheless want to ground their faith in the evaluation of scientific work in the principle that the validity of such work is in due time confirmed or disconfirmed. Hence it matters less that quantum theory and string theory were for a period of time after their emergence greeted with skepticism by in-field physicists; what matters is that these innovative theories eventually proved their worth. The time line for field validation is less than indefinite and indeed usually very short. Institutionally, the natural sciences are set up to produce a field consensus very quickly, sometimes even before rather than after the fact of publication. In the humanities, by contrast, most work needs to be published before it can even come to the attention of the field, and then it requires a period of time to be absorbed before there is a possibility of consensus about its value. Finally, controversies about work within humanities disciplines can linger over a long term, long enough to raise a doubt for the scientists about the ultimate resolution of disagreement and therefore about the knowledge claims of humanities scholarship. I return to this question at the end of this chapter.

In the scene that I am calling internal, there is no procedure for resolution of some kinds of disagreement about scholarly work for deep reasons, which have to do more, I suggest, with the historicity of humanities disciplines than with the bias of judges (though the latter may sometimes be an expression of the former). Inside the black box there is visible only the contest of individual evaluations, which must then be overcome by a procedural mechanism of peer review. At this point deans and administrators, whatever their fields of expertise, are obliged to accept the force of subjective judgments rendered institutionally objective.

Let me stress here, against what might seem the tendency of my argument, that I am not recommending a thorough skepticism about the process of evaluation. To say that judgment is subjective is as tautological as saying that water is wet. To say this is to say almost nothing—it is not yet to have opened the subject of evaluation. I am arguing rather that the social condition of intersubjectivity is not actually transcended by the procedure of externalization, which is misunderstood as an attempt to transcend bias. The purest objectivity in that sense—the absence of bias—belongs to simple ignorance. Yet we do not ask someone whose name has been chosen at random from the general population to evaluate a scholarly book. Such a person would possess a worthless objectivity. Conversely, it would be even more ludicrous to say that our randomly chosen judge is inadequate to the task by virtue of being too subjective. Neither of the terms objective or subjective describes the actual social and institutional conditions of evaluation, which are much better captured by the spatial concepts of externality and internality and by the presumptive intersubjectivity of the immanent evaluative scene. The spatial terms locate the subjects of judgment as they transfer judgment from the scene in which the subjects of a discipline are engaged with the immanent problems of making arguments in that discipline to that external or institutional scene where tenure is awarded or rewards are distributed. In the external scene, the substantiality of scholarly work thins out; it can become no more nor less thick, finally, than the CV, a surface on which is recorded the visible marks of accomplishment in a field but where the works of scholarship themselves appear only as titles.

MAKING SCHOLARSHIP PUBLIC

From the perspective of this analysis—which sets out from the interplay between internal and external, subjective and objective in the scenes of evaluation—it will be possible to characterize more accurately the pressures that result from the identification of scholarship with publication, understood as the objective evidence of achievement. Publication is what we desire for our scholarship, but publication itself, the fact of it, is not what we really mean (or should mean) by a "contribution to scholarship." The evaluation of scholarship in the context of tenure or other contexts ought not merely to ratify the fact of publication as the only truly objective form of scholarship, but that is precisely the institutional tendency of the modern disciplines, as we have known now for a long time and conventionally acknowledge in the phrase "publish or perish." Once work is published, it gains a limited immunity from subjective evaluation; it makes a stubborn claim to constitute accomplishment and therefore to merit reward, whether or not the work is ever read, whether or not it matters to anyone. Publication thus makes a claim to be scholarship and not just a means to make public scholarly work. I attempt now to describe the long-term consequences of this slippage between scholarship and publication for our understanding of humanities scholarship and for our ability to communicate its value to those outside our disciplines.

If scholarship aims rightly to be made public, it is unhappily the case that the pressure to publish as a requisite of professional advancement often makes publication the reason for scholarship and not the other way round. Writing for the sake of publication is not the same as aiming to *make scholarship public* and sometimes results in poor scholarship. Setting aside an analysis of the complex developments underlying the triumph of the productivity model in the university—what many call the "university of excellence" and what I would call the modern university as such—I want to underscore here that the misrecognition of scholarship as publication has particular disadvantages for humanities scholarship, which sometimes requires long reading and thinking and therefore a deferral of publication. The tenure clock prohibits this expenditure of time for younger scholars. Moreover, competition among institutions, when it is expressed in the determination to "raise standards," is premised too often on the conflation of scholarship with publication and is therefore understood by scholars themselves as a demand for more publication. As a systemwide tendency, raising standards by demanding more publication is paradoxically likely to result in a decline in the quality of scholarship and a creeping cynicism about publication.

In truth, the humanities disciplines were cast up on this bleak shore long before the troubles of the university presses. That crisis has exacerbated the competition for acquiring the objective signs of achievement because it reduces the availability of book publication as a means by which judgment can be relayed from the immanent site of field evaluation to that of institutional externality. Without publication, the way to translate evaluation into objective measures is blocked. And yet, whether one evaluates an unpublished manuscript or a published book, the object of evaluation remains the same, namely scholarship.

Humanities departments have unfortunately colluded in propagating the misrecognition of scholarship by steadily universalizing the "gold standard" of the published book as the requisite for tenure across the breadth and depth of the postsecondary system. In some Research I institutions the gold standard has been superseded by a platinum standard, a book plus a substantial installment of a second book. It would seem to follow from these two contradictory tendencies—diminished publication venues and rising tenure standards—that we should see a decline in the rate of tenure. But this is not the case, for reasons that are not easy to explain. Two studies of tenure rates from before the turn of the century, one conducted in 1973, the other in 1992, revealed that the rate of tenure across all academic fields, averaged across the postsecondary system, remained remarkably stable, at about 70 percent.[4] But there is no available breakdown of which I am aware for individual fields or for institutional tiers. I would guess that the rate of tenure has probably remained constant in recent decades, but con-

4. Richard P. Chait, ed., *The Questions of Tenure* (Cambridge, MA: Harvard University Press, 2002), 75. See also Basmat Parsad and Denise Glover, "Tenure Status of Postsecondary Instructional Faculty and Staff, 1992–98," *National Center for Educational Statistics, Education Statistics Quarterly* 4, no. 3 (2003), http://nces.ed.gov/programs/quarterly/vol_4/4_3/4_7.asp.

versely, the sale of monographs has seriously declined. Perhaps this fact can be attributed in part to internet dissemination of published work, which makes it possible to read many monographs without purchasing them.[5] But one might still raise a question about how seriously works of scholarship are read today, when we take into consideration the difference in engagement between owning a book and consulting one online. Despite the hyperbolic claims for so many scholarly works, the publication of books in disciplines such as literary study might have some time ago exceeded a threshold of marginal utility, resulting in a decline in wide readership for all but a few monographs.

Internet publication draws attention to the underlying problem of how to translate acts of evaluation into objective measures. The book possesses the quality of objectivity in part because it is a material object. It objectifies accomplishment in a literal way. Electronic publication will have to compete with this tacit sense of objectivity, which in the end may be more difficult to replicate than the procedures of peer review.

Meanwhile the objectification of measures proceeds apace, yielding to pressures emanating from below and above, within and without humanities disciplines. Chairs often complain justly about the increasing pressure from their administrations to quantify achievement in humanities scholarship. Purely quantitative measures are often resisted, as intrinsically opposed to humanistic thought, yet it seems increasingly difficult for many humanities departments to resist even the most mechanical systems of quantification. This development is especially troubling if the book and even the "book plus" have become universal standards for tenure. If the demand for more publication is understood as the way to raise standards, this tacit equation of publication and scholarship drives evaluation as quickly as possible out of the sphere of immanence in favor of counting publications. Both the judgments of the department's own experts and those of external reviewers fail by this standard to achieve the degree of objectivity realized by the sheer fact of publication, the objectness of the book or article. Yet the evaluation of scholarship, as I have suggested, is much the same intellectual exercise whether it is done in the context of review for publication or some other context. Because the scene of review for publication has the advantage, however, of possessing a greater measure of objectivity—that is, its subjectivity is more deeply immersed in the black box of anonymous

5. The "tenure monograph" is a subject of continued controversy, which I cannot consider in detail here. On the "tyranny of the monograph," see Lindsay Waters, *Enemies of Promise: Publishing, Perishing, and the Eclipse of Scholarship* (Chicago: Prickly Paradigm, 2004).

reviewing—departments have been increasingly driven to outsource evaluation to university presses. The presses in turn wonder why they have been asked to do the work of ad hoc tenure committees.

If this system has been steadily deteriorating, this is not to say that we can dispense with all externalizing procedures, such as outside letters of reference, but we should always remember that the shell game by which we write for one another's tenure candidates does not deliver objectivity by virtue of a letter's being external. Evaluation is always a social interaction and cannot be wholly externalized, objectified, or quantified. To entertain the delusion that judgment can be removed from its intersubjective matrix is irresponsible; it is to deny the necessity of *responsibility* in the act of judgment. Those who judge must be capable of answering when questioned. This is what responsibility means.

Yet for other reasons than the institutional pressure exerted by the university of excellence, some humanities disciplines themselves have come to rely just as much as the sciences on the objectification of judgment. Inasmuch as the humanities have become so diverse in subject matter and methodological options, objective measures have become increasingly attractive as a means of dealing with epistemological anxiety about disciplinary knowledge. For this reason, too, it has become difficult for humanities disciplines to resist pressure from above to express the value of scholarly enterprise as much as possible in external or objective terms, in publication, prizes, fellowships, and the like. Again, these measures are not fraudulent; they do indicate something. But relying too much on these measures vitiates the case for quality over quantity, a distinction on which rests the very possibility of evaluating scholarship.[6] If we cannot make this distinction, we have no adequate basis for making evaluation fully answerable.

Granted the understanding of "subjective" offered here—by which is meant the social condition of intersubjectivity in judgment—I believe we must reject the line of argument that simply concedes the primacy of objectivity by naming the object of judgment as nothing other than professional success. According to this line of argument it is only the signs of professional recognition that we can recognize as the legitimate basis for evaluation—publication above all. We cannot finally judge scholarly work

6. For a study of the quality-quantity problem, with a sensible argument for the necessity of keeping quality always in the picture, see Michael F. Middaugh, *Understanding Faculty Productivity: Standards and Benchmarks for Colleges and Universities* (San Francisco: Jossey-Bass, 2001). See also Robert Scholes, "The Evaluation of Faculty Members in the Culture of 'Excellence,'" *MLA Newsletter* 36, no. 2 (2004): 3.

itself, apart from the visible signs of accomplishment recorded in the CV, because we can no longer make our judgments about scholarship objective in some epistemological sense of incontestable. But this sense is just the opposite of what I mean by responsible or answerable. The unavailability of incontestable judgments or transcendental criteria has furthermore been widely confused with the postmodern condition of knowledge, taken to provide a kind of global justification for the very slippage from scholarship to publication I have been at pains to critique. I offer here an exemplary statement of this position, atypical only by virtue of its honesty, from an essay by Barry Sarchett:

> Professionalism is all that remains for us to use as a set of criteria to judge the relative merits of graduate and subsequent careers in literature when our discipline itself, which has never been as coherent as the sciences, becomes so fragmented as to virtually disappear. How can we judge a candidate's disciplinary competence if there is no discipline-wide set of criteria by which to judge? My hypothesis is that when English has effectively immolated itself as a discipline in order to advance, when even disciplinarity itself is regarded as constraining and politically suspect, when no clear repertoire of knowledge can be tested, when only multiple competing methodologies and objects of our attention can be found, when even these change rapidly as we move to the next big thing—we still must have some way to judge our peers at every step of their professional lives. We are thus left with purely professional standards: How well has each person succeeded in objectively accruing the signs—papers read, books and articles published, lectures invited, conferences organized, students' evaluations evaluated, committees served—of professional competence?[7]

Let us hope that Sarchett overstates the difference between humanities disciplines and the sciences with respect to disciplinary integrity. Ironically for a statement that means to celebrate our discipline, or lack of

---

7. Barry Sarchett, "Preprofessionalism and Disciplinarity," *ADE Bulletin* 133 (2003): 44. On the relativization of judgment in the literary disciplines, see Michèle Lamont, *How Professors Think: Inside the Curious World of Academic Judgment* (Cambridge, MA: Harvard University Press, 2009), 58–64: "Fields such as English literature and anthropology, where post-structuralism and the 'theory wars' have been fought, are more likely to take a relativistic stance toward evaluation, as well as to have a weaker consensus on what defines quality" (58–59). Lamont's interviews with literary scholars confirm their reluctance to apply standards common to other disciplines or at least to express these standards openly.

discipline, Sarchett concedes too much to science. Even more ironically, celebrating the groundlessness of knowledge in literary study delivers our discipline over to the shallow objectivity of a kind of board game in which the counters are the only things we recognize or reward, the only things we count. Groundless subjectivity flips over into its opposite, as objective a ground for judgment as one could ever hope to have. How well each person has succeeded in "objectively accruing the signs" of professional success is only a matter of counting. If we can no longer say anything in response to the question of why a given scholarly work is good or bad—never mind that what Sarchett means by "criteria" is not what I mean by responsibility—if evaluation can no longer be made to speak and we are condemned to tally mutely the objective signs, then how does scholarly work come to be recognized in the first place? Was no one articulating a judgment at any point about the quality of the work? These acts of judgment have simply disappeared into a black box the size of the profession itself, from which emerges, somehow, the successful scholar.

It is easy to demonstrate the ill effects of relegating judgment to the objective domain of professional achievement, chiefly the fact of publication. Each of these harms deserves to be discussed at greater length, but I consider them briefly here.

First, the practice of ratcheting up requirements for tenure and promotion must be seen in its real relation to the quantification of scholarly accomplishment. These two tendencies are mutually reinforcing. It should be obvious that as junior professors have the same amount of time they ever had to prepare for tenure, the ratcheting up of standards will inevitably be expressed as a demand for more publication in less time. Junior scholars are thus increasingly torn between allocating time for scholarship and time for other activities conceived as competing, such as teaching and service. Furthermore, it is doubtful that raising standards for untenured professors will result in work of higher quality, even if it results in more publication. The possibility of an ever-widening disparity between the quantity and the quality of publication is the risk in this demand.

Second, and a corollary of the first harm, is the mismatch between the stated expectations of hiring committees, which usually cite teaching ability and program fit as the primary desiderata of new hires, and the expectation of tenure committees, which almost exclusively reward publication.[8]

8. On the expectations of hiring committees, see Walter Broughton and William Conlogue, "What Search Committees Want," *Profession 2001*, 39–51, and the MLA Ad Hoc Committee on the Professionalization of PhDs, "Professionalization in Perspective," in *Profession 2002*, 87–210.

This disparity is widely attested by junior faculty members as a bait and switch between hiring and tenuring.[9]

Third, the demand for more publication militates against undertaking long-term projects, or projects that require acquisition of a time-consuming knowledge base such as a new language. For the same reason, the pressure to publish quickly and copiously militates against undertaking intellectually risky projects that do not conform to proven successful models for publication. It also militates against doing work in fields that are relatively arcane, where the knowledge base required for scholarly work is possessed by only a small group of scholars. Manuscripts in these fields are particularly difficult to publish, exacerbating the potential gap between good scholarship and the objective sign of professional success, quantity of publication.

Fourth, humanities disciplines have increasingly lost the capacity to recognize scholarship in any form other than book publication (or secondarily, refereed journals, with the qualification that journal articles are increasingly becoming advance installments of books). Although the AAUP and other advocates of the professoriate have made strenuous efforts to acknowledge these other forms (such as exhibition catalogs or websites), the most obvious venue of scholarship that fails to be captured by this tendency of evaluation is the classroom. We all know that there are brilliant scholars among us whose scholarship goes into the classroom and not onto the page. I am speaking here not of popular teachers, whose success is easy to measure, but important teachers, whose effects are long term and connected immediately to the depth of their scholarship. The failure of the profession to devise ways to recognize this kind of scholarly achievement, which at moments in the history of humanities disciplines has been enormously important, is not difficult to understand, but it is also not right to excuse. The existence of this and alternative modes of scholarship must be acknowledged and rewarded if scholarship is to survive in all the forms in which it can be expressed. So let us acknowledge once and for all, with the appropriate implications for our evaluative procedures, that teaching is a venue for making scholarship public.

I am speaking only indirectly here to the relative weighing of scholarship and teaching in the context of tenure and promotion (setting aside altogether the assessment of service).[10] Although the question of how to

9. See Eugene Rice and Mary Deane Sorcinelle, "Can the Tenure Process Be Improved?," in *The Questions of Tenure*, ed. Chait, 101–24.

10. For a vigorous defense of teaching as a form of scholarship (a position I would endorse), see Charles E. Glasic, Mary Taylor Huber, and Gene I. Maeroff, *Scholarship*

assess teaching is of enormous importance in the humanities, it is just as important in the sciences. The strict distinction between the creation of knowledge and the transmission of knowledge betrays a misunderstanding of the most fundamental aims of education in both the humanities and the sciences. Recognizing teaching as a form of scholarship—when it can be demonstrated as such—is one way in which teaching might be revalued without having to make the weaker case for considering teaching and scholarship as separate but equal achievements in the context of tenure. It is unwise to redress the emphasis on the objective standard of publication by simply tilting the scale toward teaching. To do that would be to lose the point that if scholarship ought not to be reduced to the fact of publication, it also ought never to be separated from the enterprise of teaching. In my experience, the best scholars are often the best teachers. Whether or not the converse of this proposition is also true, it is not good for the humanities to distinguish scholarship and teaching absolutely, as teaching depends on, and should depend on, the advances of scholarship just as much as scholarship depends on teaching to transmit its arguments and to perform a kind of beta testing of those arguments.

Fifth and finally, the equation of scholarship with publication has had the effect of evacuating public venues of evaluation, such as journals and reviews. The practice of reviewing scholarly works in public venues has atrophied because reviewing takes place more and more often in the context of tenure and promotion and of anonymous reviewing for presses. Correlated with this tendency are journals that increasingly delegate reviewing to younger scholars because advanced scholars are tapped for so many confidential letters of reference, indeed tapped out. In effect, reviewing by senior scholars is often taking place in a nonpublic way, with a resulting loss of vitality and intellectual exchange in public venues. These venues make possible answerable or responsible evaluation just because they are not premised on anonymity.

If it is said, nonetheless, that confidential letters of reference are more reliable by virtue of their confidentiality, one might reply that the reverse is often true. These letters are written for the eyes of tenure review committees—for the external scene of evaluation—and hence written with an anxious awareness that any criticism at all of a candidate's work might

---

be sufficient to provoke denial of tenure. Confidentiality frees referees from one anxiety, exposure of their name, only to shackle them with another, the awesome consequence of the confidential letter in an age of apparently rising demands. The further result of this procedure is to induce in members of promotion and tenure committees an anxious reading between the lines of letters, a distrust of confidential letters that the condition of confidentiality was supposed to be proof against. To step outside of this vicious circle, it will be necessary at the least to restore public venues of evaluation as a counterweight to anonymity. It is difficult to see how this intention can be realized, however, without reengaging with the practice of reviewing. It is likely that only in these public venues can we recover our ability to cultivate a language of evaluation that is fully responsible. But as long as the work of scholarship continues to be equated with the fact of publication, for so long the practice of evaluation is likely to take cover behind the sheer objectness of publication and continue to be drained of the descriptive richness it needs to cultivate.

A POETICS OF SCHOLARSHIP

This survey of the institutional vicissitudes of humanities scholarship hints at a surprising conclusion: that scholarship as publication is overvalued within the humanities disciplines and for that very reason undervalued without. The reduction of judgment to the ratification of professional success makes uninteresting or of merely secondary concern the question that should be the basis of evaluation: What is the contribution of this work to scholarship, to the humanities as disciplines of knowledge? If the evaluation of scholarly work fails to convey plausible answers to this question, it is not surprising that even good works of scholarship fail to find readers or that the purpose of humanities scholarship fails to be understood except in terms of professional success.

The discourse of evaluation perhaps cannot be expected on every occasion to rise to the defense of scholarship itself, but we can reasonably demand that evaluation not descend always to the impoverished idiom of hyperbole, according to which every new work of scholarship upends the shelf on which it sits, completely revises or overthrows every precedent venture on the subject. The prevalence of such a hyperbolic idiom in the advertising of monographs betrays only too obviously that the purpose of evaluation is often less to engage scholarship than to ensure the scholar's survival in a competitive struggle, a struggle in which only the most hyperbolic praise catches the attention of possible readers or members of promotion committees. In addition to the impossibility that such hyperbole can be true in all cases, its prevalence obscures the genuinely revisionist work, which is fairly rare, and devalues genuinely good scholarship that is too honest to make hyperbolic claims for itself. When there is too great a disparity between the extravagant claims of scholarly work within a specialized field and the actual interest the work provokes, it calls into question the very value of scholarship.

At this point it is necessary to qualify my assertion above that individual works of humanities scholarship are best judged by those within the field. While the condition of immanence is a necessity imposed by the division of the disciplines, by the ongoing specialization of knowledge, immanent judgment should not produce an irreversible black-box effect. While it is neither possible nor desirable to dispense with immanent evaluation or even, for that matter, with objective measures of achievement, these two institutional procedures are unhappily implicated in a damaging correlative effect: the failure of the humanities to provide a generally accessible account of what it is that scholars do, an account that might be circulated beyond the humanities disciplines and that would mediate between scenes of immanent evaluative discourse and external scenes of reception or promotion.

I have attempted in another essay in this volume (chapter 4, "Monuments and Documents") to give a descriptive account of what scholars in the humanities do, which I will call here a "poetics" of scholarship. As a historical discourse, poetics was principally concerned with describing the genres of writing and the principles of judgment proper to specific genres. In this context, we can observe that in the humanities, disciplines are roughly correspondent to genres, which cannot be reduced to the same principles of evaluation. Here I return to the second part of the hypothesis with which I began this essay, concerning the distinction between scholarship and research, which I suggested was crucial to what is at stake in the problem of evaluation in the humanities and in the problem of the relation between the humanities and the sciences.[11] Research is the dominant concept governing the system of rewards in the academy today; it names the dominant position of science among the disciplines, confirmed in the conventional narrative about the "rise of the research university."[12] I want

11. Peter Burke, *A Social History of Knowledge: From Gutenberg to Diderot* (Cambridge: Polity, 2000), points out that "research" is a term that emerges in relation to scholarship during the eighteenth century (45–47). It was originally associated with the law (we still use the expression "legal research").

12. Hugh Davis Graham and Nancy Diamond, *The Rise of American Research Universities: Elites and Challengers in the Postwar Era* (Baltimore: Johns Hopkins University Press, 1997).

to suggest, however, that scholarship is a better term than research to describe the work of humanities disciplines. Research is better understood as a *component* of scholarship. I define it here as the discovery, collation, and synthesis of textual and other artifactual or evidentiary materials relating to a given object of inquiry. If archival work can constitute an achievement in itself, sometimes a great one, the achievement is limited if it does not proceed to interpretive argument or theoretical reflection. Research must be succeeded by an exercise of thought that requires wide learning, the ability to draw connections between disparate points in time, in social space, and in the universe of concepts. Learning has both depth and breadth, and our sense of the value of a work of scholarship should engage both aspects of the learning that goes into it.

This may seem obvious, but the obviousness of it hides a subtler point concerning the historicity of archival research, as the archive's dusty corners yield to ever more light, though not always to greater understanding. Not so obviously, the archive is constructed *in discovery*; that is, it is an advancing horizon of unexamined materials, textual or artifactual. Once brought to light, an archive ceases to be the object of discovery and can only be constructed as archive again by interpretation or reinterpretation or by the discovery of related archival materials that call for revision of the already illumined (hence the trope of "new light" in scholarship).

Just as scholarship is not only research, neither is it only interpretation. For that reason, the value of humanities scholarship does not rest finally on the demonstrable validity of the interpretive claims made in a work of scholarship or conversely on the falsifiability of these claims. Because these claims are enmeshed in genres of writing that orchestrate research, interpretation, and theoretical reflection, a work of scholarship can survive even the disconfirmation of its particular hypotheses. The best scholarly works succeed in the long term by reorienting research and interpretation, by turning the object round for a different view, whether or not their assertions are confirmed. The best works of scholarship—let us propose Burckhardt's *Civilization of the Renaissance in Italy* as an example—are imperishable because their provocation to succeeding scholars inheres in the *writing itself*. Few scholars today would accept Burckhardt's thesis unrevised. Some do not accept it at all. But the book survives its thesis and continues to provoke scholarship, even to define the terms of the very repudiation of its claims.

A poetics of scholarship might serve as the basis for understanding evaluation without denying or apologizing for its subjectivity and so liberate it from its black box. Such a poetics would enjoin us to inquire into the minute particulars of scholarship, its themes, its figures, its syntax, as well as its larger structures, its methods and modes of argument. All these features can be observed and studied for themselves and for the sake of understanding everything that goes into our acts of evaluation as they arise out of our recognition of scholarly discourse. There are few precedents for this poetics, but I offer as one example Anthony Grafton's study of the footnote, in which we see a mirror held up to scholarship and a question posed: What does the footnote tell us about what scholarship is?[13]

Although the humanities disciplines are self-reflective in many ways, often celebrating the diversity of their methodologies and even the carnivalesque dissolution of their disciplinary norms, I am more impressed by enduring signs of generosity and interdependence in scholarship, such as the footnote. It has somehow survived many revolutions in theory, hanging on at the bottom of the page or banished to the rear of the book, without ceasing to mark scholarship with a sign that elicits instant recognition. Nor does the footnote even need the book or the article to manifest itself within this discourse. It can be heard in the speech of the scholar, in the charmingly complementary themes of learning and pedantry. A poetics of scholarship would understand the survival of the footnote, in whatever form, as revealing something distinct about scholarship as a species of discourse. Such continuities, even if we are disinclined to speak of them, engage us at the deep and inarticulate level at which we make judgments about scholarly work and seek a language for our judgment.

13. See Anthony Grafton, *The Footnote: A Curious History* (Cambridge, MA: Harvard University Press, 1999), and Anthony Grafton, *Defenders of the Text: The Traditions of Scholarship in an Age of Science, 1450–1800* (Cambridge, MA: Harvard University Press, 1991). See also Rudolf Pfeiffer, *History of Classical Scholarship, 1300–1850*, 2 vols. (Oxford: Clarendon, 1976).

CHAPTER 11

Composition and the Demand
for Writing

ETHOS

In homage to the late, great art of rhetoric, I am going to divide my pre-sentation into the three parts of the classical oration: *ethos, logos,* and *pathos*.[1] No one who works in literature, rhetoric, or composition will need to have these terms defined, but I will explain why I would like to structure my re-marks by invoking these ancient concepts of Greek rhetoric. Although I am very grateful for the opportunity to speak on the subject of composition, I am also aware that my qualifications in this field are dubious at best. I have never taught a composition course, and it is quite unlikely at this date in my career that I ever will. Yet I have long been interested in composition, both as a pedagogic enterprise and as an institutional formation. Over the years I have written several versions of an essay on this subject, but I discovered on the occasions of delivering these earlier efforts as talks that my speaking at all about composition provoked some skepticism among the composi-tion professors in my audience. I recognized, in other words, a challenge to my "ethos" as speaker. These earlier versions of my essay were no doubt deficient, not the least for failing to take the necessary pains to establish my *bona fides*, my standing in the case. Bearing that failure in mind, I want to begin this latest attempt with a brief argument from ethos.

My interest in the history, theory, and practice of composition is long-standing and is part of continuing work on the history of literary study in the Anglo-American university. The emergence of the composition course in the later nineteenth century is a singularly important event in that his-tory. I believe that it is essential to our understanding of literary education that we should be able to account for the conditions leading to the forma-tion of a new kind of course, focused almost exclusively on writing, and

---

1. Prefatory note: I composed this essay as a mimetic "oration" on the occasion of the Stanford English Department's search for a new director of their Expository Writing Program. I reproduce my text for oral delivery here, in order to underscore the opposi-tion between speech and writing addressed in the argument. To this end, I abbreviate references as much as possible, and have appended instead a bibliographical note.

housed for many years almost exclusively in departments of English. I have been reading in the history of composition for many years, which I have found to be in some respects a more illuminating source of information about the development of literary study than one finds in most histories of criticism. I'm greatly indebted, as a result, to the scholars in composition history, such as Robert Connors, James Berlin, Michael Halloran, Albert Kitzhaber, James Murphy, John Brereton, and others.

At the same time that I commend these scholars, I must also register my sense that this history is too narrowly defined for my purposes in constructing a big picture of literary study, a judgment confirmed for me by the relative absence in accounts of composition's history of certain other scholars who have been important in the history of education. I've come across, for example, only one reference in my reading to Kenneth Cmiel's *Democratic Eloquence*—this in Sharon Crowley's *Composition in the University*—even though in my view Cmiel has given us the most insightful account currently available of the origins of the composition course in the context of social developments in American society. But Cmiel is not the only figure of significance in this broader social context. I miss more than anything else in composition history and theory what I would call a sociology of writing, an analysis of the relation between writing and the social forms of modernity; such an analysis as can be found, for example, in the work of Alvin Gouldner, whose theory of the professional-managerial class as a "speech community" based on what he calls a "culture of critical discourse" begins to explain the *demand for writing* in the modern era, which in turn begins to explain the origin and also the travails of the composition course.

I will return to the question of a "speech community" later, but I do want to note here, in support of my argument from ethos, that the possibility of developing a sociology of writing motivates work I have done on the generic form of the memorandum, which I believe to be the principal genre of writing in modernity—not the novel, not the journal article, not even the scientific paper. Outside the specialist field of business and technical writing, there has been less attention in composition theory to informational genres, by which I do not mean what composition calls expository writing. In all probability the lack of interest in genres such as the memo is the result of the orientation of the composition course historically toward "basic writing." For that reason, the work of a business historian such as JoAnne Yates on the history of the memorandum is as far afield for composition scholarship as it is for literary study. One of the exceptions to this generic limitation of the scholarship, I'm happy to add, which I discovered only after completing my work on the memorandum, is the major work by

Lisa Ede and Andrea Lunsford, *Singular Texts / Plural Authors*, on the issue of collaborative writing.

The second point I would like to make in support of my argument from ethos is that I approach composition from the perspective of a scholar of rhetoric. I regularly teach a course in the history of rhetoric, which is also a subject of my scholarly research (see chapter 5 above on the decline of rhetorical education). Although my course on rhetoric is concerned to acquaint students with the "old rhetoric," as Roland Barthes calls it, my syllabus includes the rhetorics of the nineteenth and twentieth century, leading up to the so-called "current-traditional" version of composition pedagogy. The question of the relation between composition and rhetoric is another way of posing the question of the origin of the composition course, or what Robert Connors calls "composition-rhetoric." His term perhaps finesses the peculiarity of this pedagogic formation, given the fact that the older concept of "composition" is a fair equivalent to the part of rhetoric called *invention*—the finding of arguments—the very part of rhetoric that disappeared from postclassical rhetoric and makes no appearance at all in composition theory and practice until the reemergence late in the twentieth century of "rhetoric" as a new version of composition (or sometimes even as an alternative to composition). The rhetorical concept and practice of "invention" has been vigorously rehabilitated in much theorizing in the rhetoric wing of "rhet-comp." Though I welcome this development, I am less optimistic than many of our new rhetoricians about reinstating rhetoric to its former place of preeminence in the curriculum.

For my purposes here, I point out that my perspective on the field of composition, while not interior to that discipline, is in a way binocular. I see composition from the vantage both of work on rhetoric and on the history of literary study. From that dual perspective, what strikes me as most in need of explanation—and I've already begun to hint at this—is not the teaching of writing or "composition," in the larger, comprehensive sense of an *art of writing*, but the institutional form of the composition course. Whatever I have to say about that institutional form must be understood as in no way denying what is for me the unquestionable importance of the art of writing. The service we render our students in teaching that art is of such consequence that it is perhaps worth suspending on behalf of that goal our acceptance of the composition course as a *given*, as the necessary institutional vehicle for the teaching of writing. By "suspension" here, I mean bracketing for the sake of argument the inevitability of that particular institutional form, the freshman writing course. Conversely, I would ask the literary professoriate to get past its indifference to the composition course, which has so often allowed literature teachers to delegate the art of writing to a subordinate or contract teaching corps. I hope, then, that my remarks will be received as I intend them, as an exploration into how we might elevate the importance of teaching the art of writing within the system of university disciplines.

LOGOS

The composition course, most scholars would agree, is a response to a social demand emanating from sectors of American society in the later nineteenth century. I would like to inaugurate my argument from logos by recalling one statement of this demand, taken from an essay published in 1891 by James Morgan Hart, a rhetoric teacher of the period: "The cry all over the country is: Give us more English! Do not let our young men and women grow up in ignorance of their mother tongue."[2] Here is the raw demand, then, the object of which is said to be *English*. But English is not so simple an object; otherwise "more English" might easily have been provided by the courses already on offer in college and university English departments. The response to the demand was, as we all know, a new kind of course, the composition course, taught at first by members of English departments, but without a clear sense of the continuity between the missions of the English department and composition. On the contrary, these two projects began immediately to diverge, never to coincide again. I argue that the reason for this divergence was that the cry for English was heard by the professoriate as a demand for *writing*. Whatever is meant by the object *English*, it was to be supplied by a course in which writing was to be the main business.

In the slippage from *English* to *writing*, we can insert the entire early history of composition, which I will try to sketch here very briefly, as my *narratio*, my statement of the facts of the case. The most important point to make about this early history is that it is a continuation of the process of *vernacularization*, that is, the displacement of Latin by English as the language in which university subjects were taught and in which the learned professions conducted their communications. (Greek was also studied, of course, in the old college but was less important to professional qualification.) The same process of vernacularization occurred in the other European nations, but I'm going to restrict my account here to the situation of the English language in the United States, as only here did the composition course as such emerge when it did. Until the later nineteenth century, far the larger part

2. Cmiel, *Democratic Eloquence*, 289.

of the college curriculum was devoted to reading a curriculum of works in Latin and Greek, among which classical rhetoricians such as Cicero and Quintilian ranked near the very top. In the eighteenth century, as earlier, this curriculum was the means by which scholars gained access to professional learning. Much of what constituted knowledge reposed in works written in Latin. Outside the universities, however, the newer sciences and discourses of expertise were moving steadily away from Latin. The schools caught up very late with this development; let us recall that Harvard only dispensed with its Latin entrance requirement in the last decade of the nineteenth century. When the classical curriculum was finally dislodged, new disciplines of knowledge very quickly established themselves in the university and set up shop in the new form of departments. With departmentalization, new forms of pedagogy were devised, especially the seminar, which was imported from the German university system. The seminar (or "course" as we now call it) replaced the tutorial system, which was the form in which Latin and Greek were usually taught, along with the complementary form of "recitation," which could be adapted either to the tutorial or the lecture.

It seems worthwhile to rehearse this narrative, even if it is well known to many or most of you, because in my view the relation between the process of vernacularization and the emergence of the composition course is insufficiently acknowledged in the available histories. These histories often give us a lineage for composition in which it is rather the relation between *rhetoric* and composition that is determinative, where the immediate precursor to the composition course is the sequence of vernacular rhetorics beginning with Blair and leading up through George Campbell and Richard Whately to the famous "big four" of the late nineteenth century: John Genung, Adams Sherman Hill, Fred Newton Scott, and Barrett Wendell. This lineage assumes the established preeminence of the vernacular when what is at issue is rather the process, uneven and convulsive, that gave us the vernacular curriculum. English rhetorics, however influential they may have been in niches of the school system, remained secondary in relation to Latin until well into the nineteenth century. The vernacular rhetorics were part of the *process* of vernacularization, not the effect of its prior realization.

The situation I am describing is one in which two structures of the older curriculum—Latin and rhetoric—can be seen as inextricably bound together and thus mutually reinforcing each other. It is not possible to understand the decline of rhetorical education in the nineteenth century without recognizing that the survival of rhetoric depended upon its embodiment in the Latin curriculum; at the same time rhetoric's alliance with Latin was a fatal weakness. When the movement to dispense with prerequisites in Latin finally prevailed, it proved impossible to translate classical rhetoric fully into an English-based curriculum. Despite the manifest accomplishment of the vernacular rhetorics of the eighteenth and nineteenth centuries, rhetoric as a curriculum, a system of language arts, disappeared with the decline of Latin. What took its place was the composition course, which for a while retained the name "rhetoric," or was sometimes labeled transitionally "rhetoric and composition," but which eventually discarded the earlier name and settled into its twentieth-century identity as "composition." The birth of composition coincided with the last breath of the old rhetoric.

The history of the relation between rhetoric and Latin gives us a more complete picture of the transitional moment. In retrospect, we can see that the Latin/rhetorical curriculum also sustained the predominant *orality* of the educational system long into the nineteenth century. This aspect of the story is conspicuous in the accounts of the composition historians, but it makes less sense without acknowledging that the oral form of instruction was *essential* to the teaching of Latin (as well as Greek), just as today it is still crucial for teaching modern foreign languages. This oral pedagogy was not seen as necessary for the teaching of English, as the presumed native language of college students. The decline of Latin was coincident with the gradual replacement of oral with written instruments of examination. By the end of the nineteenth century, most examinations were written rather than oral, a spectacular change in the method of postsecondary teaching. The reasons for this change are difficult to explain, and unfortunately, I will have to resign myself to a very cursory account. Clearly this change has epochal significance. It was driven in part by a growth in the size of the college population, but only in part. There were periods in the later nineteenth century when the university population grew very little. The change had more to do with the weakening of faith in rhetorical pedagogy itself, after its last efflorescence in the elocution movement, which was more an extracurricular phenomenon than an integral part of the college curriculum. In the form of "recitation," oral performance continued to thrive for some time at the lower levels of the school system. We are speaking, then, about a pedagogic formation with three legs—Latin, rhetoric, and *orality*; this triumvirate stood together, and fell together.

What arose in its place was another troika: English, composition, and *writing*. But we have not accounted fully for the place of writing in this troika until we observe the peculiar importance of writing for the vernacularization of professional discourse. Writing facilitated the growth of new professions and new fields of expertise, but this was not writing as understood in literary culture generally. This was not the writing associated with belles lettres, which modeled norms for correct and elegant use of language, both spoken and written. In new professional, managerial, bureaucratic, and technical settings, English was shaped to new ends, quite different from the literary, but at the same time developing new possibilities of writing. Still, the demand for writing could be expressed publicly as the demand for English: "Give us more English." The two demands for English and for writing reached the university at the same time and swept over it like a great wave. But departments of English were embarrassingly unable to respond to either demand, because at this time the discipline of English was dedicated at the highest level of the university system largely to the study of the English *language*—and that in its *early* forms, Anglo-Saxon or medieval. "English" named the discipline of the philologists, often trained abroad in the German universities, and not the subject of the grammarians and the belletrists.

The demand for English could hardly be met by courses that were vehicles of Germanic philology. And yet who was to respond to this demand? By the 1880s, the demand had become hystericized, a social panic. The collegiate system moved quickly but ineptly to respond to the panic by instituting new entrance requirements, in English now rather than Latin, and then by instituting a new freshman course for the remediation of English, which we now know as composition. No doubt the inventors of this course thought that they were responding to the demand for English, meaning the rectified version of the vernacular, or standard English, but why was that standard not the product of an oral pedagogy, a system of tutorials and recitations? In that event, there would have been no composition course. The turn to written examinations by the latter half of the century ensured that henceforth teachers would gain access to the language of their students not by hearing them speak but by reading their writing. The new pedagogy was retroengineered from the form of the written exam. The difference between the instrument of pedagogy and the instrument of examination was erased.

The professoriate at the time was strongly persuaded that incoming students spoke English poorly. But entrance examinations and the freshman composition course revealed something even more shocking: student writing diverged from the vernacular standard far more than their speech. Standardization as an *oral* project sought to eradicate dialect variation, primarily by correcting pronunciation, speech. The domain of error was somewhat circumscribed by speech itself. The new pedagogy of writing, on the other hand, exposed many new and different kinds of error, specific to writing: spelling, punctuation, sentence construction, paragraphing, along with myriad rules for usage. The speech of a student would never have revealed these errors, but writing never failed to betray them, fixed indelibly by the ink on the page. The graphic error endured, both the crime and the evidence of the crime.

Even as pedagogy became more dependent upon writing, on the "theme" as both pedagogic exercise *and* means of examination, writing was becoming ever more important for the growing professional and managerial classes. As organizations became larger and more complex, and face-to-face communication was supplemented more and more by written communication, the social significance of writing itself changed. That significance was no longer best indicated by the concept of *literature*, writing that possessed permanent cultural value. The center of cultural gravity for writing shifted from the domain of literature to the domain of instrumental or informational genres, such as the memorandum or the report. As writing became more necessary for more people, it became both more ephemeral and more socially consequential. The emergence of this form of writing coincided with the new concept of *literacy*, replacing the old concept of *letters*. Henceforth it would be necessary that large numbers of people know how to write, where previously this skill was required of only a very few. The new composition course was a response to a *demand for writing*.

The difficulties facing the teachers of writing were many, beginning with their understanding of the very concept of writing. Responding to a rapid escalation of demand, they had difficulty sorting out the different modes of writing hidden in the demand for "English." The written exercise or "theme" seemed to be the best response, a form of writing that was not exactly literary nor exactly bureaucratic. Later theorists settled on the category of the "expository" as an appropriate designator. The theme was understood as providing immediate access to the language skills of students, who arrived at the colleges and universities with increasingly diverse class and ethnic backgrounds and indifferently prepared by the American high school. The social pressures driving the universities to institute the composition course, and to coerce a sector of the professoriate to teach this course, were difficult to resist, much less master. It is possible to see in retrospect an inevitable mismatch between demand and response. The composition professoriate responded to the perception of linguistic deficiency, which, at the most basic level, appeared as the transgression of grammatical rules governing the vernacular standard. But even mastery of these rules did not guarantee that students would acquire the ability to write. Despite the fact that specimens of writing in the themes of early composition gave access to grammatical error, these exercises did not easily evince the impediments to fluency in writing. This was perhaps because the nature of writing itself as a medium was poorly understood, or at least poorly conceived in the context of pedagogy. Even students who spoke fluently and grammatically might fail at writing, as they still do today, because the transition from speech to writing entails crossing over into a new medium. This crossing produces anxiety and inhibition. The construction of writing as "basic writing," that is, writing outside the disciplinary context and even outside of most genre constraints, did little to assuage these anxieties, and may even have exacerbated them by asking students to produce what seems to be "unmotivated" writing.

In fact, however, basic writing did not escape genre altogether, and the early composition course evolved the theme as a version of the personal essay, an extension of the *literary* into the new order of modern writing. The genre of the personal essay seemed at least flexible, lending itself to various kinds of argument or expression, ranging from something like the editorial at one end of the spectrum to autobiography at the other. Yet this generic flexibility, which was intended to bridge the transition from basic writing to the more sophisticated forms of writing found in university disciplines, proved difficult to motivate, and hence the problem of deinhibiting writing remained. The goal of deinhibiting the medial shift from speech to writing animates later theoretical innovations such as "process theory," which suspends judgment of writing as "product," as well as "writing across the curriculum," which provides motivation by drawing it from the disciplines themselves. Without stepping further into this controversial arena—I myself think that writing across the curriculum is a better strategy than the personal essay that grounded process theory—let me name and underscore here the problem that emerges from this analysis: it is the gap between basic writing and the motivated, generic forms of writing that are its real-world expressions. College students are expected to leap this gap as soon as they settle on a course of study in a major, which always brings with it new demands on writing.

In the composition course, "basic" writers were neither inducted into the informational forms of writing that dominated modernity nor asked to produce "literary" writing. The evolution of manuals and textbooks offered models for imitation within a narrow range of generic types, mainly the personal essay and the argumentative essay. This narrowing of models for imitation resulted in the exclusion of literary works early on from the syllabus of composition. I am aware that many second thoughts have been expressed about this policy, which seems to have been enforced in part to distinguish the professional identity of the composition professoriate from that of the literary professoriate. But it is worth pointing out that the exclusion of literary genres was matched by the exclusion of purely informational writing as well—easier to exclude because this writing is highly contextual and because the interest of such writing outside of its institutional context of production is nearly zero. And yet it was competence in precisely this kind of writing that seemed secretly, or not so secretly, to be the *social* justification of the composition course, as Edward P. J. Corbett acknowledged in his defense of excluding literature from the composition classroom: "The main objective of the writing course," he famously wrote, is to "teach students how to write the kind of utilitarian prose they will be asked to produce in their other college classes and later on in their jobs."[3]

Corbett's statement is usefully frank—it specifies the demand for writing as a demand for a *kind* of writing—but it also begs the question of exactly why writing has come to be so necessary for what students will do "later on in their jobs." I will push Corbett's point a little further and give a name to this group of workers who write. I will call them the "scribal class." They bear very little resemblance to the scribes or literati of the premodern era, who acquired a competence that was extremely technical and very rare. Although these early writers were certainly employed sometimes to produce "utilitarian prose"—for example, the bureaucratic letters that bound together the governing sites of the ancient, medieval, and early modern states and empires—this kind of prose was also far more rhetorical than its successor and indeed much closer to the kinds of writing we call literary than to memos or the successor to the memo, the email. Our latter-day scribal class knows how to write, but this writing is fundamentally different in its features and norms from the rhetorical prose of the premodern world.

In attempting to characterize this writing more precisely, I would first of all observe that it has to be produced by a literate population no longer immersed, as their predecessors were, in the most complex literary examples of the medium of writing. Or to put this point more pointedly, the *reading* that is demanded of this population is both quantitatively less and qualitatively simpler than what might seem desirable as the basis for producing competence in writing. The medial shift from speech to writing is surely best facilitated by long-established habits of reading that *immerse* readers in the medium of writing. The beneficial effect of immersion is proven by the fact that so many writers of English literature became superlative writers with little or no instruction in writing. The transitional genre for them was the "familiar letter," which was seldom formally taught; the "business letter," however, did find a place in later writing pedagogy. The rhetorical training of premodern writers involved instruction in composition, but not

3. Edward P. J. Corbett, "Literature and Composition: Allies or Rivals in the Classroom," in *Composition and Literature: Bridging the Gap*, ed. Winifred Bryan Horner (Chicago: University of Chicago Press, 1983), 168.

in our sense of the word. Composition was rather an elaborate art involving all the "parts" of rhetoric, of which one, *inventio*, the finding of arguments, was closest to what we mean by composition today. In combination with intensive reading (often in multiple languages), this pedagogy seemed to smooth out the transition from speech to writing, an effect confirmed by the fluency of so many writers of letters in the centuries before the twentieth. This fluency was an effect of a different relation to the medium of writing, a relation determined by the time dedicated to reading.

By contrast to premodern pedagogy, the modern composition course must somehow produce the *effect* of intimacy with the written word, of ease and comfort with written language, in the very process of pulling students across the forbidding threshold of written expression. The efforts of composition teachers toward this end are never less than heroic, a struggle against conditions that are nearly Sisyphean. For students, stumbling at the threshold of writing seems inevitable. This inhibition is the result not only of the innate difficulty of writing but also of too slight an acquaintance with reading. Many grammatical errors, stylistic infelicities, peculiarities of diction, and flaws in argumentation betray not so much a failure to assimilate the rules of grammar or the canons of logic as a failure to internalize the norms of writing in the course of time spent reading. From its inception, the composition course was forced to accept this lack of engagement with reading as a given and to address its effects *upon* writing by a pedagogy devoted exclusively *to* writing. If early composition pedagogy was thus a version of "treating the symptom," its original deflection from the practice of reading both persisted and came to define the field of composition, its claim to a distinct professional identity.

The effect of the deflection from reading to writing is, I hasten to admit, very well known; it was brilliantly examined years ago by Mina Shaughnessy in her indispensable study, *Errors and Expectations*, in which she argues that the fundamental hurdle for "basic writers" is that they "have read very little and written only for teachers." Limited familiarity as readers with the medium of writing produces writing effects that diverge wildly from the models used by writing instructors and often converge upon styles of writerly prose that express a premature identification with the scribal class. It is predictable, for example, that basic writers will imitate a mode of writing that is modeled by the speech they recognize as "official" or "bureaucratic." As a fundamentally mimetic activity, the writing of basic writers is vulnerable to an imitative drive that overleaps the speech of the teacher to grasp at a fetishized *writerly speech*. If the writing instructor cannot successfully intervene in this circuit of imitation, it is likely that the bureaucratic mode of writing (and speaking!) will be reproduced, so to speak, over the heads

of writing instructors. I defer here to Mina Shaughnessy's careful reconstruction of this process, which I don't think has been bettered: "Unwitting, and out of a tentativeness that is not of his making, the inexperienced
writer draws upon the same passive constructions, the same circumlocu-
tions and evasions as the bureaucrat, who uses these syntactic strategies
deliberately, as a way of blurring or suppressing information. How ironic
it would be if so-called 'remedial' English were to produce no more than a
mastery of bureaucratic syntax." [4] Given the fact that "bureaucratic" writing is prevalent in the scribal class, it seems obvious that the composition
course *has* failed to produce and disseminate an alternative mode of writing. This is not the fault of composition teachers, who have, as I have said,
a nearly impossible task: to induce in students a kind of superliteracy, the
extraordinarily complex skill which is writing, on the sandy foundation of
an underdeveloped basic literacy.

The task of teaching writing has only become more difficult with the
emergence of new technologies such as the smartphone, which have re-
distributed finite time from reading to engagement with new visual and
aural modes of communication and entertainment. I do not intend in this
chapter to address this problem further, as it can be seen from the vantage
of my argument as an exacerbation of conditions that have long prevailed
in the modern world. My point is rather to draw attention to the establishment of the composition course more than a century ago as the means to
respond to the social demand for writing. This demand still emanates from
many sites in our society and comes to focus all too intensely on the single
point of the composition course.

Deferring for a moment the question of how this demand might be answered *otherwise* than in the composition course, I would like to offer here
a brief account of the language world of the scribal class. This world has
an ideal, almost utopian side to it, perceptively described by Alvin Gouldner in his pioneering work, *The Future of Intellectuals and the Rise of the
New Class*. Gouldner argues that the professional and technical classes
have developed a language competency that is peculiarly their own, which
he calls the "culture of critical discourse." The notion of a "culture," or as
Gouldner also calls it, a "speech community," points to what linguists call
a "sociolect," in this case a mode of speech and writing that is localized
not geographically but in occupational fields: the scientific, professional,
technical, and managerial fields. Although it is my sense that Gouldner's

---

4. Mina P. Shaughnessy, *Errors and Expectations: A Guide for the Teacher of Basic
Writing* (New York: Oxford University Press), 86–87.

notion of "critical discourse" idealizes the speech community by aligning it too closely with the skeptical-scientific attitude, I believe that his formulation provides us with a means of grasping the norms of clarity, precision, and economy that govern the most effective speech and writing of the scribal class. Unfortunately, this sociolect is also vulnerable to constant deformation, which I have considered in work on the form of the memo as the tendency of bureaucratic speech and writing toward verbosity and empty technical jargon. This jargon is in part a consequence of the disappearance of the Latin curriculum, which made it possible thereafter for English words derived from Latin to circulate as technical-sounding terms, whether or not such terms actually do much work in communication. Bureaucratic speech emerges when speakers or writers recycle words with Latin roots that have lost their concreteness and that by virtue of their abstractness give the impression of a technicity intelligible only to a closed speech community.

Instead of attempting here to analyze in greater detail the sociolect of the professional-managerial class, I would like to offer a homely example of it, the *most homely* such example I have been able to find. You may have chanced to notice, when brushing your teeth some evening, that on the back of your tube of toothpaste (if it happens to be Crest) is a rather officious-sounding message from the American Dental Association: "Crest has been shown to be an effective decay-preventive dentifrice that can be of significant value, when used in a conscientiously applied program of oral hygiene and regular professional care." When I was a child I puzzled over this statement; it seemed to challenge me with its aura of being English and not English. Surely this is not what James Morgan Hart was calling for when he said, "Give us more English!" Here the professional sociolect advertises its principal features: its impersonal subject position and passive constructions, its adverbial flair, its use of subordination, its redundancy, its Latinate diction, even its self-legitimating bow toward the authority of professional expertise. The example confirms that circumlocution is the dominant rhetorical device of the sociolect (in the terminology of the old rhetoric, this would be *periphrasis*). As I contemplate this text, I think that even as a child I recognized that it was a kind of poetry, quite unlike the fluency of literary prose, yet sonorously fluent in its own way. If it is nonetheless bad poetry, one has to admit that it is linguistically powerful, capable of producing tremendous mimetic effects, both in writing and speech.[5]

5. One very interesting mimetic effect of the professional-managerial sociolect is the shift from Anglo-Saxon to Latinate diction in formal social contexts. Examples abound,

With regard to the latter point, I would underscore just how impressive the sociolect really is. It is likely that it is reproduced as much by speech as by writing, although this is a kind of speech that can be called *writerly*. The scribal class speaks in a writerly fashion. Both the speech and the prose of this class are very different from the prosaic facility of nineteenth-century standard English, the ideal espoused by the belletristic rhetorics of the period, as well as by composition in its "current-traditional" form. The composition professoriate, however, has understandably declined to bear the standard of belles lettres into battle against the bureaucratic speech of the scribal class.

The point of my example is that the demand for writing in modernity is much bigger than the response of the composition course. That course has the impossible task of deinhibiting writing at the front end and heading off imitation of bureaucratic prose at the back end. All in one semester, or sometimes two. It is no wonder, then, that the sociolect of the scribal class is an English that almost no one speaks well, because nearly everyone has learned it in a hurry. There is no question of finding a way back to the fluency of the nineteenth-century belletrists, and that may not even be desirable, because the technical jargons of the professions can and do perform work that cannot be accomplished in belletristic English. The writing of modernity makes a legitimate demand on the educational system to produce a skill that the scribal class genuinely needs. The failure to acquire that skill, not its debased imitation, has real consequences in a society that runs on communication, where the technology of communication seems to be far more reliable than the messages sent along these channels. Those messages frequently fail to communicate effectively or at all, and so we are thrown back upon the question of pedagogy, of how we teach our students to read and write.

PATHOS

If you have not been sufficiently persuaded by the argument I have just presented, I will close with a very brief presentation of an argument from pathos. The emotion I should probably invoke in all honesty is *despair*, but as that would be highly unstrategic, I will attempt to elicit the opposite emotion of *hope*. I would describe hope as a "cognitive" emotion, because it projects a future based on the analysis of past occurrence. Hope

---

but here is one: at a famous trial, a witness giving testimony wanted to say something like, "At this point, I got out of the car." But this utterance was not formal enough for the occasion, and so what the witness actually said was, "At this point, I exited the vehicle."

is a Bayesian emotion. My analysis of composition's past discloses a certain problem in the development of the composition course as a response to the demand for writing. Again, this problem is not in any way the fault of the composition professoriate, for the reasons already enumerated. But the composition professoriate *is* a problem for me in the sense that what I would like to propose will require that the professoriate suspend for the sake of argument its accession to the inevitability of the composition *course*. I understand that this will be difficult, but I would like to suggest an argument in support of this suspension, setting out from the fact that the status of the composition professoriate has always been depressed by the disesteemed place of the composition course in the college curriculum. I don't believe that composition, as the art of writing, can achieve a fully disciplinary status when it must focus all of its theory and practice on a (usually) single predisciplinary freshman course. Even given the emergence of "rhet-comp" courses in the upper division, the effort is still vastly smaller than the task. The art of writing is too important to relegate to a single freshman course.

The question I would like to put to the "rhet-comp" professoriate is whether the composition course was the wrong response to the historical demand for writing. The course, after all, was an adventitious repository for composition, an artifact of a moment—the 1880s and 1890s—when the curriculum was being restructured in a way that removed the older forms of the tutorial and the recitation. To put this point in more precise historical terms, I want to question the wisdom (in hindsight) of the aboriginal conflation of the writing exercise with the written examination. The requisite of detecting and chastising error left an unhappy stigma on composition pedagogy. What is needed now is an effort to imagine teaching the art of writing without privileging the freshman course, which is assumed to be like any other course, a seminar with a textbook and the usual set of papers to be graded. If what needs to be taught to freshmen is a predisciplinary *basic* writing, why should this writing be graded at all? Surely removing the grade would help to deinhibit writing. Happily, efforts are being made to "ungrade" composition and I would hope that the result eventually will be a pedagogy without grades.

As the composition professoriate is moving in this direction, I would propose going even further and acknowledging that the composition course itself is an inadequate tool for producing the cognitive skill of writing in students who are insufficiently acquainted (through their reading!) with the medium of writing. A possible alternative might be a suite of tutorials, workshops, and laboratory exercises, all designed to catch students at different phases of writing acquisition, as well as to target different kinds of writing problems and to address them by different pedagogic means. By "laboratory," I do not mean the writing labs common on college campuses, although these institutional forms are helpful. What I have in mind is something more like the language lab of foreign language programs. Alternative pedagogies abound, but ultimately tethered to the first-year composition course. I suggest that the motive driving new pedagogic strategies can also be related to the uncomfortable fact that we do not have sufficient evidence even now to confirm that the long-reigning composition course—with its multiple sections of freshman writing—has been entirely successful in inducing the superliteracy of fluency in writing. What if the teaching of writing was conceived from the beginning as analogous to the teaching of languages? What would the pedagogic implications be of such a reimagining? Unfortunately, the freshman composition course is so dominant that it is difficult even to imagine such an alternative pedagogy. The same impediment applies to the use of the tutorial. And yet we know how effective one-on-one instruction can be, when we are able to meet individually with students to address unique writing problems. Of course, the tutorial model has practical issues, beginning with cost. But for the sake of a thought experiment, the reason for its possible effectiveness is worth contemplating.

Let us imagine, then, a discipline in which the composition course would not be the only institutional form in which the art of writing is taught but one of several forms. The pedagogy that might emerge from reconceiving composition in this way might be analogous to the teaching of languages, as well as to the teaching of reading. In my imaginary and hopeful projection of teaching the art of writing, I would also align it with communications studies, which already overlaps considerably with the rhetoric side of composition. Composition so conceived might become a fully disciplinary field with a full array of courses at all levels. At the upper levels of this discipline, where major courses are offered, composition would establish links with education and with communications, while perhaps also serving as a bridge between English departments and these other faculties.

Now I recognize that some of these projected futurities have already been envisioned by the most forward-thinking of rhetoric and composition theorists. The critique of the freshman composition course is not new. But there is still no discipline that is the equivalent of the two I have cited as cousins to composition. In the meantime, composition is mired in conditions of employment that are themselves tied to the freshman course. The professional identification of the composition professoriate is not likely ever to be successfully acknowledged if the majority of composition teachers continue to be drawn from graduate programs in English or other disciplines or continue to have the status of adjunct labor. I don't believe that fully disciplinary status can be achieved for the teaching of writing without putting the freshman composition course, so to speak, on the table, without recognizing this course as the historical residue of a difficult moment in the longer history of vernacularization, the demand for writing in modernity, and the emergence of the scribal class. The composition course was a result of the fact that the demand for writing had to be answered before a discipline could be imagined to answer that demand. We are still waiting for that discipline to take its rightful place among the system of university disciplines.

BIBLIOGRAPHICAL NOTE

Scholarship in composition and rhetoric is voluminous, and I will not attempt here to acknowledge even a small fraction of it. Nor will I attempt to list all the works I have consulted during my research into this topic. Composition theory, and its lively correlate, rhetorical theory, continue to develop apace, and consequently any bibliographical representation of the field is likely to be out of date as soon as it is set down on the page. My purpose in this note is only to inform those who are not familiar with scholarship in the field of the work that I have found most useful. My scholarly interest is chiefly in the origins of the composition course, as this history crucially intersects with the origins of literary study in America. Readers of chapter 5, "The Postrhetorical Condition," can find a fuller bibliographical record of scholarship in composition and rhetoric than I offer here.

As composition moved away from the literary professoriate, it also moved away from its original model in "current-traditional rhetoric." Still, this early form of composition is closer to my interest in the histories of rhetoric and criticism than later developments in twentieth-century composition scholarship, such as the "process" movement (Janet Emig, Peter Elbow, et al.), the incorporation of political thematics into composition pedagogy (Patricia Bizzell, Linda Brodkey, Susan Miller, John Trimbur, et al.), the return to rhetoric in recent decades (Janet Atwill, Sharon Crowley, Cheryl Glenn, Andrea Lunsford, et al.), or "writing across the curriculum" (C. A. Knowblauch, Christopher Thaiss). I have tried to be aware of these movements, and how far some of them have traveled from the original composition course of the late nineteenth century. Although I would endorse many ideas in these later versions of composition theory, I'm interested primarily in the survival of the freshman composition course, which I believe has been problematic for many reasons, including the impediment it has been for the full professionalization of the composition professoriate.

For the history of composition pedagogy, I have relied on the following standard works: Robert J. Connors, *Composition-Rhetoric: Backgrounds, Theory, and Pedagogy* (Pittsburgh: University of Pittsburgh, 1997); James Berlin, *Rhetoric and Reality: Writing Instruction in American Colleges, 1900–1985* (Carbondale: Southern Illinois University Press, 1987); Michael Halloran, *Oratorical Culture in Nineteenth-Century America: Essays in the Transformation of Rhetoric* (Carbondale: Southern Illinois University Press, 1983); Albert Kitzhaber, *Rhetoric in American Colleges, 1850–1900* (Dallas: Southern Methodist University Press, 1990); James Murphy and Christopher Thaiss, *A Short History of Writing Instruction from Ancient Greece to the United States* (London: Routledge, 2020); John Brereton, ed., *The Origins of Composition Studies in the American College, 1875–1925* (Pittsburgh: University of Pittsburgh Press, 1997). I cite Edward P. J. Corbett, *Classical Rhetoric for the Modern Student* (Oxford: Oxford University Press, 1956) for the standard model of composition pedagogy, which looks backward to the conditions for composition at the turn of the century and forward to the "utilitarian prose" dominant in the modern world.

My perspective on the history of composition is inflected by a view of writing in modernity expressed more fully in my essay "The Memo and Modernity," *Critical Inquiry* 31 (2004): 108–32, to which the reader is directed for further bibliography. I mention above the work of JoAnne Yates on the forms of business writing, *Control through Communication: The Rise of System in American Management* (Baltimore: Johns Hopkins University Press, 1989). In the background of this concern is the work of Alvin Gouldner, *The Future of Intellectuals and the Rise of the New Class* (New York: Continuum, 1979). My understanding of oratory and rhetoric in nineteenth-century America is indebted to Kenneth Cmiel, *Democratic Eloquence: The Fight for Popular Speech in Nineteenth-Century America* (New York: William Morrow, 1990). Cmiel's work is acknowledged by Lisa Ede and Andrea Lunsford in *Singular Texts / Plural Authors: Perspectives on Collaborative Writing* (Carbondale: Southern Illinois University Press, 1992).

My understanding of inhibition and deinhibition in writing is indebted to Mina Shaughnessy's foundational study, *Errors and Expectations: A Guide for the Teacher of Basic Writing* (New York: Oxford University Press, 1977). Skepticism about the institutional form of the freshman writing course is expressed by Sharon Crowley, *Composition in the University: Historical and Polemical Essays* (Pittsburgh: Pittsburgh University Press, 1998). It is not possible within the space of this essay to pursue the latter question further; it is only possible for me to offer a view from the other side, that of the literary professoriate.

The divorce between composition and literary study seems at this point to be irreversible, but I believe it is nonetheless worth continuing to think about what a remarriage would look like. Here I would recommend Jason Maxwell's interesting effort in this direction, *The Two Cultures of English: Literature, Composition, and the Moment of Rhetoric* (New York: Fordham University Press, 2019). Maxwell turns to rhetoric as the possible common ground for the two disciplines, an idea that has considerable credibility. My own sense is that the institutional form of the composition course has to be rethought first, especially as it stands in the way of parity for the literary and composition professoriates. I hope that this view is understood as expressing my belief that the teaching of writing should occupy a much larger place in the disciplinary universe than it does today.

CHAPTER 12

The Question of Lay Reading

Is this "reading" activity reserved for the literary critic (always privileged in studies of reading), that is, once again, for the category of professional intellectuals (*clercs*), or can it be extended to all cultural consumers?
MICHEL DE CERTEAU, "Reading as Poaching"

As if the notion of pleasure no longer pleases anyone.
ROLAND BARTHES, *The Pleasure of the Text*

LAICUS LITTERATUS

Among the many moments in which the subject of reading comes up in Boswell's *Life of Johnson* is the following celebrated anecdote, from 1763:

On Saturday, July 30, Dr. Johnson and I took a sculler at the Temple-stairs, and set out for Greenwich. I asked him if he really thought a knowledge of the Greek and Latin languages an essential requisite to a good education. JOHNSON. 'Most certainly, Sir; for those who know them have a very great advantage over those who do not. Nay, Sir, it is wonderful what a difference learning makes upon people even in the common intercourse of life, which does not appear to be much connected with it.' 'And yet (said I) people go through the world very well, and carry on the business of life to good advantage, without learning.' JOHNSON. 'Why, Sir, that may be true in cases where learning cannot possibly be of any use; for instance, this boy rows us as well without learning, as if he could sing the song of Orpheus to the Argonauts, who were the first sailors.' He then called to the boy, 'What would you give, my lad, to know about the Argonauts?' 'Sir, (said the boy,) I would give what I have.' Johnson was much pleased with his answer, and we gave him a double fare. Dr. Johnson then turning to me, 'Sir, (said he) a desire of knowledge is the natural feeling of mankind; and every human being, whose mind is not debauched, will be willing to give all that he has to get knowledge."[1]

Absent from Boswell and Johnson's sense of "learning" is an acknowledgment of the ability to read and write in one's native tongue. The study of Greek and Latin is one that demanded extraordinary effort, far more than acquiring the ability to read in English. If the boy were "literate" in the language he speaks, he might learn something about the Argonauts, even if he could not hear the songs of Orpheus in the Greek of their imagined origin. Johnson draws a hopeful message from the boy's willingness to give what he has for such learning as the distinguished occupants of his little boat possess, a strong affirmation of the knowledge the boy is in no position to acquire. He lives on the other side of a divide that is far wider than the Thames, but what is that divide? Is it defined solely by his ignorance of the classical languages? Or of reading and writing as such?

Boswell and Johnson have no concept of "literacy" by which they might refer to the case of someone who can read English but not a classical language. The word *literacy* did not become current until later in the nineteenth century, when the ability to read one's native tongue was becoming universal; at the same time the study of classical languages was disappearing from the colleges. For nearly two millennia before Boswell and Johnson's trip to Greenwich, the classical languages thoroughly engrossed the concept of "learning." After the fall of the Roman Empire, those who could read were known by the word *litteratus*, or "lettered," referring only to someone who read Latin, the language of the mass, the sacraments, the Catholic Bible, and theology. Someone with no Latin was called *laicus*, the word that descends to us as "lay." This word was derived from the Greek *laikos*, meaning "of the folk." The transposition of the Greek word into Latin refunctioned this word to signal the linguistic distinction between the clergy and the laity. It was the business of the cathedral schools to teach Latin to a very small number of boys; the transmission of vernacular literacy was more casually managed in the household, not usually the concern of the school.

By virtue of the knowledge to which their ability to read Latin gave them access, the clergy became members of a *profession*. There were only two other such professions: medicine and law. These learned cadres professed different bodies of knowledge, but their learning was founded on a common linguistic base, the ability to read and write Latin. The spread

1. James Boswell, *Boswell's Life of Johnson* (Oxford: Oxford University Press, 1904), 323.

of vernacular literacy in the later medieval era complicated this scheme, with consequences that reach all the way into what is unspoken in Boswell's story, the possible or impossible circumstance that the boy might read English. Further complications were imminent, as new professions emerged in the century after Boswell and Johnson, most of which no longer transmitted their knowledge in Latin. The classical languages, Greek especially, became instead a social credential for the aristocracy and commercial upper class, with no direct relation to professional knowledge. Although the turn to the vernacular among the professions in some ways opened their learning to wider access, expertise in a profession continued to be registered by the opposition of the professional to the *laicus*, or "lay person." But this was a new kind of laity, no longer defined by ignorance of Latin or Greek; every new kind of professional knowledge became *unreadable* to the lay person, that is, to anyone not instructed in that profession's peculiar lexicon and conventions of communication. Each new profession generated a new "laity," a new group of persons "illiterate" in relation to that professional knowledge.

If the distinction between "professional" and "lay" persons was no longer a question of the learned languages, this distinction carried over something of the stigma in the older sense of *laicus*, of not knowing Latin. The vernacularization of literate culture and the rise of new professions were processes that moved in opposite directions, the one enlarging access to knowledge, the other restricting it, thus creating a frictional interface that every member of our professional society experiences, not excepting professionals themselves, who are lay persons in relation to all other professions than their own. We see indications of this dilemma already in the later Middle Ages, when the spread of vernacular readers and writers occasioned the recognition of a contradictory new type, the *laicus litteratus*, the literate lay person.[2] This contradictory figure is implicit in Boswell's question to Johnson, which raises the possibility that knowledge of Greek and Latin is perhaps not essential to "education." Waiting in the wings was a new social type, the man or woman learned in English (or other vernacular languages). Could one imagine "learning" without the classical languages?

There is one other complication I would like to tease out of Boswell's anecdote, which is signaled by the story of the Argonauts. We are obviously intended to see "learning" in the story as like the Golden Fleece. A "good education" is a "great advantage" in life, Johnson observes, which

2. See Anne Hudson, "*Laicus Litteratus*: The Paradox of Lollardy," in *Heresy and Literacy, 1000–1530*, ed. Peter Biller and Anne Hudson (Cambridge: Cambridge University Press, 1994), 222–36.

must mean that it promises wealth and status. Utility is always available as a justification for the effort of acquiring knowledge, but it is not the only one. Orpheus and the Argonauts are cited not only for that purpose, important though it is, but for something else the boy desires, namely the *pleasure of a story*. If it is only a question of reading stories, vernacular literacy might well close the gap partway between the learned and the lay person. The pleasure of reading is not acknowledged directly in Boswell's anecdote, but it is perhaps reflected in Johnson's delight with the boy's willingness to give what he has for "knowledge." What does the boy have, after all, to give? Assuming his financial resources to be minimal, a safe enough assumption, the only thing he really has to offer is the effort, the *pain*, of acquiring knowledge. This pain is what everyone must "give" in order to get at least one of the "advantages" this kind of learning promises, the pleasure of reading a story.

The ratio of pain to pleasure in acquiring the ability to read is a matter that does not quite break the surface of the text, but I want to bring it out here at the beginning of this chapter because it is where we want ultimately to direct our attention. The fact of pleasure in reading vexes the distinction between the professional and the lay person. Literary study is forced to confront this question, because the object of its knowledge is *all Argonauts*, all story. The pleasure to be had in works of literature is available to anyone who can read at least their native tongue—but not without some pain. This is just where our discipline of reading lays down a marker. Literacy today is a passport to all the professions, but it is also a means of deriving pleasure. This is not to deny that other kinds of learning promise their own kinds of pleasure, but it is easy enough to demonstrate that literary study is different, that it has a unique ratio of pleasure to pain built into its discipline by virtue of its object, literature. The study of this object intensifies both the pains and the pleasures of reading by submitting reading to *discipline*.

THE IMAGINATION'S LATIN

Literary study is distinguished from other disciplines by the fact that it foregrounds a discipline of reading as its core practice. All disciplines, of course, depend upon the textual transmission of knowledge and the ability to decipher texts in complex and self-reflexive ways, but literary study deploys reading as its *constitutive* disciplinary practice, which is to say, as both means and end. This reading practice is by no means the only possible mode of reading, but the role of reading in literary study has the peculiarity of appearing to its practitioners sometimes in the guise of *reading as such*, rather than as one practice of reading among many. For this reason, reading is the occasion of more or less continuous methodological debate in the discipline. The conflict of "theories" in the later twentieth century can be seen in retrospect as a phase of particularly vigorous struggle between different versions of reading for the status of reading as such, as in J. Hillis Miller's claim that "deconstruction is nothing more or less than good reading as such."[3] This generalization of disciplinary reading distinguishes literary study even as it takes for granted the actually rarefied social and institutional conditions in which "reading as such" occurs.

If there is one thing about which literary scholars might agree, it is that the practice of reading works of literature can be raised to the level of a discipline and further, a profession. Literary scholars and teachers in this way move reading literature beyond a merely intuitive practice. This movement beyond intuitive practice contradicts the assumption of lay readers who believe they already know how to read such works. By contrast, the reading that is done in other disciplines tends in most circumstances to be confined to practitioners. Legal, technical, bureaucratic, and scientific writing abound in our society, in quantities much greater than works of literature, but these forms of writing generally do not offer themselves simultaneously to the professional reader and to the general reader.[4] This is a problem for literary study that is difficult to acknowledge, much less to address. It accounts for a certain resistance to the discipline that must always be overcome, the assumption that literature is a kind of writing that does not require discipline to read.

I intend to affirm in this essay the premise of reading in literary study, that it is both possible and desirable to submit the reading of literature to a discipline. This premise is, in my view, identical to the assumption that any discipline makes about its object of study. Anything in the world can be studied, and everything should be studied. In the case of literature, the pre-

3. J. Hillis Miller, *The Ethics of Reading: Kant, de Man, Eliot, Trollope, James, and Benjamin* (New York: Columbia University Press, 1987), 10.

4. For the sake of economy, it is necessary for me to express this opposition more categorically than it appears in reality. Professional discourse is in fact disposed along a spectrum of legibility. At one end of this spectrum, writing in the hard sciences is almost completely unreadable for lay persons, as the abundance of technical terminology alone represents an insurmountable impediment. At the other end of the spectrum, one can locate the writing of history, which is oriented to narrative and is relatively more accessible to lay readers than perhaps any other professional discourse. Literary scholarship, though it sometimes takes narrative as an object of analysis, is not a form of narrative writing. It also depends on many concepts that are indisputably technical and often unfamiliar to lay readers. The development of a technical terminology for analyzing works of literature is of course very old, at least as early as Aristotle's *Poetics*.

dominance of pleasure in the object of study does not invalidate lay reading any more than it renders the study of literature superfluous. Lay reading, however, has a history that is largely unspoken in the discipline, although it has recently become part of a major subfield in its own right, the "history of the book." Inquiry into the history of reading practices is generally conducted now under the rubric of this subfield. For reasons I have discussed in chapter 3, literary study has been provoked into an awareness of "nondisciplinary" reading, as well as new respect for the modes of what I am calling lay reading.

The history of the book and correlated projects in the history of reading have informed us about the diverse practices of reading, both past and present. This scholarship has been of great value, although it is not my aim to supplement it. It is my purpose rather to examine the relation between professional reading and lay reading in the hope of devising a better understanding of this relation as a problem for literary study. I will propose two hypotheses about this relation: first, that lay reading is a *condition* of professional reading, more specifically, an *antithetical origin*. As we shall see, this condition results in lay reading's construction as the other of professional reading, even its antagonist. The second hypothesis, which will seem to contradict the first, is that lay reading is a *back-formation* of professional reading, analogous to the concept of "orality" as the antecedent to literacy. Although it would be accurate to say that lay reading and professional reading are concurrent formations, I want to argue that posing the relation as conflicting accounts of their priority to one another gives us a better way of approaching what is problematic for literary study in this relation.

It is not my purpose, then, to give an account of the history of reading practices, which is beyond my scope or competence, but rather to derive from the work of historians such as Roger Chartier, Paul Saenger, Robert Darnton, Ivan Illich, Janice Radway, Leah Price, and others a sense of the universe of possibilities to which the distinction between lay and professional reading belongs.[5] To this end, it will be necessary first to acknowl-

5. See Roger Chartier, *The Order of Books: Readers, Authors, and Libraries in Europe between the Fourteenth and Eighteenth Centuries*, trans. Lydia G. Cochrane (Stanford, CA: Stanford University Press, 1994); Chartier, *Forms and Meanings: Texts, Performances, and Audiences from Codex to Computer* (Philadelphia: University of Pennsylvania Press, 1995); Chartier, *The Culture of Print: Power and the Uses of Print in Early Modern France*, trans. Lydia G. Cochrane (Princeton, NJ: Princeton University Press, 1989); Guglielmo Cavallo and Roger Chartier, eds., *A History of Reading in the West* (Amherst: University of Massachusetts Press, 1999); Paul Saenger, *The Space Between the Words: The Origins of Silent Reading* (Stanford, CA: Stanford University Press, 1997);

edge certain precursors of both professional and lay reading, if only to distinguish them from the modes of reading oriented in our own time toward works of "literature" as a supergeneric concept that emerges in modernity. I have considered this question in chapter 7, "The Location of Literature," and refer my reader to the account there of the successive delimitations of the concept of literature resulting in the aggregation of genres we study in our discipline. The concept of literature has a history that can be recovered independently of the question that I pursue in this essay, but for the purpose of this argument, I will posit the conception of literature that founds the discipline: a body of writing oriented toward aesthetic values and consisting largely but not exclusively of poetry, novels, drama, essays, and the like.

To begin, then, with what must be the most cursory survey, let us recall that the most socially significant mode of reading in premodern society is a ritual orientation to the text—whether a scroll or a codex—as an object of physical rarity and metaphysical authority, what we usually mean by "scripture." The religious or clerical mode of reading is in certain respects the precursor of professional reading, by virtue of the fact already noted, that it constitutes the clergy as a profession at the same time that it projects the nonreader as *laicus*. But with the translation of the Bible into the vernaculars and the explosion of devotional writing, the "scriptural" mode of reading rapidly came to dominate much if not all lay reading by the end of the Middle Ages. In the modern world, the scriptural mode of reading characterizes many sites of lay reading. Reading scripture for application of lessons to one's religious or moral life or for allegorical prognostication is a practice more or less continuous with the transmission of such writing. If this mode of reading is unlike what literary scholars do, neither is it like the kind of lay reading we find in the reception of literature—this, even though lay reading often retains a certain residually pious orientation to great works of literature, an effect of what we might call "scripturalization."

Historians of reading are aware of a second quite different feature of premodern reading, which is that it was most often reading aloud, the alien

---

Robert Darnton, *The Forbidden Best-Sellers of Pre-Revolutionary France* (New York: W. W. Norton, 1995); Ivan Illich, *In the Vineyard of the Text: A Commentary to Hugh's "Didascalicon"* (Chicago: University of Chicago Press, 1983); Janice Radway, *A Feeling for Books: The Book-of-the-Month Club, Literary Taste, and Middle-Class Desire* (Chapel Hill: University of North Carolina Press, 1997); Leah Price, *How to Do Things with Books in Victorian Britain* (Princeton, NJ: Princeton University Press, 2012); and Price, *What We Talk about When We Talk about Books: The History and Future of Reading* (New York: Basic Books, 2019). See also Alberto Manguel, *A History of Reading* (New York: Penguin Books, 1996).

quality of which Ivan Illich vividly evokes in his depiction of the monastic scriptorium, filled with the murmur of reading monks, quite unlike the silence of the modern library.[6] Paul Saenger argues that the spread of silent reading was an enabling condition of scholastic theology, in that it permitted scholars to read much more rapidly, to cross-reference more efficiently, and hence to produce argument and refutation on doctrinal matters.[7] Silent reading would seem to be a distant condition for professional reading in modernity, but its relation to lay reading is harder to specify. The practice of reading aloud, to oneself or others, continues into the present, if attenuated by comparison to former ages. Yet lay reading is for the most part done silently, much like professional reading. Silent reading is assumed to be faster, which is certainly an advantage in some contexts of professional reading. Whether this feature matters in lay reading seems largely a matter of situation and the content of reading matter.

More promising, perhaps, as a precursor condition for lay reading is the emergence of solitary reading, which assumes the wider availability of manuscripts in the later Middle Ages and then printed books in the sixteenth century. For much of the Middle Ages, books were shared and could only be read in conditions of restricted access, as in the scriptorium or the lecture room. Solitary reading requires different social, institutional, and even architectural conditions. The difference between Montaigne's study, for example, a private library, and the medieval scriptorium is striking in this context and certainly has long-term consequences. But Montaigne's reading is neither lay reading nor professional reading in the sense in which I am using it—or perhaps, a premonitory fusion of the two. There is little difference between Montaigne's method of reading and that of the most scholarly readers of the period, the "humanists"; at the same time, Montaigne is not a "professor," a creature of the school. More revelatory, perhaps, than Montaigne's capacity to embody diverse forms of reading in his period is the fact of his commitment to the vernacular. Readers who possessed "small Latin and less Greek" were able to read Montaigne, whose work flowed into the great stream of vernacular writing, spreading across social strata to the aristocracy, the prosperous commercial classes, and above all to women, who more and more acquired the ability to read in vernaculars but were still largely excluded from learning

6. Illich, *In the Vineyard of the Text*, 87.

7. Scholasticism revived an agonistic mode of reading, more like the sectarian conflict of late Greek philosophy than like scriptural reading. This agonistic mode was enabled by certain material innovations, such as the introduction of paper into the late medieval classroom. Teachers and students could take notes rapidly on paper and thereby develop arguments with greater facility.

Greek and Latin. Here we might return just briefly to Boswell's question to Johnson, recognizing that vernacular literacy, as yet nameless, drives the fractioning of reading populations in modernity. The ultimate precursor of the lay reader is the figure of the *laicus litteratus*, at once a reader but excluded from the languages of the professions. This reader was no longer a figure of the school but of the domestic spaces in which solitary reading took place.

To this condition we can add a new emphasis in the early modern period on pleasure in reading, conspicuously declared in Dryden's criticism, wherein he insists on *delectare*, or "to delight." as the chief aim of a certain kind of writing: "For delight is the chief, if not the only end, of poetry: instruction can be admitted but in the second place."[8] "Poetry" is standing here for a larger aggregation of writing than verse writing, though not yet identical to what we call "literature." By the eighteenth century, the traditional *topos* by which the pleasure of reading was justified as the vehicle of its moral purpose was no longer entirely adequate to account for all the scenes of reading, though it must be admitted that instruction or edification never ceased to be extolled, for reasons that will concern me presently. Additionally, one must remark the effects of the growing heterogeneity of reading matter, which spurred habits of reading adapted to the rapid scanning of many different kinds of writing, including ephemeral works such as newspapers, chapbooks, periodicals, and other kinds of print publication. Some historians refer to the transition between "intensive" and "extensive" reading, not without some unease with the sharpness of the distinction. But even the cautious Roger Chartier allows that something like "extensive" reading did appear in the eighteenth century.[9] This kind of reading happily coexisted with the kinds of "immersive" reading the romances and novels of the eighteenth century occasioned.

It makes sense to speak of "lay reading" at this point as oriented to vernacular literature, in the sense of poetry, plays, novels, essays. These are the forms in which pleasure was most to be found, as distinguished from the writing of the professions. I would emphasize that lay reading was also intimately connected with the emergent discourse of *criticism*, the main purpose of which was to instruct lay readers in the development of their taste and judgment. The ambiguous status of the critic as "expert" in a practice that was not itself professionalized—critics cannot yet be described

8. John Dryden, "A Defense of an Essay of Dramatic Poesy," in *John Dryden: Of Dramatic Poesy and Other Critical Essays*, 2 vols., ed. George Watson (London: Everyman's Library), 1:113.

9. Chartier, *Forms and Meanings*, 17.

as professional readers, even if they might be described as professional writers—is a fact that is easy to forget when criticism from Dryden to Eliot is simply annexed to the prehistory of academic criticism. Suffice it to say that we cannot speak of "professional reading" in the contemporary sense until we can point to the existence of professional readers and to the sites and procedures of their credentialization in the university (or other types of schools or academies). If the eighteenth- and nineteenth-century critic attempted to instruct the taste of the reading public and to impose upon its members a more refined reading practice than they might have been inclined to embrace on their own, the critic's mode of reading was not professional reading. It remained, in fact, a version of lay reading. The critic sought to instruct the reading public *as one of them.*

By contrast, when the discipline of literary study crystallized in its present form in the twentieth century, its professional reading practice was defined precisely by the deliberate cultivation of a difference from lay reading and even by the expression of antagonism toward that mode of reading. The significance of this transition is unfortunately distorted by the received history of criticism, which posits a continuous discourse of criticism from Aristotle to the present. The history of criticism, however, as a formalized discourse of judgment, is really only datable to the Renaissance and the spread of vernacular writing. By contrast, works in Greek and Latin—the classics—did not require the same effort of judgment as works newly written, performed, or published. Criticism was a response to the latter fact of contemporary literary production.

As historians of our discipline have been at pains to demonstrate, the emergence of a discipline of literary criticism coincided with the recession of criticism as a form of periodical or journalistic writing. This kind of writing did not disappear, but it retreated to a space within the public sphere that was far less commanding than had previously been the case in the era of the great reviews and quarterlies of the previous two centuries. "Reviewing" and "literary criticism," once indistinguishable from each other, separated into two forms of writing with two locations. In the university, as I have discussed in chapter 2, the form of literary criticism fused with forms of historical scholarship that presupposed judgments about any vernacular writing that survived long enough to acquire canonical status. Already by the eighteenth century, vernacular literature had its own classics to celebrate. Scholarship in "English" literature was still largely pursued outside the university system, but this scholarship ultimately established a curriculum for the discipline that began gradually to enter the schools from the later eighteenth century to the beginning of the twentieth. This is a story that is of course well known. My point here is that criticism, even in its "predisciplinary" form, had an important role to play in the transition to professional reading in the twentieth century.

This role was to set the stage for a debate between those who rejected and those who embraced "modernist" literature. This literature often seemed to confound the understanding of the lay reader and to demand a readership with specialized skills of interpretation. The alienation of the "common reader" was an event that was entangled in the complex fractioning of the cultural domain, affecting all forms of cultural production. Without attempting to represent this development in any way adequate to its complexity, I will attempt briefly to indicate the position of the "lay reader" in the literary scene of this transformation. No topos of modernism is more common than the recognition of its "difficulty." Wallace Stevens raised this feature to the status of a poetics in "Notes toward a Supreme Fiction," which he telegraphed as "the imagination's Latin."[10] The difficulty of modernist writing contrasted with other cultural work in new media such as film and radio that seemed much easier to "consume." New media artifacts contended more or less successfully in competition for consumers with "high modernist" literature, art, and music—despite the fact that there was far more traffic between the "high" arts and new media than might at first have been apparent to consumers or to scholars. When this struggle began, its outcome in a thoroughgoing distinction between lay and professional modes of reading was by no means obvious or perhaps even assured. In any case, a defense of modernism such as we find in Robert Graves and Laura Riding's important *Survey of Modernist Poetry* projected a reading public that was rapidly bifurcating into those who were receptive to the experiments of the modernists and those who were resistant, those Graves and Riding called "plain readers."[11]

And yet it would be inaccurate to say that it was the professional readers, the academics, who were the chief defenders of the modernists. On the contrary, the opposition of modernism and mass culture was a conflict occurring largely outside the university, in a final phase of the old public sphere of periodical criticism. Only when the literary professoriate (or a sector of them) took up the cause of modernist literature was it possible

10. Wallace Stevens, "Notes toward a Supreme Fiction," in *The Collected Poems of Wallace Stevens* (New York: Alfred A. Knopf, 1974), 397. The stanza in which this phrase occurs reads, "The peculiar potency of the general, / To compound the imagination's Latin with / The lingua franca et jocundissima." Stevens describes here an interchange between the metaphorized languages of Latin and the vernacular that comes closer to the actual practice of modernism than is indicated by the concept of difficulty.

11. Laura Riding and Robert Graves, *A Survey of Modernist Poetry* (Garden City, NY: Doubleday, Doran, 1928), passim.

to speak of the professors and the "plain readers" as standing on opposite sides in mass society. While we certainly know this story in its outlines, in my view we have not yet taken in the significance of the fact that professional reading did not emerge until a cadre of professors found the means of defending modernism by developing an autonomous reading practice, removed from the immediate aim of instructing the lay reader and addressed primarily to other scholars of literature.

Making reading professional entailed both the institutional relocation of criticism and its redefinition. As I discussed in chapter 2, criticism was reoriented in the 1940s and '50s from the *judgment* of literature to the interpretation of literature. The necessity of interpretation was occasioned initially by the difficulty of the modernists, but interpretation proved to be too interesting and generative to be restricted to new writing. It very quickly came to be the means of recovering the intelligibility of older literature that was rendered "difficult" as a result of cultural and linguistic changes wrought by the passage of time. Eventually all literature was reconceived as *inherently* difficult. The transition from judgment to interpretation gave rise to considerable confusion, evinced by the fact, for example, that early readers of William Empson's famous *Seven Types of Ambiguity* denied that it was criticism at all, because Empson was concerned with interpreting rather than judging literature.[12]

The distinction between judgment and interpretation traces the line of demarcation between lay reading and professional reading, even today. All lay readers are judges of what they read and, when called upon to defend their judgments, can usually summon arguments. But lay readers are often resistant to interpretation, for reasons that are at once obvious and hard to address. It is just here that the gap between lay and professional readers yawns widest, enlarging into a no-man's land of mutual hostility. There is a surprising irony in this situation, when we consider the uses to which interpretation has been put since the later nineteenth century. For professional literary critics, interpretation has *become* criticism. Our discipline has appropriated the name of criticism as the aim of interpretation, or what we now call "critique." We do not recognize that, in fact, criticism is what lay readers practice intuitively, whenever they judge the works they read to be good or bad, even when that judgment is expressed in the simple

---

12. In the preface to the revised edition of *Seven Types of Ambiguity* (1930; New York: New Directions, 1947), Empson cites a review by James Smith, complaining that "it is not his [the critic's] main, or even his immediate, concern that a word can be interpreted, that a sentence can be construed, in a large number of ways; if he makes it his concern, there is a danger that, in the enumeration of these ways, judgements of value will be forgotten" (xii).

terms of liking or disliking. At the same time, lay readers often *suspect* interpretation, disabling at the outset the agenda of literary scholars who want
interpretation to do the work of criticism, to bring readers to the higher
criticism of "critique." This situation of mutual misunderstanding has long
occasioned a backlash among lay readers, for which Susan Sontag's famous
essay "Against Interpretation" provided a kind of manifesto. A version of
this resistance has been reasserted in the "postcritical" manifestos of Rita
Felski, Sharon Marcus, Stephen Best in recent years, discussed in chapter 3
above.[13] But rather than continue hostilities between lay reading and interpretation, it seems to me more advisable to recall the historical circumstances that gave rise to this problem.

The divergence between the old aim of criticism, to instruct the taste
of the lay reader, and the new aim, to develop an autonomous, professional, interpretive reading practice, underlies the mythologized version
of the narrative of professionalization that circulates today. This narrative
is often enough written as a story of decline or as the abandonment of the
critic's social role.[14] But it is important to remember that the situation of
literature in modernity was vastly complicated by the adjacency of new
media, to which modernist practice was compelled to respond. Or let us
say that "modernism" is the name of the response. This movement gave
birth to a discipline of reading even as it rescued older vernacular literature
in English from oblivion. Older works of literature seemed to be written
in *another language*, not quite so different as Greek or Latin but requiring
the aid of teachers in its transmission. Modernist difficulty replicated linguistic otherness, "the imagination's Latin." For better or worse, English
literature—both old and new—needed the school to survive. In this enormously complex cultural situation, the unhappy but inescapable result was
the division between the professional reader and the lay reader, the situation acknowledged poignantly by Michel de Certeau in the essay quoted as
an epigraph to this chapter.[15]

HYPOCRITE LECTEUR

There is now an enormous gap between reading as it is practiced within
and without the academy. I want to give a very schematic picture of this

13. Felski, *The Limits of Critique*; Sharon Marcus and Stephen Best, "Surface Reading: An Introduction," *Representations* 108 (2009): 1–21.

14. For a version of this argument, see Morris Dickstein, *Double Agent: The Critic
and Society* (New York: Oxford University Press, 1992).

15. Michel de Certeau, *The Practice of Everyday Life*, trans. Steven Rendall (Berkeley: University of California Press, 1984), 171.

division in reading practices, by which I refer as much or more to the social conditions of reading as to the methods of reading. This schematic depiction is, of course, an abstraction from social conditions that are vastly more complex than can be detailed here, and therefore my reader is cautioned to take this schema as a heuristic aid. Here, then, is a description of the disciplinary mode of reading, "professional reading," as characterized by four very particular features, to be followed by an enumeration of the contrasting features of lay reading:

First, professional reading is a kind of *work*, a labor requiring large amounts of time and resources. This labor, reading for a living, is compensated as such, by a salary, along with all the perquisites attached to the professional career.

Second, it is a *disciplinary* activity; that is, it is governed by techniques of interpretation and procedures of research developed in the context of a university program of credentialization, at both the undergraduate and the graduate level. These techniques take years to acquire; otherwise, we would not award higher degrees to those who succeed in mastering them.

Third, professional reading is *vigilant*; it stands back from the experience of pleasure in reading, not in order to cancel out this pleasure but in order necessarily to be conscious of it, so that the experience of reading does not begin and end in the unexamined pleasure of consumption but gives rise to a certain sustained reflection.

And fourth, this reading is a *communal* practice. Even when the scholar reads in privacy, the act of reading is connected in numerous ways to the communal scenes of a profession. Accordingly, it is often dedicated to the end of producing a publishable work of scholarship, a secondary artifact of writing that presupposes the literary artifact. Professional reading envisions an audience of students or scholars, in the classroom or in print. These performed "readings" thus submit to the response and judgment of other professional readers.

Outside the academy it is very difficult to engage in a practice of reading such as I have just described. This does not mean that some aspects of it cannot be replicated there, but lack of time and resources alone are insuperable impediments to its replication for most nonprofessional or lay readers. Lay reading can be characterized by four features that are both opposed to those of professional reading but also simply different, or incommensurable:

Lay reading is first of all practiced at the site of *leisure*. Many of the same literary works that we read in the academy in the course of our teaching and research are also read by lay readers who in no way regard this reading as work. I exclude here from the category of lay reading the kind of reading that occurs in work situations, the reading of memos, emails, reports, manuals, etc. This practice of reading has its own interesting protocols, which are not those of what I am calling lay reading.

Second, the *conventions* of lay reading are very different from those of disciplinary or professional reading. One has only to invoke the relation between the occasions of reading—breakfast, bedtime, weekends, vacations, commuting, in the waiting room—and the reading matter sometimes taken up on those occasions (newspapers, magazines, fiction and "bestsellers," self-help books, along with myriad new forms of internet writing) in order to see that lay reading is indeed organized by conventions that are situationally determined by the disposition of leisure time.[16] The conventions of lay reading are not restricted to works of literature but spread out over all the kinds of reading that might possibly be done outside the context of work.

Third, lay reading is motivated primarily by the experience of *pleasure*, which may be not only a necessary but a sufficient motive for reading. Lay reading might involve a number of other ends—informative, moral, or edifying—of which I shall speak presently, but the experience of pleasure will ordinarily be the first and necessary motive of lay reading. It is a paradox of lay reading, however, that when pressed to justify the reading of literature, lay readers will often omit the experience of pleasure and cite instead the kind of moral or edifying function that professional readers tend to regard with greater caution.

Fourth, lay reading is largely a *solitary* practice. Its scenes of communal reading are seldom formally organized but rather occur by chance or by virtue of the considerable effort it takes to overcome the condition of solitariness. I do not mean, then, to dismiss reading groups or other communal scenes of reading, though they are surely less common than the communal occasions to be found in earlier, less widely literate societies. Those societies, just because the ability to read was rarer, cultivated practices of recitation that brought many nonreaders into communal contact with vernacular literature.

Given the relative incommensurability of professional and lay reading in my schematic account, it should be evident why contemporary literary study has been tempted to resort to a political fantasy in order to describe its effects in the world. Those of us who are professional readers cannot hope to see our reading practice simply replicated outside the academy. On

16. On this and related questions, see the interesting conversation between Roger Chartier and Pierre Bourdieu, "La lecture; une pratique culturelle," in Roger Chartier, ed., *Pratiques de la lecture* (Paris: Payot, 1985), 218–39.

the contrary, the difference between professional and lay reading grows ever more pronounced, given, on the one hand, that professionalization is an ever more complex process and, on the other, that so many other activities compete with reading for leisure time. It is in these circumstances that a certain mutual misunderstanding has arisen between lay and professional readers, a sense, on the one side, that the professors have betrayed their traditional duty as *critics* to offer guidance to lay readers and, on the other, that sophisticated and politically vigilant techniques of reading can have transformative effects vastly beyond the sphere of their practice.[17]

It seems to me altogether unrealistic that we should expect those outside the academy to exercise the same vigilance in relation to their pleasure as we do in the context of professional reading. But it is also very unfortunate for our society that lay reading so often falls to the level of ephemeral consumption, with no other end than pleasure or distraction—or rather, that kind of pleasure that aims merely to distract. Again, I am describing here lay reading and professional reading as they generally are, not as they always are, and certainly not as they must be.[18] The mutual incomprehension of these two practices of reading is painfully evident to those of us—I mean those teachers of literature—who want our most brilliant students to go on to graduate school, even when the market for new PhDs is nearly nonexistent, for are we not thinking, as are they, that they will never again be able to read as they have learned to read under our professional tutelage, unless that tutelage is continued? And those readers outside the academy who have escaped our seduction, do they not suspect that we would like nothing better than to deprive them of their pleasure, to impose upon them a joyless and disillusioned vigilance, when they are eager for some more uplifting pleasure whose content they cannot name, except by naming great works of literature?

It has become very difficult indeed to locate or develop intermediate sites or practices of reading, between the poles of mere entertainment on the one side and vigilant professionalism on the other. Professional reading and lay reading have become so disconnected that it is difficult to see

17. This is an example of what Bourdieu calls the "scholastic fallacy." See Bourdieu, *Pascalian Meditations* (Stanford, CA: Stanford University Press, 2000).

18. I am mindful here of the argument of Michel de Certeau in *The Practice of Everyday Life* that we should not underestimate lay reading, which he rightly regards as an activity of production as well as consumption. Nonetheless I would suggest that when de Certeau describes this reading, he tends to project onto it a certain transgressive desire that may or may not characterize any individual act of lay reading. The analogy of reading to "poaching" in his account, however appealing, projects the political desire of the professional reader onto lay reading practices.

how they are both reading, which is why it has become a temptation for the most sophisticated practitioners of professional reading to condemn lay reading as a failure to "read," either in the higher sense of to interpret, or in the sense of the politicized classroom, to make reading an occasion for the criticism of society.

Having underscored this difference, I would like now to argue the other way round, and to assert that at a deeper level lay reading and professional reading are not simply noncoincident, or antithetical, but that lay reading is in fact the inescapable condition of professional reading in at least two of its features: (1) the comprehension of sentence meaning and (2) the experiential pleasure of reading, however one understands the psychology or politics of that pleasure. Since at least the first of these two features might be described as a universal characteristic of reading, it is not surprising that when reading has been studied as a practice, it is usually basic comprehension of sentence meaning that offers itself as *identical* to reading, as essentially what reading is. The equation of reading with the achievement of such comprehension is otherwise known as "literacy." But let us admit that the equation of literacy with reading as such underestimates what reading can be. Reading has no terminal point, at which one might say, "Now I know how to read." Reading is a practice that can be developed indefinitely, that can always be improved and deepened.[19]

Both comprehension and the correlated pleasure of reading a work of literature are aspects of lay reading that are systematically alienated in the interpretive modes of professional reading. But in this alienation from intuitive comprehension and from an immediate "consumer" pleasure, professional reading preserves within it a version of lay reading as its inevitable occasion, its necessary point of departure. Such alienation would be pointless were the pleasure of lay reading to be simply destroyed rather than subsumed into the "work" of professional reading. This should be news to no one: all sophisticated play becomes labor. It is unfortunate that profes-

---

19. I would note that reading has also been a subject of interest to anthropologists. See, for example, A. W. McHoul, *Telling How Texts Talk: Essays on Reading and Ethnomethodology* (London: Routledge and Kegan Paul, 1982); Eric Livingston, *An Anthropology of Reading* (Bloomington: Indiana University Press, 1995); Jonathan Boyarin, ed., *The Ethnography of Reading* (Berkeley: University of California Press, 1992). Within the discipline, literary reading is examined in Norman Holland, *5 Readers Reading* (New Haven, CT: Yale University Press, 1975), and many works by Wolfgang Iser, among which I will cite *The Act of Reading: A Theory of Aesthetic Response* (Baltimore: Johns Hopkins University Press, 1978). The bibliography here is too voluminous to cite further.

sional reading sometimes constructs lay reading as nonreading.[20] The intensity of professional readers' derogation of lay reading betrays the fact that literary scholars must alienate not only the *other's* but also *their own* practice of lay reading.

A THEORY OF LAY READING IS WANTED

Every profession creates its own laity as a back-formation of its expertise. But, as we have just established, literary study is distinct by virtue necessarily of sublimating lay reading into its professional process. This necessity obtains, no matter what particular method of interpretation is applied to a literary text. If professional reading is an operation upon lay reading, a systematic alienation of it, literary critics would do well to acquire a better sense of what lay reading actually is, or can be at its best. I would like to propose here what may seem at first a novel or puzzling historical conjecture, the aim of which will be to show why lay reading has been seen variously as both a naïve and a rich experiential mode. Reading in modernity, I will argue, belongs to the category of what I will call *ethical practice*, by which I mean a practice of self-improvement, achieved in and through the experience of pleasure. This practice is the condition for the distinction between lay and professional reading, as also for the bad conscience of both, the tendency of lay reading to fall to the level of mere consumption or entertainment, and the tendency of professional reading to express frustration in the face of the lay reader's resistance to having naïve pleasure called into question. I suggest that professional reading has never completely alienated the practice of lay reading, which it hopes still to instruct, even though it understands the aim of instructing the laity too narrowly and unrealistically as the imposition of its own reading practice upon lay readers.

At this point I must set before my readers what I hope will be a plausible, if radically abbreviated, account of what I mean by reading as an ethical practice. To accelerate this exposition, I would like to invoke very briefly a certain turn in the later work of Michel Foucault toward the subject of what he called the "ethical," which he distinguishes, as I would like to do, from

20. Livingston, in *An Anthropology of Reading*, proposes a version of this hypothesis: "When the literary critic discusses a reading of a poem, 'reading' refers to a subtle distortion of the laic skills of reading, a kind of alchemy of the practices of ordinary reading" (xvii). I depart from Livingston's development of this thesis, however, inasmuch as he is concerned to demonstrate that what I would call "interpretation" can be reduced to "the laic skills of ordinary reading" (43), for which "expert knowledge" is finally a dubious supplement.

the category of morality. Foucault's turn to the ethical occurred between the first and subsequent two volumes of *The History of Sexuality*. This turn coincided with a surprising movement away from the subject of sexuality itself, which Foucault had conceptualized in political terms, as a premier instance in modernity of the power/knowledge complement, or "bio-power." In the second and third volumes of *The History of Sexuality*, sexuality itself recedes somewhat from the foreground of Foucault's interest, along with the political. Instead sexuality is assimilated to a range of other everyday life practices, among them physical exercise and diet.[21] Foucault described these practices as the "care of the self," or as "techniques of the self," practices that took as their aim a mastery of the body or mind for the sake of enhancing pleasure or well-being.[22]

The larger aim of Foucault's argument was clearly to remove sexual practice from the domain of morality, which Foucault attempted to distinguish as sharply as possible from the realm of the ethical. Unfortunately, morality and ethics are consistently confused in ordinary usage, and that confusion has troubled the reception of Foucault's later work as well.[23] It is not my purpose here to import into my own argument any more of the baggage Foucault's name invokes, and indeed, I might have made my case for the distinction between the ethical and the moral by invoking Pierre Hadot's

21. See Michel Foucault, *The Use of Pleasure*, trans. Robert Hurley (New York: Vintage Books, 1985), and Foucault, *The Care of the Self*, trans. Robert Hurley (New York: Vintage Books, 1986).

22. This turn was very surprising indeed; it allowed Foucault to remark in late interviews that "sex is boring," by which, presumably, he meant when sex became the object of knowledge and as such could be delivered over to the disciplinary society of the doctors and the psychiatrists. In short, the sex that is boring is the sex that is political. See Foucault, "On the Genealogy of Ethics: An Overview of Work in Progress" (1983), in *Ethics: Subjectivity and Truth*, in *The Essential Works of Foucault, 1954–1984*, 3 vols., ed. Paul Rabinow (New York: The New Press, 1994), 1:253.

23. This confusion is all the worse because it is so discordant with philosophical usage. In English, "ethics" tends to refer to a wider domain of reflection on right and wrong than "morality," and it thus names an area within the discipline of philosophy. "Morality" tends to be used commonly to refer to specific moral systems, such as "Christian morality." But in the German idealist tradition, from which philosophical thought on ethics largely descends, the principal terminological distinction is between *Moralität*, as the domain of reflective and conscious choice between right and wrong, and *Sittlichkeit*, or the "ethical," which refers to the domain of customary morality and does not necessarily entail reflective and conscious choice. In adopting Foucault's use of "ethics," despite his occasional misconstruction of this concept in antiquity, I would emphasize the continuity of ethics with *Moralität*, as a domain of choice, and its distinction, as the choice between goods. It is also distinct from *Sittlichkeit*, or custom.

work on ancient philosophy as a "way of life," from which Foucault himself borrowed liberally, or Bernard Williams's analogous attempt to rehabilitate the field of ethics as the question of "how to live," which he sees rightly as very different from morality's prohibitions or categorical imperatives.[24] But the difficulty Foucault and others have had in demarcating a realm of the ethical from the moral is one that cannot really be avoided and is quite instructive in the context of reading, especially as it has become fashionable to speak of an "ethics of reading," a notion that unhappily reduces ethics in the usual way to a version of morality. Between the Greeks and ourselves, Christianity erected the great wall of morality, meaning the choice between good and evil, right and wrong. But for the Greeks, an ethos or "way of life" implied rather a *choice between goods*, a cultivation of the self not based on notions of sin or prohibition. Since these choices were not burdened by the consequence of salvation or damnation, the domain of the ethical in antiquity resembled what we call morality somewhat less than is usually supposed.

This point might seem at first to be unrelated to the question of reading as a practice, but it is my purpose here to argue that lay reading is best understood as a practice that belongs to the ethical domain. To put this point as explicitly as I can, I would like to argue that we should regard lay reading, or reading for pleasure, as belonging to the same category of practice as physical exercise, cooking, conversation with friends, sexual activity, or any number of other pleasures which enlarge our experience and

---

24. For Pierre Hadot, see "Reflections on the Notion of the 'Cultivation of the Self,'" in *Michel Foucault: Philosopher*, trans. Timothy J. Armstrong (New York: Routledge, 1992), 225–232; Hadot, *Philosophy as a Way of Life*, ed. Arnold I. Davidson (Oxford: Blackwell, 1995); and Hadot, *What Is Ancient Philosophy?*, trans. Michael Chase (Cambridge, MA: Harvard University Press, 2002). Foucault was strongly influenced by Hadot's depiction of philosophical culture, which he appropriated in a philosophical project that had its origins elsewhere, in a meditation on the emergence of the regime of sexuality in the later nineteenth century. This goes some way toward explaining the strong link between antiquity and the later nineteenth century in his final works, since he tended to identify the aestheticism of Wilde and others of that period with the lifestyle philosophers of antiquity. The Greeks were for him "other Victorians," rather like those Victorians whose aestheticism set itself against the regime of sexuality, with its moralization (and thus politicization) of sexual practice. The problem with this association, as Hadot points out, is that Greek ethical practice was more normative than transgressive. For Bernard Williams's attempt to institute a rigorous distinction between morality and ethics, in which ethics is defined by the question of "how to live" and morality is circumscribed as a special kind of ethics, see Williams, *Ethics and the Limits of Philosophy* (Cambridge, MA: Harvard University Press, 1985).

enrich our sensibilities.[25] These pleasures include, of course, our engagement with the other visual and musical arts.

Unfortunately, it is very difficult either to name or to isolate ethical practice in modernity, in the sense in which I'm using the term, without taking the risk of having this practice reduced to some version of morality. This reduction occurs every time we conceive what should be regarded as an ethical practice as a question of sin or abnormality—every time, for example, we call overeating a sin or every time we wonder whether indulging in a sexual fantasy makes us abnormal or sick. Ethical practice is in truth very hard to see in our society, but it is far from absent. I would like to invoke in this context the general category of "therapy," specifically self-therapy or self-help, as the perhaps degraded form of Foucault's ethical practice, and to be sure, a massified or commodified form of that practice. Our "therapy culture" has in fact been responsible for resurrecting recognizably ethical practices in the Greek sense, for example, physical exercise—surely our most Greek ethical practice.

Lay reading belongs to the field of the ethical because it is a practice on the self and because the experience of pleasure in reading is capable of being cultivated or refined, in precisely the sense of what was called in the early modern period *self-improvement*. What I would like to propose is that the practice of lay reading belongs to the domain of a *practice* of pleasure, where the assumption is that the practicing of pleasures will both intensify them and make them better for us.

The development of reading in modernity was marked, as I have suggested, by the gradual and very uneven demarcation of pleasure as a legitimate end of reading, as an end in itself. At the same time, reading was moving out of the domain of the clergy into the world of the laity and into the field of leisure or entertainment. The latter domain was often still the site of communal reading, of reading aloud before groups, but it was also the site in which the solitary reader appeared. Solitary reading for pleasure was initially regarded as socially threatening, subject to suspicion and surveillance. It was not clear at all during the early history of the novel, for example, whether the pleasure of novel reading was sufficiently justified by the moral doctrine novels were supposed to contain. The historians Thomas Laqueur and John Brewer have reminded us that a connection was often

25. For an interesting philosophical version of this argument, see Alexander Nehamas, *The Art of Living: Socratic Reflections from Plato to Foucault* (Berkeley: University of California Press, 1998). And for the historical sense of how an ordinary practice such as "conversation" could be elaborated into a formal art, see Burke, *The Art of Conversation*.

made between novel reading by women and masturbation, an association that conveys very vividly how suspect solitary reading could be.[26] Thomas Laqueur, in his study of the history of masturbation, has demonstrated beyond question that masturbation and solitary reading were widely associated in the eighteenth century. "Private reading," he observes, "bore all the marks of masturbatory danger."[27] Now given such an association, we might think that reading is obviously located in the domain of the moral, as a practice that presents one with a choice between right and wrong. But I suggest that this is in fact not what the association means at all, since it is not a question of whether to read or not to read but of what to read and how to read. Despite the distorting mirror of a reductive morality, we have to learn to see the emergence of lay reading as an ethical practice, the possibility of improving oneself by legitimate pleasure.

In solitary reading, an act of self-pleasuring occurred, and this act had to be understood as potentially improving in order to protect it from capture by the regime of morality. It was to be several more centuries before solitary sex itself, that kind of self-pleasuring, would escape the prison of morality and come to be regarded as a harmless and even beneficial indulgence. Solitary reading was already too prevalent by the eighteenth century to be prohibited, and the motive of pleasure in reading was far too obvious to be suppressed in favor of reading solely for morality or devotion. The failure of the latter attempt to moralize reading is wittily portrayed in Sheridan's 1775 play, *The Rivals*, where the heroine, upon being told that her guardian is approaching her bedchamber, rushes to hide her copies of *Roderick Random*, *Peregrine Pickle*, *The Sentimental Journey*, and *The Man of Feeling* and to replace them on her desk with an open copy of Fordyce's *Sermons*.

We might say that the problem of justifying the pleasure of solitary reading was the occasion in the eighteenth century for *problematizing* reading, for devising the terms by which lay reading might be defended. Of course, it is necessary to emphasize here that this problem could only have arisen with the emergence of what we now call literature—the aggregation of the genres of pleasurable writing: poems, novels, and plays. The possibility of self-improvement in lay reading had to be seen as an effect of the very genres of writing that were coming to be increasingly demarcated from de-

---

26. Brewer, *The Pleasures of the Imagination*, xxii. See also his citation of John Cannon, who "claimed to have learned to masturbate as a result of reading *Aristotle's Masterpiece*, a standard work of sexual instruction" (186). For further discussion of this association, see Thomas Laqueur, "Credit, Novels, Masturbation," in *Choreographing History*, ed. Susan Leigh Foster (Bloomington: Indiana University Press, 1995), 119–28.

27. Thomas Laqueur, *Solitary Sex: A Cultural History of Masturbation* (New York: Zone Books, 2003).

votional, scientific, and bureaucratic writing. For literary works, pleasure was less and less capable of being justified as the sweet shell of the moral kernel. One cannot stress too strongly that it was rather the experience of *pleasure itself* that was to produce the improving or refining effect of reading. Here is one early lay reader, Eliza Haywood, making just this claim in the opening sentences of her subscription series of 1744, *The Female Spectator*: "It is very much by the choice we make of subjects for our entertainment, that the refined taste distinguishes itself from the vulgar and more gross. Reading is universally allowed to be one of the most improving as well as agreeable amusements."[28] It would be an anachronism, I suggest, to expose Haywood's defense of pleasure as merely an expression of a class system of distinction. A less anachronistic analysis would recognize the game of distinction as itself a version of ethical practice, an attempt to enlarge one's social being in an emergent class society, wherein the ability to read was no longer controlled by professionals. The utility of that game was precisely its capacity to save the pleasure experienced in reading from the fate of moral condemnation. Haywood's "choice" among subjects for entertainment is not a choice between good books and evil books but between good books and bad books, between works that enlarge and those that diminish her very self. But this is not to say, of course, that Haywood's successors have not labored mightily to show how bad books are really evil books. It is rather to say that this effort might well end in tossing some of the best books on the fire.

In lay readers such as Haywood we can see the ethical emerge in its typical modern form, which involves an uneasy or defensive relation to the moral. While it is still possible and even common for lay readers to justify their reading by invoking the end of self-improvement, all too often self-improvement is understood in narrowly moral terms, as apprehending and internalizing the "moral" of a work. It remains difficult to see pleasure itself, or the quality of a pleasure, as self-improving, as the substance of a practice on the self. We all know, for whatever this most banal knowledge is worth, that pleasure too often bears the stigma of the immoral. This stigma is imprinted on even the most rigorous aestheticism, as in the inverted moralism of the Gidean "immoralist." In retrospect, the emergence of the category of the aesthetic can be seen as having been necessitated in part by the absence of a distinction between the ethical and the moral; the dismissal of the aesthetic as trivial or immoral is the residue of this problem. The practice of reading has suffered in a peculiar way the effect of this unresolved

28. Virginia Walcott Beauchamp et al., eds., *Women Critics: 1660–1820: An Anthology* (Bloomington: Indiana University Press, 1995), 68.

problem, which is nothing other than the spectacular failure of professional reading to recognize lay reading.

If it is also the case that professional reading always presupposes lay reading, the pleasure of lay reading is not eradicated in the stance of vigilance but both diffused and intensified through a labored disciplinary practice. The rarified pleasure of professional reading, which comprises the labored pleasure and pleasant pains of research and scholarly writing, is nonetheless subject to a moralistic reduction when the laborious aspect of its practice is offered as a metonymy for reading as such. When J. Hillis Miller, for example, remarks that reading "is extraordinarily hard work" (3), he is reducing professional reading to a version of the "work ethic," and to a distinction between work and play belied by the real complexity of professional reading practices.[29] The pleasure of scholarly reading is not just different from lay reading; it is also a confirmation of the continuity between lay and professional reading.

The failure to recognize this continuity is equally evident when professional readers invoke certain political aims as a justification for professional reading, when reading is justified in relation to its presumed social or political effects. Suppose we rather conceived the practice of reading as an ethical practice, whose object is first of all oneself. Would such a practice exclude political consequence? If we are tempted to think that it would, then I would say in response that we have not understood lay reading, that we are still inclined to oppose pleasure to the political in the same way that we wrongly oppose pleasure to the moral. On this subject Barthes's meditation on reading in *The Pleasure of the Text*, from which I have drawn the second epigraph to this chapter, remains for me a definitive statement, still ahead of our most earnest theorizing. Barthes understood very well that in the "foreclosure of pleasure" nothing less than a "political alienation" was at issue. He deplores not the inability of readers to read as professionals do but the fact that our society is "ridden by two moralities: the prevailing one, of platitude; the minority one, of rigor (political and/or scientific). As if the notion of pleasure no longer pleases anyone."[30] Our most advanced theoretical defense of pleasure tends to celebrate it only when it comes dressed in the garb of a transgressive politics. To politicize pleasure is once again to moralize it and thus to misplace the politics of pleasure, which resides in

29. As a student long ago of the late J. Hillis Miller, I can attest that Miller's picture of an ethics of reading does not do justice to his teaching, which at every point communicated the pleasures of reading.

30. Roland Barthes, *The Pleasure of the Text*, trans. Richard Miller (New York: Hill and Wang, 1975), 46–47.

the question of *what social conditions must obtain* in order for individuals to develop the possibilities of pleasure, including the pleasure of reading.

If the failure of both lay and professional readers to recognize reading as an ethical practice underlies their mutual antagonism and miscomprehension, I have, alas, no program for reconciling these practices. In my view, the autonomy of professional reading as a university discipline must be defended, whether or not its practices can be disseminated much beyond the academy. The work of scholarship is justified for many reasons in addition to the instruction of lay reading. Conversely, I suggest that lay reading must be defended too, whether or not it can be brought into closer relation to the reading of literary scholars. In the present circumstances of literary study, it is difficult to be sanguine about the possibility of establishing intermediate practices of reading, which would presumably sophisticate lay reading without yielding to the fantasy of replicating professional readers. Yet if lay reading is defined by a pleasure that is in itself improving, it seems obvious that this improving pleasure has no upper end or terminal point. Many lay readers very much desire the improvement of their reading experience, a desire that is widely expressed in lay engagement with the other arts as well. The prevalence of this desire confronts the literary professoriate with a demand, however difficult it will be to imagine a response to this demand, a new relation to lay readers. Such a response can only be undertaken with a better sense of what lay reading is, a practice that literary scholars have held so close as not to see it at all.

Ratio Studiorum

You've been too long in the institution.
FINE YOUNG CANNIBALS, "Like a Stranger"

THE ADVANCEMENT OF LITERARY LEARNING

The study of literature—in the premodern sense of any writing that has been preserved or valued—is very old, the oldest kind of organized study in Western history, excepting only rhetoric. Reading and writing, along with the arts of speaking, once constituted all there was to learning. Contemplating the proliferating discourses of knowledge in his own day, Francis Bacon proposed in the Latin version of his *Advancement of Learning* a summary "history of literature" (*historia litterarum*) that would survey all learning, everything written since antiquity.[1] Even in the seventeenth century, this would have been an impossible task, but in the modern world it would be meaningless. On the one hand, documents have accumulated by factors unimaginable for Bacon, filling the contents of paper and electronic archives with uncountable volumes of writing. On the other hand, "literature" is no longer the name of this accumulation, no longer identical to writing as such. The domain of what is called "literature" has steadily contracted over the centuries since Bacon to the genres of writing defined mainly by notions of the "imaginative" or the "fictional." This sense of literature has no correspondent in antiquity or early modernity. Even in its modern sense, a history of literature in all languages and locations would likely defeat any effort to undertake it, but the delimitation of literature compels us to understand its history as in part the history of that delimita-

---

1. Francis Bacon, *De dignitate et augmentis scientiarum*, ed. and trans. James Spedding, in *The Works of Francis Bacon*, vol. 4, *Translations of the Philosophical Works* (New York: Cambridge University Press, 1858). The phrase "*historia litterarum*" translates literally as the history of "letters" or "writing," not "literature" in our sense. Because the semantic domain of "literature" in the premodern era comprised all of writing, the most precise translation for our purposes would be the "history of learning."

tion. This history is a condition for the emergence of a discipline—literary study—that is and can only ever be one discipline among many.

Still, it will be helpful to remember the "history of literature" in Bacon's grand conception when we consider the question of what constitutes the reason for being of literary study, the scope of its possible aims. The reason for being of the discipline is difficult to bring out from the practices of any moment in its history because these reasons are deeply rooted in the entire history of literature, in precisely Bacon's sense. I mean to expose this difficulty and this embedded history by resurrecting an old expression for "curriculum," *ratio studiorum*. I refunction this borrowing from Renaissance usage not as a model for current practice but for its correlation of reason (*ratio*) to studies (*studiorum*). If the pretension of the Latin phrase can be forgiven, the concept of *ratio* will be useful for its semantic density, its compression of three significations that define the working conception of a discipline: *ratio* in the sense of (1) "reason for being," (2) a "plan of study" or curriculum, and (3) a relative measure or proportion of one thing to another, the current sense of the English word "ratio." I will explain the pertinence of this third term presently.

The first point I will assert, then, is that the study of literature is a rational procedure for establishing what can be known about an object. In current terms, literary study is a *discipline*. This is worth saying, however obvious, because literary study has sometimes been relegated in both past and present controversies to an ineffable expression of taste or the intuitive cultivation of sensibility rather than a disciplined set of procedures for the production and transmission of knowledge. Although literary study long ago moved beyond the positivism of earlier university disciplines, it still struggles, as do the humanities generally, with asserting the mode of its rationality. I have attempted in chapter 4 above to deal with this question in the larger context of humanities disciplines; my purpose here will be to address the subject with reference to literature as a mode of writing.

The second sense of *ratio studiorum* activates its meaning in Bacon's day as a "plan of study," that is, a curriculum. Early treatises on the curriculum circulating under this name listed the authors, books, and subjects studied and the methods of their study. This is what Erasmus sets out in his *De ratione studii* (1511), as does Vico, in his *De nostri temporis studiorum ratione* (1708).[2] Erasmus, Vico, and their contemporaries assumed that the curriculum made a kind of sense when considered as a plan or system of interrelated studies. In the premodern school, the curriculum was still a

---

2. See also the Jesuit plan of 1599, *The Ratio Studiorum: The Official Plan for Jesuit Education*, trans. Claude Pavur, (Saint Louis: The Institute of Jesuit Sources, 2005).

unitary structure, presumptively the same for all the students in a school. The knowledge that was foundational for this structure was the ability to read, write, and speak Latin (or sometimes both Latin and Greek). This linguistic coherence disappeared from the educational system with the vernacularization of learning and is now to be found only at the primary level of the school system, where it is identified with literacy in one's native tongue. The unitary language curriculum rules until students develop interests in particular subjects and eventually, careers. A unitary curriculum at every level of the educational system would be as impossible for us today as the Baconian "history of literature." But the question of *coherence* in the curriculum has not entirely ceased to concern educators, as incoherence increases with the ramification of the forms of knowledge and expertise. It is problematic that any two students in almost any university can make their way through four years of study without ever taking the same course. The theory of curriculum in the modern era is nothing other than an effort to establish a "ratio" between the coherence and incoherence of the curriculum, a negotiation between the commonality and diversity of its offerings. This third sense of the Latin word, as proportion or measure, alerts us to what is most difficult in a theory of curriculum, the source of the perennial struggles over what to teach, and how.

If the cohering force of the curriculum is radically attenuated from the perspective of the educational system in its totality, it still persists within individual disciplines, in the collegiate form of "majors" or programs of study and in the disciplines that oversee these programs. Yet even there, the coherence of the curriculum, its ratio, is not easy to determine. Literary study today allows considerable specialization among periods and topics and great diversity in methods. This tendency follows from the dynamic of specialization discussed in chapter 1; it can be countervailed only up to a point. While the effort to conceptualize a ratio between coherence and incoherence in literary study may be quixotic, it is worth attempting. The fortunes of any particular discipline depend to a certain degree upon the strength of self-definition, a measure of coherence expressed in the capacity of a discipline to define its object of study and to develop a set of methods appropriate to that object. It seems obvious that literary study is by this standard a weakly defined discipline, for all the reasons discussed in earlier chapters. But there is a certain paradox inhering in this weakness. Our discipline has achieved a measure of coherence only by selecting as its object a small fraction of written artifacts. At the same time, this delimitation has posed the question of the reason for being of the discipline in an acute form: Do these genres of writing really need a discipline dedicated to their study? Literary criticism, as it came to be defined in the twentieth century, seems never to have articulated an answer to this question that would establish a ratio of coherence to incoherence in its plan of study. It has rather been the tendency of the discipline, as we have seen, to digress from its object, to range widely over the whole cultural field. At the same time, the concept of literature continues to define all of the organizational features of the discipline: period specializations, the undergraduate major, journals, conferences, hiring priorities, and professional associations.

The insistence of the "ratio" problem contrasts with the situation of the sciences, which happily divide and multiply disciplinary subfields, defining new and ever more specialized objects of study without sacrificing the presumptive unitary role of scientific method. The multiplicity of scientific specializations somehow only increases their strength as disciplines. It would be tempting to credit the scientific method alone for the strength of the sciences, but for reasons too complex to enter into here, I do not think this explanation is necessary or even correct. The sciences have problems of their own, but they seem able to assimilate considerable incoherence without suffering a loss of status; they continue to be perceived as the embodiment of procedural rationality. The study of literature, by contrast, is troubled by a foundational doubt about its object of study, and this uncertainty has undermined its strength as a discipline. The delimitation of the literary object, which was a condition for the formation of the discipline, does not seem to impart to its various specializations a counterbalancing coherence or strength.

If a troubled ratio of coherence to incoherence is a persistent feature of literary study, the resulting institutional weakness poses interesting questions about the nature of its object, as well as creating problems on the ground of practice. I have touched in other chapters on the difference of literary study from the situation of the visual arts and music history, which seem to be less conflicted about the nature of their objects. This difference is perhaps less than it seems, but on the face of it, literary study requires a somewhat greater effort to account for its reason of being than the other arts. In my view, this question has to do with the nature of writing as a medium, at the least its greater capacity for ideational content than visual images or music. But I will defer that question until its appropriate moment. In the meantime, it will be helpful to bear in mind throughout this concluding essay the three notions of *reason* (for being), *plan* (of study), and *ratio* (of coherence to incoherence) that translate the Latin *ratio*. For the sake of an economy of presentation, I will henceforth indicate this compression of senses by the term "rationale." I can attempt here only the most schematic presentation of "rationale"—or rather "rationales"—beginning with the proposition that there are multiple rationales for literary study and that these rationales can be distinguished for the purpose of assessing them individually. At the same time, I concede that in most circumstances of teaching, as in most works of scholarship, these rationales will be fused or intertwined. I want to explore in this conclusion the possibility of putting forward multiple rationales for literary study, arguing that we scholars and teachers of literature can and should affirm the reason of literary study, both its core rationality and the possibility of its "advancement" in the Baconian sense.

THE RATIONALES

It sometimes seems that literary study is berated for continuing to do what it no longer does, and for not doing what it has always done. A better understanding of the rationales for literary study will perhaps clear away some misconceptions that arise from the response of scholars to the exigencies of the moment, which distort their understanding of the reasons for the discipline itself. The rationales I propose to describe here are not defined by the agendas of our present moment but by a longer timeline of *literary knowledge* extending deep into Bacon's hypothetical history of literature, the long prehistory of the discipline. These rationales survive in the disciplinary form of literary study, but they are often not recognized, or misrecognized. They will seem at first glance to be unrelated to topics or agendas that are current, that constitute the advance guard of the discipline. It will be necessary to set these contemporary movements to one side in order to make visible the operation of the rationales. Understandably, scholars like to point to what is *new* in order to express a sense of the value of disciplinary work, but I argue that what is new in the discipline is built on very old foundations, which *make possible* what is new. I will not, for this reason, be concerned to discuss at any length the diverse tendencies or movements in literary study today, such as postcolonial studies, race and ethnicity studies, digital analysis, disability studies, animal studies, indigenous studies, ecocriticism, cognitive studies, evolutionary studies, new materialisms, book history, affect studies, or new formalisms. The rationales for literary study must be conceived rather according to the metaphor of "sedimentation," which has been a useful if overworked trope for grasping the survival of older forms of concept formation and practice into later forms. The recovery of these long-durational forms discloses the extent to which our understanding of what we do fails to respond to more than the surface of practice or its moment.

One of these moments is that of "literary criticism" itself as a university discipline. If we truly believe in the value of literary study in its disciplinary form, then we might as well buckle down for the labor of examining closely what this effort actually accomplishes. My model for this kind of analysis is again Baconian, on the supposition that Bacon called for a history of knowledge that has only in the last half century become a disciplinary project in its own right. Such a history, in Bacon's prescient description, enjoins us "to inquire and collect out of the records of all time what particular kinds of learning and arts have flourished in what ages and regions of the world; their antiquities, their progresses, their migrations (for sciences migrate like nations) over the different parts of the globe; and again their decays, disappearances, and revivals. The occasion and origin of the invention of each art should likewise be observed; the manner and system of transmission and the plan and order of study and practice (*tradendi mos & disciplina; colendi & exercendi ratio instituta*)."[3] Bacon declares this history of learning to be unfortunately lacking—not surprisingly because it implies a kind of metaknowledge, a history not of what is known but of how knowledge was produced and transmitted. The tools for such a history did not exist in Bacon's time, but we do now have models for a synoptic history of knowledge in the work of Michel Foucault, Peter Burke, Anthony Grafton, and many other scholars. I will not adhere to any one of these models in particular, though I have been influenced by many of them, nor am I interested in summarizing the "history of criticism." My purpose is rather to understand the reason of literary study as it emerges from the long-durational history of literature in the Baconian sense, as one of the "kinds of learning and arts" that have "flourished" in certain "ages and regions of the world." The terms of Bacon's project are of particular utility: literary study is at once a kind of *learning* and the cultivation of an *art*. The rationales will confirm this dual aspect of the discipline as, in more modern language, a combination of positive knowledge and cognitive training.

I do not assert that the schema to follow is exhaustive or that there are not other ways to describe the conceptual structures that underlie the discipline. But we must begin somewhere, and so I propose for consideration these five rationales:

1. Linguistic/Cognitive
2. Moral/Judicial
3. National/Cultural
4. Aesthetic/Critical
5. Epistemic/Disciplinary

3. Francis Bacon, *De dignitate et augmentis scientiarum, Translations of the Philosophical Works*, 5: 300.

This enumeration might appear to be both familiar and unfamiliar. The conceptual domains represented obviously do not correspond in any direct way to the areas of topical interest that currently dominate the discipline. The rationales operate at an infrastructural level of conceptual organization, deeper than, for example, period specialization, or topical foci. But, as we shall see, the rationales do not disallow the projects that go by all the familiar names in our discipline. On the contrary: these projects always express one or more of the rationales, which sustain teaching and scholarship even when they are not explicitly invoked.

A second point to be underscored before I look at the rationales individually is that they constitute very roughly a time line. The linguistic/cognitive and moral/judicial rationales are the oldest, the epistemic/disciplinary the most recent. The third and fourth rationales, the national/cultural and the aesthetic/critical, can be dated to the early modern period. This historical unfolding of the rationales can be recovered by means of a metaphorically geological effort, which is not the same as tracing the sources or influences of particular ideas. It involves rather exposing the concepts and practices built into the infrastructure of the discipline by procedures of transmission and refunctioning.

Finally, my naming of the rationales with paired concepts requires some word of explanation. It might have been adequate to assign the rationales a single name, which would be the first term in each pairing. But the second term allows me to specify the rationales in such a way as to indicate a little more precisely the programmatic implications of the first term. Even so complicated, the rationales as I have enumerated them in this schema are necessarily abstract, merely a schema. In order to keep the schema as simple as possible, I refrain from offering examples of scholarly work for the rationales, as this procedure would have sunk my effort under the weight of bibliography. But my hope is that the schema will bring out or make visible the conceptual infrastructure of literary study, the immaterial analogue of departmental offices and classrooms. This conceptual infrastructure is equivalent to what we would otherwise call an *institution*, a structure that organizes practice. We have been living in this institution so long that we no longer see it.

The Linguistic/Cognitive Rationale

The first rationale, as I have already remarked, has the deepest roots in Bacon's *historia litterarum* by virtue of demarcating a selection within the total production of written artifacts; at its origin, this selection was nothing other than a claim to *preservation*. The success of preservation, however, was subject to contingencies of innumerable kinds, related both to the fragility of material inscription and to the vicissitudes of human history. By chance or design, a body of writing survived, in which preservation constituted a de facto form of canonization. In the modern world, by contrast, in which archives in electronic form are potentially infinite and eternal, the canonical motive is more difficult to assert and sometimes almost desperate. Preservation and canonization no longer converge.

Looking back over the history and prehistory of literary study, a very large fact emerges: the delimitation of literature selects certain language artifacts that engage the *medium of writing itself* in an elaborated practice. I introduce the concept of "medium" into the argument here because, as we shall see, it is only this concept that makes sense of the aggregation of works in a possible history of literature. Literary works make a claim for recognition, not only in the sense of being documents but in another more elusive sense. The electronic medium has compelled us to recognize something about the medium of writing that is very difficult to appreciate fully, which is that the forms and genres of writing have usually been imposed upon writing after the fact, as a means of organizing an otherwise overwhelming accumulation. Writings in antiquity that we would assign today to categories such as "physics" or "theology" seem to belong to literature in the delimited sense; we continue to read these works for their interest *as writing*. The same cannot be said of later works in such disciplines as physics or theology, which are clearly distinguished from literature in the manner of their composition and the modes of their transmission and reception. Here is the first clue to the history of literature: the concept of "literature" changes continually according to a time line with a long periodicity, but *generally in the same direction*, toward the exclusion of more and more genres of writing.

No individual or group determines this history, but surveying its millennial trajectory, we can see that the works descending to us from the premodern era are far more generically diverse than the writing that defines "literature" today. This body of premodern writing survived by virtue of being *sufficiently wrought*, that is, having crossed a certain threshold of interest as specimens of writing. This threshold in antiquity was not necessarily marked by any explicit judgment of a separable "aesthetic" quality of the writing; the works that elicited the motive of preservation were more likely regarded as *doing something well*. The notion of "sufficiently wrought," as a minimal description of this accomplishment, can be further specified as the equivalent of a *techné*, an art. Although it was difficult in the earliest years of writing to distinguish this art from its material instantiation—the preparation of surfaces and instruments of inscription and the arduous task of mastering the visual symbols of inscription—this distinction was in fact the most important condition of preservation. This is why the works preserved include examples of poetry, drama, and romance but also history, laws, devotional and prophetic writing, prayer, philosophy, letters, medical treatises, and many other kinds of writing. These works draw a sometimes blurry, sometimes bold, line of demarcation from the vast production of writing in the millennia since human beings have engaged in this practice.

The possibility of raising the practice of writing to the level of an art was not new with writing, but was analogically extended from the older, more advanced arts of speaking in metrical or nonmetrical modes, poetry or oration. These verbal arts (sometimes accompanied by music) were already the repository of stories and of performative speech that human beings admired and wanted to remember. In this aboriginal moment, disappearing into an irrecoverable past, the history of literature finds its first rationale, as *an art of writing parallel to an art of speaking*. Writing in this sense was not the "representation" of speech, but its companion art. The arts of speaking took as their material substance the spoken language, alongside which arose the art made possible by the technology of inscription. The Greeks named this artifactual potential of language *poiesis*, from which we derive the first of the names of literature. All of this is too well known to belabor further, but it is the ultimate ground of literary study and needs to be so acknowledged.

The concept of *techné* or "art" is not equivalent to our notion of the "high arts," such as painting, music, or literature. Nor is the concept of "art" translated adequately by "skill," which is the usual point of entry for pedagogic theory. The arts, as I will understand them here, following Greek usage, refer to cognitive abilities and not to the objects that such abilities might bring into existence. Our notion of the "cognitive," which was not available in antiquity, is closer to what the Greeks meant by art than the English word "skill." From that perspective, literary study takes as its object not only language in the largest sense of a universal human phenomenon, but *artifactual language* in particular, that is, language wrought into object. The early institution of this artifactuality discloses the nature of the relation between written artifacts and language itself, or language as a *substance* of art. This relation does not tell us everything we need to know about language, which has endless other functions. But the artifice of writing, its technicity, institutes a specific *relation* to language, a working upon it that requires cognitive abilities that have to be taught, that are beyond intuitive practice. What Bacon calls "literature" is the result of this working upon language.

In denominating a "linguistic/cognitive" rationale, I mean to indicate, then, that the study of literature is the site for the development of modes of cognition specific to language use. These modes refer to potentialities in all the modes of language use—*listening, speaking, reading,* and *writing*—when these practices are wrought beyond their intuitive base.[4] Listening and speaking can be paired as the cognitive abilities that must be developed in order to respond to, or to create, highly wrought instances of speech. Reading and writing have notional zero degrees in the forming of letters and their "decoding," but beyond this zero degree lie cognitive abilities that must be intensively developed in order to understand or to create wrought instances of writing. This systematic analogy of speaking and writing in the language arts constitutes a rationale for literary study that is immense in its aim, hardly in need of exaggerating its effects, because it transformed the world.

On the one hand, I suspect that this rationale must seem merely obvious, and that is as it should be. On the other hand, I would ask why this rationale does not come immediately to the lips of literary scholars when they feel compelled to describe or defend what they do. It is as though we no longer see what we do, even though we have always been engaged in the transmission of this art. Perhaps the cognitive abilities I describe are assumed by the university professoriate as the mission of the lower levels of the educational system; if so, I would insist that this assumption is a grievous mistake. These modes of cognition are capable of development at every stage of literary study in a program of study that is, or should be, *continuous* from the earliest to the latest phases of the educational system. In any case, the cognitive/linguistic rationale has an obvious relation to "cognitive studies," which has recently become a lively field of research in the literary disciplines. There is no reason why this research should not be reconnected to the origins of literary study in antiquity.

It might be said that some version of the rationale I have described is foundational for all the disciplines. But the disciplines are founded not only on the distinction of object but on the cognitive abilities developed specifically in the study of that object. This is, to recall the argument of chapter 1, an occasion of specialization, which has the possible or inevitable cost for each cognitive project of underdeveloping some other aspect of our mental function. That is certainly the case for literary study, which neglects

---

4. The presence of "listening" among these faculties will perhaps give pause, as less likely than the other practices to be given programmatic treatment. I think it is safe to assume that rhetoric, as the art of speaking, entailed a tacit process of educating auditors in the best means of listening to artful speech. The four practices I discuss here are, in my view, inseparable in theory, as they should be in practice.

cognitive functions that are important for other disciplines, such as those founded on mathematical thinking. Still, no one can deny the importance of language arts among the modes of cognition. In this context, literary study has an enviable position that is sometimes even acknowledged in the university curriculum, in the centrality of English or foreign language study, the peculiar and not wholly complimentary way in which teachers of reading and writing can be regarded as "essential." Literary study can at the same time be assigned the contrary social value as a "luxury," a contradiction that will be addressed below in my discussion of the epistemic rationale. While this essential relation to language arts is "served" in other ways by other disciplines, there should be no need for literary study to justify what might seem otherwise the merely pleasurable task of reading novels or, relatedly, why scholars are concerned with such apparently trivial matters as the caesura in the heroic couplet. These practices of the discipline can always be reconnected to their roots in the "history of literature" and more deeply to the cognitive aims of the discipline in its engagement with artifactual language.

In antiquity, the cognitive basis of literary study was in some respects more obvious than it is today, despite the absence of a psychological lexicon comparable to our own, because the practical activities associated with literary study were organized coherently by a single program of language study. It is worth recalling briefly how this curriculum arranged the arts of language, not in order to resurrect it, but in order to understand the paradox that arises from the specialization of knowledge discourses. As different language-related subjects and practices were assigned to different disciplines or teaching cohorts, progress was accelerated for individual disciplines but at the cost of losing touch with the cognitive foundation of *all* the language-related disciplines.

The example of what was called *grammatica* in Roman antiquity will demonstrate this point. Both "grammar" and "rhetoric" were devised by the Greeks and Romans as organized programs for the transmission of linguistic knowledge, the former corresponding to the couplet of reading/writing, the latter to listening/speaking. I will set aside the subject of rhetoric for the present to consider "grammar," which has been reduced in modernity to a small part of what it once was: a total program for the teaching of reading and writing. In his study of *grammatica* and its broad signification in Roman antiquity, Martin Irvine remarks that "*grammatica* reveals the extent to which modern forms of textuality and critical discourses are part of longer suppressed or forgotten histories." He further describes *grammatica* as a "deep, but now historically unconscious, layer in modern uses of writing and texts."[5] *Grammatica* consisted of four main parts: *lectio*, rules for reading, recitation, construing, and other related practices; *ennarratio*, rules for interpretation; *emendatio*, rules for establishing the authenticity of texts; and *iudicium*, the critical evaluation of texts. What we mean today by grammar, the notion of "correct" or conventional norms of speech or writing, does not even appear in this scheme, though it is given a place elsewhere in rhetoric. The various practices that constitute literary study today can be traced to these precursors, but running along parallel tracks that do not necessarily intersect or converge. Interpretation, textual editing, evaluative judgments (criticism)—these are functions that have been distributed to distinct cohorts. The question for us is not whether the specialization of tasks in literary study is justified, but whether the common cognitive basis of these tasks can be, to draw a lesson from Irvine, unforgotten.[6]

The discipline of "English" today usually assigns the teaching of reading and writing to distinct cadres, which have been structured in ways that institutionalize unequal status and compensation. In response to this asymmetry, the composition professoriate asserts its disciplinary autonomy by identifying with rhetoric, despite the orientation of rhetoric originally to performative speech. This represents a distortion that was probably impossible to avoid, perhaps even to rectify. I have considered in chapters 5 and 11 above the complex moment of transfer between speech and writing that gave birth to composition, but my point here is that this event created incoherence in the curriculum of English or, rather, produced a ratio of coherence to incoherence that had unintended consequences. I take note of the problem as an instance of how difficult it has become to see the scope of the linguistic/cognitive rationale, which ought to be inclusive of both writing and reading.

The relation between literary study and disciplines such as "media studies" and "communications" is another instance of incoherence in the formation of disciplines. These two disciplines have demarcated objects of study that might well be integrated conceptually with a "history of literature." Indeed, this is a matter of some urgency for literary study, as literature in its delimited sense inhabits a world of proliferating media that perform many functions of entertainment, edification, and information once

---

5. Martin Irvine, *The Making of Textual Culture: "Grammatica" and Literary Theory, 350–1100* (Cambridge: Cambridge University Press, 1994), 21.

6. Absent from the program of *grammatica* is "translation," which names a practice of immense importance and complexity, and which has become a distinct specialization for moderns.

nearly exclusive to genres of writing. If literary study does not in the near future succeed in establishing a more engaged and rationalized relation to the system of the media, its place within that system will continue to contract. Literature itself is a medium, a subset of the medium of writing, and a medium in which questions about the future of writing can be explored. Writing is not going away, but neither is it staying the same.

If the theoretical effort to bring literature into relation to the media system fails, literature will continue to contract in *social* significance, just as it has contracted *generically* for our incoming students, who sometimes simply equate literature with the form of the novel. This generic contraction is a remarkable reversal of the earlier identification of literature with the form of poetry, which even as late as the beginning of the twentieth century prevented the novel from being taught in literature courses at all. And let us recall too that poetry was once refracted into dozens of genres that have all but disappeared in modern practice. A "poem" today exists only in a form descending from the Romantic lyric, the remnant of an atrophied genre system. Such long-durational shifts have become almost invisible in the discipline, as the organization of the curriculum has turned away from the history of literature. The recovery of that history in something closer to its Baconian sweep is, I suggest, a possible way forward for the discipline. At the origin of that history, after all, is the *first* technical medium, writing. The arts of reading and writing were arguably the first versions of media studies in Western education. These arts are equally the deepest foundation for the future development of literary study.

The Moral/Judicial Rationale

The moral/judicial rationale is as old as the linguistic/cognitive, but it subjects the accumulation of writing to greater selection. Those artifacts of writing that concern human actions insofar as such actions can be *judged* constitute a large portion of surviving writing, though far from the whole of it. At the same time, this selection of writing is still quite a long way from the modern conception of literature. The moral/judicial rationale informs a body of writing in antiquity that includes (again, to take my examples from ancient Greece), philosophical works such as Plato's *Republic* or Aristotle's *Nicomachean Ethics*, as well as nominally "literary" works such as the Homeric epics and Athenian drama. To these kinds of writing, we can add the form that straddles writing and speech: the "oration," the generic instantiation of rhetoric. The occasions of rhetoric in ancient Greece—the forensic, the deliberative, and the epideictic—largely involved moral judgments, expressed in highly structured arguments. The commonality of the judicial motive across these forms of writing and occasions of speech raises a question about the notion that works of literature have a *special* relation to the moral or ethical domain. This assumption is programmed into the teaching of literature from the moment of its introduction to children, when the first genuinely interpretive efforts in response to a narrative take the form of identifying "the moral of the story." Of course, I am acknowledging that "literature" for most readers today means "narrative." Some nonnarrative genres are less obviously motivated by explicit moral aims, which is not to say that such aims are ever entirely absent but that action capable of being judged as right or wrong has the status of a manifest *content* in most narrative writing. The possibility that such content might be less conspicuous in genres such as lyric poems suggests that the moral/judicial rationale has a relation to form or genre that requires further clarification. This observation in turn reminds us that moral issues are foregrounded to lesser degrees in the visual arts and in forms of music without words.

The moral/judicial rationale is characterized by its prevalence in works of literature, especially narrative, but also by its many analogues in other forms of discourse, such as the law, which is virtually coterminous with moral concerns. In antiquity, the parts of an oration in forensic rhetoric included a *narratio*, or "story of the case" which, despite the claim to be a statement of facts, shared the discursive signal of narrative with what we now call literature. Those who presented legal cases in antiquity (as still today) understood that this presentation needed to possess some of the pleasurable and cohesive features of fictional narration. The commonality of motive and technique across different forms and occasions of discourse tells us why Bacon's concept of the "history of literature" remains valid even after the forms of writing and speaking have been divided up among the disciplines. It is worth exchanging our disciplinary spectacles for a moment to recall that for scholars in "classics," it is still common to include works such as Plato's *Republic* in the category of literature. For vernacular literary study, that inclusive perspective is less available, though not wholly out of bounds with respect to writers such as Plato (translated), and a few other philosophers in the Western tradition. In any event, the movement of philosophy in the disciplinary era away from literature (or vice versa) reminds us of the difference *argument* makes in philosophical discourse. The relative absence of argument in fictional narrative encourages readers to rely on their intuitive responses. As teachers of literature know very well, younger readers are inclined to trust their judgment on matters of right or wrong, good or evil, and can be quite resistant to moral ambiguity or moral dilemma, which call for suspending judgment until positions can be deliberated. The difficulty of moving beyond intuitive response is further exacerbated by canons of realist narration that are widely assumed for all fictional narrative and that tempt readers to reduce moral issues to a question of liking or disliking characters, the standard we now know by the term "relatability."

Moving beyond intuitive responses to narrative—to say nothing of other genres of literature—entails directing attention to the fact of *representation* in literary works. Representation generates problems of interpretation that are different from the judgment of real human actions and not always resolvable with the logical resources of philosophical or legal argument. In this context, we might revise our suggestion that narrative is a signal of literature; it would be more accurate to say that representation is this signal. Unless interpreters attend continually to the fact of representation, judgment can default to its intuitive base, where it often echoes contemporary norms and biases. To this point I shall return.

The history of responses to representation tells us that interpreters frequently stumble over this question, perhaps even Plato himself, the greatest critic of representation, despite (or because of) his reliance on narrative in his philosophy. Here I would like to borrow an insight into the relation between representation and moral judgment from Shakespeare's *Hamlet*, a play that famously confounds the relation between the representation of its title character and the work that goes by his name. In the scene of instruction to the players, the prince offers a rather platitudinous version of the moral/judicial rationale, asserting that the purpose of playing is "to hold, as 'twere, the mirror up to nature, to show virtue her own feature, scorn her own image, and the very age and body of the time his form and pressure (*Hamlet*, 3.2.24–26)." These high-sounding lines declare a moral aim for the drama belied by the story Shakespeare himself is telling. Hamlet's play within the play, "The Mouse-Trap," disastrously fails to hold a mirror up to Claudius, who sees in Hamlet's play not a reflection of his own evil deeds but a taunting declaration of Hamlet's desire to kill him. Shakespeare understood very well that the moral/judicial rationale has interpretive complications that arise from the nature of representation itself.

The moral/judicial rationale is ubiquitous in literary study, the obvious opening gambit for much interpretation, as well as the occasion for the conceptual break that brings representation into view. This break is not to be understood, however, as a moment or an epiphany; it is rather a process, very uneven for most readers of literature. Teachers know that the impulse to judge characters in literature is difficult to resist and that it often precipitates judgment of the work. Such an outcome alerts us to the fact that the moral/judicial rationale can be heavy-handed, an overwriting of the literary work by unexamined moral attitudes. Moreover, the moral norms of earlier societies often strike us as immoral in themselves, a fact that can elicit a dismissive response to older works of literature but should be the motive for a deeper inquiry into the historicity of moral precepts. Only a little progress in this direction would reveal, for example, the difficulty of distinguishing between custom and morality in the narratives of earlier societies. Custom presses upon behavior with the same force as morality and tends only to become distinguishable from morality after changes in the society rob it of its power. Moral precepts then appear to be universal by contrast to the local embeddedness of custom. Another turn of the screw brings us to the vertiginous threshold of relativizing all moral systems, as Nietzsche sets out to do in *The Genealogy of Morals.*

The latter possibility points in the direction of what we now call "critique," in one version of which moral systems themselves are capable of being judged as screens for systems of oppression, or in the familiar term, as ideology. With critique, another conceptual break is inaugurated: it is no longer a question of judging individual human actions in a narrative but of exposing the social structures that produce effects of exploitation or oppression. These structures transcend the agency of characters and even of authors, but they are supposed to be reflected or represented in literary texts and so bring representation itself into question. Whether in the guise of ideology critique, or other "suspicious" modes of analysis, this version of the moral/judicial rationale aims to reveal the complicity of literary texts in social effects that can be adversely judged. This is a question of considerable complexity, which I have discussed at length in part 1 of this volume. Here I would only insist that it is better to acknowledge frankly the essentially moral impulse behind what we call critique. On the other hand, I would caution that the "postcritical" movement in literary study, discussed in chapter 3, risks authorizing a regression to the baseline of readers' intuitive moral judgments, which can lead to a judgment against the work as severe as that of critique. For both critique and its naïve analogue, there is the same temptation to conflate the moral *contents* of a literary work with its moral *effects.* This is a problem with no easy solution, given that the moral/judicial rationale is an ineradicable component of response to literature.

This reflection on the relation of the moral/judicial rationale to critique is intended to clarify the reason for my speaking of a "moral/*judicial*" rather than a "moral/*critical*" rationale. I have reserved the term "critical" instead for the programmatic component of the "aesthetic" rationale, returning the terms "critical" and "critique" to their early modern origin in the judgment of literary or other works of art. Disambiguating the judicial and the critical will, I hope, only momentarily perplex the reception of my schema. The notion of the aesthetic, introduced prematurely here, reminds us that in antiquity there was no such concept and that writing tended *universally* to be judged in moral terms. Whether a work was "good" or "bad" might involve concepts that we would call aesthetic, such as the notion of "beauty," but judgment ultimately rested on the determination of whether a work discriminated appropriately between good and evil or was conducive to good actions.

The domination of the moral over other terms of judgment has been a continuous feature of the reception of literature, and it would be tedious to produce examples in any number. Let it suffice to note that some works of literature have been appropriated wholly for the function of moral exemplum, such as Harper Lee's *To Kill a Mockingbird*, which is only distinctive by virtue of performing this exemplary function so well. I would, however, like to consider further one instance of how literary works themselves problematize the moral/judicial rationale, this taken from the later Middle Ages. In *The Canterbury Tales*, Chaucer connects two words that are suggestive for the purpose of exploring the entailments of the moral/judicial rationale: these words are *sentence* (meaning moral axiom) and *solas* (referring to a kind of pleasure, such as we might take from a story). We first hear these words when the host, who proposes that the pilgrims each tell a tale on the road to Canterbury, offers to reward the pilgrim who tells "Tales of best sentence and most solas." These words recur at other moments in *The Canterbury Tales*, providing an abbreviated poetics for the work as a whole. Such a poetics is helpful to bear in mind because the tales vary so widely in genre and tone, from the most scurrilous to the most serious, from the dirty jokes of the Miller and the Reeve to the sermons of the Pardoner and the Parson. We might expect the pilgrims to prefer the mode of *solas*, as more entertaining, but in fact, they like both kinds of story. At one moment in the frame narrative, in advance of the Pardoner's turn to tell a tale, they seem to express fatigue with the joke-like stories and beg the Pardoner to give them "some moral thing." Chaucer is aware that a choice is being made between modes of narration that appear to be contradictory. In the famous "retraction," he rejects the scurrilous tales altogether, deferring to the moral superiority of *sentence*. (I set aside the question of whether Chaucer intended his retraction seriously.) The "Retraction's" nod to an unforgiving moralism casts a curious light in retrospect on the concept of *solas*, as a signal of the literary artifact. The problem is that although this pleasure is most conspicuous in the tales that tend toward the comic, it is just as much an effect of the tales that foreground *sentence*. This is so because it is representation itself that produces *solas*, collapsing thereby the moral contradiction between *solas* and *sentence*.

The question emerging here is the adequacy of the moral/judicial rationale to apprehend all of the possible ways in which the effects of literary works might be described. If pleasure is regarded as incompatible with the "sententious" motive, or at best as the sweet shell of a narrative's moral kernel (in the immemorial trope), literary works that seem wholly dedicated to producing the effect of pleasure bring representation itself into suspicion. The effect of *solas* has implications down the line, as it were, for the history of literature, most conspicuously in the problem of the "immoral" work. As I have hinted, the possibility of so constructing literary works reaches all the way up into the stratosphere of critique, where works of literature are judged as moral agents themselves, collusive or resistant as the case may be. It requires a fine sense of how to qualify the impulse to moral judgment in order not to imperil representation itself. In other social sites than that of literary study, there are fewer reservations about judging representation. The imputation of moral agency to representation, for example, can elicit censorship by the state; this is what critique looks like when it is exercised by the state. The state's mode of critique is by no means only an expression of reactionary politics. Its clumsiness as a mode of interpretation can ensnare one generation's moral exemplum in another's net of judgment; a witness here would be Mark Twain's *Huckleberry Finn*.

Solas and *sentence* are also generic signals, suggesting that the question of genre is a locus for deepening our understanding of the moral/judicial rationale. It would be possible to show, for example, that there is a royal road from genre to critique. At the furthest limit of this generic modalization, all literary works become moral allegories, elaborate analogues of their social worlds, Hamlet's "age and body of the time." For the moral/judicial rationale, *sentence* is the chief purpose of all literary genres, even those "low mimetic" genres, such as the novel, which otherwise might be regarded as dedicated to pleasure, to *solas*. Interestingly, the tendency of modern scholarship is to favor genres like the novel as opposed to those genres in which moral aims are explicit, as in satire or the "moral essay." The novel challenges scholars to devise subtler, more allegorical modes of interpretation, which transmit moral effects through the filter of the "social," or the "political." There may be a clue here to the delimitation of literature in modernity, the contraction of its domain. The dispersion of moral agency seems to be a feature of fictional forms of writing that other genres do not necessarily exhibit to the same degree.

It is safe to say that the moral/judicial rationale is inextricable from literary study; conversely, this is why literary examples are so often invoked in arguments about moral issues. To this I would add that the judgment of moral action has a bias toward the question of genre that is worth pondering further. Insofar as genres might be distributed on a spectrum according to the degree of their *moral seriousness*, the genre system itself draws attention both to the necessity and to the limitations of the moral/judicial rationale. The distinction between "tragedy" and "comedy," for example, is our shorthand acknowledgement of the contradiction that drives generic oscillation in the history of literature. The tendency toward the mutual exclusion of tragic and comic modes dominates the judgment of literary works (as also work in the other arts) and subjects them to a preliminary ranking that is questionable. Can comic works ever be as great as tragic? There is something wrong with this question, the residue of our continued struggle with the moral/judicial rationale. Without crediting Aristotle's solution to this problem in the *Poetics*, we might recover from his argument what seems to be its enduring remainder, the pleasure experienced in tragic action itself. This problem has never in fact been resolved, but the example of tragedy confirms the entanglement of the moral/judicial rationale with the problem of genre. Historically, the effort to specify the nature of the pleasure elicited by highly wrought forms of writing—both comic and tragic, and everything in between—was not possible until the invention of a discourse, the aesthetic, addressed to the uniqueness of that pleasure. That discourse did not solve the problem but at least clarified its scope.

The National/Cultural Rationale

The concepts of *nation* and *culture* in the senses familiar to us today did not become current in Western society until the latter end of the early modern period. The rationale I name by linking these terms is very different from the former two, both in the fact of having its origin in modernity and in its early focus on "national literatures." These literatures are the complement of that other object of literary study, national languages. Further, we understand both the literature and the language of nations as belonging to a larger domain of *culture*. "National literature" seems properly a subset of "national culture," the language, beliefs, customs, manners, rituals, values, traditions, and even "character" of a people. But as Raymond Williams and Benedict Anderson have argued in different ways, the vernacular literatures of European nations preceded and were a condition for the modern conceptualization of culture, as also of the nation. Thereafter, everything that constituted culture, including literature, could be seen as an expression of the culture of the nation. On the horizon of this development, the convergence of culture and nation resulted in the form of expression we know as "nationalism." It is through the filter of this expression that we look back on the history of national literatures.

Insofar as it excludes writing in Greek and Latin, the idea of national literature implies a radical selection from the totality of Bacon's "history of literature." Vernacular literacy gave a new group of readers, no longer literate in the classical languages, access to writing, despite the fact that vernaculars such as English were divided into many dialects, some of which were unintelligible to others. Over time, vernacular publication muted, as it were, aspects of dialectal difference, encouraging readers to imagine that the language they encountered in written English was the true embodiment of the language. The idea of the "English language" circulated as an abstraction from the reality of language use and a precursor to the even more abstract entity that is the "English nation." The same process of abstraction governed the other modern languages, but for convenience of exposition I will continue to use English as my reference case in discussing the national/cultural rationale.

Although the copula that gives us "national literature" is easy to call into question on empirical grounds, it nonetheless established a rationale for literary study that has never been wholly superseded. The desire to move beyond it is very strong in the literary disciplines today, a development acknowledged in the preface to The Modern Language Association's volume of 2007, *Introduction to Scholarship in Modern Languages and Literatures*: "In recent years, many scholars in modern languages and literatures have questioned the conceptual coherence of national literatures and have sought new ways to understand the circulation of languages and literatures both transnationally and within national contexts."[7] This moment of reckoning in the history of the discipline was inevitable and even in some ways belated. In this section I would like first to describe the operation of the national/cultural rationale in predisciplinary and disciplinary phases of literary study and, second, to assess the waning of the rationale in the present context of globalized cultural transmission.

The notion of the "transnational" that literary scholars favor at present is at once a repudiation of the "national" and at the same time an invocation of it. As this contradiction is unavoidable, it seems to me necessary to acknowledge this historical condition as crucial to the emergence of literature as an object of organized study. In the millennia prior to the emergence of nation-states, "nation" and "people" were interchangeable concepts; "nation" referred only to a people with ethnic or other characteristics shared with those who lived not too far away.[8] If the study of national

---

7. David Nichols, *Introduction to Scholarship in Modern Languages and Literatures* (New York: Modern Language Association of America, 2007), vii.

8. On this earlier sense of nation, it is worth recalling the oft-cited line of Macmorris, in Shakespeare's *Henry V*, responding to a perceived slight in Fluellen's reference to his

literatures today is no longer implicated in *nationalist* agendas—happily so, in the view of the professoriate—literary study is still oriented by its antinationalism to the *existence* of the nation-state. Further, the early modern reconceptualization of the "nation" was the ground for the emergence of the discourse of *culture*, which has become a crucial concept for literary study. Linked by vernacular language, the compound of nation and culture constituted the rationale for the study of literature in the early modern period and was the precursor of its disciplinary form. This is why I have named this rationale the "national/cultural" and why I believe we must recognize even "postcolonial studies" as grounded in the national/cultural rationale. Literary study can only liberate itself from its bond to national languages by thinking through its own origins.

Although medieval society had no "nations" in the modern sense, it had "states" in great number, kingdoms and empires that sprawled across territories occupied by people of different ethnic self-identification and speaking different languages. The hypothetical union embodied in the later form of the "nation-state" confronted enormous obstacles to its formation, perhaps above all the multiplicity of languages. Early modern states set about to promote a dialect of the vernacular as an instrument of administration, a motive that did not initially involve the promotion of a national literature or national consciousness. And the learned elites remained, until very late in this story, committed to pan-European Latin and Greek literacy as the linguistic marker of their cultural entitlement. In these circumstances, one has to speak of "English" as an ideal, even a fantasy, that projected a social unity in advance of the nation itself. The vernacular language had in some way to become "national" before the nation-state could will itself into existence.

And yet efforts to cultivate something like a national vernacular began as early as Dante, with landmark statements later by Joachim du Bellay in France and Sir Philip Sidney in England. Literature became the means to press language into a national form, long before this goal could be formulated in fully political terms. Histories of literature in English, such as Sidney offers in his *Defense of Poesy*, describe an object in some ways more real than the English "nation." England was still in Sidney's time a kingdom, or small empire, overseeing mutually hostile populations, with different cul-

---

Irish nation: "What ish my nation? Who talks of my nation?" (*Henry V*, 2.2.124–26). Shakespeare makes a point of the fact that Henry's army consists of English, Scottish, Welsh, and Irish soldiers. Henry himself was French. From William the Conqueror on, no monarch of England has been of English descent. Coincidentally, it was during Henry's reign that the English court made a transition from French to English in the conduct of its business.

tural traditions and speaking different languages. The historical priority of English literature to the concept of nation is for this reason not so much an absurdity as a condition for the conceptualization of that abstraction which is the "nation-state" of England. Once this abstraction was in place, it became possible to construct *English* literature retroactively as a *national* literature.

For a sense of the larger context of this recursive process, I turn briefly to Benedict Anderson's indispensable account of the origins of nations and nationalism, *Imagined Communities*, in which he identifies three sets of conditions operating more or less simultaneously in the wake of a transition to what he calls "print-capitalism." These conditions are: (1) the spread of writing in the vernacular, which allows for communication across popula- tions "below Latin and above the spoken vernaculars"; (2) the greater fixity of textual transmission as a result of print technology; and (3) the selection of one dialect of the vernacular as a "language of power."[9] Print-capitalism occasioned an explosion of vernacular publication in the sixteenth and seventeenth centuries, as vernacular literacy and the market for vernacu- lar writing entered into a period of mutual stimulation. Without endorsing Anderson's emphasis on print-capitalism as an exclusive causal agent—the tendency toward privileging a single vernacular dialect for literary pur- poses, for example, had already begun before the invention of the printing press—I suggest that his analysis is extremely useful for understanding the importance of vernacular writing to the experience of "national conscious- ness." The novel and the newspaper are the crucial examples in this con- text, connecting people across wide distances and differences in situation.

And yet neither the novel nor the newspaper entered into the category of writing circulating at the time as "English literature." The question of what constituted English literature was as complex in the early centuries of vernacular publication as it has become once again in our own time. We cannot take for granted that either of these terms possessed a very stable signification. Nevertheless, writing in English was sufficiently esteemed by the eighteenth century for a predisciplinary form of literary study to crys- tallize: *literary history*. Along with philology, this scholarly practice laid the basis for departments of "modern languages" in the university of the later nineteenth century. I have discussed these disciplinary forms in several of the chapters above at greater length. Here I want to observe how "English literature" came to include certain forms of writing and exclude others, evincing the contingencies that entered into conceiving the first versions of English literary history.

9. Anderson, *Imagined Communities*, 44.

Looking back on the emergent construction of English literature, we can spread out its components and consequences as a sequence of social abstractions:

vernacular speech > selected dialect > vernacular writing/publication > English literature

These four sets of terms lay down the conditions for the summary rewriting of the entire sequence as the history of English as a "national literature," a notion that was inconceivable in the early modern period. "Nation" in the modern sense was still in the future, simplifying our task for the moment. At this point, we are concerned only with the ongoing effort in the early modern period to gather writing in English within a category that made an implicit claim for the greatness of English authors; until the eighteenth century this category was not yet *literature* but the older concept of *poetry*. The category of poetry was interpolated between the concepts of vernacular writing and English literature as a kind of gatekeeper, opening or closing entry into the latter class. In operation, poetry was a weak gatekeeper but still consequential. Sidney famously argued in his *Defense* that poetry was not restricted to verse, thus making an opening for prose romances such as his own *Arcadia*. Later, the Addisonian essay would be the beneficiary of this inclusive definition. Still, the concept of poetry exerted a certain pressure on early histories of English literature in favor of verse over prose. In the eighteenth century, the bias in favor of verse made it possible to exclude both novels and newspapers from the history of literature, the two genres Anderson singles out as expressing the experience of time and space most closely resonating with an emergent consciousness of nation. It is obvious why newspapers were excluded, but novels presented a complication that would take nearly two centuries to resolve. In the meantime, novels were relegated to an ambiguous zone *between* poetry and newspapers.

The gatekeeper function of poetry can be understood as an example of what I will call "selection pressure." Although this notion sounds vaguely Darwinian, my point is simply to underscore the impersonality of the selection process, which is removed from the control of individual agents. Any candidate for inclusion in a history of English literature had to meet certain requirements of genre and language, even before judgments of quality entered in. These requisites were determined above all by the modeling function of classical literature, which set a standard for imitation that was quite difficult to meet and often ignored by writers of the sixteenth and seventeenth centuries. The "classicism" of the following century encouraged a somewhat stricter adherence to classical norms, but this selection pressure proved even weaker than the bias in favor of poetry.

The universally acknowledged superiority of Greek and Roman literature seemed also to imply that the greatest literature in human history was the earliest, a judgment that affirmed the genre system of antiquity, in which epic and tragedy occupied the highest ranks. The consequences of the classical analogy were everywhere manifest in attempts during the eighteenth century to write the history of English literature. The analogy gave epic and tragedy an advantage that was difficult for other genres to overcome; it also implicitly privileged earlier writing in English literary history, a bias that came into conflict with another standard that was equally derived from the modeling function of classical literature and was concerned not with particular authors or works but with the state of the *language*.

In England, as on the continent, humanist scholars advocated tirelessly for a purer standard of Greek and Latin transmission than was prevalent during the medieval era, a norm of linguistic refinement that was routinely transferred to vernacular writing. From the perspective of literary historians writing in the eighteenth century, it was undeniable that the English language had progressed in refinement over the preceding two centuries, a conclusion that would seem to advantage later works over earlier in any process of selection and hence to contradict the bias in favor of earlier writing. This contradiction is well known to scholars, who will recognize in my account an extremely abbreviated rehearsal of the debate between "the ancients and the moderns." I invoke this famous controversy in order to highlight the opposing selection pressures that complicated efforts to identify the best of English literature. These selection pressures privileged older literature for some reasons, later literature for others. One effect of combining these contradictory standards was the exclusion of Chaucer from the highest rank and of medieval literature generally. Although English writing of the sixteenth and seventeenth centuries was recognizably more refined than its predecessors, it was still regarded as imperfect by reason of its profusion of genres and its imperfect conformity to the stylistic norms espoused by the humanists. The category of English literature coalescing in the eighteenth century was in the end a compromise formation, selecting works *between* the Middle Ages and the eighteenth century. Literary historians of the time called this middle period "the last age."[10] A trio of poets—Spenser, Shakespeare, and Milton—emerged from this process as the greatest English poets, not without reservations about the relatively

---

10. Early references to the "last age" include Dryden, *An Essay on Dramatic Poetry of the Last Age* (1668), and Thomas Rymer, *Tragedies of the Last Age* (1678).

unpolished aspects of their language by comparison to their successors.[11] This version of literary history removed contemporary writing from consideration for canonicity on the assumption that the canonical worthiness of this writing would be confirmed in the future. In the nineteenth century, the "last age" became the age of the Addisonian essay and of a poetry that exhibited the correctness and polite elegance of Addisonian prose. It was the literature of this new "last age" that gave us "standard English," the basis for a national language.

Over time, successive drafts of literary history produced a tenuously stable configuration, a perennial present for English literature, but only at the upper end of the hierarchy, where the greatest English authors were identified. Ultimately, canonical selection made possible the conversion of great literature into a property of the nation. Anyone who has visited Westminster Abbey knows what this means. The great writers of England survive today as *national icons*. This reframing of English literature became a permanent feature of literary history after the eighteenth century, without at the same time closing the curriculum to revision. Visitors to the abbey can see that the canonical choices of the eighteenth century were followed by choices based on other principles, other selection pressures. The "last age" is a movable feast, and permits canonical selection to evolve over time. Otherwise we would not be able to explain such a gambit as F. R. Leavis's "great tradition," a canon of the novel promoting four authors to the top stratum: Austen, Eliot, James, and Conrad. Why only four? In the process of canonical selection, something like Zipf's law obtains, a principle of rank distribution that elevates a very small number of figures to the top tiers, below which other authors are disposed in rapidly declining rank.[12] At the

11. The standard reference on literary history is Wellek, *The Rise of English Literary History*. The major figures of relevance to my argument include John Dennis, *The Grounds of Criticism in Poetry*, 1704; John Upton, *Observations on Shakespeare*, 1746; Thomas Warton, *Observations on the Faerie Queene of Spenser*, 1754; Joseph Warton, *Essay on Pope, 1756*; Richard Hurd, *Letters on Chivalry and Romance*, 1762; Hugh Blair, *Dissertation on the Poems of Ossian*, 1763; Thomas Percy, *Reliques of Ancient English Poetry*, 1765; Thomas Warton, *History of English Poetry*, 1774.

12. Zipf's law is a discovery in the statistical analysis of natural languages that the frequency of word use in a natural language is inversely proportional to its rank. That is, the most frequent word is twice as frequent as the second most frequent word, three times as frequent as the next most, and so forth. Although the canon does not strictly follow the rank distribution of words in a natural language, the tendency of ranking to fall rapidly from the top figures is interestingly resonant with Zipf's law and suggests a quantitative pressure on canonical selection of which we should be aware. For a discussion of the "trio" of Spenser, Shakespeare, and Milton, see Jonathan Brody Kramnick, *Making the English Canon: Print-Capitalism and the Cultural Past, 1700–1770*, 2.

top, there is only room for a few figures, as with the eighteenth century's trio of Spenser, Shakespeare, and Milton. We have only to advance the calendar to our own time to see that Spenser and Milton have both suffered a significant loss in readership, if not the esteem of period specialists, but other writers have replaced them, most notably Jane Austen. Among earlier writers, Chaucer has displaced Spenser, a shift in status that might be attributed in part to a selection bias for the novel, or more precisely, for realist narrative (many social determinations hide behind this bias). The consequent change in the status of an author such as Spenser tells us nothing about the interest of *The Faerie Queene* or Spenser's other works; the same can be said of Milton, whose influence in literary history was immense, for very good reasons. In the cases of both Spenser and Milton, their status depends as much on the status of poetry itself as on the quality of their work. The churn in rank distribution tells us about the *present*, about the selection biases that prevail today, among which the extraordinary inversion of the relation between poetry and prose is most conspicuous.

The literary history composed in the eighteenth century, the first draft of "English literature," attempted to bring literature and language into a relation of congruence, which proved to be difficult at best. Not surprisingly, countercurrents began to flow, with the resurrection of much older models of English literature, oriented toward generic formations such as the "Gothic" and later to stylistic aberrations such as the "sublime." I propose now to look at these opposing forces in literary history from a more theoretical perspective, suggested by the two terms discussed earlier: *preservation* and *canonization*. These are motives of literary history, but they are, like literature and language, at cross-purposes. The goal of canonization is to select from the past for the sake of the present. The aim of preservation is to preserve everything, so that nothing from the past is lost.

The latter version of literary history descended from the seventeenth-century genre of "antiquarian" writing, of which William Camden's *Britannia* (1607) was the most famous example, and far more influential than its present reputation would suggest (Camden has a place in Westminster Abbey). For the antiquarians, every artifact or document was precious, every survival from the slow erosions or sudden storms of history. Their fascination with these survivals was uncritical, free of the canonical motive. Literary antiquarianism began in earnest in the sixteenth century, with lists of authors and biographies of poets and other writers. These researches laid the basis for a counternarrative to canonical literary history, redeeming work otherwise regarded as rude and primitive, such as the "gothic" and "romance" forms derogated by the selection bias of classicism. The strategy of preservation created a vast penumbra of literary works that were at once easy to forget but also *available* to be remembered. This archive of literary works was extremely important to subsequent canonical history. As some literary works sank into obscurity, they did not disappear altogether but suffered the ambiguous fate of preservation. These works in the shadow of the canon could always be rediscovered, even moved back into the canonical sunlight. The motives for such revisions have been many over the centuries and not always immediately based on judgments of quality. In the case of writers such as Aphra Behn or Margaret Cavendish (two not entirely arbitrary examples), works that were largely forgotten (*Oroonoko* and *The New Blazing World*) have become essential to literary history for our present moment. Examples of this sort can of course be multiplied. Such revisions necessarily introduce incoherence into the curriculum in that they represent the assertion of new selection biases in tension with the old. The *ratio* of this incoherence to the coherence that is its necessary complement is a matter of negotiation. It is not always obvious what this ratio should be, a circumstance that is reflected in the conflicting motives perennially unsettling the literary curriculum.

To the extent that preservation makes possible canonical revision and thus produces incoherence, it is both a necessary component of literary study as a discipline and a link to the social externalities of the discipline that impinge upon it and create new selection biases for canonization. The authors and works occupying the highest stratum have a certain security, but the degree of this security falls off rapidly further down the hierarchy. The excitement generated by a rediscovery is a powerful solvent of canonical security. Given this condition, we can get a better sense of the dissatisfaction troubling the national/cultural rationale at present. Let us begin by recognizing that preservation was for a long time an important support of national consciousness and by no means incompatible with the motives of canonical selection. The research of scholars in the seventeenth and eighteenth centuries into the traditions, both oral and written, rooted in folk experience, discovered a source of "Englishness" that could seem more authentic than the refined practice of canonized authors. In truth, of course, these two spheres of cultural expression were much more intertwined than the distinction between canonization and preservation would suggest. The recycling of the ballad form is a nice example of this interaction of cultural levels, famously instanced by the uptake of the ballad into the elite (and elitist) experiments of Wordsworth and Coleridge in *Lyrical Ballads*.

The different values attached to the transmission of works in the two traditions had further important historical consequences. The recovery of folk traditions was spurring new concept formation throughout Europe, most notably in the work of Herder, who refunctioned the conception of "culture," bringing language and literary expression into a new relation to the idea of a nation. This is to put the transition far too simply, but my point is to show that the idea of "national literature" is founded in both high and low domains of transmission, spanning the gap, let us say, between Pope's classical imitations and Thomas Percy's *Reliques of Ancient English Poetry.* The questions raised by this complexity of the text tradition is old; it belongs to literary history, not only in its eighteenth-century forms but properly as a subfield of literary study as a discipline. Many of the issues troubling the discipline today arise from our inattention to the long-durational dynamic of literary history, the slow or fast transformations of form and genre that alienate works of the past and so impair our understanding of the present.

No one today would deny that literature is a form of cultural expression that witnesses, in Raymond Williams's deceptively simple phrase, the "whole way of life" of a people.[13] Over the course of his career, Williams unravels the various strands of the culture concept, only to have some clever Penelope knit them up again. The concept of culture has a long bibliography attached to it, but among its myriad sites of operation, it has a point of intersection with literary history that transforms canonical selection into "national literature." This schema is always complicated by the fact of its simultaneous operation in both high and low spheres. Canonical selection supports a "high" concept of culture, a mode of cultural experience aimed at the sophistication of sensibility and judgment, and the effect of education. This sense of culture, which in its origins also expressed a certain resistance to industrial civilization, progresses through Coleridge, Carlyle, and their contemporaries and culminates in Matthew Arnold's *Culture and Anarchy.* The difficulties facing this notion of culture in its succeeding incarnations are well known and have only become more serious. On the other hand, there is the mode of cultural expression that is perceived to arise from the life of the people. The "lower" version of culture is what Percy and his like set out to preserve. This is the culture that Herder raises to theoretical consciousness and that eventuates in new disciplines, such as anthropology and archaeology. In both high and low versions, culture has become an inescapable concept, the name for every regularity of belief or practice that can be assigned to any distinguishable group whatsoever. This is the concept we confront in notions such as folk culture, popular culture, mass culture, the culture industry, and cultural elites, as well as the thou-

13. Williams, *Culture and Society,* 43.

sands of niche cultures scattered across the landscape of modernity. The radical fracturing of culture beyond even its high and low forms, of which the "culture wars" is a late expression, eventuates in a paradoxical condition for all forms of culture: it is the proliferation of cultures that dissolves cultural unities, including that of national culture.

By far the greatest consequence of this refraction has been the liberation of culture from its original task of defining the "whole way of life" of the nation. A chaotic assemblage of cultural expressions now performs this function, insofar as it possible to conceive it at all. The heterogeneity of "mass civilization" throws into sharp focus the service once provided by literature to the state as a means of projecting an English or national culture. The history of this projection can be recovered, in its aspirational form, in many dozens of educational documents between Macaulay's *Minute on Indian Education* of 1835 and the *Newbolt Report* of 1921. The citation of Macaulay reminds us of the role of English literature in colonial government but also of the unintended consequences of the attempt to impose English culture on the colonies. Some of the language taken up by anticolonial actors was transmitted with this culture, even the concept of the nation itself. This point is of considerable importance in accounting for the vicissitudes of "national literature" in literary study today.

Correlated with its political function, English literature also served in the schools as the vehicle for nationalizing the language, in the form of standard English. As I argued in *Cultural Capital*, literary works rarely set out to embody or celebrate these dual forms of cultural and linguistic nationalism. That was the task of literary pedagogy, which, when it faltered in its directly political aims, reverted to holding the line on the national language. Teachers of literature have often fallen from their role as the docents of literature to the prefects of grammar. If the cultural reality of the nation-state was supposed to be enforced through literary pedagogy, this mission was always a struggle against the real conditions of literary transmission— even in the eighteenth century, when the English had to come to terms with Swift as an Irish writer or Hume as a Scottish writer. Like many colonials, no writers in English were more scrupulously correct than Swift or Hume, but even this scrupulosity fell short of the motive of nationalism. The stresses against the seams of the nationalist motive were always felt, if not always acknowledged. With later writers such as Yeats or Joyce, and later still with authors such as Walcott or Achebe, writing in English was less serviceable than ever as a prop for British nationalism.

As objects of study today, both the English language and literature in English are global in reach. Revolutionary nationalisms have severed directly political ties of subordination to the imperial center, though not to its language, and only partially to its literature. This not to say, of course, that other modes of subjugation, both economic and military, do not continue to operate globally. It is rather to acknowledge that the situation with "culture" is more ambiguous. The transition from a national to a transnational English literature throws a cultural bridge across a political breach, enabling traffic in both directions. For that reason, the national/cultural rationale retains a certain legitimacy as the record of historical fact. The facticity of the English language and of literature in English exceeds the motive of nationalism, just as it once fell short of this motive. At the same time, the volume of literary production in English creates the conditions for a ruthless narrowing of canonical selection, with candidates drawn from dozens of nation-states rather than one. This process of revisionist selection has been underway for a very long time in the United States, which inherited the English language and British literature at the same time that it was producing a "national" literature of its own. The slow rise of American literature to parity with British literature in the United States tells us how complex and enduring is the operation of the national/cultural rationale.

Establishing a plausible ratio of coherence to incoherence in the literary curriculum will require new conceptions of the relation between language and literature in the global condition of cultural transmission. But let us admit that cultural production today is no longer principally constituted by works of literature. That place has been taken by all the forms of new media and mass media that collectively constitute national cultures and even something close to a global culture. Literature is only one medium among many, and it does far less work of representation today than other forms of mass media with global circulation.

With reference to the curriculum, I suggest that the continuity of the earliest English literature with global English is a historical fact. The curriculum should acknowledge this fact, however imperfectly "departments of English and American literature" capture the reality of literary history in its latest form as postcolonial literature. Other narratives of global dispersion must be devised for the "modern foreign languages," but I believe that these narratives would disclose their own ambivalent mutualities of influence and contradictory effects of dissemination. I discuss these contradictions as they characterize global English in chapter 8 above. For my purpose here, I want to insist that literature in English no longer belongs to one nation, neither to the imperial powers nor to the nations from which literature in English is now pouring forth. The truth of that supranational situation has been evident for a long time, at least since the American nation appropriated English literature for its own nationalist purposes. The Astor Place Riot of 1849 offers an astonishing, if violent, instance of this appropriation, when a relatively trivial dispute between a British and an American actor, performing on different stages in New York at the same time, somehow led to a riot in which nearly two dozen people died. A number of social tensions were entrained in the violence, but among these was the feeling of the Americans that Shakespeare belonged as much to them as to the British. To whom does Shakespeare belong? The riot did not answer this question, but it might serve as a caution for us in assessing the viability of the national/cultural rationale in literary study today.

The Aesthetic/Critical Rationale

The concept of the "aesthetic" entered into Western discourse by way of Alexander Baumgarten's treatise, *Aesthetica*, published in two volumes between 1750 and 1758, but it arguably refers to an aspect of human existence that is immemorial. Baumgarten launched the term on a new career by channeling the Greek term *aisthesis*, meaning sensory experience, to the context of response to natural or artificial beauty. The word was quickly embraced in European philosophy, though it has seldom been integrated fully into philosophical systems. My purpose in this section is not to argue for a particular theory of the aesthetic but to bring this term into relation with the slightly older term "criticism." The latter concept was introduced by Julius Caesar Scaliger in 1561, in a section of his *Poetici Libri Septem* entitled "Criticus," offering a comparative study of the merits of ancient authors. Scaliger latinized the Greek term *kritikos*, meaning the ability to judge, applying it to the restricted context of literary achievement. Thus defined, the word was widely adopted in the seventeenth century and soon came to define a new genre of writing, the description of the "beauties" and "faults" of literary works. The genre was first popularized by French authors, who called it *critique*; this term was anglicized by the addition of the suffix "ism."[14] Like the aesthetic, criticism might be seen as immemorial, in that it refers at base simply to judgment. The nearly concurrent appearance the new terms *aesthetic* and *criticism* suggests a new condition of culture, as the premodern West had no words adhering precisely to the narrower contexts of their use in the seventeenth century.

The first difficulty we will face in presenting the aesthetic/critical rationale is the fact that the concept of the aesthetic was and remains extremely controverted in philosophy. Even its status as a domain of philosophy is not

14. The most influential work was René Rapin, *Reflections on the Poetics of Aristotle and on the Works of the Ancient and Modern Poets*, which was translated into English in 1706 as *The Whole Critical Works of Rapin*.

always acknowledged. I will take advantage of this radical uncertainty to sidestep most debates on this subject, focusing instead on those issues connecting the aesthetic to the early history of literary criticism. The concept of the aesthetic, we may conjecture, must have responded to some need of the moment; otherwise, it would have sufficed for eighteenth-century writers to make do with the notion of "beauty," which had correlatives in every known language and in antiquity. There must have been some insufficiency in this concept that occasioned the turn to the more technical term, *aesthetic*. A similar question can be posed about the relation between the word *judgment* and its specialization in the concept of *criticism*. We know that the Greeks were keenly interested in the judgment of drama and that the performances of tragedies and comedies were actually contests, with a panel of judges to award prizes. In his *Poetics*, Aristotle attempts to raise the principle of judgment to the level of theory with criteria that were essentially generic: works were deemed successful or good that *conformed to a form*. Aristotle had no other way to establish literary form except inductively, from actual plays, and hence generic criticism from its inception was characterized by a circular logic. Until the early modern period, the judgment of literature, as of the arts in general, was oriented to this principle of conformity to form. Treatises on "poetics" assumed the primacy of genre and were designed as guides for composing in given genres. Any theorization of "beauty," as the name for what was being approbated in a play or sculpture or painting, was thus likely to return in the end to the circular principle of conformity to form.

As I suggested earlier, however, the judgment of literary work was dominated by another principle, the moral, referring not to form as such but to the representation of human action. These two principles of the moral and the formal might be reconciled, though not without some difficulty. As I noted earlier, for most purposes of judgment, it sufficed to say that a work of art was good if it induced good in those who perceived it; this moral reduction, as we have also noted, had a remainder, the pleasure that was experienced in representation itself. Such pleasure might be linked to the appearance of beauty, but in this context, the fact that beauty can be found both in nature and in products of human art is problematic for any theory of the aesthetic. The absence of immediate moral signification in the former is perhaps not fatal for linking morality and beauty, especially within the frame of a creationist theology. Still, the perception of beauty in nature raised questions that were different from those arising from the moral intentions of human art. If the perception of beauty in nature was properly the concern of aesthetics, that discourse was troubled by the question of how beauty inhered in an object of perception, such as the accidental arrangement of elements in a landscape. (Not surprisingly, landscape entered into painting at this time as a favored subject.) Kant's notion of the "subjective universality" of the perception of beauty deployed a new philosophical vocabulary in order to resolve this problem but at the cost of sacrificing the objective status of aesthetic judgment.

In the late seventeenth and early eighteenth century, both the discourse of beauty and the discourse of poetics were transformed. The discourse of beauty was folded into that of aesthetics, while poetics was displaced by criticism. Associated with these transitions and complicating them was a metaphorization of judgment in debates about the "standard of taste." In retrospect, debates about taste enabled a pivot away from the rule-bound generic system of poetics, with its principle of conformity to form. Although the standard of taste was typically defended as rational, or confirmed by the judgment of time, taste was also generally understood as the peculiar possession of certain individuals. The retreat from universal rules to an ineffable judgment might in some ways appear to be a theoretical regression, but the opposite was the case. Kant revolutionized aesthetics along just these lines in his assertion that aesthetic judgment is "without concept."

The psychologization of judgment was a condition for the transition from poetics to literary criticism, a discourse in which disagreement about the quality of a literary work was constitutive and, indeed, generative. Judgment was not a single speech act but the beginning of a debate without conclusion. Poems and plays but also paintings, sculpture, architecture, music—everything that would come to be called a "work of art"—would be submitted to debate. Although disagreement about the merits of particular authors or works was certainly possible before the early modern period, it became in this first age of criticism a pastime and a passion. A new mode of reception for literary works was emerging—in retrospect, the social condition for the aesthetic/critical rationale. This mode of reception organized criticism paradoxically as an *unorganized* proliferation of discourse about literature among those who claimed a right to judge on the basis of their ability to persuade others of their opinions. Criticism remained very close to conversation, replicating its loose style of argument. Dryden's instinct in producing the first major published work of criticism as a dialogue, his *Essay of Dramatic Poesy* (1668), confirmed this discursive condition, as did the use of the essay as the generic infrastructure for criticism in the following century.

If the essay form made possible a more refined mode of criticism, as in Addison, this mode was always, again as in Addison, a refunctioning of conversation, which ran like a murmuring stream under the published works of criticism. Pope's "Essay on Criticism" classicized the genre with its allusion to Horace's "Ars Poetica" but only by distancing the cacophony that appears full-voiced in *The Dunciad*. Closest to the oral idiom of criticism is Richard Brinsley Sheridan's comedy *The Critic* (1779), which offers portraits of two critics, Mr. Dangle and Mr. Sneer, commenting on the rehearsal of a new (and very bad) play. Mr. Dangle fancies himself the "head of a band of critics, who take upon them to decide for the whole town, whose opinion and patronage all writers solicit, and whose recommendation no manager dares refuse."[15] Though he does not write for the newspapers, Mr. Dangle's opinions have something close to the force of publication. But as Mrs. Dangle reminds her husband, whatever "the managers and authors" might think of his views, they must accede in the end to a higher authority: "The PUBLIC is their CRITIC." And yet the public could express its opinion without articulation, by purchasing or not purchasing admission to a play. The absence of articulation created the social space for the critic, a site of intellectual convection at which criticism irrupted into the public sphere.

As Sheridan understood, the critic was a new *social type*, at once a representative of the public and yet set apart from it as the purveyor of expert opinion. This expertise was, as noted in chapter 2, self-authorized, but it had a great future before it. In the seventeenth century, criticism was relatively unconcerned with religious controversy, topics in philosophy, or political debate, but in the eighteenth century, critics began to write increasingly about all of these matters, with the consequences I and other scholars have recounted. The critic occupied a unique position of authority, sustained by the popular press but otherwise unsupported by the school. The discourse of criticism made judgment a kind of expertise but without relying upon a procedure for its credentialization. Samuel Johnson conjured this figure (whom he also embodied) as *Idler 60*'s "Dick Minim," meant to show that "all can be criticks if they will."[16]

This unusual social condition obtains for criticism in some of its expressions down to the present. The division in the twentieth century between the literary professoriate and the sphere of reviewing reaffirmed a long-established differentiation of function but now rendered asymmetric by the diminished role of criticism in the public sphere and the professionalization of the literary scholar. This is a story that many others have related,

15. Richard Brinsley Sheridan, "The Critic," in *The School for Scandal and Other Plays*, ed. Eric Rump (London: Penguin Classics, 1989), 125–84.

16. Samuel Johnson, *The Works of Samuel Johnson*, 9 vols. (London: William Pickering, 1925), 4: 325.

and I allude to it here in order to bring out its implications for judgment, a universal cognitive function, also universally capable of being refined with practice. For the professoriate, aesthetic judgment has been relegated to a tacit assumption of scholarship, a condition that is often lamented but that in fact has been an enabling condition for the specialization of scholarship. Scholars have experienced the freedom from judgment as a liberation. This benefit has been undeniable, but there is also a cost to literary culture with the contraction of the sites of judgment. Surely the greatest possible distribution of informed and practiced judgment is desirable; unfortunately, the practice of judgment is difficult to train and therefore to credentialize. For that reason, the critic in the public sphere continues to be self-authorized, even today.

Conceding the difficulty of *teaching* judgment, I would nonetheless want to insist that the aesthetic/critical rationale entails just this task. Our discipline is, or should be, committed to developing the capacity to judge among readers of literature. It has been too easy for the discipline to relegate judgment to the unspoken, or even to disparage it as just a ruse of ideology. This position has become more difficult to assert in recent years. For a discipline fatigued with its usual aims—rightly or not—the aesthetic/critical rationale has recovered a certain appeal. The revival of interest in the aesthetic, though it has something of a perennial aspect, appears of late to be in earnest, a reassertion of judgment as the legitimate practice of all readers of literature—scholars, reviewers, students, and the reading public, whoever they are.

This very sketchy account of criticism in its relation to the aesthetic, and to the practice of judgment, raises certain practical questions that will be impossible to address at any length here. In a sense, my account of criticism only insists tautologically on the meaning of the word, but having said that, there is one final point that needs to be made (or underscored), concerning the grounds of judgment in the experience of pleasure. Almost always, as we have seen, this pleasure is justified when allied to moral norms. Invoking again Sheridan's play, Mr. Dangle's fellow critic, Mr. Sneer, mounts a familiar critique of public taste on the grounds, or higher ground, of moral purpose: "I am quite of your opinion, Mrs. Dangle: the theatre, in proper hands, might certainly be made the school of morality; but now, I am sorry to say it, people seem to go there principally for their entertainment" (*School for Scandal and Other Plays*, 137). Mr. Sneer is probably less scandalized than he pretends, but he puts the question in its most enduring form. His description of the theater as "entertainment" sounds like an early warning about the depravations of consumer culture. The quality of the pleasure experienced in cultural works varies, to be sure, but a theory of aesthetic pleasure should begin from the premise that all instances of this pleasure are consubstantial, regardless of whether the work at issue belongs to high or low domains of culture. The experience of aesthetic pleasure is of enormous psychological complexity, with numerous modes and intensities. Further, this pleasure is not ancillary to engagement with a work of art; it is the principal aim, which is to say that all art is entertainment. The *quality* of this aesthetic pleasure depends on many variables and is not reducible to a single principle of commensuration. In my view, there is no interest in comparing works like *Middlemarch* or *Beloved* with a television sitcom or a thriller purchased in an airport bookstore. This is not because the latter forms are "bad" but because they belong to a different locus of production and consumption. The exercise of judging the quality of any particular artifact of this sort must assume a ground of cultural similitude in order to be credible. At the same time, the *pleasure* given by these works, regardless of whether they are seen as "serious" or "trivial," has to be acknowledged as equally "aesthetic." This kind of pleasure extends across a vast domain of objects, far too differentiated in function to be ranked as though they were all attempts to produce "high art."

The best effects of aesthetic pleasure might be described with the quaint eighteenth-century term "improving," a word that has the advantage of a certain open-endedness. If we do not know exactly "what" is being improved, we know that the reason we have literature is that we are changed by our experience of reading it. Whatever other benefits the work of literature might offer—and there are many possible names for these—the experience of pleasure is evidence, like radiant heat from an oven, that something is happening in the reading mind. We can only observe such mental events indirectly, but conceding this ignorance, we might take a hint from Kant's conjecture that pleasure in natural beauty is the experience of "free play" among the cognitive faculties. This was an ingenious hypothesis, whether or not it holds up under neurological scrutiny. We are still a long way from understanding the psychological basis of pleasure in the experience of natural beauty, much less the experience of pleasure in works of art. Kant's preference for examples drawn from nature simplifies the task of explanation for him by restricting it to the sphere in which aesthetic experience is unschooled, the intuitive possession of all human beings. The induction of pleasure in works of art is vastly more challenging. As teachers of literature and all the other arts know, the experience of pleasure in our engagement with works of art is neither intuitive nor necessary. The possibility of aesthetic pleasure depends upon effort and knowledge; it is the result of *educated* experience.

We are speaking, then, of literary education and its aims. These aims might fail to be realized for many reasons, beginning with the situation of literature as a medium in our time. The greatest problem for teachers of literature today is the fact that literature is no longer, as it once was, the principal source of entertainment for those able to read. Nor is it the principal means of achieving cultural distinction of the sort that once motivated the European bourgeoisie. The waning of literary culture is a "media situation" that is probably irreversible, but it does not mean that literature has ceased to be entertainment. It means rather that creating the conditions for aesthetic pleasure in the ancient technology of writing has become more difficult, more likely to fail. For those who make the effort to read, failure can be related to many causes: the alien cultures represented in older narratives, the difficulty of literary language, the density of information content, or a break with the dominant aesthetic modes of the moment. All of these eventualities frustrate our desire to induce in our students, in the reading public, and even in ourselves, the pleasurable response that is the condition of everything else that comes after, including the work of scholarship. Nor can it be said that this induction of pleasure is only a question of pedagogy, as distinct from the higher vocation of scholarship. More than ever, the uncertainty of aesthetic pleasure in literature calls for a sophisticated theory of cultural transmission in all of its sites, but above all in the classroom, where all the ladders of the discipline find their start.

The Epistemic/Disciplinary Rationale

I begin with a large question about the discipline of literary study suggested by a small hypothetical scenario: knowing that the discipline is recent, dating only from the nineteenth century, it is not impossible to imagine that it might someday cease to exist. In the event of that existential threat, what might we say to justify the continued existence of literary study in its avowedly highest form, as an organized research enterprise? For I am thinking in this scenario mainly of scholarship, and of all the professional responsibilities and privileges that follow from its organization as a discipline. If the teaching of literature in some form or other is very old, literary study today is a *discipline* because it claims to produce knowledge about its object.

The most obvious response to my existential question is that we no longer conceive of teaching in the universities apart from the activity of scholarship. If there is to be the teaching of literature, there must be scholarship, and equally logically, if there is to be scholarship, there must be teaching, the transmission of knowledge. Historically, disciplines were an innovation, a fusion of research and teaching. This is the model bequeathed to us by the famous classical scholar Friedrich Wolf, inventor of the "seminar." It was possible to conduct research without teaching before Wolf instituted his seminar in Halle in 1783, and it was equally possible, and indeed common, for teachers in the universities to pursue a career in teaching without being active scholars. But we cannot conceive, after the establishment of disciplines in the universities, that a discipline can exist that is exclusively one or the other, teaching or research. The disciplines were a solution to the problem of advancing the production and transmission of knowledge *together*, in a single institutional form.

As it happens, my hypothetical scenario of a disappearing professoriate was entertained at the height of the "science wars" in the 1990s. At the time, the relatively new field of "science studies" was greeted with alarm by some scientists, who saw this field as an attempt to undermine the epistemic claims of science. The conflict was quickly assimilated into the ongoing culture wars, which are unhappily still with us, our domestic forever war. In the glory days of the conflict, two of the combatants on the side of science, Paul R. Gross and Norman Levitt, published a rebuttal of "science studies" entitled *Higher Superstition*, in which they suggested that if the humanities faculty at MIT were one day to "walk out in a huff, the scientific faculty could, at need and with enough released time, patch together a humanities curriculum, to be taught by the scientists themselves."[17] Of course, this is just a tired bit of "two cultures" rhetoric, but my aim is not to debunk the fantasy. I want rather to force the question raised by the underlying assumption in Gross and Leavitt's book: that if the humanities, including literary study, can be taught by the scientists on relatively short notice, that is presumably because there is no real knowledge in these disciplines. I take this to be the implied assertion, though it is not stated explicitly. The question, therefore, subdivided with reference to literary study, is whether there is real knowledge in literary scholarship. And assuming there is knowledge, what is its nature?

I want to affirm in this section that literary scholarship is most definitely a form of knowledge. Our problem in my view is not so much the status of scholarship as knowledge but the difficulty of formulating a response to its being questioned. In the context of the science wars, the conflict was starkly posed as the difference between scientific knowledge and disciplinary aims that do not rise to the status of knowledge at all. Scientists produce truths about the natural world. Teachers of literature, on the other hand, communicate moral lessons, or love for great literature, or something called

17. Paul R. Gross and Norman Levitt, *Higher Superstition: The Academic Left and Its Quarrels with Science* (Baltimore: Johns Hopkins University Press, 1997), 243.

critical thinking, but these aims, however laudable, do not exactly constitute knowledge in the sense in which it can be *accumulated* or *progress*. The
terms of the debate, which are only too familiar, are not wholly inaccurate;
teachers of literature do concern themselves with the aims stated. I have
discussed versions of these aims and others in connection with the other
rationales, as modes of knowledge defined by cognitive ability, or *techné*—a
mode of *knowing how*. Where, then, does that leave scholarship, as a mode
of *knowing that*? This is a question that continues to trouble the discipline
in its negotiation with the natural and social sciences, as well as with university administrations. Anyone who has served on a tenure and promotion committee will attest that the scientists do indeed wonder whether
disciplines such as literary study produce knowledge. The question of the
"epistemic" would not be worth addressing if literary scholars had a ready
way to describe knowledge in their discipline.

To these obvious and even crude questions, we must add the queries
internal to the discipline itself, many of which seem unanswerable in terms
that would support the epistemic claims of literary study. To begin, literary
scholars do not have at their command an obvious answer to the question
"What is literature?" As I have tried to demonstrate in this conclusion, and
in other essays above (see chapter 7, "The Location of Literature"), this object is a constantly moving historical target. What we can say about it at this
moment is that "literature" defines an object that was once all of writing,
Bacon's *historia litterarum*, but which has contracted over time to the genres
identified as "imaginative" or "fictional." Even so limited, the discipline does
not lack a significant object of study. Works defined by these qualifiers have
been produced for millennia and throughout the world in great numbers.
Literary study produces knowledge about this object, not because it is a
"natural kind," in the parlance of the sciences but because it aggregates artifacts in a way that makes knowledge about those artifacts possible.

This knowledge begins very humbly with facts, some of which are difficult to establish and valuable for that reason. Other facts are easier to come
by and are the necessary counters for argument. It helps at the very least
to know who is the author of a work, when and where it was written, how
the work was disseminated, its generic affiliations, how it was received by
its early audience, what allusions and references need to be explained—and
thousands of other facts besides these. Facts deserve immense respect, as
they are the bricks of knowledge, but they will never be of great interest
if not taken up into an argument that builds with them, that establishes
relations among them. Unfortunately, it is just on this matter of argument
that the epistemic claims of literary study defy an easy defense. An abyss of
uncertainty seems to swallow up arguments in literary study because they

so often contradict one another and are not capable of confirmation in the manner of scientific hypotheses. Literary scholars are thought to employ a mode of argument that conforms to a less rigorous epistemic standard than the sciences, and that typically goes by the name of "interpretation." But this category too is problematic, in that it includes many different and incompatible modes of argument. Interpretation invites the methodological conflicts that supposedly constitute the discipline's history and that confront its initiates with a puzzling series: formalism, Marxism, structuralism, post-structuralism, deconstruction, feminism, race studies, gender studies, queer studies, new historicism, postcolonial studies, and so on. In dozens of "theory" manuals, lists such as these introduce students to the discipline, but the list makes no sense at all as an account of literary study as a discipline. There must be something behind this parade that constitutes the *reason* of the discipline and that supports its knowledge claims.

My characterization of the epistemic situation of literary study is no doubt familiar but not very helpful as an account of the epistemic/disciplinary rationale. Let me begin again by restating my observation about the role of fact in the discipline: the *interest* of arguments in literary study is for the most part inversely related to the proportion of fact constituting the argument. Much as the discipline values research, the presentation of new facts is insufficient in itself to function as an argument in literary study. An argument must be *made*, and it can be made well or badly, regardless of the facts. The reason for this inverse relation is that the object of argument is not just fact but *artifact*. Textual artifacts constitute what is given for literary study; they are themselves data of a particular sort. The evidentiary distinction of the literary artifact is that it consists wholly of *meaning*, that it can only be *known* by being *understood*. Now, this formulation too will likely strike scholars as obvious, just what we do when we "interpret" literary works, when we put them into relation to one another, to forms and movements in the history of literature, to historical contexts, to problems that potentially transect the whole realm of human experience. Interpretation entails *understanding*—not only in literary study but presumably in all the cultural disciplines. Many other scholars before me have developed the notion of understanding in relation to human artifacts far more elaborately than I can begin to consider here. Often scholars in humanities fields have proceeded by distinguishing understanding from *explanation*, the concept that is supposed to define the aim of scientific inquiry. I am happy to accept some version of this distinction, but my point is somewhat different. We literary scholars do not credit sufficiently as the premise of our scholarship the possibility that understanding *need not be articulated at all*. Works of literature can be "consumed" without expressing understanding in words,

and so they have been, for much of their history. As audiences in the sixteenth or seventeenth century exited the theaters, did they undertake "interpretations" of the plays they saw? Did they ask themselves, what was
Molière or Jonson trying to say in that play? We have no "exit polls" that
would recover such hypothetical acts of interpretation, only chains of in-
ference from remarks that usually express no more than an opinion about a
work's success or failure. These are hints, but they fall very short of articulating understanding. Still, there is no question that audiences experienced
plays as meaningful, because a literary artifact such as a play is *all meaning*;
it is nothing but meaning embodied in the words, sounds, movements of
bodies, and all the material supports for staging a play.

Meaning was experienced, then, but understanding was not necessarily
further articulated. And why should we, after all, want it to be? Most engagements with literary artifacts, even today, involve no such articulation
of understanding. What does the absence of articulation mean? Now, I am
not suggesting that no one ever undertook to disclose meaning in writing before the discipline of literary study. The long history of commentary
tells us otherwise; so does the history of biblical interpretation, as well as
legal discourse. But these practices were quite rarefied; the circumstances
of biblical interpretation, or debates in law, suggest that interpretation was
usually driven by high social stakes. For most kinds of writing, and certainly
for most works in the form we recognize today as literature—poetry, plays,
novels, essays—there was less urgency, or none at all. If our understanding
of literary works seems to demand articulation, this felt need might require
an explanatory conjecture about the evolution of our relation to meaning
in the whole history of literature. Something is different for us now; a tilting point has been reached that brings literature into a new mode of social being. As literary works recede into the past or confront us with the
unimaginable complexity of the present, understanding is now challenged
to speak; we want to know *and to say* what works of literature mean. This
change in our relation to meaning itself is doubtless connected with many
other conditions of modernity, but especially, I would argue, with the increased visibility of the aesthetic as a domain that not only defines works
of art but permeates large areas of production and consumption. The later
nineteenth-century movement known as "aestheticism" confirmed this
epochal shift by employing this concept to name a dominant style that
traversed the fine arts and the decorative arts and extended even to the
manner of living in the figure of the "aesthete." Concurrently, the sociologist Georg Simmel explored this mutation of culture in a body of work that
specified the domain of the aesthetic as a privileged condensation of culture's role in modernity.

With this admittedly underdeveloped speculation in mind, let us return to the moment of transition, in the early modern period. At this time, interpretation began to move beyond the ancient practice of commentary, or glossing; its first site of expansion was in the humanist practice of editing, in the new techniques of "textual criticism." The mode of interpretation exhibited in the great editing projects of these centuries rarely attempted, however, to grasp the meaning of a work as a whole; editing remained rooted in commentary. Still, in the practice of editing we can discern the emergence of a recognizably interpretive practice; there, a foundation was laid for literary study as a future discipline. Appearing first in the historical and philological fields, the practice of interpretation was, we might say, *protodisciplinary*. It was the province of scholars who could devote to it considerable learning and effort, and it proved to be highly absorbing. Not surprisingly, scholars across the cultural fields seized upon it and sought to bring the practice into theoretical consciousness and finally to name it. Interpretation found its moment, appearing variously in the form of philology, as in the work of Wolf; in a new conceptualization of historical evidence, associated with Ranke; and in the extension of biblical hermeneutics to literature, in the work of Schleiermacher. Nor was it possible to limit the extent of its domain. By the early nineteenth century, not only religious texts and historical documents but works of vernacular literature began to be submitted to interpretation. If Renaissance audiences were silent on the problem of Hamlet's delay, questions of this kind two centuries later provoked *total* efforts of interpretation, readings of whole works and of whole oeuvres. Eventually, even works that were first dismissed as ephemeral, such as novels, yielded to the demand for interpretation. This practice was different from the "criticism" discussed in the previous section, as also from literary history, discussed in connection with the national/cultural rationale. With Dilthey's statement, following Schleiermacher, that the goal of interpretation is "to understand an author better than he understood himself," the primacy of interpretation in the cultural disciplines seemed assured.[18]

In the event, the fortunes of interpretation have been more uncertain, as its advocates had to defend its epistemic value against a strongly positivist movement in the emergent social sciences, occasioning the well-known "method war" that raged intermittently through the twentieth century. At the same time, interpretation had to be deracinated from its origins in Ger-

18. Wilhelm Dilthey, *Hermeneutics and the Study of History,* vol. 4 of *Selected Works,* ed. Rudolf A. Makkreel and Frithjof Rodi (Princeton, NJ: Princeton University Press, 1996), 255.

man Romanticism and idealist philosophy, which would have limited its possibilities. What we call very loosely by this term today includes an enormous range of procedures and is not reducible to any one of its expressions, not even "close reading." Fascinated as we are by these methodological debates, we do not see the great change in the conditions of cultural transmission that underlay them. The climacteric only becomes visible when we recall that most readers in the nineteenth century and early twentieth century still felt under no compulsion to interpret the literary works they read. As widely disseminated as interpretation was becoming in the cultural disciplines, it was not until the inception of "literary criticism" in the interwar period of the 1920s that the interpretation of literature was possible to conceive in fully disciplinary terms. Only then could literary education be devised on the basis of this practice, and the literary professoriate reconstructed as a corps of professional interpreters.

In rehearsing one last time the story of our discipline's origins, the one point that I want most to bring to light is that the articulation of understanding can be communicated as knowledge but not as fact. This is a difference between the sciences and the cultural disciplines that is worth affirming, even celebrating. For most of us who are not scientists, science comes to us in the form of facts, which we are unable to confirm by our own efforts. We accept these facts because the natural world and the social world would make no sense otherwise. This is the social condition in which scientific knowledge is disseminated, and though it is adequate in most circumstances, it can fail. We know this from the case of climate change and too many other such cases. The epistemic claims of literary study, though dependent on facts and on research, are founded equally on the epistemic principle of understanding, the kind of knowledge that in its simplest expression takes the form: "I know what you mean." The goal of certainty is irrelevant here, and in most exchanges of this kind would even be offensive. And yet, understanding is knowledge: I *know* what you mean. The proof of that knowledge is the ability to articulate understanding—to *say*, in other words, *what you mean*. Of course, this formulation simplifies interpretation by invoking an implicitly oral scene of communication, leaning as well on a psychologism that is ultimately inadequate to the complexity of textual transmission. Conceding the limits of this epistemic analogy, we can only gesture toward the "in other words" of interpretation, the quasi-translational language that constitutes interpretation of the written artifact.

For artifacts as complex as works of literature, literary scholars want to articulate understanding for reasons that have to do with our debt to the past and our interest in the future and many other motives besides but also for the sake of those nonscholars who want to produce knowledge for themselves, who want to express their understanding of literary works *in other words*, that is, their own words. Although this feat is difficult to accomplish, as we know from our experience in the classroom, it responds to a genuine desire among those we teach, both during and after their time in the school. But how far beyond the classroom, or beyond the professional society of the teachers and scholars, does this effort reach? This is a question that is very hard for the literary professoriate to answer, or even to face.

In the nature of our society, there are limits to the dissemination of Bacon's dual forms of "learning" and "art"—or in our less elegant technical terminology, "accumulated knowledge" and "cognitive ability." The production of knowledge about literature in our society is necessarily a specialized practice. It has to be this before it can be anything else. Literary study is not, then, just the expression of opinion. I have attempted in the chapters above to chart the vicissitudes of literary study as a specialized practice, its formation and deformation. Here I want briefly and finally to recall the social theory that supports my analysis, which I will cite in this instance as the "the differentiation of functions," another way of viewing the phenomenon of specialization, and the correlative forms of discipline and profession. Differentiation of function was one of the great themes of classical sociology, of Durkheim, Weber, and Simmel, and many other scholars who have studied the history of professions. Our society likes to study itself, and among the multitudinous possible objects of study, literary artifacts solicit a particular kind of study, a particular kind of expertise. This is again something that we all know; it is not news. What we do not like to acknowledge, as I have argued, is that literary artifacts do not need to be interpreted. We scholars study them because we want to, because we have the resources to do so. And to whatever extent we transmit scholarship to those we teach, we can reasonably claim to have enhanced their ability to understand literary works, to take pleasure in these works, and to comprehend how complex a literary artifact can be, how interconnected with its social environment, how much meaning can be condensed in how few words. And we can, moreover, hope to enable readers of literature to articulate understanding for themselves. I do not know how we might measure the effect of such cultural transmission; I only suggest that our society would be the poorer without it, however limited its dissemination. This statement of the discipline's aim, I hope, resists overestimation; it expresses a certain realism about the social effects of literary study, a reserve that I believe is more credible as a response to my hypothetical scenario of extinction than the grander claims literary scholars are so often tempted to make.

The fact that scholarship in literature requires considerable education to produce ensures that its field of dissemination will be limited, and that is just what is to be expected in a social condition in which specializations have multiplied nearly beyond numeration. This is a world in which some of us can specialize in the study of cultural artifacts, and within this category to specialize in literary artifacts, and within literature to specialize in English, and within English to specialize in Romanticism, and within this period to specialize in ecocriticism of Romantic poetry. Or some other topic, or some other period, and similarly for all the cultural disciplines. It would be useful once in a while for scholars to follow this path back up to its beginning, to see what our specializations look like from outside the institution. There we might give some thought to the problem of how to moderate the centrifugal tendencies that make it so difficult to communicate what we do, not only to an abstract "public," but to others in the university, and even to colleagues in our own departments.

The condition of functional differentiation that makes the discipline of literary study possible also makes possible a future in which literary scholarship might be regarded as unnecessary, a luxury that can no longer be afforded. It is with full awareness of this hypothetical future that we must understand our relation to knowledge and explain this relation to ourselves and others. I repeat, then, with emphasis, that the invidious comparison between literary scholarship and scientific research is not really our problem. Nor is the conflict between types of interpretation, nor even between interpretation and other ways that literary scholars might want to talk about literary works. The conflicts between methodologies that fascinate and trouble literary scholars are in truth the result of a knowledge explosion, materially witnessed by a proliferation of books and articles that is only now, in a disquieting sign, beginning to diminish. If the production of literary scholarship is a luxury of our society, it is also evidence of the growth of knowledge or what Bacon called, in the idiom of his time, the advancement of learning.

Acknowledgments

I am grateful for permission to reprint in whole or in part the following essays:

"Monuments and Documents: Panofsky on the Object of Study in the Humanities," *History of Humanities* 1 (2016): 9–30.

"Literary Study and the Modern System of the Disciplines," in *Disciplinarity at the Fin de Siècle*, ed. Amanda Anderson and Joseph Valente (Princeton, NJ: Princeton University Press 2002), 19–43.

"The Location of Literature," in *A Companion to Literary Theory*, ed. David Richter (Chichester: Wiley Blackwell, 2018), 153–64. © 2018 John Wiley & Sons Ltd.

"Evaluating Scholarship: Principles and Procedures," *ADE Bulletin* 137 (2005): 18–33. Reprinted by permission of the copyright owner, The Modern Language Association of America (www.mla.org).

"The Ethical Practice of Modernity: The Example of Reading," in *The Turn to Ethics*, ed. Marjorie Garber, Beatrice Hanssen, and Rebecca L. Walkowitz (New York: Routledge, 2001), 29–46.

All of these essays have been revised for this volume. "Literary Study and the Modern System of the Disciplines" has been retitled "Two Failed Disciplines: Belles Lettres and Philology" (chapter 6). "The Ethical Practice of Modernity" has been retitled "The Question of Lay Reading" (chapter 12).

It is in the nature of a book of this sort that its debts to individual scholars cannot always be acknowledged by name. In the years during which I was composing these essays, I delivered versions of them as lectures or seminars at many institutions. The questions and comments I received on those occasions were invaluable to me in the task of revision and in raising questions for further research. Collectively, these responses amounted to a kind of collaboration, for which I am very grateful. It was also my privilege to serve on a number of MLA committees, when I was able to hear the views of colleagues and students from every type of institution. Those discussions contributed in no small measure to my efforts to understand our discipline.

Some of my friends and colleagues commented on drafts of my work. I am most grateful to Scott Newstok, first reader of these essays and a better scholar than I; he has improved nearly every page of my book. I thank also David Laurence for sharing his thoughts and his experience over many decades and many hours of conversation. Helen Small and Jonathan Kramnick read the manuscript for the press and offered invaluable suggestions for revision. Those I have taxed to a lesser but hardly negligible extent include Margaret Ferguson, Lisa Gitelman, Richard Halpern, Langdon Hammer, Geoffrey Galt Harpham, Phil Harper, Paula McDowell, Franco Moretti, Jeff Nunokawa, Mary Poovey, and Bruce Robbins. Many other scholars offered useful observations in conversation, sometimes in response to lectures, sometimes to written work, and sometimes in the midst of more broad-ranging conversations about academic life. Many of these conversations were crucial to the development of my argument, although I expect that some of my interlocutors have long forgotten them. I thank here: Kwame Anthony Appiah, Michael Bérubé, Rens Bod, Bill Brown, Christopher Cannon, Mary Carruthers, Kent Cartwright, Stefan Collini, Henry Cowles, Andrew Delbanco, James English, Leonard Cassuto, James Chandler, Una Chaudhury, Wai Chi Dimock, Rosemary Feal, Juliet Fleming, Frances Ferguson, Angus Fletcher, Paul Fry, Andrew Goldstone, Kevis Goodman, Dayton Haskin, David Hoover, Amy Hungerford, Yohei Igarashi, Adrian Johns, Paula Krebs, Wendy Lee, Günter Leypoldt, Alan Liu, Andrea Lunsford, Robert Matz, Paula McDowell, Mark McGurl, W. J. T. Mitchell, Haruko Momma, Richard Müller, Karen Newman, Ross Posnock, Elizabeth Renker, David Richter, Catherine Robson, David Simpson, Cliff Siskin, Helen Small, Michael Warner, R. John Williams, Michael Witmore, and Robert Young.

I want to thank especially some friends, several of whom I also thank above for their responses to my work, for support of another kind. Phil Harper and Una Chaudhuri sustained my good cheer in these last difficult years, over regular drinks and dinner. Henry Abelove reminded me of the joys of intellectual conversation beyond the academy. My colleague Paula McDowell has been equally a great friend and a great colleague, as we both ventured into new fields of study. Richard Halpern, oldest of friends, held me to the highest intellectual standard. Lanny Hammer makes every conversation a source of long-term sustenance. For their support over the years, however rarely we manage occasions together, I thank also Margaret Ferguson, Kevis Goodman, Karen Newman, and Mary Poovey.

I was fortunate to have three superlative undergraduate research assistants, who made substantial contributions to my project: David Alworth, Ari Liberman, and Ethan Sapienza. They have gone on to distinguished careers, but I want to remember their labors here.

Alan Thomas waited a very long time for this book. I thank him for his patience, as well as his sage counsel over the years. I'm grateful to the team at the University of Chicago Press, especially Randolph Petilos and George Roupe.

And, finally, I am lucky in the faithful companions of my study, Lily and Emma; and for his fidelity and more, my husband, Wynn Fitzpatrick. This book is dedicated to my students, who still surprise me.

Index

CPSIA information can be obtained
at www.ICGtesting.com
Printed in the USA
BVHW030945170123
656435BV00002B/6